Linguistic Turns in Modern Philosophy

This book traces the linguistic turns in the history of modern philosophy and the development of the philosophy of language from Locke to Wittgenstein. It examines the contributions of canonical figures such as Leibniz, Mill, Frege, Russell, Wittgenstein, Austin, Quine, and Davidson, as well as those of Condillac, Humboldt, Chomsky, and Derrida. Michael Losonsky argues that the philosophy of language begins with Locke's *Essay Concerning Human Understanding*. He shows how the history of the philosophy of language in the modern period is marked by a dichotomy between formal and pragmatic perspectives on language and that modern philosophy has not been able to integrate these two aspects of human language. Language as a human activity and language as a syntactic and semantic system remain distinct and competing focal points, although the interplay between these points of view has driven the development of the philosophy of language.

Michael Losonsky is professor of philosophy at Colorado State University. He is author of *Enlightenment and Action from Descartes to Kant* and coauthor and coeditor, respectively, with H. Geirsson of *Beginning Metaphysics* and *Readings in Mind and Language*.

THE EVOLUTION OF MODERN PHILOSOPHY

General Editors:
Paul Guyer and Gary Hatfield (*University of Pennsylvania*)

Published Books in the Series:
Roberto Torretti: *The Philosophy of Physics*
David Depew and Marjorie Grene: *The Philosophy of Biology*
Charles Taliaferro: *Evidence and Faith*

Forthcoming:
Paul Guyer: *Aesthetics*
Gary Hatfield: *The Philosophy of Psychology*
Stephen Darwall: *Ethics*
T. R. Harrison: *Political Philosophy*
William Ewald and Michael J. Hallett: *The Philosophy of Mathematics*

Why has philosophy evolved in the way that it has? How have its subdisciplines developed, and what impact has this development exerted on the way that the subject is now practiced? Each volume of "The Evolution of Modern Philosophy" will focus on a particular subdiscipline of philosophy and examine how it has evolved into the subject as we now understand it. The volumes will be written from the perspective of a current practitioner in contemporary philosophy, whose point of departure will be the question: How did we get from there to here? Cumulatively the series will constitute a library of modern conceptions of philosophy and will reveal how philosophy does not in fact comprise a set of timeless questions but has rather been shaped by broader intellectual and scientific developments to produce particular fields of inquiry addressing particular issues.

Linguistic Turns in Modern Philosophy

MICHAEL LOSONSKY
Colorado State University

CAMBRIDGE UNIVERSITY PRESS

CAMBRIDGE UNIVERSITY PRESS
Cambridge, New York, Melbourne, Madrid, Cape Town, Singapore, São Paulo

Cambridge University Press
40 West 20th Street, New York, NY 10011-4211, USA

www.cambridge.org
Information on this title: www.cambridge.org/9780521652568

© Michael Losonsky 2006

This publication is in copyright. Subject to statutory exception
and to the provisions of relevant collective licensing agreements,
no reproduction of any part may take place without
the written permission of Cambridge University Press.

First published 2006

Printed in the United States of America

A catalog record for this publication is available from the British Library.

Library of Congress Cataloging in Publication Data
Losonsky, Michael.
Linguistic turns in modern philosophy / Michael Losonsky.
p. cm. – (Evolution of modern philosophy)
Includes bibliographical references and index.
ISBN 0-521-65256-1 – ISBN 0-521-65470-X (pbk.)
1. Language and languages – Philosophy – History. I. Title. II. Series.
P107.L67 2006
149'.94 – dc22   2005009634

ISBN-13 978-0-521-65256-8 hardback
ISBN-10 0-521-65256-1 hardback

ISBN-13 978-0-521-65470-8 paperback
ISBN-10 0-521-65470-X paperback

Cambridge University Press has no responsibility for
the persistence or accuracy of URLs for external or
third-party Internet Web sites referred to in this publication
and does not guarantee that any content on such
Web sites is, or will remain, accurate or appropriate.

> There are some qualities – some incorporate things,
>   That have a double life, which thus is made
> A type of that twin entity which springs
>   From matter and light, evinced in solid and shade.
> There is a two-fold *Silence* – sea and shore –
>   Body and Soul. One dwells in lonely places,
>   Newly with grass overgrown.
>
> E. A. Poe, Sonnet – Silence

Die *Sprache*, in ihrem wirklichen Wesen aufgefasst, ist etwas beständig und in jedem Augenblicke *Vorübergehendes*.

[*Language*, regarded in its real nature, is an enduring thing, and at every moment a *transitory* one.]

W. v. Humboldt, Über die Verschiedenheit
des menschlichen Sprachbaues

Perhaps neither of these abstractions is so very expedient: perhaps we have here not really two poles, but rather an historical development.

J. L. Austin, How to Do Things with Words

Contents

Preface		*page* xi
1	Locke's Linguistic Turn	1
2	The Road to Locke	22
3	Of Angels and Human Beings	52
4	The Form of a Language	83
5	The Import of Propositions	116
6	The Value of a Function	148
7	From Silence to Assent	190
8	The Whimsy of Language	229
Bibliography		253
Index		269

Preface

The pioneering historian of linguistics R. H. Robins began one of his essays with this important warning:

> The selection of what is significant within the history of a subject and the reasons for such significance, and even what falls within the bounds of the subject whose history is being traced, must be affected by the author's current standpoint, in part at least the product of his own upbringing.
>
> Such an approach may be deliberate and explicit, and is probably justified if the readership aimed at is wide... in that it provides a unifying and easily grasped viewpoint from which to interpret and assess the work of earlier generations; but it does reinforce the theme of unitary development. Earlier scholars are noticed, and commended or criticized according as they comply with working precepts in current favour and to the extent that a contemporary scholar can view their work without serious change in the attitude towards his subject. Persons, and the topics they discuss or expound, are selected for attention as "milestones" (notice the implications of this common metaphor) in the progress of the subject up to the present day. (Robins 1976, 14)

This warning holds for anyone preparing to read or write a history of any field or discipline, but it applies especially to the study of language, which is still ruled by several competing paradigms. It also applies to the history of philosophy, where the diversity of paradigms is as great as philosophers' convictions that they are traveling on the only road worth taking. So, anyone writing on the history of the philosophy of language embarks on a doubly treacherous journey.

Nevertheless, in this book I deliberately take the approach of finding milestones in the history of the philosophy of language in the modern period. I aim to describe the characteristic features at each milestone and then look backward and forward to see where the road came from and where it leads. What I find is surely influenced by my current standpoint and past training, yet I have been careful to recognize diverse developments and distinct roads with their own milestones and also to appreciate the many roads that crisscross this philosophical landscape.

I am particularly interested in milestones on important crossroads, which mark the distances of several directions. What stands out for me in the history of philosophy is that important contributions are such milestones, and the history of the philosophy of language in the modern period is no exception. John Locke's *Essay Concerning Human Understanding* begins the evolution of the philosophy of language and linguistics in the modern period (Chapter 1). Not only is Locke's work a culmination of a long-term turn to natural language (Chapter 2), but it also initiates two distinct lines of development (Chapter 3). One begins with the work of Leibniz, who highlights the underlying formal structure of natural language, particularly its logical form, which is distinct from the empirical appearance of language. The other begins with Condillac, whose focal point is the empirical appearance of language in human action: language as human behavior on a continuum with cries and gestures.

What Leibniz and Condillac separated, Wilhelm von Humboldt attempts to reunite in his work on human language as dual aspects of language: it is a determined, rule-governed formal and biological system as well as a free, undetermined human activity beyond the scope of science (Chapter 4). Although Humboldt is concerned with form and develops the Leibnizian idea of a linguistic form that underlies linguistic appearances, he is concerned not with logical form but with the phonological structure of natural language. It fell to John Stuart Mill to rekindle work on the logical form of natural language within a naturalistic framework (Chapter 5). In the twentieth century, the logical form of natural language becomes the centerpiece of the philosophy of language, but only after Frege purges it of Mill's psychologism and interprets form in terms of mathematical function (Chapter 6). Ironically, the evolution of the philosophy of language in the twentieth century – for example, the work of Wittgenstein, Carnap, Quine, and Davidson – is an ongoing attempt to renaturalize logical form and function (Chapter 7). The various attempts to naturalize logical form on the basis of linguistic appearances, however, could not sustain a robust conception of language as a formal semantic system and instead encouraged various forms of irrealism about semantic structure. In fact, the turn to linguistic performance as the guide for linguistic theory threatens the very idea of a theoretical treatment of natural language (Chapter 8).

Accordingly, my understanding of the philosophy of language is ecumenical. I do not identify the philosophy of language with a discipline that has its "beginnings...in the work of the German philosopher and mathematician, Gottlob Frege" (Searle 1971, 2). Frege's work is certainly an important milestone, but so are the works of Condillac, Humboldt, and Saussure. Similarly, it is a mistake to maintain that "Condillac is the first real philosopher of language" (Trabant 1990, 27), because for him language does not simply mirror human thought and cognition, but is an essential or constitutive part of thought and cognition. Neither is it right that a philosopher of language must believe that there is a "logical necessity that the structure of a thought be reflected in the structure of a sentence expressing it" (Baker and Hacker 1984, 66). It should be possible for a philosopher of language to arrive at the conclusion that there is a gap between the structure of thought and the structure of language.

The primary limit I have placed on the subject matter of this book is that the philosophy of language is concerned with natural human language. Thus I agree that "to qualify as a philosopher of language one must...investigate...ordinary language" (Baker and Hacker 1984, 67n). Accordingly, the philosophy of logic, for instance, even when understood as the philosophy of the languages of logic, is not, as such, part of the philosophy of language. It is treated here only as far as work in logic and the philosophy of logic is explicitly understood as shedding light on the workings of natural language.

What I wish to document is how natural language becomes an object of philosophical and then scientific theory, and how significant features of natural language seem to resist the net of theory. Two competing poles dominate the study of natural human language in the modern period. On the one hand, human language can be seen as something human beings do voluntarily to achieve certain ends, typically communication. I find this to be Locke's perspective, and on this issue he is a successor to the philosophy of language that defines Renaissance humanism. On the other hand, human language can be seen as a structured syntactic and semantic system, whose structure can be studied apart from the particular uses human beings make of this system. This perspective stands out in the philosophy of Scholasticism, and it is the perspective that Leibniz resurrects and develops in light of the critique that logic is irrelevant to understanding the nature of natural language.

In the latter case, to borrow from Austin's *How to Do Things with Words*, the focal point is locution: the construction of the linguistic utterance or inscription together with its literal meaning – for instance, its sense and reference. In the former case, the focal point is what a writer or speaker aims to do with the locution, for what ends we produce meaningful utterances and inscriptions, that is, the linguistic performance. Perhaps both of these poles are abstractions and, as Austin notes, "neither of these abstractions is so very expedient," but as Austin adds, "perhaps we have here not really two poles, but rather an historical development" (Austin 1975, 146). I take Austin's observation as my point of departure and try to show that these two poles are two intersecting lines of historical development.

Moreover, I believe there is a lesson to be learned from this history. Although these may just be abstractions from "the total speech situation... the *only actual* phenomenon which, in the last resort, we are engaged in elucidating" (Austin 1975, 147–8), without these abstractions a theory of human language is not sustainable. The actual phenomenon of the linguistic performance of a speaker or writer has a tendency to resist theory and undermine the idea that language is a determinate and rule-governed system.

Even the abstraction to what Austin calls "locution" – the sentence with its literal meaning – is insufficient to preserve the systematicity of natural language. Language as a system requires a further abstraction from locution to a structure of possible locutions. The actual locution as a unit of analysis needs to be placed in a system of all possible as well as actual locutions of a language, but actual locutions by themselves do not determine such a system. Language as a rule-governed system, if there is such a thing, will be an abstract structure distinct from actual locutions or performances. But that also means that language as a system will be distinct from the empirical basis for its study – the phenomena of human linguistic activity, that is, human linguistic performances. This distinction has the paradoxical consequence that the empirical basis of the study of language tends to undermine the very idea that language is a system that can be represented by a theory.

This paradox is especially striking because philosophers in the modern period have turned to language in order to solve philosophical problems, particularly problems of mind and cognition, on an empirical and, ultimately, naturalistic basis. Part of the empirical and naturalizing trend in philosophy is to turn to language to better understand the human mind. This is the essence of Locke's linguistic turn, which,

I argue, begins a series of linguistic turns that motivate and sustain both the science and philosophy of language in the modern period. But the empirical linguistic phenomena by themselves undermine those components of language, particularly linguistic meaning and structure, which could best serve as evidence for the nature of mind and cognition. The view that language is a system with a determinate semantic and syntactic structure is best sustained when this system is understood to be an abstract object that is the object of primarily formal, and not empirical, investigations.

Of course, some linguistic turns, such as Frege's turn to language, were reactions to naturalism and turns to Platonic objects. Following Leibniz's lead, Frege turned to the systematicity of concepts and propositions that language, when properly constructed, represented, and he believed that an accurate representation of this structure would contribute to advancement in philosophy and the sciences. Unfortunately, this turn to systematicity is a turn away from, to adapt Austin's words, "the *only actual* phenomenon which, in the last resort, we are engaged in elucidating" – namely, actual linguistic activity. Therefore, it labors under the suspicion that it is irrelevant to understanding linguistic performances. Moreover, its conception of language is so rich that it cannot well serve as a neutral source for resolving fundamental philosophical disputes. The dispute between Platonism and nominalism, for instance, cannot be resolved by an appeal to an abstract noncausal structure that is the subject of nonempirical knowledge.

It is the contention of this book that modern philosophy was not able to integrate these two faces of language. Language as human activity and language as system remain distinct focal points despite various attempts to develop a unified view. The various attempts to bring these perspectives together have contributed to the development of the philosophical and scientific study of language and have engendered various paradigms for this study, but no consensus has emerged regarding the integration of system and performance, suggesting that these are dual aspects of language that cannot be integrated. This conclusion is contingent, based on the persistent diversity of competing views and historical development, but I believe it is the one best supported by the evidence so far.

I must thank several people for their assistance and support during this project. At the head of the list are Paul Guyer and the late Terry Moore. Their confidence, patience, and encouragement made this book possible. I am also very grateful to Beatrice Rehl, who succeeded Terry at Cambridge University Press, and to my production editor, Brian MacDonald. Finally, I thank Steve Daniel, Heimir Geirsson, Fred Johnson, Jane Kneller, Jim Maffie, Lex Newman, John Rogers, Bernard Rollin, Donald Rutherford, and Ron Williams for the numerous ways in which they have supported the writing of this book.

Linguistic Turns in Modern Philosophy

ONE

✦

Locke's Linguistic Turn

The genesis of analytic philosophy in the twentieth century has been characterized as "the linguistic turn" in the history of philosophy. It is true that a philosophical movement emerged in the beginning of this century that drew on the groundbreaking work of the philosopher and logician Gottlob Frege (1848–1925) and held that "philosophical problems may be solved (or dissolved) either by reforming language, or by understanding more about language we presently use."[1] Nevertheless, the definite article in "the linguistic turn" is inappropriate because there were other significant turns to language besides Frege's.

Language was as central to the Prague Linguistic Circle as it was to the Vienna Circle, and the Prague Circle was also interdisciplinary, including not only linguists but also literary critics, anthropologists, and philosophers (Steiner 1982, ix–xii and 83). Rooted in Ferdinand de Saussure's (1857–1913) groundbreaking theory of language, the "Theses of the Prague Circle" was an important milestone in the history of structuralism and had a profound influence on European thought. The idea that language and its structural properties are appropriate models for understanding other fields of study, including philosophy,

---

[1] See Rorty 1967; 1992, 3. Other statements of the fundamental tenet of what is also known as "linguistic philosophy" include "the theory of [linguistic] meaning is the fundamental part of philosophy which underlies all others" (Dummett 1973, 669); philosophy "should be defined...as the '*pursuit of meaning*,'" namely the meaning of propositions (Schlick 1932, 48); "a great part of philosophy can be reduced to something that may be called 'syntax'" (Russell 1945, 830); "the business of philosophy, as I conceive it, is essentially that of logical analysis" (Russell 1988, 9:176); "a careful study of language may lead to positive philosophical conclusions" (Copi 1949, 65); and "Preoccupation with the theory of meaning could be described as the occupational disease of twentieth-century Anglo-Saxon and Austrian philosophy" (Ryle 1963, 128).

still reverberates in discussions of texts and subtexts. No less influential was the linguistic hypothesis formulated by Edward Sapir (1884–1939) and Benjamin Lee Whorff (1897–1941) that human languages have incommensurable differences that cause human beings to perceive the world in radically different ways. This hypothesis has been so influential that it is considered a ruling paradigm in the contemporary social sciences. This cannot be said of philosophy, but linguistic relativism has also left important marks on European and North American philosophy.[2]

Not only was analytic philosophy's linguistic turn one among several in twentieth-century philosophy, but, like all the other contemporary turns to language, it gathered significant momentum from a series of earlier evolutions. Without Wilhelm von Humboldt's (1767–1835) turn to the phonological form of a language, Saussure's work is hardly conceivable, and the same is true of Frege and the groundwork for a theory of linguistic meaning laid out by John Stuart Mill (1806–73). Moreover, the turns to language of the twentieth century that still in one form or another play a role today are also culminations of a shared development. Despite their important differences, they have common ancestors. The earliest of these ancestors, and the one that can be credited with making the first linguistic turn not only in the modern period but in the history of philosophy, is John Locke (1632–1704).

Locke's *Essay Concerning Human Understanding* is a recognized epistemological landmark devoted to understanding the nature and limits of human knowledge and doing so in terms of ideas. The concept of ideas plays such a fundamental role in Locke's *Essay* that he apologizes for its frequent use, yet he is also willing to describe his approach as a "new way of ideas." But there is another distinctive feature about this work. Although Locke's primary aim is to use ideas to develop an account of sensation, reflection, perception, memory, knowledge, and the objects of knowledge, the same themes that exercised his successors and critics such as Berkeley, Hume, and Reid, the *Essay* also includes an equally significant turn to human language. Locke devotes an entire book of the *Essay* to language, a work that has justifiably

---

[2] On the social science paradigm, compare Pinker 1995, 56–7 and 405–7. The Sapir-Whorff hypothesis plays a role in various forms of linguistic relativism, including the relativism of Feyerabend and Kuhn. The linguistic turns in existentialism and phenomenology, particularly in the works of Heidegger (1944) and Merleau-Ponty (1964), should also be mentioned.

been called "the first modern treatise devoted specifically to philosophy of language" (Kretzmann 1967, 379; also Kretzmann 1968). But why does Locke turn to language? The answer to this question shows why Locke's *Essay* marks the beginning of the philosophy of language in the modern period.

From Epistemology to Psychology

Locke's book III of the *Essay* has the title "*Of Words*" and begins with a chapter called "Of Words or Language in General." The preceding book II, "*Of Ideas*," begins with an account of the mind's basic elements and operations, such as simple ideas, complex ideas, sensation, reflection, perception, memory, composition, and abstraction, and then continues with an account of some key ideas, such as the ideas of space, power, substance, causality, identity, and difference. Locke concludes this book on the structure of the human understanding with these words:

> Having thus given an account of the original, sorts, and extent of our *Ideas*, with several other Considerations, about these...Instruments, or Materials, of our Knowledge, the method I at first proposed to my self, would now require, that I should immediately proceed to shew, what use the Understanding makes of them, and what Knowledge we have by them....[B]ut upon nearer approach, I find, that there is so close a connexion between *Ideas* and Words; and our abstract *Ideas*, and general words, have so constant a relation one to another, that it is impossible to speak clearly and distinctly of our Knowledge, which all consists in Propositions, without considering, first, the Nature, Use, and Signification of Language; which therefore must be the business of the next Book. (1975, 401, II.29.19)

Locke in fact does postpone the discussion of the nature, extent, and degree of human knowledge to book IV.

This account of the development of the *Essay* is repeated later in Locke's discussion of the "*Imperfection of Words*":

> I must confess then, that when I first began this Discourse of the Understanding, and a good while after, I had not the least Thought, that any Consideration of Words was at all necessary to it. But when having passed over the Original and Composition of our *Ideas*, I began to examine the Extent and Certainty of our Knowledge, I found it had so near a connexion with Words, that unless their force and manner of Signification were first well observed, there could be very little said clearly and pertinently concerning Knowledge. (1975, 488, III.9.21)

Locke's claim that he had planned to turn to knowledge right after his discussion of ideas in book II but decided instead to turn to language first is not made for dramatic effect. The earliest known draft of Locke's *Essay*, written in 1671, has very little to say about language. It addresses language primarily in connection with propositions that "are only verball but are not Instructive" (1990, 55). For instance, a Roman might signify with the word *homo* the idea of something rational and risible, and then his utterance in Latin that all men are rational and risible is universally true. But this does not tell us anything about humanity, but only that "this word Homo in his country comprehended" both the idea of rationality and capacity for laughter (1990, 56). But the second draft, written a few months later, already has a much richer discussion of language. In his discussion of substances, Locke recognizes that we use language not only to communicate or to record something but "also even to think upon things" (1990, 166). Yet the second draft also does not have a unified and self-contained discussion of language. Instead, the discussion of language is woven throughout Locke's discussion of substances, kinds, and other classifications, where Locke believes words play a role in our thinking.

Only in the published *Essay* does Locke devote a whole book to language. Even the third known draft of the *Essay*, written in 1685, does not contain a book on language. However, the last paragraph of Draft C already matches the last paragraph of the published *Essay*. Locke announces in Draft C that after having discussed

> the instruments or matter of our knowledge it will probably now be expected that I should immediately proceed to shew what knowledge we have by them. This was that I confess I at first proposd to my self & thought would be my next & only worke as soon as I had dispacht the Consideration of our Ideas. But when I began to apply my self to that which was my chief end viz what use the understanding made of these Ideas & what knowledge it attaind by them I found words by constant use soe neare a Connection with them & were by inadvertency soe often put for our Ideas that it was impossible to speake clearly & destinctly of our knowledge which all Consists in propositions without considering first the nature use and signification of language which therefor must be the businese of my next booke.[3]

---

[3] I am very much indebted to John Rogers for information about Draft C.

This strongly suggests that it was during the writing of this draft that Locke came to believe that language was so important that he needed to insert a distinct section on language before he could go on to discuss the nature, degree, and extent of human cognition.

The seeds for this decision, however, were already sown in the second draft of the *Essay*, where Locke writes that human beings use language not only to communicate and record, but "also even to think upon things" (1990, 166). That language is needed for thinking, particularly "*to comprehend several particular Things*" – that is, to think about "a multitude of particular existences" (1975, 402, III.1.3) – becomes a central thesis in the *Essay*. This concept is so important for Locke that in the concluding chapter of the *Essay*, where he gives his overall "Division of the Sciences," he recommends that one of the three branches of science is "σημειωτική, or *the Doctrine of Signs*, the most usual whereof being Words" (1975, 720, III.21.4). This branch of science is concerned with "the Nature of Signs, the Mind makes use of for the understanding of things" (ibid.).

That Locke had expressly connected epistemology to semantic inquiry has been recognized as a new and unique contribution of Locke's *Essay* (Kretzmann 1967, 379). Of course, the stature of Locke's *Essay* as a philosophical masterpiece that "inaugurates an 'epistemological turn' which was to launch philosophy on the road to Kant" is beyond all doubt (Jolley 1999, 14). It has also been noticed that Locke has very practical reasons for engaging in, to use Hume's words, "abstruse philosophy" (Hume 1996, 1:3). It is not an exaggeration to say that "Locke intended his epistemology as a solution to the crisis of the fracturing of the moral and religious tradition of Europe at the beginnings of modernity" (Wolterstorff 1996, 227). Locke begins his inquiry into the human understanding because "five or six friends" who regularly met in his apartment ran into "doubts" and "difficulties" that, Locke writes, could be resolved only after an examination of "what Objects our Understandings were, or were not fitted to deal with" (1975, 7, Epistle). The topic of these discussions is not known with certainty, but it is highly probable that they were discussing morality and religion (Woolhouse 1983, 7–8). Locke came to believe that in certain areas, particularly morality, religion, metaphysics, and also science, human beings "extended their Enquiries beyond their Capacities" (1975, 47, I.1.7). The task of the *Essay* was to show what our cognitive capacities are, or how far they can reach, and thus avoid the many disputes that Locke thought marked his age.

But what is frequently overlooked in assessing Locke's philosophy is that his epistemic concerns do not lead him straightaway to discuss justification, belief, and knowledge. Only in the last book of the *Essay*, book IV, does Locke turn to the theory of knowledge. What precedes Locke's epistemology is a theory of mind in book II devoted to the elements and operations of the human understanding.

This psychological turn marks the opening sentences of the *Essay*. Locke writes that he is going to begin by investigating human understanding, which, like the eye, "takes no notice of itself" and requires "Art and Pains to set it at a distance, and make it its own Object" (1975, 43, I.1.1). Locke turns to the human mind because he believes that to know the limits and extent of human cognitive capacities, one needs to know something about how cognition works: "This was that which gave the first *Rise* to this Essay concerning the Understanding. For I thought that the first Step towards satisfying several Enquiries, the Mind of Man was very apt to run into, was, to take a Survey of our own Understandings, examine our Powers, and see to what Things they were adapted" (1975, 46–7, I.1.7). That epistemology must rely on psychology is a basic assumption of Locke's *Essay*. Therefore it is a misunderstanding of Locke's project to suppose that he is confusing epistemology and psychology, as some have argued.[4] Locke fully understands the difference between the psychological inquiry of books I and II and the epistemic questions concerning justification in book IV.

In sum, Locke's epistemological turn is combined with a psychological turn, and Locke's psychological interests lead him in the first instance to language. So an important feature of Locke's linguistic interests is that it is tied not only to epistemic concerns but also to his psychological inquiries. As Locke writes, he turns to language because after his psychological investigations, that is, after examining "Instruments, or Materials, of our Knowledge," he realized he cannot discuss epistemology (i.e., "proceed to shew, what use the Understanding makes of them, and what Knowledge we have by them") until he looks at language (1975, 401, II.33.19).

---

[4] Kant was the first philosopher to accuse Locke of confusing questions of fact with questions of justification. He writes that Locke does a "physiology of the human understanding" (Kant 1904, 4:Aix), and a "physiological derivation ... cannot strictly be called a deduction" (Kant 1904, 4:A87).

Psychology and Philosophy of Mind

Before we examine Locke's linguistic turn more closely, it is important to be clear about the nature of Locke's psychological turn. He does not care about the biology of the mind: he will not "meddle with the Physical Consideration of the Mind" or study "by what Motions of our Spirits, or Alterations of our Bodies, we come to have any Sensations by our Organs, or any *Ideas* in our Understandings" (1975, 43, I.1.2). He will also not discuss the traditional mind-body problem: "I shall not... trouble my self to examine, wherein [the mind's] Essence consists" and whether "*Ideas* do in their Formation, any, or all of them, depend on Matter, or no." Instead, Locke announces that he will "consider the discerning Faculties of a Man, as they are employ'd about the Objects, which they have to do with" (1975, 43–4, I.1.2).

Locke believes he can consider the "discerning faculties" without examining the physical properties of the brain. To understand what he has in mind, it is useful to look at what Locke means by "faculty." Locke is not fully comfortable with this term because he believes that referring to various faculties of the mind suggests that the mind has distinct agents responsible for its various powers. Claims that the human intellectual faculty is responsible for cognition or that the elective faculty, or will, is responsible for human conation do not advance knowledge, he maintains (1975, 243, II.21.20). Nevertheless, Locke recommends keeping the term "faculty" because it is widely used but emphasizes that he is *not* using it to refer to "distinct Agents" responsible for distinct capacities or abilities such as cognition, conation, and digestion.[5] For Locke, "*Faculty, Ability*, and *Power*... are but different names for the same things" (1975, 244, II.21.20).

What Locke aims to examine are certain powers or abilities of the mind – the discerning powers – that we are aware of without knowing anything about the mind's physical structure. We exercise these powers consciously and are able to experience them in our own case. Specifically, he wants to consider the discerning powers, which he characterizes later in the *Essay* as the capacity to distinguish and identify ideas (1975, 155, II.11.1). Discernment, however, is only one among several

---

[5] This suggests that Locke would reject the modularity thesis, namely that the mind is a collection of semiautonomous agencies (Gazzaniga 1985) or independent processing systems devoted to well-defined tasks, such as language acquisition or memory (Chomsky 1980; Fodor 1983).

mental capacities we have, so Locke appears caught in one of the many discrepancies of the *Essay*, which was written and rewritten over the span of almost two decades. Nevertheless, Locke's intentions are clear. Human beings are conscious of certain powers that, broadly speaking, are the powers that characterize the human understanding. These powers include abilities such as recognizing, distinguishing, comparing, and remembering things, and Locke aims to examine these more closely.

Locke's interest in the mind's powers from a first-person point of view suggests that he is also concerned with what might reasonably be called a "phenomenology of mind." Relying on introspection or reflection, Locke describes mental phenomena and analyzes them into their apparent components. Locke can also be described as doing what has been called "descriptive metaphysics" (Strawson 1959, xiii). He is, to use Strawson's terminology, describing the "actual structure of our thought about the world," namely that part of the world inhabited by human minds. So Locke's aim is to give an empirical theory of the mind, but the empirical evidence he uses is subjective. For Locke, empirical evidence is not limited to objective, publicly accessible evidence (Searle 1987). Because he does rely on first-person evidence, however, Locke's psychological project is not sharply distinguished from what today we might think of as the philosophy of mind.

Locke's linguistic turn, then, has two significant features. First, it is tied to his epistemology. To understand the scope of human knowledge, we need to understand human language. Second, it is tied to his psychology and philosophy of mind. Language is relevant to human knowledge because language plays a crucial role in how we think about the world, and this feature is something we can recognize in our own case.

Knowledge and Propositions

As we saw, Locke turns to language because he believes "there is so close a connexion between *Ideas* and Words" (1975, 401, II.33.19). One reason for this close connection, according to Locke, is that all human knowledge "consists in Propositions" (ibid. and 488, III.9.21). Although Locke believes that propositions can be either mental or verbal because "there are two sorts of Signs commonly made use of" in propositions, namely ideas and words (1975, 574, IV.5.2), verbal propositions are what Locke has in mind here.

Locke gives several reasons for why he had to consider verbal propositions more closely. First, treating verbal propositions separately is very difficult because they must be used when discussing mental propositions, "and then the Instances given of *Mental Propositions*, cease immediately to be barely Mental, *and* become *Verbal*" (1975, 574, IV.5.3). To consider a mental proposition, one would have to consider only ideas without any words, and once we express a proposition using language, the mental proposition ceases to be pure. Locke believes that once language is used to express a proposition, the words of the verbal proposition come to replace the ideas not only in our discussion but also in our thinking about the proposition.

The second problem is more serious because it affects human thinking not just in the special case where we are talking or writing about propositions. Most human beings, if not all, Locke writes, "in their Thinking and Reasonings within themselves, make use of Words instead of *Ideas*" (1975, 574, IV.5.4). This occurs primarily when people have thoughts involving complex ideas. As is well known, Locke distinguishes between simple ideas that are received passively and complex ideas that are products of the workmanship of the understanding (1975, 163, II.12.1; Losonsky 1989). In a complex idea, various simple ideas are tied together to form a new idea. For Locke, all ideas of substances (e.g., animals, minerals, and plants) are complex ideas, as are ideas of space, duration, number, power, and causality. These ideas are the sources of many problems, and for Locke the fact that human beings typically rely on words when thinking about subjects that involve complex ideas is "great evidence of the imperfection and uncertainty of our *Ideas* of that kind" (1975, 574, IV.5.4).

The problem with complex ideas is that for the most part they are imperfect. For example, in the case of ideas of substances, the number of ideas the human mind "combines, *depends upon the Care, Industry, or Fancy of him that makes it*" (Locke 1975, 456, III.6.29). Because the amount of care, industry, or imagination that is exercised changes from occasion to occasion and from person to person, ideas of substances can differ depending on the context and who has them. In fact, Locke writes that "[m]*en are far enough from having agreed on the precise number of simple* Ideas, *or* Qualities, *belonging to any sort of Things, signified by its name*" (1975, 457, III.6.30). For this reason,

> when we would consider, or make Propositions about the more complex *Ideas*, as of a *Man, Vitriol, Fortitude, Glory*, we usually put the Name for the *Idea*:... we reflect on the *Names* themselves because they are more clear, certain, and distinct, and readier to occur to our Thoughts, than

the pure *Ideas*: and so we make use of these Words instead of the *Ideas* themselves, even when we would meditate and reason within ourselves, and make tacit mental Propositions. (1975, 575, IV.5.4)

So although, for example, we are thinking to ourselves about man, we usually do not use the complex idea of man but instead rely, Locke writes explicitly, on the name "man."

Locke's claim that words are a "*Medium* through which visible objects pass" and they "impose upon our Understandings" (1975, 488, III.9.21) – that words "interpose themselves so much between our Understandings, and the Truth... that... their Obscurity and Disorder does not seldom cast a mist before our Eyes" (ibid.) – poses a problem. This role he appears to assign to words conflicts with his central view that "*the Mind*, in all its Thoughts and Reasonings, hath no other immediate Object but its own *Ideas*" so "our Knowledge is only conversant about them" (1975, 525, IV.1.1). Consequently, "'Tis evident, the Mind knows not Things immediately, but only by the intervention of the *Ideas* it has of them" (1975, 563, IV.4.3). If words "interpose themselves... between our Understandings, and the Truth," then ideas are not the only immediate objects of our understanding.

This conflict also infects Locke's discussion of propositions. As we saw, Locke claims that all human knowledge "consists in Propositions" and that sometimes these propositions are verbal, that is, propositions in which "*Words* [are]... *put together or separated in affirmative or negative Sentences*" (1975, 575–6, IV.5.5). So sometimes knowledge consists of sentences (1975, 488; III.9.21), but this does not square with the claim that knowledge has only ideas as immediate objects. If knowledge consists only of ideas, then it cannot *consist* in sentences.

One way of resolving this conflict is to suppose Locke was careless and that, strictly speaking, Locke is proposing that when we rely on language in our thinking, the *immediate* objects of such thoughts are *ideas* of words, not words themselves. For example, when the word "gold" comes to replace the idea of gold, strictly speaking what happens is that the idea of the word "gold" replaces the idea of gold in thinking and reasoning about gold (Losonsky 1994).

Unfortunately, Locke is not clear about this issue, and the historical context offers few clues. As we will see later, both Hobbes and Leibniz assign an important role to language in human reasoning, particularly abstract reasoning. Unfortunately there is too much room for interpretation whether they meant literally that words themselves are constituent parts of these thoughts or held the weaker view that *ideas* of words are constituents of these thoughts and that words only function as causes of these ideas.[6] Condillac is clearly committed to the stronger thesis and his work has been called a *"a Supplement to Mr. Locke's Essay on the Human Understanding"* (Condillac 1971), but he interprets this emphasis on the role of language in thought as a correction of what he believes is a deficit in Locke's philosophy.

Kretzmann (1968, 196) offers some textual evidence that suggests Locke held the weaker thesis. Locke defines words as articulate sounds (1975, 224, II.18.3; and 402, III.1.1), and Kretzmann maintains that Locke holds that every sound is an idea and so words are ideas (1968, 190). Further evidence, I believe, is the passage from book IV quoted earlier, in which Locke argues that we use names instead of complex ideas, such as the idea of *man* or *vitriol*, "because they are more clear, certain and distinct, and readier occur to our Thoughts, than the pure *Ideas*: and so we make use of these Words instead of the *Ideas* themselves, even when we would meditate and reason within ourselves and make tacit mental Propositions" (1975, 575, IV.5.4). The fact that Locke writes that words play a role even in the unspoken ("tacit") mental propositions that we use when reasoning "within ourselves" strongly suggests that Locke has *ideas* of words in mind, because mental propositions "within ourselves" can only consist of ideas.[7] The distinction between pure and impure ideas corroborates this reading, suggesting that when we think with language we are still thinking with ideas, although they are impure because ideas of words are not ideas of qualities ascribed to the objects of which we are thinking. For example, unlike the ideas of tall or tanned, the idea of the word "woman" is not an idea of a quality ascribed to a woman.

Still, these passages are not decisive, because there are passages where Locke clearly distinguishes words and ideas. In the concluding chapter of the *Essay*, Locke describes "*Ideas* and *Words*, as the great Instruments of Knowledge" (1975, 721, IV.21.4). Locke also writes that "Words, by their immediate operations on us, cause no other *Ideas*, but their natural

---

[6] See Dascal 1987; Losonsky 2001, 160–3 and 171–3; and Pécharman 1992.

[7] Locke also writes that "when we make any Propositions within our own Thoughts, about *White* or *Black*, *Sweet* or *Bitter*, a *Triangle* or a *Circle*," in these latter cases "we can and often do frame in our Minds the *Ideas* themselves, without reflecting on the Names" (1975, 575, IV.5.4). The use of the phrases "pure *Ideas*" and "reflect on the *Names* themselves" supports Kretzmann's reading. For Locke, reflection consists only of ideas of the mind's own operations (1975, 105, II.1.4).

Sounds" (1975, 224, II.18.3), that they are "external sensible Signs" that allow us to communicate "invisible *Ideas*" (1975, 405, III.2.1), and that "Words... do really exist without me" (1975, 634, IV.11.7). These passages not only distinguish words and ideas, but they suggest that words are qualities or powers in objects that produce ideas in us, and not just ideas in the human understanding (1975, II.8.8). After all, if words were ideas, which for Locke are private, invisible, and inaudible to others, they could not be used to communicate our ideas to other people. For these reasons, the judicious conclusion is that Locke simply had not worked through this issue carefully, but he clearly was committed to the idea that language is essential to human cognition.

Language and Classification

The claim that "Locke's major theses concerning the metaphysics and epistemology of classification can be understood independently of his teachings about language" (Jolley 1999, 162; also see 144) would in fact distort Locke's *Essay*. In Locke's philosophy, language plays a key role in classification because complex ideas require the support of language. Language plays a central role in Locke's argument against the traditional Aristotelian views on species and natural kinds (Guyer 1994, 116).

Locke challenges the view that the way human beings classify natural objects into species rests on a natural and objective classification that is independent of the mind's activity. Locke's argument regarding classification begins with the puzzle that on the one hand "[a]ll Things, that Exist... [are] particulars," but "[t]he *greatest part of Words*, that make all languages, *are general Terms*" (1975, 409, III.3.1). Locke solves this puzzle by arguing that general terms are made to signify general ideas, and general ideas are constructed by the mind using the process of abstraction. Generality and universality, then, "belong not to the real existence of Things; but *are the Inventions and Creatures of the Understanding*, made by it for its own use, *and concern only Signs*, whether Words, or *Ideas*" (1975, 414, III.3.11). Ideas are general "when they are set up, as the Representatives of many particular Things," and words are general "when used for Signs of general *Ideas* (ibid.). For Locke, "such a manner of sorting of Things, is the Workmanship of Men" (1975, 462, III.6.37).

It must be noted that Locke extends his view that all things are particular to ideas and words themselves: "[U]niversality belongs not to things themselves, which are all of them particular in their Existence, even those Words and *Ideas*, which in their signification are general" (ibid.). So even ideas and words are particulars, and insofar as they are grouped into sorts and kinds, this grouping is also a product of the workmanship of the human understanding.[8]

So far, it appears that Locke has a two-tiered account of classification in which general ideas play the fundamental role, while language, specifically general words, play a secondary role that can easily be detached from the more fundamental work performed by general ideas. A closer reading of Locke's text, however, reveals that his thinking on this subject was more complicated. For instance, Locke writes that "to be of any Species, and to have a right to the name of that Species, is all one" (1975, 414–15, III.3.12), "*abstract* Ideas, *with Names to them ... are Essences* (1975, 419, III.3.19), and "*each abstract* Idea, *with a name to it, makes a distinct Species*" (1975, 463, III.6.38). After discussing how general names and ideas are first formed, Locke writes: "To conclude, this whole *mystery* of *Genera* and *Species*, which make such a noise in the Schools, and are, with Justice, so little regarded out of them, is nothing else but abstract *Ideas*, more or less comprehensive, with names annexed to them" (1975, 412, III.3.9). Here again Locke maintains that genera and species are "nothing else but abstract *Ideas*... with names annexed to them."

The annexation of names appears throughout Locke's discussion of classification. For instance, Locke writes that "the abstract *Idea* or Essence, to which the name Man belong[s]" is not "of Nature's making," but "the uncertain and various collection of simple *Ideas*, which the Understanding puts together, and then abstracting it, affixed a name to it" (1975, 416, III.3.14). He emphasizes the annexation of names in the conclusion to his discussion of general terms:

> To conclude, this is that, which in short I would say, (*viz.*) that all the great Business of *Genera* and *Species*, and their *Essences*, amounts to no more than this, That Men making abstract *Ideas*, and settling them in their Minds, with names annexed to them, do hereby enable themselves to consider Things, and discourse of them, as it were in bundles, for easier and readier improvement, and communication of their Knowledge. (1975, 420, III.3.20)

He repeats this in his discussion of the names of substances: "The measure and boundary of each Sort, or *Species*, whereby it is constituted

---

[8] Hence Chappell (1994, 42) is wrong to suppose that for Locke ideas are not particulars.

that particular Sort, and distinguished from others, is what we call its *Essence*, which *is* nothing but that *abstract* Idea *to which the Name is annexed*" (1975, 439, III.6.2). For instance, "Why do we say, This is a *Horse*, and that a *Mule*; this is an *Animal*, that an *Herb*? How comes any particular Thing to be of this or that *Sort*, but because it has that nominal Essence, Or, which is all one, agrees to that abstract *Idea*, that name annexed to" (1975, 443, III.6.7).

The reason Locke regularly mentions the annexation of names in his discussion of classification is that annexation contributes to the formation of general ideas. This is particularly true in the case of the ideas of what Locke calls "mixed modes." Mixed modes are general ideas that combine ideas that are very different from each other, do not appear to coexist in nature, and are "scattered and Independent" (1975, 288, II.22.1; also 208, II.16.7). For example, Locke believes that there is no more special connection between killing and a human being than between killing and a sheep, but we have a special idea and word for the former – murder – but not the latter. Similarly, Locke maintains that the idea of incest combines scattered and independent ideas that are connected only in the mind, not in nature (1975, 432, III.5.7).[9] Because these general ideas are "made *very arbitrarily* ... without Patterns" in nature (1975, 429, III.5.3),[10] the mind needs something that keeps the disparate ideas together, and Locke maintains that names perform this function:

> *The near relation* that there is *between Species, Essences, and* their *general Names*, at least in *mixed Modes*, will farther appear, when we consider, that it is the Name that seems to preserve those *Essences*, and give them their lasting duration. For the connexion between the loose parts of those complex *Ideas*, being made by the Mind, this union, which has not particular foundation in Nature, would cease again, were there not something that did, as it were, hold it together, and keep the parts from scattering, Though therefore it be the Mind that makes the Collection, 'tis the Name which is, as it were the Knot, that ties them fast together. What a vast variety of different *Ideas*, does the word *Triumphus* hold together, and

---

[9] All the examples of mixed modes Locke gives are tied to moral, legal, political, and social practices: obligation, lie, triumph, apotheosis, appeal, reprieve, adultery, incest, sacrilege, murder, parricide, justice, gratitude, and procession.

[10] Locke writes that "'tis the Mind, that combines several scattered independent *Ideas*, into one complex one; and by the common name it gives them, makes the Essence of a certain Species, without regulating it self by any connexion they have in Nature" (1975, 430, III.5.6).

deliver to us as one *Species*!...I think, that which holds those different parts together, in the unity of one complex *Idea*, is that very word annexed to it. (1975, 434, III.5.10)

Names have a smaller role to play in the construction of general ideas of substances, but they still play a role:

This then, in short, is the case: *Nature makes many particular Things, which do agree* with one another, in many sensible Qualities, and probably too, in their internal frame and Constitution: but 'tis not this real Essence that distinguishes them into *Species*; 'tis *Men*, who, taking occasion from the Qualities they find united in them, and wherein, they observe often several individuals to agree, *range them into Sorts, in order to their naming,* for the convenience of comprehensive signs; under which individuals, according to their conformity to this or that abstract *Idea*, come to be ranked as under Ensigns: so that this is of the Blue, that the Red Regiment; this is a Man, that a Drill: And in this, I think, consist the whole business of *Genus* and *Species*. (1975, 462, III.6.36)[11]

Although ideas of substances are regulated by patterns of coexisting qualities that come together in our experience – and thus ideas of substances have "a lasting Union" compared with ideas of mixed modes (1975, 465, III.6.42) – human beings have a greater need for order than is found in experience, even in the case of substances.

The patterns of nature are more fluid than is required for human conduct, and thus the ideas combined in general ideas of substances are simpler and more rigid than the patterns on which they are based. Nature does not make "precise and *unmovable Boundaries*" and instead produces many specimens that fall outside any boundaries we might set with the general ideas we make (1975, 454, III.6.27). But by combining several ideas and annexing a name to it, our ideas of substances are supposed to remain steady through the mutations particular substances are liable to undergo (1975, 419, III.3.19). Moreover, the ideas human beings collect into general ideas are simpler than the patterns found in nature. Human beings limit themselves to "a few sensible obvious Qualities" (1975, 456, III.6.29; also 452, III.6.25), whereas nature, even as we experience it, is much more

---

[11] A little later Locke writes, "*the making of* Species *and* Genera *is in order to general names*, and... general Names are necessary, if not the Being, yet at least to the completing of a *Species*, and making it pass for such" (1975, 463, III.6.39).

complex.[12] In fact, "[t]*he more general our* Ideas *are*," Locke writes, "*the more incomplete and partial they are*" (1975, 459, III.6.32). For Locke, important evidence that general ideas of substances are the workmanship of human beings, not nature, is the fact that human beings usually do not agree on what the precise number of qualities is that a substance comprehends. The disagreement is due to the complexity of nature's patterns. "It requires much time, pains and skills, strict enquiry, and long examination," Locke writes, "to find out what, and how many those simple *Ideas* are, which are constantly and inseparably united in Nature, and are always to be found together in the same Subject" (1975, 457, III.6.30).

By relying on a few obvious properties and a shared name, we impose an order that makes communication possible. In fact, it seems that Locke believes that classification is driven by our linguistic needs. We have a "need for general Words," because we make complex ideas out of individual simple ideas (1975, 449, III.6.21). We "*range*" the simple ideas we find more or less together "*into Sorts, in order to their naming*" (1975, 462, III.6.36). He writes:

> But Men, in making their general *Ideas*, seeking more the conveniences of Language and quick dispatch, by short and comprehensive signs, than the true Nature of Things, as they exist, have, in the framing of their abstract *Ideas*, chiefly pursued that end, which was, to be furnished with store of variously comprehensive Names. (1975, 459–60, III.6.32)

In fact, according to Locke, "[t]*his all* [is] *accommodated to the end of Speech*," and a purpose of language is to be "the easiest and shortest way of communicating our Notions" (1975, 460, III.6.33). The second purpose of language is to aid human beings to record their thoughts, and classification is also driven by that need: "[O]bserving several particular Things to agree with others, in several of those simple *Ideas*, we make that collection our specific *Idea*, and give it a general name; that in recording our own Thoughts and in our Discourse with others, we may in one short word, design all the Individuals that agree in that complex *Idea*" (1975, 458, III.6.30).

In sum, for Locke there is such a close tie between classification and language because, first, classification itself is driven by the human need

---

[12] Locke's attack on using the obvious appearances of objects to classify them is central to his attack on Aristotelian classification of species and genera in terms of their salient perceptual qualities. See Guyer 1994, 116.

to record and communicate, and language is essential to these activities; and second, in most cases classification is unstable – either because in the case of mixed modes classification does not rest on any pattern in nature or because natural patterns are too complex or fluid for our classificatory needs – so that human beings must rely on the stability of outward signs, particularly words, to keep the ideas combined in general ideas. For these reasons, as Locke puts it, "there is so close a connexion between *Ideas* and Words" that he cannot properly discuss human knowledge without focusing on language.

Language and Confusion

Locke identifies two broad categories of problems with language. On the one hand, there are abuses that are "*wilful Faults and Neglects*, which Men are guilty of" and, on the other, there is "the Imperfection that is naturally in Language" (1975, 490, III.10.1). Both lead to obscurity and confusion and to problems in a variety of domains, including politics as well as science, but they have significantly different roots.

The abuses due to negligence or malice were familiar at least since Francis Bacon's discussion of the "Idols of the Market Place." According to Bacon, the marketplace is the locus of human intercourse and communication, and language is its primary tool. Language becomes an idol in human exchange when human beings assume that their words refer to something when in fact they do not, and when human beings use words that are ill-defined (Bacon 2000, 42). The abuses Locke discusses also fall into these two categories. The abuses of "using of Words, without clear and distinct *Ideas*" (Locke 1975, 490, III.10.2), equivocation (491, III.10.5), "*affected Obscurity*" (493, III.10.6), and the assumption that "the Speaker and Hearer had necessarily the same precise *Ideas*" (503, III.10.22) are all problems of definition. For instance, affected obscurity is willfully using words with unusual meanings or structuring words in such a way that their ordinary meanings change.

Abuses of reference are "*taking* [words] *for Things*" (1975, 497, III.10.14) and "*setting them in the place of Things, which they do or can by no means signify*" (499, III.10.17). It is important to point out that simply using words that lack a referent – for instance, mistakenly believing that unicorns exist and saying so – is not an abuse of language. What is abusive, according to Locke, is to assume that our words refer to things unmediated by ideas that are the workmanship of the understanding. Locke's famous distinction between real and nominal essences is helpful here. The real essence of a substance is its "real internal... Constitution," that is, the properties that constitute the inner structure of a substance and that are responsible for their observable properties and patterns of properties (1975, 417, III.3.15). Nominal essences are the properties that human beings sort together along with names in their general ideas and general names. It is an abuse of human language to suppose that one is referring to a real essence when in fact and at best one is referring only to a portion of nature that satisfies the general ideas we constructed. For instance, it is abusive to suppose that when I say, "Gold is malleable," I am saying something about the real, internal constitution of gold, namely gold's real essence. The proper stance is to admit that all I am saying is that *"what I call Gold is malleable"* (1975, 499, III.10.17).

These confusions of meaning and reference are abuses because they undermine the purpose of language. The purpose of language, when used in communication, is to inform others what one has in mind; to do this quickly and easily; and, by quickly and easily informing others of what one has in mind, *"to convey the Knowledge of Things"* (1975, 504, III.10.23). So when people use language obscurely or ambiguously, they are abusing language because they are not informing others quickly and easily of what they have in mind. Such abuses, Locke implies, are avoidable because human beings can speak carefully or remain silent when their ideas are deficient.

Besides these abuses due to the intentional misuse of language, language has inherent and practically unavoidable imperfections. "[T]he very nature of Words," Locke writes, "makes it almost unavoidable, for many of them to be doubtful and uncertain in their signification" (1975, 475–6, III.9.1). The reasons for this uncertainty are because "Sounds have no natural connexion with our *Ideas*, but have all their signification from the arbitrary imposition of Men," and because words can signify the inherent diversity of ideas (1975, 477, III.9.4). For instance, if the phonetic structure of a word was naturally connected to a certain set of ideas, human beings could decipher a word's signification simply by hearing it. Moreover, lacking such a natural connection, if at least ideas were uniform and stable, then once a person learned what the conventions are that tie words to ideas, she could rely on the conventions and the stability of ideas to decipher the meaning of words. But with words being tied to ideas only by human convention and the ideas themselves changing and unstable, the meaning of language is a source of instability.

The signification of a word is uncertain because learning and retaining their signification is difficult in these four cases:

First, The *Ideas* they stand for, are very complex, and made up of a great number of *Ideas* put together.

Secondly, Where the *Ideas* they stand for, have no certain connexion in Nature, and so no settled Standard, any where in Nature existing, to rectify them and adjust them by.

Thirdly, Where the signification of the Word is referred to a Standard, which Standard is not easy to be known.

Fourthly, Where the signification of the Word, and the real Essence of the Thing, are not exactly the same. (1975, 477, III.9.5)

Needless to say, Locke believes that these four conditions are part of the human condition. Ideas of mixed modes are "*so complex*" and "*have no Standards*" (1975, 478, III.9.6 and 7). Moreover, the convention or "*common Use*, that is the Rule of Propriety," for words signifying such ideas is, Locke writes, "no where established, and often a matter of dispute" (1975, 479, III.9.8). Ideas of substances do have standards in nature that can help stabilize these general ideas, and so the general names tied to them. Nevertheless, this standard is itself a source of uncertainty. The standard "*either cannot be known at all, or can be known but imperfectly or uncertainly*" (1975, 482, III.9.11). If the standard is taken to be the real internal constitution of things – the real essence – then the signification of these words can never be adjusted and established, because, very simply, real essences are "utterly unknown to us" (1975, 482, III.9.12). Of course, relying on this standard is really an abuse of language because this is a case of using words "*in the place of Things, which they do or can by no means signify*" (1975, 499, III.10.17), but the proper standard is not much help either because knowledge of it is imperfect or uncertain.

The proper standards for ideas of substances are the patterns of coexisting simple ideas human beings experience – for instance, that malleability, fusibility, and the color yellow (among other qualities) are found together in our experience of gold.[13] But these simple ideas that coexist in a pattern or "archetype" are "very numerous" (even "almost infinite"), and all of them have an "equal right to go into the complex, specifick *Idea*" that human beings construct from this pattern

---

[13] As Locke writes at the outset of his discussion of language, "*Words in their primary or immediate Signification, stand for nothing, but the* Ideas *in the Mind of him that uses them*" (Locke 1975, 405, III.2.2).

(1975, 482, III.9.13). Locke refers to the great variety of properties a metal can have when heated and "in the Hands of a Chymist, by the application of other Bodies," and so the properties that coexist are "not easy to be collected, and to be completely known." Accordingly, different people, depending on their skill, attention, and circumstances, will construct different general ideas of gold, and this holds for all substances. Locke concludes "that the complex *Ideas* of Substances, in Men using the same Name for them, will be very various; and so the significations of those names, very uncertain" (ibid.).

This imperfection of our substance terms, Locke believes, is at the root of many disputes. Locke recounts the time he witnessed a dispute among learned men about "whether any Liquor passed through the Filaments of the Nerves" (1975, 484, III.9.16). After the debate went on for a while without resolution, Locke asked for the signification of the word "liquor" and it turned out that they all had different meanings for this term and that the meanings they had assigned to the term were not certain. Thus they discovered that their dispute was not about what passed through the nerves but about the meaning of a word. Locke maintains that "this is the Case in the greatest part of Disputes, that Men are engaged so hotly in" (1975, 485, III.9.17).

This is no less true when it comes to the imperfection of moral and political language, where there are no standards in nature. Many a controversial debate "concerning *Honour, Faith, Grace, Religion, Church*, etc. . . . is nothing but this, that they are not agreed in the signification of those Words" and "all the contests . . . are only about the meaning of a Sound" (1975, 480, III.9.9). Paying attention to the imperfections of language will not only help solve many philosophical, scientific, legal, moral, and theological disputes, but it will improve humanity. In a striking passage Locke writes that, "I am apt to imagine, that were the imperfections of Language, as the Instrument of Knowledge, more thoroughly weighed, a great many of the controversies that make such a noise in the World, would of themselves cease; and the way to Knowledge, and, perhaps, Peace too, lie a great deal opener than it does" (1975, 489, III.9.21).[14]

---

[14] The idea that the study of language can also serve the aims of political progress is echoed in Habermas 1981. For Habermas, however, the source of progress lies not in the study of the imperfections of language but in the study of the fundamental assumptions of successful communication.

Conclusion

In sum, Locke turns to natural language because the human understanding in its pursuit of knowledge relies on language. Knowledge requires generalizing and classifying, and the mind's activity of sorting the world under general ideas rests on human language. Words are the "knots" that bind our conventional ideas needed in our moral, legal, and other social institutions. Here words offer the stability that these ideas cannot have without them. Moreover, even when human beings rely on experienced patterns of nature, as in our ideas of substances, words are needed to construct general ideas that are simple and clear enough to facilitate communication and memory. Communication and memory, at least in most ordinary situations, require a degree of speed, simplicity, and constancy that nature, at least as far as human beings can know, does not offer.

Finally, although language is a source of strength because it contributes to the communication and recording of knowledge, it is also a source of confusion. Language is not just prone to be abused by sloppy human beings, but language by its very nature is imperfect. If we pay attention to these imperfections, however, we can solve many theoretical and practical disputes, because often they are not about things but about language and its meaning.

Locke's linguistic turn, then, is significant for four reasons. First, Locke is not concerned about symbol systems in general or about reforming natural language, but his interest is in the powers and limits of natural language. Second, his turn to natural language is tied to his epistemology. Locke turns to language in order to understand the nature, extent, and limits of human knowledge. Third, Locke's linguistic turn is tied to his psychological interests in that he believes that mind and language are so closely tied that one cannot be understood without the other. Finally, language by nature is systematically misleading, and greater attention to the philosophy of language will rectify many disputes that are, at bottom, linguistic in nature. These features of Locke's discussion of language in the *Essay* place it at the very beginning of the evolution of modern philosophy of language and dramatically distinguish Locke's discussion of language from that of his predecessors.

TWO

◆

The Road to Locke

John Locke's linguistic turn in his *Essay Concerning Human Understanding* was the culmination of an intellectual evolution from Plato to Hobbes that steadily moved natural language to the center stage of philosophy. An important feature of this development is the legacy of Renaissance humanism. Reacting to the distortions of ordinary language when seen through the prism of syllogistic logic, the humanists elevated the role of natural language by making ordinary usage of natural language a standard for philosophical style and critique. The needs of formal logic distorted natural language, whereas ordinary usage, which included public oratory, preserved natural language. By turning to the diversity of purposes people have when ordinarily using language, humanist writers also began to tie language to psychology instead of logic. The concern for the systematic features of language and its underlying logical structure that marked Scholastic philosophy was to be transformed later by Leibniz in light of Locke's linguistic turn, as we will see in Chapter 3, but the road to Locke is a road that leads away from traditional logic and, as Locke put it, to "another sort of Logick and Critick, than what we have been hitherto acquainted with" (1975, 721, IV.21.4).

Plato

Before Plato (427?–347? B.C.E.) there is some discussion of linguistic issues. For example, Pythagoras argued that the connection between names and their referents is natural, not arbitrary; Parmenides distinguishes between true and false names in his argument against the existence of real difference and change; and the Sophists, particularly Protagoras, paid attention to the grammatical structure of natural language.

However, the earliest surviving work devoted to language is Plato's *Cratylus*, probably written in 388 B.C.E.

The central theme of this dialogue is a debate between what have been called conventionalists and naturalists on the question of naming. Cratylus and then Socrates argue that names are natural, not conventional, whereas Hermogenes argues that the connection between names and objects is established purely by convention. What Socrates has in mind is that the letters and syllables of a name express the form or essence of the names' object, or that there is a "natural fitness of names" (*Crat.* 390e–391a).[1] Socrates speculates that a name expresses the essence of its object by consisting of letters and syllables that "imitate" or resemble the essence of the named object (425d). Although Socrates admits that his speculation is "wild and ridiculous," he believes that this is the best available explanation (426b).

Socrates' reasoning about names has two major elements: an argument to show that names must have a natural meaning, and an explanation or theory of natural meaning in terms of resemblance. To show that names are naturally connected to their objects, Socrates pursues two lines of reasoning. First, if the relation is arbitrary, then names cannot be true. Yet names in true propositions are true, so the relationship cannot be arbitrary. Second, naming is an action and, as any action, has a standard of correctness. Just as there is a proper way of sawing wood, there is a proper way of naming an object. But if naming is arbitrary, Socrates concludes, then there is no proper way of naming an object, so conventionalism about names is false.

Once Socrates settles on the view that conventions alone cannot yield standards of correctness for names and that "names ought to be given according to a natural process" (387d), Socrates, prodded by Hermogenes, who resists this conclusion without more detail about this natural process, looks for such a theory. Socrates is clear that he really does not know what this natural process is, but he is willing to think about it (391a). Although Socrates does outline the view that certain sounds have natural meanings – for example, "the letter ρ appears to me to be the general instrument expressing all motion" (426b) – it needs to be pointed out that he limits this view to only a certain class of names. Socrates distinguishes between secondary names and primary names, and only primary names' sounds resemble or imitate their objects

---

[1] All translations of Plato's text are from Plato 1971.

(422d–423c). Secondary names are derived from primary names, and often in secondary names the original meaning is lost.

In fact, a consequence of this account is that most ordinary names are not correct, as Socrates suggests when he shows that Hermogenes has an incorrect name because he is not the descendant of Hermes (429c). Moreover, Socrates believes that many names are corrupted with letters that are inappropriate, and human beings do rely on convention or custom to determine meaning when names are incorrect or corrupted (434d–435d). So Socrates' theory of natural meaning applies to "the most perfect state of language," whereas ordinary languages rely on convention and are imperfect (435c).

But even a perfect language based on resemblance can be imperfect. In fact, the ideal language that is the root of contemporary language is imperfect because the original givers of names contradicted themselves (438c). Whereas some names express the rest and stability of reality, other names resemble the flux of appearances. Socrates suggests that the original name givers were guided by the mistaken belief that all things are in flux and fell "into a kind of whirlpool" that they "want to drag us in after them" (439c). The resulting problem for human beings is that we need some other standard of truth besides language to resolve this "battle of names" (438d). This other standard, Socrates argues, is the named object itself. "The knowledge of things is not to be derived from names," Socrates declares, "No, they must be studied and investigated in themselves" (439b).

Although this dialogue addresses key issues in the philosophy of language, primarily the reference and conventionality of language, Plato's and Locke's foci are significantly different. First, whereas Locke is concerned with natural, existing language, Plato ultimately is laying out a theory about ideal names, not real names in natural languages, which are mostly corrupted and incorrect. Second, whereas Locke ties the study of language to epistemology and argues that we cannot lay down the principles of knowledge without getting clear about the nature of language, Plato by the end of the *Cratylus* concludes that language does not play a role in the proper pursuit of knowledge. Third, although Socrates briefly mentions that "custom and convention must be supposed to contribute to the indication of our thoughts" (435b), the *Cratylus* has next to nothing to say about the relevance of language to human thought. Finally, unlike Locke, Plato does not see the study of language as relevant to solving philosophical problems. Both agree that natural language is systematically misleading – Plato because its names are tied to the less-than-real realm of fleeting appearances, and Locke because names require greater stability than reality or experience has to offer. But only Locke believes that many theoretical and practical disputes are really linguistic in nature and can be resolved by paying more attention to the nature of natural language.

Consequently, if these are the hallmarks of modern philosophy of language – concern for the structure of natural languages, tying the study of language to epistemology and the philosophy of mind, and seeing the study of language as a source of solutions to philosophical problems – then Plato's *Cratylus* does not mark the beginning of the philosophy of language. Of course, this dialogue is the first theoretical treatise on language, and the significance of this must not be underrated. If philosophy of language is simply philosophical reflection on language, then of course the philosophy of language begins with the *Cratylus*. But this would obscure a substantial and real divide that separates the evolution of the philosophy of language after Locke and the philosophical study of language before Locke. Perhaps the clearest evidence of this divide is the difficulty in seeing how in the ground prepared by Plato the philosophy of language could grow into a field with pretensions to be First Philosophy. Locke's discussion, in contrast, pushes language close to the center of philosophical focus, and it is much easier to see how, on the basis of Locke's discussion, philosophers come to believe that the core problems of philosophy in epistemology, metaphysics, and even ethics can be solved if they are recast as problems in the philosophy of language.

Plato, particularly in the *Parmenides*, does at times turn to language to gain greater clarity about philosophical issues. For example, in his discussion of existence and nonexistence, Plato, in the voice of Parmenides, asks "What, then, is the meaning of... 'if a one does not exist'?" and writes "suppose one says, 'if largeness does not exist,' or 'if smallness does not exist,' or any other statement of that type" (*Par*. 160b–c). Plato assumes that these statements are meaningful and concludes from the meaningfulness of the supposition that "if a one does not exist" that we can know that something does not exist (160d). This reliance on language in the *Parmenides* to resolve ontological issues does illustrate the point that ontological puzzles are easier to think about and discuss when they are recast in linguistic terms, and this point plays a key role in the evolution of the philosophy of language in the twentieth century (Quine 1960, 270–6). But Plato's reliance on linguistic insights is not the product of a strategy, program, or even a central commitment on his part. In fact, Plato quickly moves back to the mode he prefers, speaking of objects by referring to "this nonexistent one."

Plato's dialogue the *Sophist* has a more direct discussion of language than the *Parmenides*. Here Plato, in the voice of a stranger, seeks to show the possibility of "saying... something which yet is not true" (*Soph.* 236e), and the reason for showing this is that Plato wants to "establish by main force that what is not, in some respect has being, and conversely that what is, in a way is not" (241d). During the argument that meaningful false statements are possible, Plato suggests that "thinking and discourse are the same thing, except that what we call thinking is, precisely, the inward dialogue carried on by the mind with itself without spoken sound" (263e). But it is important to be clear about Plato's intent here. Plato is arguing that just as we can assert and deny in language, we can make judgments in the mind; and just as our spoken assertions and denials can be true or false, our mental judgments can be true or false (264a–b). The point Plato is after is that propositions can be affirmed or denied in thought and in language, and consequently it is possible to affirm and deny falsehoods in language, and not only in thought. There is no suggestion here that natural language – "spoken sound" – is part of human thinking or somehow determines or structures how we think. Unlike Locke, Plato does not turn to language because he thinks that human language is the key to understanding the human mind and its knowledge.

Aristotle

Language receives a much more fine-tuned treatment from Plato's student Aristotle (384–322 B.C.E.). Aristotle recognizes the conventionality of public language: words and the "inarticulate sounds of wild animals" mean something, but the words of a human language signify in virtue of human conventions. Aristotle also has a much deeper appreciation than Plato of the significance of the various parts of speech, and he recognizes that declarative sentences are the bearers of truth-values, not names. At the same time, Aristotle recognizes that not all sentences have truth-values – for example, prayers (*De Inter.* 17a).[2] In many ways, Aristotle's appreciation of the grammatical structure of language is much more refined than Locke's, which lacks much discussion of logical and

---

[2] All translations of Aristotle's text are by J. Ackrill in Aristotle 1984.

grammatical structure. Still, it is in Locke, and not Aristotle, that we find the beginnings of the philosophy of language.

Most of Aristotle's discussion of natural language is in *De Interpretatione*. He begins with the assertion that "spoken sounds are symbols of affections in the soul, and written marks symbols of spoken sounds" (16a). While language, both written and spoken, differs among human beings, the affections in the soul are "the same for all." The affections of the soul are images or likenesses of actual things, and these too are the same for all. It seems, then, that for Aristotle language refers to objects in virtue of mental states that resemble those objects.[3] This rudimentary psychological account of linguistic meaning survived into the modern period, in the work of Hobbes and Locke, for instance, and it still plays a role today (Avramides 1998; Apel 1976, 36).

However, there is a fundamental difference between Locke and Aristotle. Whereas Locke brings his discussion of language into the center of his discussion of mind and knowledge, Aristotle draws a sharp distinction between his linguistic studies and psychology. After he mentions that language symbolizes states of the soul, which are the same for everyone, Aristotle adds that "these matters have...been discussed in the work on the soul and do not belong to the present subject" (*De Inter.* 16a). Aristotle's *De Anima* as well as his other psychological writings in the *Parva Naturalia* contain almost nothing about human language. In *De Anima* Aristotle mentions assertion on two occasions (*De An.* 431a and 432a), but he is not thinking specifically about language. For example, he writes that "imagination is different from assertion and denial; for what is true or false involves a synthesis of thoughts" (432a). Clearly his point here could just as well have been made referring to judgments, because all he wants to say is that imagination lacks truth-value.

When Aristotle does connect mind and language, he always argues as follows. If a certain distinction can be made in thought, then a similar distinction must be made in language. For instance, he argues that because "there are in the mind thoughts which do not involve truth or falsity, as well as those which must be either true or false," speech must also have units that do not have a truth value and units that do" (*De Inter.* 16a). The same line of argument is used later in the treatise: "[I]f, in thought, that judgment is contrary of another...the same must needs hold good either regard to spoken affirmations" (23a). Aristotle then switches to discussing the nature of contrary judgments, and the

---

[3] Compare Arens 1984 and Coseriu 1971.

topic of language is left behind for the remainder of this treatise. In fact, except for the first four chapters, where Aristotle discusses the meaning of language, parts of speech, sentences, and declarative sentences, *De Interpretatione* is primarily devoted to topics central to syllogistic logic: affirmation, negation, universal and particular propositions, contradiction, and contrariness.

Aristotle makes a famous detour into metaphysics in this treatise on logic and language. He considers the argument that the law of the excluded middle – that necessarily a proposition is either true or false – appears to entail determinism: that "there are no real alternatives; everything takes place of necessity and is fixed" (18b). Aristotle in the end rejects this argument on the basis of the metaphysical intuition that obviously we can effectively deliberate about the future and that alternatives are indeed available to us when we deliberate about the future. He concludes from this that "it is plain that it is not necessary that of an affirmation and a denial, one should be true and the other false" (19a). The law of the excluded middle does not hold for propositions about the future and other potentialities. So here again Aristotle does not let linguistic or even logical intuitions drive his metaphysics, but instead he adjusts his logic in light of his metaphysical intuitions.

In sum, what Aristotle develops is what has been described as a "logical conception of language," because its fundamental categories are logical categories and his theory of language is developed primarily in the context of a logical inquiry, namely Aristotle's theory of syllogisms (Arens 1984, 14). Although we do find in Aristotle a psychological theory of linguistic meaning, it would be false to say that Aristotle develops a psychological conception of language because his brief inquiry on human language is not motivated by the desire to attain a better understanding of mind and cognition. This difference between Aristotle and Locke is fundamental and is what separates Aristotle from the philosophy of language in the modern period.

The Middle Ages

The sharp division that Aristotle draws between his linguistic and psychological inquiries fades and dissolves in medieval thought. This is evident immediately in the writings of Boethius (480–524), whose Latin translation of and commentaries on *De Interpretatione*, together with his translation of the *Categories*, served as Europe's source of Aristotle's philosophy until the arrival of Arabic and Hebrew translations in

Spain and Sicily in the twelfth century. Where Aristotle mentions the soul only in *De Anima* and sharply distinguishes its subject matter from the subject of *De Interpretatione*, Boethius takes an excursion into the topic of the soul, its notions or affections, and how they are related to external objects on the one hand and spoken language on the other.

Although this excursion served to bring the two domains closer together, the fundamental characteristic of this encounter is that Boethius raises psychological issues in order to be clearer about language, not vice versa. However, in an interesting passage in Boethius's commentary on *De Interpretatione*, he endorses the view, attributed to Porphyry and the Peripatetic school, that "discourse [*oratio*] was threefold: one written with letters, one produced by the voice, and once connected in thought; one consisting of notions, one of voice, and one of letters" (Arens 1984, 170). This echoes Plato's suggestion that thinking is inward discourse, a view found again in Augustine's *De Trinitate*, where Augustine refers to "the word that sounds outwardly" and "the word that gives light inwardly," that is, mental words or locutions, which for Augustine are more fundamental. But Boethius, citing Porphyry, develops this doctrine further by suggesting that "if there are three kinds of speech, the parts of speech must also be threefold" (ibid.). So a noun is not just a category for written or spoken language but applies to mental discourse as well.

Boethius's description of thought as a kind of discourse played an important role in medieval philosophy and anticipates the idea that language can serve as the model for understanding human thinking. Still, for Boethius mental and linguistic discourse are distinct, and spoken or written language is in no sense constitutive of mental discourse. Boethius endorses Aristotle's view that the impressions of the soul, or what Boethius glosses as notions or concepts and which are the constituents of mental discourse, are the same for all people, whereas spoken or written language varies from nation to nation (Arens 1984, 174–6). Not only is mental discourse distinct from written or spoken discourse, but the latter acquires its meaning and structure solely from the former. Just as a piece of copper becomes a coin only because it is the value of something, vocal sounds become words only when they "are instituted for the signification of notions" (Arens 1984, 171). In fact, linguistic meaning is wholly parasitic on human thought, and human thought is constituted independently of language: "From the things which were before our eyes and which we determined in their proper substance, arise notions. The notions are always notions of things, and when they have been constituted, the signification of the word soon originates. Beside the concept, the word signifies absolutely nothing" (Arens 1984, 162). Finally, nowhere does Boethius appear to suggest that language is in some sense systematically misleading or that the study of human language will lead to solutions to philosophical problems.

The role Boethius assigns to language in his philosophy is preserved throughout medieval philosophy. For instance, Anselm of Canterbury (1033–1109) distinguishes in the *Monologion* between external verbalization or locution (*locutio*) using spoken language and inward locution that relies solely on imagination or understanding. Each kind of locution relies on "its own kind of word," but the inward words "are natural and hence the same for all peoples," whereas spoken words are invented and diverse. Moreover, if we have inward natural words for an object, we do not need any other words to think about it; but the arbitrary words of speech, without these natural words, are useless. Finally, "natural words are truer insofar as they resemble and designate their objects more manifestly," and "therefore the natural word ... is correctly said to be the most proper and principal word for its object" (Anselm 1998, 24: *Mon.* par. 10).[4] In fact, Anselm claims that possibly this kind of verbalization "exists in the supreme substance, and that it existed before its objects, in order for things to be created through it" (ibid.).

Although Anselm affirms the primacy of mental locution over language, he also suggests that there is another kind of locution that combines internal and external states, namely when human beings "think of the name 'man' but not say it aloud." In this sort of case, I am thinking of "outwardly perceptible signs," but "within myself, imperceptibly" (1998, 23: *Mon.* par. 10). This case differs from pure mental locution because we do not use the perceptible signs of language "either perceptibly or imperceptibly" (ibid.). Here Anselm anticipates the view that evolves in the modern period that language is integrated into human thinking. Although this contribution should not be underestimated, the idea does not play a central role in Anselm's philosophy. Anselm does not see imperceptible thinking of spoken words as essential or important to human thought, and it clearly is to be shunned for proper cognitive activity.

---

[4] The primacy of the understanding is also reflected in Anselm's willingness to violate ordinary language (*usus loquendi*) in order to better express true understanding (*intelligere*) (Henry 1974, 11–14, 181–96).

Anselm's younger contemporary Peter Abelard (1079–1142) also emphasizes the independence of thought from human language in his *Glosses* on Aristotle's *De Interpretatione*. Abelard also denies that different languages require different concepts and adds:

> [T]he things or the things of the intellect lose none of their identity because of the diversity of language, neither concerning their essence nor the function. But words and the letters through the diversity of languages are diverse essentially in their proper forms of sound and writing as well as diverse in their significative function [*officium significandi*]. (1933, 324)

The things of the intellect or notions are distinguished from sensations and images. Sensation and imagination focus on the "thing itself" – for example, it appears in perception and the image we have when remembering it – but the intellect observes "its nature or property" (1933, 317). Sensation and imagination simply encounter or are acquainted with the object or image, but they do not discriminate anything in it (1933, 329). The task of the intellect is to discriminate or discern the various properties the object has and to determine its nature. This activity of discernment and discrimination yields the notions, and it is the intellect's notions that give language its meaning (1933, 321).

Abelard characterizes language use in terms of three types of situations: a questioner and a respondent, a teacher and a learner, and a narrator. He writes that the "interrogator and the teacher and the one who makes a continuous speech" use the following order: first they "look at the thing, then, considering its nature or property, conceive the notion, and at last, to manifest that notion, speak a word; they proceed from the things to the notion, and from the notion to the spoken word" (1933, 324). The other three, he continues, act conversely: "[F]irst they hear the word, from it they conceive the notion, and by the notion they are led to the thing to heed" (1933, 324–5). Although this second type of situation that proceeds from words to notions might have been an opening for a discussion of how language can help construct or constitute our notions, Abelard does not discuss this. Abelard most certainly believed that the word causes the hearer to think of notions conventionally associated with the heard word.

Still, Abelard has been credited with explicitly turning the problem of universals into a semantic problem and offering a semantic solution (Kretzmann 1967, 369). Abelard suggests that universality – for example, that distinct individual roses all have the property of being a rose – consists in "words [*vocibus*] alone" (1933, 16). However, it is important to notice that Abelard recognized that the term "word" is not univocal and that in his writings he struggles with this ambiguity. In his *Glosses* Abelard notes that "Aristotle did not well to state... that the notions were always the same, but not the words," because "words, too, might, in some way, be said to be identical like notions" (1933, 323). What he has in mind is that words can be identified in terms of their meaning: "[T]he words of different languages happen to be the same on account of the same mode of signification concerning the same thing. '*Anthropos*' signifies the same thing as 'homo,' and in the same way: as a rational mortal being" (ibid.). So although words in different languages "are diverse essentially in their proper forms of sound and writing" (1933, 324), they can also be identified by their mode of signification.

Elsewhere Abelard attempts to capture the ambiguity of "word" with his well-known distinction between the uttered word or *vox*, which for Abelard, following Boethius, is a physical accident, namely a quantity of air, and *sermo*, which is the mode of signification of a word, or the word in regard to its meaning. With this distinction in place, Abelard does not identify universals with uttered words anymore; instead, a universal is the mode of signification of a word (*Universal est sermo*; 1933, 522). So strictly speaking, Abelard is not relying on language to solve the problem of universals. In fact, he is relying on signification to explain universality, and for Abelard, throughout his writings, words signify in virtue of the mind's concepts (1933, 308–9; Marenbon 1997, 182). Therefore, it is more accurate to call Abelard's position about the nature of universals "conceptualism," in order to highlight the fact that concepts or mental names, not names of public languages, underwrite universality for Abelard.

Abelard's treatment of universals is often seen as a modification of more radical positions according to which universals literally are uttered words. Roscelin of Compiègne (1050–1120), who was probably one of Abelard's teachers, is one of the first medieval philosophers associated with nominalism in its "naïve and complete sense" (Copleston 1952, 144). There is nothing left of Roscelin's writings except a letter to Abelard, but according to Anselm, as well as John of Salisbury (1115–80), Roscelin taught that universals are "merely vocal emanations" (*flatus vocis*) (1998, 237; Rogers 1997, 115). However, we know too little about Roscelin to be sure what he meant with this claim.

The philosopher who is usually associated with a linguistic account of universals and whose writing we do know is William of Ockham.

It is tempting to state that Ockham simply denies that universals are "extra-linguistic objects" and that for him "universals are elements in language" (Loux 1974, 3).[5] After all, Ockham does in fact write that "a spoken word...is a universal" and "a conventional sign is a universal" (1974, 79 and 82; *Summa Logicae* I.14 and 15). Moreover, Ockham departs from the orthodox medieval view, found in Boethius and Thomas Aquinas, that words signify concepts directly and objects indirectly, whereas concepts signify objects directly (Broadie 1987, 6–7). Ockham agrees with his Franciscan brother Duns Scotus that spoken words of ordinary language signify the very same things as mental concepts, and that words, like concepts, signify their objects immediately (1974, 50; *Summa Logicae* I.1)

Nevertheless, Ockham is very clear about the primacy of mental concepts: "I say vocal words are signs subordinated to mental concepts or contents." Although spoken words signify objects directly, Ockham still affirms the medieval orthodoxy that "the concept signifies something primarily..., whilst the word signifies the same thing secondarily" (ibid.). The signification of public language depends completely on its associated concepts, and when concepts change their signification, their conventionally associated words "immediately, and without any new convention," also change their signification.

A crucial difference between words in public language and concepts, or what, following the tradition of Boethius, Ockham also calls "conceptual terms" or "mental words," is that "a concept or mental impression signifies naturally whereas a spoken or written term does not signify anything except by a voluntary convention [*voluntariam institutionem*]" (ibid.). For Ockham a decision or agreement can change what the words of public language signify, but no decision or agreement can alter the natural signification of conceptual terms. Concepts signify objects not in virtue of agreement or convention, according to Ockham, but in virtue of similarity, and for Ockham the similarity between concepts and objects is a natural relation, not a conventional one (Ockham 1957, 41 and 44; also Adams 1987, 121–33).

---

[5] In fairness, it must be stated that Loux goes on to write that for Ockham language includes more than written and spoken languages, but less informed accounts omit this qualification and attribute to Ockham the view that "They are simply useful terms which we can employ to sort the world" and "species, category, or archetypes are not valid properties...; they are ways of describing similarities we notice among objects" (Magee 1996).

This difference plays an important role in Ockham's treatment of universals. While Ockham does say that a spoken word such as a common noun can be said to be universal because it can be predicated of many things, it is universal only by convention. Because concepts signify naturally, they are universal by nature, and Ockham's discussion of universals treats only universals by nature (*Summa Logicae* I.14). The reason for this is simple. Ockham *rejects* the view that "nothing is universal of its very nature..., but only by voluntary convention" (1970, 2:271). Ockham believes that an object belongs to a genus and species by its very nature and that "a universal expresses or indicates the nature of a substance" (1974, 86; *Summa Logicae* I.17; also see Adams 1987, 109–10). If all universals were conventional, then nothing would be of a certain kind by its nature but only by convention.

Consequently, as with Abelard, it is appropriate to call Ockham a "conceptualist." He is a nominalist in the sense that he argues that only individuals exist and that universals are really individuals, but he does not reduce or characterize universals in terms of spoken or written symbols. For Ockham, the spoken and written words of public language are parasitic and subordinate to mental words that, Ockham writes citing Saint Augustine, "belong to no language; they remain only in the mind and cannot be uttered aloud" (1974, 49–50; *Summa Logicae* I.1).

An important topic of scholastic logic developed with particular clarity was the supposition (*suppositio*) of terms. Signification and supposition were considered to be two components of the meanings of terms: signification was what the term signified or indicated by itself, whereas supposition was aimed at treating terms in the context of a proposition. Scholastic logicians recognized that terms can have different meanings in different contexts, and theories of supposition were devoted to understanding the apparently different meanings terms have in the context of a whole proposition. For instance, to use Ockham's illustration, the theory of supposition attempts to explain the differences in signification of "man" in "Man is a species" and "Man is an animal."[6] The proper supposition of a term could be either formal or material. The proper material supposition of a term was the term itself, as is the case for "man" in the proposition "Man is a noun." The proper formal supposition of a

---

[6] To see the difference notice that whereas "Man is an animal. This is a man. So this is an animal." is a valid argument, the following argument is invalid: "Man is a species. This is a man. So, this is a species."

term was either an individual, for example, Socrates in the proposition "Socrates is an animal," or the form or essence of an individual, for instance, manhood in the proposition "Man is a species." The theory of supposition is an account of the different objects terms can stand for, depending on how they are used in a proposition, and thus it appears that this doctrine is an early form of the doctrines of connotation and denotation or sense and reference that we will encounter in Mill and Frege.

The Renaissance

Humanism, naturalism, and the "restoration" of Greek and Roman literature are central if not defining features of the Renaissance, and these involved a new appreciation of natural language. The study of classical texts, the concern for the nature and values of human beings, and the recognition of the importance of nature and the place human beings have in nature all conspired to direct attention to the role that natural language plays in human life. This new appreciation of natural language is such a central feature of Renaissance philosophy that it has been claimed that there is a connection between "Renaissance philosophers of language" and the "central philosophical concerns... of recent Anglo-American philosophy" (Copenhaver and Schmitt 1992, 351). This includes "turning to language as the main or only object of analysis" and examining language not simply for its own sake but for the light it sheds on philosophical problems.[7]

Renaissance thinkers developed a critique of philosophy, particularly Scholastic logic, that appealed to customary speech (*usus loquendi*). For example, Lorenzo Valla (1407–57) in his critique of Aristotelian logic and metaphysics, *Retilling Dialectics and Philosophy* (*Repastinatio dialecticae et philosophiae*), exhorts the reader: "Let us conduct ourselves more simply and more in accordance with natural sense and common usage. Philosophy and dialectic... ought not to depart from the customary manner of speaking" (Valla 1962, I.679).

Valla recommends the orator's approach to reasoning as persuasion, particularly as found in Quintillian's *Institutio Oratoria*, over the

---

[7] Copenhaver and Schmitt (1992, 351) cite Ayer, who writes in *Language, Truth and Logic*, that "the philosopher, as an analyst, is not directly concerned with the property of things" but "only with the way we speak about them" (1946, 57).

logician's perspective on reasoning as formal demonstration. He cites the Roman rhetorician Quintillian throughout his writings (Mack 1993, 26) and relies on Quintillian's discussion in *Institutio Oratoria* of proofs, evidence, enthymemes, induction, and modal statements, among other things, to develop his own views on logic. For instance, Quintillian's emphasis on persuasion over validity underlies Valla's rejection of syllogisms that were considered deductively valid, namely syllogisms in the third figure, because they do not belong to common usage and have no persuasive force. All the valid syllogisms in the third figure have conclusions such as "Some men are mortal" and "Some mortals are not men," and Valla claimed that these indefinite particular conclusions are awkward and cannot be found in arguments that convince in a real dispute. In fact, Valla calls such syllogisms "entirely insane" (Valla 1962, II.739; Ashworth 1974, 9; and Copenhaver and Schmitt, 226–5).

By relying on linguistic usage (*consuetudo*), particularly the grammar and style of the Latin or classical Roman texts, Valla generates a critique of Scholastic doctrine of supposition. Valla suspected, correctly, that the doctrine of supposition was needed to make sense of abstractions, as is the case with the term "man" in the statement "Man is a species." In the *Elegances of the Latin Language* (*Elegantiae Linguae Latinae*), Valla suggests that an analysis of possessive pronouns and adjectives (*meus/mei, tuus/tui*) undermines the need for a doctrine of supposition.

In general, Valla was wary of abstraction – he even disliked the use of formal notation in logic – and attempted to reduce or eliminate the number of abstract ideas that played a role in medieval philosophy. He rejected the distinction between form and matter; he attempted to reduce Aristotle's ten basic categories – substance, quantity, quality, relation, place, time, position, state, action, and affection – to only three: substance, quality, and action; and he attempted to eliminate terms such as "the good" (*bonum*) or "being" (*ens*) in favor of the apparently simpler term "thing" (*res*) (Valla 1982, II.370–82). The emphasis on "*res*" expressed Valla's commitment to the nominalist view that only individual things exist and that even abstract concepts cannot be thought of without thinking of individuals (Trinkaus 1970, 152–3).

So Valla is not simply interested in promoting better Latin style and rhetoric. Instead, he believes that the usage of the classical Latin authors and orators should play a foundational role in the study and teaching of logic and, moreover, that it provides a criterion for adjudicating philosophical issues (Jardine 1982, 797–9; 1988). The Spanish humanist Juan Luis Vives (1492–1540) is "another Quintillian" (Tobriner 1968, 1) who echoes Valla's promotion of traditional rhetoric over traditional logic in philosophy. He criticizes the traditional methods and problems of logic – including the use of variables – because "Cicero, if he were resurrected, would not understand" (Vives 1964, 3:41). Cicero (106–43 B.C.E.) was seen as a father of the rhetorical tradition that, building on Aristotle's *Topics*, replaced logic with rhetoric and made rhetoric into the primary instrument of philosophical reasoning. For Vives, Cicero's understanding, as well as the understanding of famous orators, rhetoricians, historians, and statesmen such as Pliny the Elder, Julius Caesar, Quintillian, Cato, or Pliny the Younger, were touchstones of what was admissible and intelligible in philosophy. Accordingly, because these rhetoricians would "be at a loss" to understand central issues in traditional logic, these issues were worthless. Vives particularly had in mind statements that expressed logical ambiguities that Scholastic logicians studied and that played a key role in widely used logic texts (1964, 3:43).[8] These typically paradoxical statements were collected under the headings of *sophismata* and *insolubilia*, which were widely ridiculed by Renaissance humanists.[9]

Vives accuses Scholastic logicians of making rules that are "against every custom of speech [*loquendi consuetudinem*]" (1964, 3:53). Even Aristotle, Vives continues, did not depart in his "entire dialectic" from the "meanings of Greek speech that scholars as well as children, little women and in fact all the common people used." The reason is that the logician "does not make and bequeath a new language, but teaches out of ancient and familiar observed rules" (ibid.). Vives argues that a Latin sentence such as *Homo est albus* is a Latin sentence not because it is so ruled by Latin grammar, and neither do rhetorical figures make speech splendid and refined because it is decreed by rhetoric. "Rather it is so because that sentence was judged to be Latin by Roman people, who spoke true Latin," and thus "the grammarian does not decree that it is Latin, but he teaches that it is" (1964, 3:42). Similarly, the principles of logic are not decreed by logicians; the logician teaches what "customary speech ... sanctions" (ibid.). The rules of logic, like the rules

---

[8] For example, Peter of Spain's (1205?–1277) *Summulae Logicales*, used in introductory logic courses, went through 166 editions and was used throughout Europe for 300 years (Mullaly 1945, 133–58).

[9] They often involved ambiguities of the syncategorematic or logical terms in a proposition. For instance, Vives cites the sentence, "Although Varro is a man, yet he is not a man because Varro is not Cicero" (1964, 3:41).

of grammar and rhetoric, are adapted to the "common usages of speech" (*usum loquendi communem*).

According to Vives, the problems and issues of various intellectual endeavors are rooted in common usage, and their resolution also rests on the ordinary use of language: "Accordingly, diligently the common use of words is observed. Out of it [the common use of words] much in all the disciplines and inquiries arises and is routed, as is seen in Aristotle, Plato and others" (1964, 3:193). His actual application and development of this idea to areas outside of logic is mostly limited to critiques of Aristotle's writing style in the *Metaphysics*.

The focus on actual linguistic usage, at least as is found in the classical Latin writers, is a genuine contribution of Renaissance humanism and anticipates ideas in contemporary philosophy of language. In fact, some have found the outlines of postmodern thought in this work. Particularly, Valla has been interpreted to hold the view that human public language is so central to human cognition that not only does it determine the structure of thought, but language also constitutes the world itself – or things (*res*), as Valla would put it. It has been argued that Valla overcomes "the steep split between word and object" and understands the world experienced by human beings as a "creation of ordinary language" (Gerl 1974, 65 and 224). Valla "collapsed all distinction between 'sign' and 'signified,'" and "he is destroying... a ripely traditional shibboleth as the dualism of sign/thing" (Waswo 1987, 108). Words "can indeed only 'signify' themselves; their meaning is their use" and so "language and the people who use it do not 'represent' a reality but constitute one" (Waswo 1987, 109–10). On this reading of Valla, "the intoxicating and terrifying possibility of *making* meaning...is...one of the...defining energies of the entire Renaissance" (Waswo 1987, 132).

If this claim is true, then the Renaissance would be the birthplace of the philosophy of language in its most radical form, anticipating views that have been associated, rightly or wrongly, with the philosophies of Wittgenstein and Derrida. These views include structuralism, or the view that the meaning of a word is determined by the word's relationships to the rest of the language in which it exists; linguistic determinism, or the view that language determines or constitutes how human beings think and know; and linguistic irrealism or idealism, namely the view that human language somehow constitutes the world.

Unfortunately, this reading of the Renaissance is highly speculative. The textual evidence for it is too thin: it depends on translations and interpretations of ambiguous passages that have competing alternatives that are much less dramatic (Monfasani 1989).[10] Moreover, this irrealist, determinist, and structuralist reading is not supported or motivated by either the narrow textual or wider historical context. First, Valla, as a humanist should, tries to write clearly and boldly. His writings are not mysterious or difficult, even when he affirms religious mystery over philosophy,[11] and he does not shrink from controversy, as shown by his best-known work, the *Declamation on the Falsely Credited and Fabricated Donation of Constantine*.[12] Thus, it is very unlikely that Valla, a clear and straightforward thinker, would express such a dramatic thesis as that mind and world are constituted by language in only an ambiguous, tentative, and convoluted manner. Second, there are no historical antecedents for this view and no historical reception of Valla's purported view that there is no distinction between word and object.[13] If Valla indeed had this idea that language constitutes mind and world, it came to him ex nihilo and was completely ignored by all his contemporary readers.[14]

[10] For instance, Gerl (1974, 17) translates *Non est verbigena nisi vera sophia* as "True wisdom is born through the word" (*Die wahre Weisheit ist durch das Wort geboren*) but more-literal, alternative translations are "There is no making of words without true wisdom" (Monfasani 1989, 312) or "No words are born unless [there is] true wisdom." Waswo interprets claims such as "the term is a thing" (*vocabulum res est*) as expressing Valla's "collapse of the venerable dichotomies between word and thing, sign and signified...that words can only 'signify' that class of 'things' called words" (Waswo 1987, 108; also 1989, 327; also Gerl 1974, 220–2). An alternative reading is that Valla only claims that words themselves are things without implying that words are everything. This alternative is supported by Valla's claim that the word "'thing' signifies a thing: the latter is signified, the former is its sign; one is not a word, the other is a word" (1982, 122–4). Waswo acknowledges this passage but believes that it might be a joke or that Valla has reached the limits of his language, which is not adequate "to describe the newly constitutive role of language" (1987, 108 and 110).

[11] For instance, in his dialogue *On Free Will* Valla argues that philosophy can show that human liberty and God's foreknowledge are compatible because knowing something does not entail causing it (1934, 40–50 and 67–70). But philosophy is unable to solve the mystery how human freedom is compatible with God's will, which only religious faith can resolve (1934, 82–4 and 88–93).

[12] Here Valla showed conclusively that a document used to justify papal territorial claims was a forgery.

[13] In fact, Vives, who follows Valla on key issues, is taken to task by Waswo for his unwillingness or inability "to follow in Valla's footsteps" (1987, 117 and 125).

[14] I think an important aspect of this reading of the Renaissance is that it is driven by an unargued but substantial philosophical assumption that somehow the recognition of the historical and conventional nature of language and relying on common usage to adjudicate philosophical issues entails irrealism, linguistic determinism, and structuralism (Waswo 1987, 94, 100–1, 122–3, 125, and 128). This assumption is false.

Nevertheless, perhaps the kernel of truth to this reading of the Renaissance is that the emergence of the philosophy of language should be located in the linguistic focus of Renaissance humanism, not in Locke's linguistic turn. Perhaps it is the subordination of both logic and philosophy to rhetoric that spawned the philosophy of language, not Locke's epistemological and metaphysical orientation in his linguistic investigations.

Although it is certainly true that the Renaissance's focus on natural language contributed to a greater awareness of the nature and structure of natural language, it still seems misleading to claim that the philosophy of language emerges with Renaissance humanism or that there is a philosophically significant kinship beyond the basic interest in language between "Renaissance philosophers of language" and the "central philosophical concerns... of recent Anglo-American philosophy" (Copenhaver and Schmitt 1992, 351).

To say that Renaissance humanists turned to natural language to solve philosophical problems is an overstatement. They turned to natural language to critique Scholastic logic, but there is no serious attempt to examine language to solve epistemological or metaphysical problems. Valla's discussion of free will, for example, does not rest on linguistic analyses of any kind, and Vives's discussion of moral philosophy in *On the Corruption of Moral Philosophy* is not based on concepts rooted in ordinary linguistic practice. In fact, Vives points to the deficiencies of language when he points out that although nobility and goodness are really distinct, they are "mixed together in all languages," and that Aristotle's discussion is unclear on this issue. Vives goes on to wonder if Aristotle judged nobility according to the senses, as does the mob, or according to reason (1964, 6:14).

The turn to natural language and ordinary discourse by Renaissance humanists is primarily motivated by the practical needs of public speakers, the needs of politicians and preachers, not by philosophical concerns. For example, Vives's *The Theory of Speech* (*De Ratione Dicendi*) begins with a brief but mostly standard Aristotelian account of language and meaning. Without speech, the mind would remain forever hidden from others, and Vives adds that "Speech is a distribution [*sortitus*], which is derived from the mind as the stream is from the spring" (1964, 2:93). Later he states that in all speech there are words and thoughts (*verba et sensa*) and that these stand to each other as body and mind. Words are like covers over the light of the soul, but "words whose thoughts are taken away are empty and dead objects" (1964, 2:94–5).

Vives has very little to say about this relationship between words and thoughts, except to mention very briefly that words have "natural signification" when they are used to signify just those things for which the words were invented, endorsing the Aristotelian view that the signification of words is conventional (1964, 2:97). Vives's real interest is not the meaning and signification of language and how these can illuminate philosophical problems. He is motivated by the value of speech in "assemblies and all of society" (1964, 2:93), and consequently he aims to teach how to use words and thoughts to achieve a proposed end (2:95). Accordingly, the subjects he discusses at length are the origin and age of words, the etiquette of word use, and various figures of speech. The topics throughout the book convey what features of language concern Vives: color, tone or dress (*color*) of speech, erudition, mores, rank, teaching, persuasion, engaging the listener, and decorum, among others.

This nonphilosophical perspective is not surprising given the very strong "anti-philosophical impulse in oratorical humanism" (Copenhaver 1988, 93). The thinkers of this period were inclined to reject philosophy and replace it with what today we might call "applied social sciences." Vives, for example, declares that the orator is wiser than the philosopher (1964, 1:799), and Valla concludes his discussion of free will by championing the practical man over the philosopher. He maintains that the philosopher is an object of ridicule and that philosophy is the seedbed of heresy, and Valla repeats this view in what was supposed to be a commemorative speech for Thomas Aquinas but was turned into an attack on philosophy.

So the significant difference between Locke's linguistic turn and the perspective on common linguistic practice in the Renaissance is that Locke turns to study the structure and function of natural language to solve basic philosophical problems, whereas Renaissance philosophers turned to natural language to reject philosophy and to promote other disciplines and practices. Moreover, Renaissance humanists were firmly rooted in the Aristotelian view that language is parasitic on thought. They did not share Locke's insight that mind and language are so closely tied that one cannot be understood without the other. Finally, whereas Locke turned to natural language because he believed it to be systematically misleading and a source of errors and disputes in philosophy and elsewhere, Renaissance humanists typically did not view natural language as a source of error. It is hard to find anything in their writings to suggest that philosophical problems are, at bottom, linguistic in nature.

Locke's linguistic turn, however, included significant Renaissance themes. The Renaissance severed the tie between the study of logic and language that was maintained throughout Scholasticism since Abelard. On this view, logic was concerned with the meaningful word – *sermo* – and hence logic was understood as the science of words (*scientia sermocinalis*). Seen through the prism of logic, language was characterized in terms of its formal properties, particularly those relevant to deductive validity. For this reason, propositional meaning and truth were the central properties of language in the Scholastic conception of language, and typically these formal properties were not apparent in ordinary usage. The logical structure was an underlying or implicit structure, and consequently a technical vocabulary was needed to reveal this structure. This meant that departures from ordinary or common usage were necessary. If the task is to make explicit the meaningful features of language that play a role in deductive relations, then ordinary usage, whose efficiency depends on leaving those features implicit, cannot be the touchstone for understanding the nature of language.

The critique of logic found in Renaissance humanism was that logic had nothing to do with language on the grounds that it introduced and was concerned with formulations that departed from ordinary usage. Classical grammar and rhetoric, according to humanism, had the proper take on language, and, seen through this prism, language was characterized in terms of its pragmatic properties. Instead of looking at the underlying features relevant to deductive relations, humanists were concerned with the role of language in influencing people and how one might properly adapt one's speech to "places, circumstances and persons" to achieve one's ends in speech.[15] This shift in focus to the actual phenomena of linguistic use pushed natural language into the philosophical foreground, and subsequent philosophy from Bacon to Locke is marked by this shift. There is an important difference, however, in the concerns of Bacon, Hobbes, and Locke. Whereas humanist texts on logic and language focused on political and literary discourse, Bacon and his successors in English philosophy were primarily concerned with the language of science.

Bacon

The sixteenth-century interest in the role of natural language in scientific reasoning is clearly documented in the writings of Francis Bacon

---

[15] For instance, see Vives 1964, 2:90.

(1561–1626). Bacon's education was guided by humanist texts, particularly Agricola's *De Inventione Logica*, and he clearly draws on the Renaissance themes that logic has to be useful to human beings and that demonstrative, syllogistic logic is too limited in this respect (Jardine 1974). However, he also criticizes humanist approaches to logic. He writes in the *New Organon* that "the logic now in use, though properly applied to civil questions and the arts which consist of discussion and opinion, still falls a long way short of the subtlety of nature" (1968, 1:129; 2000, 10).

Falling short of the "subtlety of nature" is also the problem with demonstrative logic: "We reject proof by syllogism, because it operates in confusion and lets nature slip out of our hands" (1968, 1:136; 2000, 16). Bacon proposes to remedy this defect in his *New Organon*, whose title already expresses Bacon's ambition to replace Aristotle's logic. He aims to focus on the process of arriving at judgments useful to scientific inquiry, and this he calls "induction": "For we regard *induction* as the form of demonstration which respects the senses, stays close to nature, fosters results and is almost involved in them itself" (ibid.). Thus Bacon aims to direct philosophers' attention to nature and to tie their reasoning to the processes of nature, rather than to its application in human affairs.[16]

An important feature of Bacon's account is how it configures the relationship between mind and language. In his critique of syllogisms, Bacon affirms the traditional Aristotelian view that words are "counters and signs of notions,... the soul of words, and the basis of every such structure and fabric" (ibid.). Bacon then immediately draws the conclusion that if these notions are "badly or carelessly abstracted from things, and are vague and not defined,... everything falls to pieces," and accordingly he prescribes a logic that considers the formation of the notions that form the basis of all our reasoning (ibid.). The first concern of such a logic is deception and error: how to correct deceptions due to the senses and how to remedy errors due to the understanding (1968, 1:138–9; 2000, 17–18).

---

[16] Gaukroger (2001, 5) argues that Bacon aims to "transform the epistemological activity of the philosopher from something essentially individual to something essentially communal." Although this is an important corrective to our understanding of Bacon and helps explain his interest in language, it is also true that for Bacon public or social interaction is a deep source of errors, and human beings need forms of reasoning whose standards are pried away from convention and instead are found in nature.

The errors due to men's understandings are Bacon's famous idols or illusions of the mind, and one of these involves language: the idols of the marketplace (*idola fori*) or, more accurately, the idols of the forum, common, or town square. These are illusions due to human association. "Men associate through talk," Bacon writes, and this causes illusions because "words are chosen to suit the understanding of the common people" (1968, 1:164; 2000, 42). A "poor and unskillful code of words incredibly obstructs the understanding," but unfortunately the technical terms and definitions that "learned men have been accustomed to protect and in some way liberate themselves, do not restore the situation at all." The conclusion Bacon draws is simple: "Plainly words do violence to the understanding, and confuse everything; and betray men into countless empty disputes and fictions" (ibid.).

Bacon finds these linguistic illusions "the most troublesome of all, because relying on the agreement of words and names they have insinuated themselves into the understanding" (1968, 1:170; 2000, 48). Human beings believe that their reason rules words, "but it is also true that words retort and turn their force back upon the understanding" (ibid.). In *Of the Advancement of Learning*, Bacon makes this point even more dramatically: "[C]ertain it is that words, as a Tartar's bow, do shoot back upon the understanding of the wisest, and mightily entangle and pervert the judgment" (2001, 137–8).

Part of the problem, as noted, is that "words are mostly bestowed to suit the capacity of the common man, and they dissect things along the lines most obvious to the common understanding," not along the lines of a "sharper understanding ... in accordance with nature," that is, science. Still, "words resist" this sharper understanding and even learned men "end in disputes about words and names." The reason for this, Bacon explains, is that language cannot be improved without improving the understanding, and this requires tying language to particular "instances" (ibid.).[17]

How language is tied to the mind and, more specifically, how language forces itself upon the human understanding are not discussed in great detail. What Bacon has to offer is that names that do not refer to anything and names that are poorly defined impose illusions on the understanding. Although the illusions due to empty names are easily

---

[17] For instance, the word "heat" needs to be tied to known instances of heat: any flame, solids on fire, natural hot baths, boiling liquids, sun's rays, especially in summer at noon, and so on (Bacon 1968, 1:236; 2000, 110).

remedied by rejecting false and groundless theories, Bacon believes that the illusions due to poorly defined names are "complex and deep-seated" (1968, 1:171; 2000, 49). Names are badly defined because they are based on "poor and unskillful abstraction," and Bacon suggests that abstraction is an inevitable source of problems because it depends on what comes "to the notice of the human senses" (ibid.). Bacon has little more to offer about the nature of natural language.

Nevertheless, Bacon has a novel perspective on language. Ordinary languages as well as more formalized, technical languages are problematic because language itself is problematic.[18] Moreover, simply turning to the mind for clarification or solution of the problems of language is also unhelpful because language ceases to be purely parasitic on the mind: language insinuates itself into the human understanding. At the same time, the mind itself, particularly its capacity to abstract, has limitations on account of which language is limited. In this way, Bacon begins to replace the Scholastic union of language and logic as well as the Renaissance affair of language and rhetoric with a new and tighter relationship between cognition and language. Due to this new bond between mind and language in which both depend and infect each other, philosophical problems, particularly epistemological problems, are tied to questions of language.

Hobbes

Thomas Hobbes (1588–1679), too, was under the influence of the Renaissance oratorical tradition but at the same time, in midlife, affirmed more-traditional syllogistic approaches to reasoning (Skinner 1996). While Hobbes's mature work does not share Bacon's disdain for demonstrative reasoning, he also assigns language a dual role. It is necessary for human civilization, but at the very same time it is a source of error and confusion.

Without language, people could not give and understand the commands of authorities, and for Hobbes without authority there is no society. Without this "benefit of speech...there would be no society among men, no peace, and consequently no disciplines (1839, 1: *De Homine* 10.3). On account of speech, particularly rhetoric (*oratio*), human beings are "drawn together, agreeing to covenants, live securely,

---

[18] So, as Dascal writes, "Paradoxically [Bacon's] critique of language will lead to an enhanced interest in language" (1993, 142).

happily, and elegantly" (ibid.). In the *Leviathan*, Hobbes broadens the scope of the benefits of speech beyond the issuance of commands to include the capacity to "declare [their thoughts] to one another for mutuall utility and conversation" (1996, 24/12).

Language also improves human reasoning because words allow us to reason with generalizations. Without words or some other sensible marks for our thoughts, "whatsoever a man has put together in his mind by ratiocination without such helps, will presently slip away from him, and not be revocable but by beginning his ratiocination anew" (1839, 1:I.2.1). Moreover, without the use of words we can reason only about particular things and particular causes (1996, 33/19). Thus any reasoning about general causal relationships, namely the sort of reasoning essential to science, will require some sensible marks, and that is why Hobbes believes that science begins with the defining of words (1996, 35/21).

In fact, in the *Leviathan* Hobbes seems to go as far as to declare language to be constitutive of all reasoning.[19] Human beings have unregulated trains of thoughts in which thoughts "wander, and seem impertinent one to another; as in a Dream" (Hobbes 1996, 20/9; also Losonsky 2001, 48–51). But thoughts can be regulated by desire or a "passionate thought," and regulated trains of thought are cases of reasoning when they are regulated by an acquired and artificial method, namely reason (Hobbes 1996, 53/35). Reason is acquired through "study and industry" and it depends on the "invention of Words, and Speech" (1996, 23/11). Reason is "consequent to the use of Speech," Hobbes writes (1996, 459/367), and so children who are not yet speaking "are not endued with Reason at all" (1996, 36/21). We reason when we regulate our search for causes and effects with an acquired method, embodied in a system of sensible symbols, that guides us from one specific thought to the next. The result of such a methodical search for causes and effects is science or natural philosophy (1996, 35/21 and 458–9/367; also see Jesseph 1996, 96–102).

Still, language is also a source of trouble, and in the *Leviathan* Hobbes lists four abuses of language (1996, 25–6/13). First, the signification of language is not stable, and consequently words can be used that do

---

[19] This appears to be a departure from Hobbes's earlier position in *De Corpore* (I.1.3), according to which there clearly is such a thing as "reasoning in silent thought without words." On this tension in Hobbes, see Losonsky (1993).

not have an accompanying conception that gives words their meaning. Meaningless words are still powerful enough to deceive both speakers and hearers into thinking that they are meaningful. The second and third abuses are due to metaphorical uses of words and lying, both of which are causes of deception. The fourth abuse of language is when we use speech to hurt or "grieve one another" (1996, 26/13).

Only the first abuse is tied to the nature of language rather than to human nature. The function of language is to "transferre our Mental Discourse, into Verbal; or the Trayne of our Thoughts into a Trayne of Words," and consequently when words do not signify mental conceptions, we are abusing language. This is why for Hobbes "words are wise mens counters; they do but reckon by them: but they are the mony of fooles" (1996, 28–9/15). Only fools use words as if they had value on their own; the wise know that words, used properly, only keep track of thoughts.[20]

Hobbes identifies various ways in which we can use meaningless names. Human beings introduce names that they have not defined, sometimes to confuse others, sometimes to hide their ignorance, and sometimes simply out of ignorance. Hobbes likes to illustrate this point with Scholastic terms of art such as "hypostatical" or "consubstantiate" (1996, 30/16–17 and 35/21). People also combine names that have contradictory signification, such as, "incorporeal substance," which for Hobbes is contradictory because the only thing "substance" can properly signify is a body (1996, 30/17). Another example of abuse is, in contemporary terminology, a category mistake (Ryle 1949). For example, Hobbes believes that the terms "general object" or "universal thing" are absurd because terms that apply only to language, namely "general" and "universal," are combined with "thing," which Hobbes maintains only refers to individual bodies (1996, 35/17).

Although Hobbes's philosophy represents the continued intensification of the philosophical pursuit of language that emerges in Bacon's work, Hobbes only takes us to the threshold of Locke's linguistic turn that marks the beginning of the philosophy of language in the modern

---

[20] Nevertheless, as counters, names are important because they allow us to do an accounting of our thoughts or reasoning. Hobbes points out that, in Latin, financial accounts are called *rationes*, accounting is *ratiocinatio*, and the items in an accounting ledger are *nomina* or names (1996, 29). Hobbes speculates that the Latin terms for reason (*ratio*) and reasoning (*ratiocinatio*) are accounting metaphors.

period. The line between Hobbes's and Locke's turn to language is a fine one, to be sure, and Locke's philosophy has the definite marks of Hobbesian influence (Rogers 1988). Yet the differences between them are strong enough to stake out the emergence of the philosophy of language in the modern period for Locke.

First, there is the issue of influence. Hobbes's discussion of language is an integral part of his methodological doctrines about the pursuit of scientific knowledge, and these doctrines had little influence at home in England or on the continent (Jesseph 1996). Hobbes's political philosophy, of course, had much greater influence, particularly in France, and the influence of Hobbes on Leibniz and Spinoza must not be underestimated. But none of these lines of influence specifically carries Hobbes's views on language. Locke's case is very different: his philosophy of language had a serious impact on his readers (Aarsleff 1994). Samuel Johnson quotes Locke 3,200 times in his *Dictionary of the English Language*, and perhaps the clearest example of this influence is Condillac's attempt to develop Locke's philosophy in his influential *Essai*.

Second, and more important, there is something to Condillac's claim that Locke was "the first who has written on this matter as a genuine philosopher" (Condillac 1947, 1:5; 2001, 8). Hobbes's conception of philosophy is a premodern conception that includes the natural and social sciences. "By PHILOSOPHY," Hobbes writes, "is understood *the Knowledge acquired by Reasoning, from the manner of the Generation of anything, to the Properties; or from the Properties, to some possible Way of Generation of the same*" (1996, 458/367). Consequently, philosophy in Hobbes's sense includes geometry, astronomy, and physics as well as first philosophy (1996, 463/371). Language plays a role in this pursuit because correct reasoning is deductive reasoning based on general principles and relying on deductive inferences, which for Hobbes is limited to the traditional syllogism. This deductive approach to the pursuit and organization of human knowledge was at odds with the "experimentalist" approach promoted by the newly founded Royal Society (Jesseph 1996).

Locke, of course, had close ties to the founding members of the Royal Society, and he was elected to be a fellow of the society in 1668, serving on the committee for "considering and directing experiments" (Woolhouse 1983, 36). Locke's philosophy captures this commitment to the role of experience and experiment in science. At the same time, Locke clearly distinguishes science and philosophy and locates his contribution within the domain of philosophy. In the Epistle to the Reader of the *Essay* Locke writes

> The Commonwealth of Learning, is not at this time without Master-Builders, whose mighty Designs, in advancing the Sciences, will leave lasting Monuments to the Admiration of Posterity; But every one must not hope to be a *Boyle*, or a *Sydenham*; and in an Age that produces such Masters as the Great *Huygenius* and the incomparable *Mr. Newton*, with some others of that Strain; tis' Ambition enough to be employed as an Under-Labourer in clearing Ground a little, and removing some of the Rubbish, that lies in the way to Knowledge. (1975, 9–10)

He goes on to explain that too many "uncouth, affected, or unintelligible terms" were introduced into the sciences and "vague and insignificant Forms of Speech, and Abuse of Language, have so long passed for Mysteries of Science." His task is "to break in upon the Sanctuary of Vanity and Ignorance" and this, Locke continues with characteristic humility, "will be, I suppose, some Service to Humane Understanding" (1975, 10).

In these passages Locke clearly signals that he does not intend to contribute to the advancement of science and that his contribution instead will be second order in nature (Jolley 1999, 16). Instead of doing science, he will investigate the terms and concepts that are used in the sciences and will offer standards for evaluating them and distinguishing the legitimate from the illegitimate ones. As we saw in the preceding chapter, this involves looking at the nature and scope of the human understanding, which leads Locke to consider the nature of language and its role in human understanding. So when he turns to language, Locke turns to it primarily as a philosopher, not a scientist, and he treats language as a philosophical problem. Hobbes, on the other hand, sees himself as contributing to the advancement of science, and he turns to language in his pursuit of scientific knowledge.

This brings us to a third and most significant difference between Locke and Hobbes on language. Locke's focus is clearly on natural language and its role in human cognition, which is not quite Hobbes's target. Hobbes is primarily concerned with what the scientist needs in the pursuit of scientific knowledge, that is, generalizations about causes and effects and a deductive calculus for using and generating generalizations. Thus, his primary concern is not the nature of natural language and its relationship to the human mind, but with the "apt imposing of Names" and "getting a good and orderly Method in proceeding from the Elements, which are Names, to Assertions...; and so to Syllogismes,...till we come to Knowledge of all the Consequences of names appertaining to the subject in hand" (1996, 35). In other words, Hobbes is concerned with symbol systems in general and does not draw sharp distinctions between natural language and formal languages, such as the languages of arithmetic, geometry, or logic.

For this reason, Hobbes begins all his major works with a discussion of language: chapters 4 and 5 of the *Leviathan*, part I, called "Computation or Logic" of *De Corpore*, and chapters 5 and 13 of the second section "Concerning Man" or *De Homine*. None of those discussions is clearly devoted to the role of language in the specific domains Hobbes is writing about: physics, psychology, and (in the case of the *Leviathan*) human society. In none of these discussions does Hobbes turn to language to solve specific physical, psychological, moral, or political problems. Instead, Hobbes's discussion of language in these works is a general methodological prelude or prolegomena that defines the general structure of a science that he will follow in his pursuit of a science of "*natural bodies,...* the *abilities and customs of humans*;...[and] the *duties of citizens*" (1839, 10).

For Locke, on the other hand, the turn to language is not a prelude for discussing the nature and scope of the human understanding. He does not discuss language as part of a methodological discussion that sets the parameters of his enterprise, as Hobbes does, whose linguistic interests are driven by his desire to define properly the key terms of his subject, to lay down the basic principles using these terms, and finally to draw the appropriate deductive consequences. Locke's turn to language is an intrinsic part of his *Essay Concerning Human Understanding*.

Moreover, Locke is concerned explicitly with natural languages and not symbol systems in general. The language he is studying and that plays a role, for good and ill, in human cognition is "Language,...the great Instrument, and common Tye of Society," that is natural language (1975, 402, III.1.1). Locke is not thinking of constructed, reformed, or purified languages, but "the *Languages* of the world" and the language of one's "own Country" (1975, 507, III.11.2). For Locke, the attempt to reform natural languages or construct philosophical languages is a "ridiculous" project and "the Market and Exchange must be left to their own ways of Talking" (1975, 507, III.11.2–3). Of course, human beings can exercise care in the use of natural language, especially in the pursuit of truth, and "deliver themselves without Obscurity, Doubtfulness, or Equivocation, to which Men's Words are naturally liable, if care not be taken" (ibid.; also 520, III.11.24). Locke wants to contribute to such careful discourse and therefore the "Consideration of *Ideas* and *Words*, as the great Instruments of Knowledge," is not a "despicable part" of any study "of humane Knowledge in the whole Extent of it" (1975, 721, IV.21.4).

THREE

✦

Of Angels and Human Beings
Leibniz and Condillac

Renaissance philosophy of language severed the Scholastic bond between the study of logic and the study of language and instead turned to the pragmatic and rhetorical dimensions of natural languages. Locke continues along this path by disparaging the relevance of logic to understanding the structure of mind and language. Locke's primary achievement, however, was to unite the study of language with the study of the human understanding, particularly its cognitive capacities. This new relationship immediately fostered new approaches in the philosophy of language. The two approaches that define the evolution of the philosophy of language in the modern period are due to Leibniz (1646–1716) and Condillac (1715–1780). Both philosophers recognized the significance of Locke's turn to language in the *Essay*, but they aimed to improve upon the *Essay* in distinct ways: Leibniz by reconnecting natural language, including ordinary usage, to an underlying logic, and Condillac by highlighting language as a human action.

Leibniz and Locke

Soon after the first publication of Locke's *Essay* in 1690, Leibniz wrote some comments on it and in 1696 asked Thomas Burnett to give them to Locke. Burnett delivered them almost a year later, but Locke had already received a copy of the comments from another source. Locke never responded to Leibniz, except indirectly in June 1704 when Locke, very ill and four months away from his death, asked Lady Masham to apologize for not writing back (Leibniz 1960, 3:351). Why Locke did not respond earlier is not known, but certainly he must have shared the

Royal Society's suspicions of Leibniz.[1] Moreover, he also thought that Leibniz was overrated. Referring to Leibniz's comments, Locke writes to Molyneux in 1697 that "this sort of fiddling makes me hardly avoid thinking that he is not that very great man that has been talked of him," that "even great parts will not master any subject without great thinking, and even the largest minds have but narrow swallows" (1976, 1:87).

Locke's failure to respond did not deter Leibniz, who continued reading and commenting on the English text of the *Essay* despite his poor mastery of English. On the other hand, Leibniz's French was outstanding, and so his work on Locke's *Essay* received a tremendous boost in 1700 when Pierre Coste's French translation was published. By the end of the summer of 1704, Leibniz had completed his commentary on all four books of the *Essay* in the form of a dialogue between Philalethes, a spokesman for Locke who quotes from the *Essay*, and Theophilus, representing Leibniz. By November Leibniz completed a draft with the title *New Essays Concerning the Human Understanding* (*Nouveaux essais sur l'entendement humain*), when he received news of Locke's death. Leibniz decided against publishing his *New Essays* because, he writes, he has "a repugnance of publishing refutations of dead authors ... for such refutations should appear during their lives and be sent to the authors themselves" (1960, 3:612; 1970, 656).[2] A brief set of reflections on the *New Essays* was published posthumously in 1720 in a French anthology of Leibniz's writings, and the whole book was published in 1765, forty-nine years after Leibniz's death in 1716.[3]

Leibniz prefaces the *New Essays* with the remark that his and Locke's "systems are very different" because Locke's philosophy "is closer to Aristotle and mine to Plato" (1962, 6.6:47). Although Leibniz recognizes that "each of us parts company at many points from the teachings of both of these ancient writers," his rough characterization of their

---

[1] Leibniz has a troubled history with the Royal Society. On several occasions he sought approval from it and its members, but he was repeatedly rebuked. Leibniz's ill-fated relationship with the English culminated in the well-known controversy with Newton over the calculus.

[2] P. Remnant and J. Bennett in their introduction to Leibniz (1982, xiii) report that Leibniz was also afraid of being accused of unfairness or cowardice.

[3] Curiously, the fact that the *New Essays* were published in part in 1720 is ignored by Bennett and Remnant in their account of the publication of the *New Essays* (Leibniz 1982, xiii) as well as Aarsleff (1982, 48–9). For more details on the writing and publication of the *New Essays*, see the introduction to Leibniz 1962, A.6.6.

differences does apply to their philosophies of language. Whereas Plato aims to develop a nonconventionalist view of human language, Aristotle sees human language as conventional. Similarly, whereas Locke proposes that words signify human ideas "not by any natural connexion, that there is between particular articulate sounds and certain *Ideas*,... but by a voluntary Imposition, whereby such a Word is made arbitrarily the Mark of such an *Idea*" (1975, 405, III.2.1), Leibniz cannot accept this characterization.

"I know that the Scholastics and everyone else are given to saying that the signification of words are arbitrary [*ex instituto*], and it is true that they are not settled by natural necessity," Leibniz concedes, "but they are settled by reasons; these reasons," he adds, are "sometimes natural ones in which chance plays some part, [and] sometimes moral ones which involve choice" (1962, 6.6:278). Leibniz continues that "[p]erhaps there are some artificial languages which are wholly chosen and completely arbitrary," but "known languages involve a mixture of chosen features and natural and chance features" (ibid). A bit later he mentions with some approval the popular seventeenth-century doctrine that there is a primitive or Adamic language of nature that Adam received at his creation and that is at the root of all languages. Available evidence about language does contradict this belief, he writes, and adds that current spoken languages "considered in themselves have something primitive about them" (1962, 6.6:281).

Sound Symbolism

What Leibniz has in mind at this point is sound symbolism or the onomatopoeic features of natural languages. Leibniz likes to give the example of the Latin *coaxare* and the German *quaken* for the sound of frogs (1962, 6.6:281–2; 1988, 151). He speculates that this term is the root of the Middle High German word *quek* for "life" or "lively," which, as he points out, is the root of the English word "quickly." He also argues that in German "the letter R naturally signifies a violent motion, [while] the letter L signifies a gentler one" (1962, 6.6:283). These examples and "any number of similar terms," Leibniz argues, "prove that there is something natural in the origin of words something which reveals a relationship between things and the sounds and motions of the vocal organs" (ibid.).

Sound symbolism played a visible role in seventeenth- and eighteenth-century Protestant religious thought. On several occasions, Leibniz mentions the writings of Jacob Boehme (1575–1624), whose religious and philosophical speculations about the Adamic language of nature (*Natursprache*) were widely read throughout Europe.[4] According to Boehme, the language of nature consists of sounds that are natural expressions of the essential qualities of real objects (1963, 1:208). Boehme elaborates that all objects have an inner essence and every object also has certain characteristic sounds that express this inner essence. These characteristic sounds are the outer sensible forms of objects, and theses sounds, according to Boehme, constitute "the language of nature, with which everything speaks according to its properties, and reveals itself"(1956, 6:4; also 1963, 1:58–9). Consequently, for Boehme all sounds signify inner forms, and all things speak the language of nature, not just Adam or, more generally, human beings. However, the language of nature for human beings is human sounds that express the inner natures of human beings, namely our souls or minds (*Gemüth*).

What is special about human beings is that their souls contain "signatures" for all things because humans are made in the image of God (Boehme 1956, 6:4–5). The human soul or understanding is brought about by God breathing the invisible word of God's power into the human understanding, which thus acquires an innate knowledge of the visible and invisible world (1956, 7:1–2). Boehme maintains that every "person has received the power from the invisible word of God to say it again, so that he can say the hidden word of God's wisdom [*Scientz*]... in the manner of temporal creatures; and this same spiritual word makes the living and growing things, through which God's invisible wisdom is modelled in different formations [*Formungen*], as it is before our eyes, so that the human understanding can... name all things according to their properties" (1956, 7:4). The sensible expression is part of the "sensual language" (*sensualische Sprache*), whereas spiritual words are part of "mental speech" (*mentalische Zunge*) (1956, 6:102, and 7:333). This mental language allows human beings to understand the true nature of things, and it is also why, by coming to know ourselves, we also come to know everything that can be known (1956, 6:7). Even though human languages became corrupted by human conventions that deviate from the God-given language of nature, the divine language is recoverable by paying attention to the soul's mental speech. By recovering it, human beings can come to

---

[4] In England, Boehme's followers – Behemists – drew Royal Society members into a heated polemic about the university curriculum. See Debus 1970.

understand the natural meanings that still adhere to the sounds of ordinary language.

Boehme's language of nature, then, is innate and universal because all human beings are given this language simply in virtue of being human. It is also natural because its meaning and structure are not human constructs or artifacts. Moreover, this language is not arbitrary because the linguistic symbols have a natural connection to their meanings in that the physical properties of a term in the language of nature express the properties of the referent. Finally, the Adamic language is accurate. Every term of the language of nature has only one meaning and it contains only terms for existing things. Therefore, anyone that knows this language, also knows something about the world and its essential features. This is why the language of nature was proposed as a cure for skepticism and an instrument for the advancement of science.

The recovery of the language of nature is a special concern of the English "Behemist" John Webster. In his critique of education, *Academiarum Examen* (1653), Webster writes that Adam had "the language of nature infused into him in his Creation, and so innate and implantate in him, and not inventive or acquisitive, but merely dative from the father of light" (Debus 1970, 29). What is infused into Adam are notions or "images or *ideas* of things themselves reflected in the mind," and that for these given notions there is an "absolute congruency betwixt the notion and the thing, the intellect and the thing understood" (Debus 1970, 29–30). He compares this congruency to a face and its reflection in a mirror and to a seal and its wax impression, which he maintains is not arbitrary or conventional but a natural relation.

Webster believes that every mind has such notions that naturally and unequivocally represent reality, and that these notions are naturally connected to certain sounds. He writes, "truly, the mind receiveth but one single and simple image of everything, which is expressed in all by the same motions of the spirits, and so doubtlessly in every creature hath radically, and naturally the same sympathy in voice, and sound" (Debus 1970, 32). Unfortunately, "men not understanding these immediate sounds of the soul, and the true *Schematism* of the internal notions impressed, and delineated in the several sounds, have instituted, and imposed others, that do not altogether concord, and agree to the innate notions, and so no care is taken for the recovery and restauration of the Catholique language in which lies hid all the rich treasury of natures admirable and excellent secrets" (ibid.). Webster's educational reform recommendation is that this language of nature be taught in the schools and universities.[5]

The Natural Order

Of course, Leibniz rejected the view that Adam's divine language survives in some form that human beings can discover (1960, 7:204–5; 1962, 6.6:281; 1988, 151). But as we saw, he did believe that natural languages have Adamic properties. Moreover, he thought that it was possible to create a symbol system that maximizes the Adamic properties that a human language can have. This Adamic ideal was at the center of Leibniz's project to develop an artificial, yet nevertheless universal, real, and rational characteristic.[6] He wanted to develop a universal symbol system that could become the basis of an unambiguous universal language in which the physical structure of its signs reflected the essential properties of the things themselves. What Boehme and other religious enthusiasts wanted to discover, Leibniz aimed to construct (1960, 7:184–5; Courtine 1980, 376).

The key to this project was Leibniz's assumption that there is a "natural order of ideas" that is "common to angels and men and to intelligences in general" (1962, 6.6:276). In fact, this order "is something we have in common with God" (1962, 6.6:397). God produced the ideas human beings have even before they think of them, and God determines when human beings think of them (1960, 4:453; 1962, 6.6:300). This natural order of ideas is not "instituted or voluntary" or subject to human control: "[I]t is not within our discretion to put our ideas together as we see fit" (1962, 6.6:149 and 294). This is not to say that God, angels, and humans have exactly the same ideas. Leibniz is very clear that human ideas are numerically distinct from God's ideas (1960, 4:453–4). Nevertheless, ideas have a natural pattern or order, and it is this pattern that all intelligences have in common. Although in ordinary thinking and speaking human beings depart from this natural order of

---

[5] For more on language of nature doctrines, see Coudert 1978 and Losonsky 1992. For more on the theory of mind in Boehme, see Losonsky 2001.

[6] For more on Leibniz's universal language project, see Couturat 1901; Cohen 1954; Rossi 1960; Heinekamp 1972; Walker 1972; Pombo 1987; Wilson 1989, 28–41; and Rutherford 1995, 226–40. For broader discussions of universal language projects, see Knowlson 1975 and Slaughter 1982. There is some doubt about the consistency of Leibniz's use of *lingua universalis*, *lingua rationalis*, and *ars characteristica* (Rossi 1960, 24).

their ideas because they must follow their contingent interests, proper reflection and analysis will uncover this natural order.

Analysis is possible because ideas are related as parts to wholes. Ideas are built out of a finite set of simple ideas that Leibniz calls "a kind of alphabet of human thought" (1960, 7:186; 1970, 222). Simple ideas combine to form complex ones, which in turn can be compounded to form more-complex ideas or decomposed into their simpler constituents (1960, 4:64–75; 1962, 6.1:194; 1966, 3). Similarly, ideas can be combined into propositions, and propositions into syllogisms. Leibniz believed that ideas, complex ideas, propositions, and syllogisms are structured so that they can be assigned unique numbers and composed and decomposed using arithmetic operations. For example, in 1679 Leibniz worked on a calculus of ideas in which every true universal affirmative proposition is one in which the number assigned to the subject can be divided exactly without any remainder by the number assigned to the predicate. If the subject cannot be divided by the predicate without a remainder, the proposition is false.[7]

Relying on this natural combinatorial structure of ideas, Leibniz analyzes truth in terms of the relationship "by virtue of which one idea is or is not included within another" (1962, 6.6:397).[8] Leibniz expresses this most emphatically in his correspondence with Antoine Arnauld (1612–94), author of the *Port-Royal Logic*: "[I]n every true affirmative proposition, whether necessary or contingent, universal or singular, the concept of the predicate is included in some way in that of the subject, the predicate inheres in the subject [*praedicatum inest subjecto*]; or else I do not know what truth is" (1970, 337; also 334). Given that truth is defined in terms of the containment relationship of ideas and ideas are a divine product, it is not an exaggeration for Leibniz to say that human knowledge is an emanation of the light of God (1960, 3:660; 1966, 410–11).

---

[7] Leibniz 1988, 78–9; 1966, 26. Leibniz illustrates this as follows. Assume that the term *wise man* is assigned the ordered pair <70, −33> while *pious* is assigned <10, −3>. Consequently, the proposition *Every wise man is pious* is: <<70, −33>, <10, −3>>. The first number in the first pair is divided by the first number in the second pair, and the same holds for the second number. So $70 \div 10 = 7$ and $-33 \div -3 = 11$. Because this division is without remainder, the proposition is true. However, *Some pious man is not wise* would be <<10, −3>, <70, −33>>, and 10 cannot be divided by 70 without remainder.

[8] This is what Leibniz had in mind when he wrote elsewhere that "truth is always grounded in the agreement or disagreement of ideas" (Leibniz 1962, 6.6:357 and 375), where an idea agrees with another if the one is contained in the other.

The combinatorial structure of ideas parallels the combinatorial structure of reality because nature, too, is composed of parts: "All things which exist or can be thought of are in the main composed of parts" (Leibniz 1962, 6.1:177; 1966, 3). The structure of reality is a consequence of the fact that God creates by reasoning, that is, by calculating. "When God calculates and exercises his thought," Leibniz writes in the margins of one of his manuscripts, "the world is made" (*Cum Deus calculat et cogitationem exercet, fit mundus*; 1960, 7:191). Leibniz tried to represent this in a commemorative coin he designed called "Image of Creation" (1966, 402; also Lenzen 1992). A table depicting the binary number system in the middle of the coin stands under the lines:

> 2, 3, 4, 5 etc. 0
> Everything from nothing and one alone can flow[9]

In a letter recommending this design, Leibniz writes that nothing "demonstrates" God's creation of all things from nothing better than the origin of numbers represented by this medal (1966, 401). He argues that does it show not only that God makes everything from nothing, but also the goodness of creation. The table shows the perfect order and harmony of the set of natural numbers in their binary form, and how they can be generated without memory or calculation simply by continuing the pattern of zeroes and ones in the left half of the table (1966, 402). Leibniz also maintains that in order to better show that this is not just about numbers but about creation (and to make it more pleasing to the eye), the medal should include "light and darkness, or as human beings represent it, the spirit of God over water" (1966, 404).[10]

The Image in the Mirror

Although Leibniz experimented with various more or less ambitious symbol systems and languages for expressing precisely that natural order of ideas, a constant throughout his philosophy was the belief that

---

[9] My translation attempts to preserve the verse of Leibniz's Latin couplet: "2, 3, 4, 5, etc. 0 [Duo, tres, quattuor, quinque, etcetera, nullum], Omnibus ex nihilo ducendis sufficit unum."

[10] The duke did not mint this coin, and it was not minted until the twentieth century in Hannover (Lenzen 1990). In 1697 Leibniz painted and published a German version of the design. This coin design also represents the binary numbers, binary addition and multiplication, as well as heavenly bodies such as the sun, moon, and Earth. In addition to the words "Image of Creation," it contains the motto "Someone made everything from nothing.... One thing is necessary."

because of the combinatorial structure of ideas, it is in principle possible to construct a universal characteristic that would be a complete algebra of concepts. Such a well-defined and rule-governed system of symbols would fully express or mirror this natural, combinatorial structure.[11] The analysis of the structure of this characteristic would "correspond exactly" to the analysis of concepts (1962, 2.1:413; 1970, 193). Moreover, by applying a finite set of rules to a finite set of symbols, this language would not only allow human beings to analyze ideas by dividing them into their appropriate components but it would also supply a method by which "everything can be discovered and judged" (1960, 7:186; 1970, 222; also Lenzen 1990 and 1992). In other words, this characteristic would serve what Leibniz, following Peter Ramus (1515–72), distinguished as both the art of discovery (*ars inveniendi*) and the art of judging (*ars judicandi*). Through its application, the characteristic would express the content and structure needed to generate all of the deductive relations that ideas have to each other.

Concern for the deductive structure of ideas informs Leibniz's thinking about natural language. For Leibniz, as for Locke, studying natural language is necessary to achieve a better understanding of the nature and structure of the human mind. In the *New Essays* Leibniz concurs with Locke "that languages are the best mirrors of the human mind, and precise analysis of the signification of words would tell us more then anything else about the operations of the understanding" (1962, 6.6:333).[12] For Leibniz this also means studying the diversity of languages. Recording the grammars and vocabularies of the world's diverse languages "will be extremely useful," Leibniz writes, "for the knowledge of our minds and of the marvelous variety of its operations" (1962, 6.6:366). But Locke and Leibniz are looking at very different images in

---

[11] Thus the universal characteristic is very much like a language of nature, except that it is established by the "wise arbitrary imposition" worthy of human beings. However, insofar as the design of a universal characteristic rests on the natural order of ideas accessible to human beings, it rests on divine illumination (Leibniz 1988, 151; Courtine 1980). Moreover, the natural order of ideas, as expressed in the human understanding, is very much like a language of nature, albeit a language of thought (Losonsky 1992; 2001, 164–7).

[12] The mirror metaphor also opens Leibniz's posthumously published booklet *Unprepossessing Thoughts Concerning the Practice and Improvement of the German Language* (*Unvorgreifliche Gedanken, betreffend die Ausübung und Verbesserung the teutschen Sprache*): "It is known that language is the mirror of the understanding," and when understanding flourishes, so does the use of language (Leibniz 1966, 449).

this mirror. Whereas Locke looks to the psychological clues language offers, Leibniz sees the structure of natural languages as a source of information about the mind's deductive structure.

For Leibniz, although natural languages depart from the natural order of ideas, they remain tied in significant ways to the mind's underlying universal logical structure. Even the argumentation of an orator with all its ornamentation has a "logical form" (*forme logique*) relevant to logical validity (1962, 6.6:480). The logicians' laws of logic merely put in writing laws of "natural good sense" (ibid.). Systems of logic designed by logicians (*logique artificielle*) are like systems of arithmetic: both are aids to human reasoning because they attempt to make explicit natural relations that anyone who must count or draw inferences will use (1962, 6.6:482 and 483–4).

Locke's and Leibniz's treatments of particles – that is, syncategorematic terms such as "is" or "but" – illustrate their different perspectives on the mirror of the human understanding.[13] Both look to particles to understand the human mind, but Locke fixes on psychological states. Particles exhibit "the several Postures of the Mind" (Locke 1975, 472). According to Locke, they are "all *marks of some Action, or Intimation of the Mind*," and to understand the particles of language properly, one must attain an understanding of "the several views, postures, stands, turns, limitations, and exceptions, and several other Thoughts of the Mind" (ibid.). For example, the word "but" can be used to indicate a variety of psychological states. When someone declares, "But to say no more," the particle "intimates a stop of the Mind, in the course it was going, before it came to the end of it" (1975, 473). On the other hand, in "I saw but two planets," the particle "but" shows "that the Mind limits the sense to what is expressed, with a negation of all other" (ibid.).

Leibniz, on the other hand, is not interested in the diverse subjective states that accompany the various uses of particles. Instead, he looks for a common, underlying meaning (Dascal 1990, 34). He suggests that the way to approach an analysis of "but" is to find a paraphrase that can be substituted for the particle in all the contexts in which it occurs (Leibniz 1962, 6.6:332). This substitutable paraphrase would then bring us closer to the meaning or signification of the particle. Leibniz suggests that the proper substitution for "but" is "and no more," so that "I saw but two planets" is paraphrased as "I saw two planets, and no more."

[13] On Leibniz and Locke on particles, see Dascal 1990 and McRae 1988.

Particles are to be studied in greater detail – in much greater detail than Locke did – "for nothing would be more apt to reveal the various forms of the understanding [*formes des l'entendement*]" (Leibniz 1962, 6.6:330). Particles are the elements of natural languages that are most intimately tied to the structure of the natural order of ideas. Particles, which Leibniz believes are often "concealed in the inflections of verbs," reveal the various forms of the understanding because they do more than serve as conjunctions that connect propositions or, as is the case with the copula "is," conjoin the component ideas of a proposition. Particles, Leibniz maintains, also "connect... the parts of an idea made up of other ideas variously combined" (ibid.). In other words, particles not only are the "cement" or "ligaments" of language, as was argued by Dalgarno (1680, 62; 1661, 78; quoted in Dascal 1990, 53) earlier, but also have a role as the cement or ligaments of the human understanding.[14]

So when Leibniz is interested in the "turns of thought that reveal themselves so wonderfully in our use of particles" (1962, 6.6:333), he is not concerned with particular psychological thoughts a speaker is conscious of while using particles. Instead, he is interested in the deductive structure of ideas. Leibniz captures this difference by distinguishing thoughts from ideas. On several occasions in the *New Essays*, Leibniz responds to Locke by accusing Locke of failing to make or ignoring this distinction (1962, 6.6:109, 118–19, 140, and 300–1). Many of Locke's claims about ideas – for example, that some ideas are arbitrary while others are not – hold true, Leibniz argues, only of "actual thoughts" or "noticeable thoughts." If we turn to ideas as "the very form or possibility of those thoughts" or as "objects of thoughts," Leibniz continues, then Locke's account of the limits of the human understanding is wrong. The realm of ideas is the realm of "possibilities and necessities," and what is possible and necessary is "independent of our thinking" (1962, 6.6:301 and 293).

This distinction plays a role in Leibniz's discussion about the nature of propositions. Leibniz rejects Locke's view that "[t]he *joining* or *separating* of signs... is what by another name, we call Proposition" (Locke 1975, 574, IV.5.2). Whether they are verbal or mental, for Locke

---

[14] This is an exciting moment in the *New Essays*, because here Leibniz anticipates Kant's fundamental claim that categories are forms of the understanding and that ideas themselves have a structure tied to the forms of judgment (Kant 1904, 3:91–2; 1965, B104–5). Kant read the *New Essays* in 1769. For more discussion on Leibniz and Kant, see Tonelli (1974).

propositions are always actual psychological entities; they are a specific thought or declaration made by a person on a particular occasion. Consequently, truth, which for Locke is a property of propositions, is either mental or verbal. It is verbal in the case of actual statements people make, and it is mental for actual thoughts that people have. Leibniz responds that if truth is distinguished in this manner, then it also makes sense to distinguish various kinds of "*written* truths." For example, it will make sense to divide truths "into paper truths and parchment ones, and into ordinary-ink truths and printer's-ink ones," which for Leibniz is an obvious absurdity (1962, 6.6:396–7).

Instead, truth should be assigned to the relationships of ideas that, as was pointed out, "we have in common with God and the angels." A dialogue Leibniz wrote in Paris in 1677 about Hobbes's conventionalism expresses the same point. A truth of geometry "is true even if you were never to think of it" and "even before the geometricians had proved it or men observed it" (1960, 7:190). Leibniz goes on to maintain that truth is a property of propositions, and he draws the conclusion that not all propositions are thoughts, that is, actual mental events. Instead, propositions are "possible thoughts."

Yet Leibniz recognizes a major dilemma here. On the one hand, ideas are natural and not conventional, and consequently propositions and their truth are independent of human thought. On the other hand, Leibniz follows Hobbes in maintaining that some kinds of human thinking are "blind" or "symbolic" in that they involve conventional symbols.[15] For example, in reasoning about a chiliagon, human beings typically do not reason with the idea of a polygon with a thousand sides. Instead, they reason with ideas of words, such as "chiliagon" and "polygon with a thousand sides." Although these words are ultimately tied to their proper signification, for instance, the idea of a polygon with a thousand sides, this idea is not necessary at the time of reasoning (Leibniz 1960, 4:424). Not only does reasoning in arithmetic and geometry "presuppose some signs or characters" (1960, 7:192), but in the *New Essays* Leibniz states baldly that all abstract thoughts require "something sensible" and that human beings "cannot reason without symbols" (1962, 6.6:77 and 212).

If human beings can think about, say, arithmetic only with the help of symbols, and symbols are conventional, how can the conventionality

---

[15] Leibniz 1960, 4:424; 1962, 6.6:275. On the constitutive role of symbols in reasoning in Leibniz's philosophy, see Dascal 1987 and Losonsky 2001, 160–3 and 171–3.

of the language of arithmetic be reconciled with the idea that the propositions of arithmetic are true no matter what anyone happens to think or do (1960 7:192)?

Language and Form

The solution Leibniz offers is crucial to understanding his contribution to the philosophy of language. Leibniz claims that although different languages and artificial symbol systems can be used to reason, "there is in them a kind of complex mutual relation or order which fits the things...in their combination and inflection" (1960, 192; 1970, 184). He adds:

> Though it varies, this order somehow corresponds in all languages. This fact gives me hope of escaping the difficulty. For although characters are arbitrary, their use and connection have something which is not arbitrary, namely a definite analogy between characters and things, and the relations which different characters expressing the same thing have to each other. This analogy or relation is the basis of truth. For the result is that whether we apply one set of characters or another, the products will be the same or equivalent or correspond analogously. (1960, 7:192–3)

Leibniz illustrates this point with the fact that both the decimal and the duodecimal systems of arithmetic preserve truths about the natural numbers.

For Leibniz, conventional symbol systems can have a structure that is not conventional, and this structure can be the same across different systems of signs. Moreover, this similarity of structure need not be explicit in the apparent structure, for example, the grammar of a language. All that is needed is that there is an equivalence or correspondence. Two structures that appear to be distinct can in fact correspond to each other because there is a precise one-to-one and lawlike mapping between the two structures. For example, as Leibniz points out, there is a correspondence between a circle and an ellipse because "any point whatever on the ellipse corresponds to some point on the circle according to a definite law."[16] On account of this correspondence, the ellipse can represent a circle.

---

[16] Leibniz 1960, 7:264. For Leibniz, "[t]hat is said to express a thing in which there are relations which correspond to the relations of the thing expressed" (1962, 7:263–4). Also see 1960, 6:327, and 1962, 6.6:131.

In the same manner, natural languages can correspond to each other and, what is more important, to the natural order of ideas. For example, a sentence in a natural language can correspond to a sentence of the universal characteristic because there is a precise mapping between the two sentences. Because the universal characteristic is a precise and perspicuous expression of the natural order of ideas, a formula of the characteristic will express exactly the proposition that was expressed confusedly by the sentence of natural language. Leibniz came to despair of his own ability to construct a universal characteristic and proposed less ambitious projects that would take an existing language – Leibniz recommended Latin – and rationalize it by reducing it to all and only the grammatical forms that are needed to express everything relevant to deductive reasoning. Although such a rationalized language is weaker than a universal characteristic, it would still be strong enough, Leibniz believes, to express the propositions of the natural order of ideas more precisely than natural languages are able to.

Of course, Leibniz would have to devote some effort to showing how the diverse grammatical forms of natural languages can correspond to the forms of a more rational symbol system, and he does. Leibniz devotes several studies to grammatical analyses of natural languages in which he argues that various grammatical forms, such as gender, case, or mood, are irrelevant to logical reasoning (1988, 286). Similarly, "the distinction between nouns and adjectives may be dispensed within the characteristic" (1988, 433). All substantive terms are equivalent to an adjective together with the terms "entity" or "thing" – for example "man" is equivalent to "human entity." In fact, Leibniz claims that "everything in discourse can be analysed into the noun substantive 'entity' or 'thing,' the copula, i.e., the substantive verb 'is,' adjectives and formal particles" (1988, 289).

The form this kind of grammatical analysis takes is the gradual substitution of equivalent phrases. In order to justify a proposition with a demonstration or to discover a new proposition, we need to be able to analyze propositions, and to do this, we have to be able to analyze the signs or characters that we use to express propositions (1988, 351). "An analysis of characters," he writes, "consists in the substitution of certain characters by others that are equivalent in use to the former" (ibid.). Typically, in an analysis one word will be replaced with a more complex phrase (e.g., as we saw, "man" with "human entity"), but in some cases phrases will be treated as one word, for example, in the case of idiomatic expressions (1988, 352). Leibniz's idea is that, by an orderly sequence of well-defined substitutions, a sentence of natural language can be transformed into a sentence of a more precise characteristic or artificial language. Then again using successive substitutions within the characteristic or language, the sentence can be subjected to various logical operations and used in logical demonstrations.

These analyses, then, are not just concerned with formal structure but with content as well. According to Leibniz, the substitutions of such an analysis must preserve signification (1988, 351). Consequently, the symbol system to be used in such analyses, whether it is a universal characteristic or a rationalized existing language, will not be just a system of formal logic that abstracts from all nonlogical content – that is, a formal calculus of logical relations where nonlogical terms are replaced with arbitrary symbols. A universal characteristic, for instance, will capture all the concepts human beings can express, which explains why it can serve as a tool for justifying and discovering propositions. Consequently, Leibniz devoted a large number of studies in various stages of completion trying to define fundamental categories or concepts, such as Reality, Possibility, or Order (Rutherford 1995:233–4). His hope was that by starting with a complete list of the broadest categories, he can work back to the basic concepts out of which all others are combined.

In short, Leibniz introduces the idea that sentences of natural language have an underlying logical form. These sentences form a structure on account of the deductive relations of the propositions they express. The deductive relations of propositions, being combinations of ideas, constitute the combinatorial structure of ideas. The structure of ideas that underwrites logical validity, Leibniz believes, can be expressed exactly in a symbol system or characteristic that can exactly and explicitly express the structure that determines their deductive properties. By expressing exactly the underlying structure a sentence has that accounts for all of its deductive consequences, a characteristic can express the underlying logical form of a sentence because the logical form of a sentence is just that structure that determines all of its deductive relations.[17] As we will see, the idea of logical form appears again in Mill's *System*

---

[17] It is helpful to highlight the fact that in order to explain the logical relations a sentence has to other sentences, a theory of logical form will not just be about the logical rules of implication and entailment but will include the nonlogical axioms and definitions that are involved in the deductive relations of a language. Consequently, a theory of logical form is not just concerned with logical relations, and it does not abstract from the domain what a language is about (compare Dascal 1990, 46).

of Logic, but it comes into its own in the philosophy of language that develops after Frege.

In this manner, Leibniz reintroduces the logical perspective on human language that had been damaged during the Renaissance. As we saw in the preceding chapter, a major cause of this damage was the wide gap between the evident grammatical structure of natural language and the language of logic. It is this gap that Renaissance humanists exploited in their parodies and critiques of Scholastic logic. Leibniz filled this gap by rejecting the assumption that natural language's logical form is located in the apparent grammatical structure of language.[18] Instead, grammatical structure is seen to be a function of the needs, desires, and other contingencies that shape how human beings actually think and speak. However, underlying this contingent human order, there is a divine or natural order accessible to human reason and explicit when human beings are particularly careful in their reasoning – for example, in mathematics, science, or jurisprudence. This order is not absent from ordinary reasoning of daily life, and it is explicitly present in the particles of natural languages, but in this setting it requires greater effort and care to uncover.

So whereas Locke found little or no room for the workings of logic in his account of mind and language, Leibniz locates logical order in the mind's abstract structure. One might say that what Locke missed by taking into account only *actual* human thought and speech, Leibniz recognized by trying to capture all that *could* be said and thought. By looking for an account of all possible judgments, Leibniz was able to add logic to the union Locke forged between philosophy, psychology, and the study of language. Leibniz's vision of logical form overcomes the disparities between formal logic and ordinary language and preserves the demands of both truth and the conventionality of human language and thought. It comes with a cost, however, which is the bifurcation of language into two components – namely, the apparent structure of natural language and the hidden, underlying form that is revealed only through chains of substitutions.

Condillac and Locke

Locke's *Essay* was available in France before it was published in England. During his second exile in Holland, Locke wrote a long

---

[18] On the distinction between surface structure and underlying form in Leibniz, see Brekle 1971 and Dascal 1987, 125–44.

summary of the *Essay*, which was translated into French and published in 1688 in *Bibilothèque universelle*. The French abridgment of the *Essay* was widely read and established Locke's influence on the continent (Bonno 1990).[19] Locke was repeatedly cited, including in Voltaire's famous letter from 1733 "On Mr. Locke" (Yolton 1990, 246–53; 1991, 39–59), and the publication of Leibniz's reflections on Locke's *Essay* in 1720 is part of a steady stream of discussion of Locke's philosophy in France (Leibniz 1962, 6.6:4–9; Weyant 1971, vi).[20] Etienne Bonnot de Condillac's *Essay Concerning the Origins of Human Knowledge* (*Essai sur l'origine des connaissances humains*), first published in 1746 and translated into English in 1756 by Thomas Nugent with the subtitle *Being a Supplement to Mr. Locke's Essay on the Human Understanding*, is also part of this important stream.

Condillac, an ordained priest who apparently never celebrated mass, was attracted to English antimetaphysical philosophy by 1740, and Voltaire's praises of Locke and Newton most likely played an important role in turning Condillac to Locke's *Essay* (Condillac 1947, 1:viii). Condillac introduces his *Essai* by distinguishing between a metaphysics that is "ambitious and wants to pierce through all the mysteries" and one that is "more reserved" and "proportions her researches to the weakness of the human understanding" (1947, 1:3; 2001, 3). He claims that philosophers have tended to devote themselves to the former kind of metaphysics, but "Mr. Locke is the only one that I believe ought to be excepted" (ibid.). Only Locke limited the scope of his study to the human understanding.

Still, Condillac claims that Locke's account has two significant shortcomings that he will remedy. First, Locke's "explication of the springs of the human understanding" fails to explain how human beings are able to "repeat, compare, and unite ideas... and so make all kinds of new complex ideas" (1947, 1:5; 2001, 7). These are the operations of

---

[19] On Locke's influence in France, also see Yolton 1991 and Aarsleff 1994.

[20] Thus it is not quite right that Leibniz has "no historical relevance to the *Essai*" and that "Locke alone came to influence the lively concern with language among the French *philosophes*" (Aarsleff 1982, 149 and 49). Leibniz's published response to Locke in 1720 is meager, but he does comment briefly on book III of Locke's *Essay* and introduces his comments on the fourth book with the claim that it "shows the usefulness" of the previous book on language, and that in both books he finds "an infinite number of beautiful reflections" that merit a book as large as the *Essay* itself (Leibniz 1962, 6.6:8). In these remarks Leibniz highlights Locke's disdain for the "forms of the Logicians" and his own esteem for logic (1962, 6.6:9).

the understanding, and Condillac argues that because infant human beings have sensations before they use these operations to turn sensations into ideas, an account of the origins of the operations of the understanding is needed. This is the missing explanation Condillac wishes to offer.

Probably inspired by Newton's unified account of mechanics, the second deficiency Condillac sees in Locke's account is that it lacks a unifying principle. He charges that Locke is not single-minded enough in following the principle that all knowledge is derived from sensation (ibid.). Condillac aims to correct this fault by relating "to a single principle everything that concerns the human understanding" (1947, 1:4; 2001, 5). This single principle is that all ideas are tied to signs, and it is by means of this tie to signs that ideas are connected to each other in diverse ways.

Condillac uses this principle to explain the origin of the operations of the understanding. The emergence of the mind's operations, he announces in the introduction to the *Essai*, depends on the use of various physical signs, including gestures, facial expressions, dance, and music, and human natural language is rooted in these kinds of physical expressions. In fact, the progression of the operations of the understanding parallels the development of language in human beings. On account of the central role natural language has in the basic operations of the human understanding, Condillac believes that the discussion of language in Locke's third book of the *Essay* should have been incorporated into the second book devoted to the origins of ideas (1947, 1:5; 2001, 7).

The Cartesian Heritage

Condillac's philosophy of mind and language not only builds on Locke's philosophy but is also a reaction to, as well as a continuation of, Cartesian views on the relationship between mind and language.[21]

Descartes' best-known and longest discussion of language is his brief argument in the *Discourse on Method* (1637) that human beings are essentially distinct from other animals. He argues that even if there were animals that imitated human behavior "as closely as possible for all practical purposes," it would be possible to tell them apart from real

---

[21] For a groundbreaking account of the role of language studies in the French Enlightenment, see Ricken 1994.

human beings on account of their language use. Such imitations could not, Descartes asserts, "put together other signs, as we do in order to declare our thoughts to others" (1985, 1:139–40). Although such an animal might be able to use words that fit their other bodily actions, they will not be able to "produce different arrangements of words so as to give an appropriately meaningful answer to whatever is said in its presence, as the dullest of men can do" (1985, 1:140).

This incapacity is tied to Descartes' other test for distinguishing human beings from other animals. Human reason is "a universal instrument which can be used in all kinds of situations" (ibid.). Accordingly, "in all kinds of situations" and "in all the contingencies of life," including completely new situations, human beings are able to produce rational responses. Beasts, to use Descartes' term for nonhuman animals, are limited to reacting with a particular action to a given particular stimulus. Although a nonhuman animal's skills might excel that of any human being in a certain domain, this skill will be limited to one domain and will not transfer to others. This shows that they do not have reason, Descartes argues, because if they had reason, they would be at least as skilled in other areas because of the universal nature of reason. Because nonhuman animals lack universal reason, they are unable to use language creatively in novel situations the way human beings do (cf. Chomsky 1966, 3–6).

The freedom human beings have in their use of language is referred to in a very short discussion in *Passions of the Soul* (1649) about the human capacity for self-control. Although due to their nature, written or spoken words are tied to particular sensory impressions of the utterance or inscription of a word, through training we can break this knot and instead tie a word to a particular meaning. Thus, when listening or reading, we think of the meaning, not the word, and when speaking, we do not think of the sound we are making but simply speak as we think (Descartes 1985, 1:344 and 348). This shows that "[t]here is no soul so weak that it cannot, if well-directed, acquire an absolute power over its passions" (1985, 1:348).

Descartes also turns to linguistic issues in a famous letter to Marin Mersenne in 1629 assessing the feasibility of a universal language. Descartes believes that a new language will not be universally adopted because it will not have a phonetic structure that will be easy and pleasant to everyone. For example, what is easy and pleasant in French is coarse and intolerable in German (1985, 3:12). Moreover, people will not learn a new vocabulary for a language for which there are neither books nor speakers. It would be much easier to get everyone to speak Latin than teach everyone a new language.

Nevertheless, Descartes endorses the idea of devising a symbol system that is like the number system for all thoughts. He writes that "all the thoughts which can come into the human mind must be arranged in an order like the natural order of the numbers" (ibid.). Then, just as people can learn in a single day to name each number in an infinite series of numbers, they can also learn to name everything that they can think of. Such a symbol system would require "the true philosophy" that reduces all thoughts to simple ones and then numbers and orders all of these simple thoughts. Nevertheless, Descartes believes that such knowledge can be discovered, and thus such a language, which will enable "peasants to be better judges of truth.... than philosophers are now," is possible (1985, 3:13).

The only other important place where Descartes faces linguistic issues is in his reply to Hobbes's Fourth Objection to the *Meditations*. Hobbes objects to Descartes' claim that Descartes' imagination does not play a role in his intellectual conception of a piece of wax. Hobbes argues that if "reasoning is simply the joining together and linking of names or labels by means of the verb 'is,'" then "reasoning will depend on names, names will depend on the imagination, and imagination will depend (as I believe it does) merely on the motions of our bodily organs." Hobbes concludes that "the mind will be nothing more than motion occurring in various parts of an organic body" (Descartes 1985, 2:125–6).

Descartes rejects Hobbes's suggestion that we reason with language. Reasoning "is not a linking of names but of the things that are signified by the names, and I am surprised that the opposite view should occur to anyone" (1985, 2:126). His opening defense is to distinguish imagination from "a purely mental conception." This is a recurring theme in Descartes' replies to Hobbes, most notably in his reply to Hobbes's claim that "we have no idea or image corresponding to the sacred name of God" (1985, 2:127). Images are part of the "corporeal imagination," Descartes writes, but ideas are "forms of perception" that even a divine mind without a body has (ibid.). This undercuts the need for language, because the instability Hobbes perceives is the instability of our mental images, not of the ideas of reason.

Hobbes's view is not only unmotivated, but it has what Descartes believes are two absurd consequences. First, it would mean that people speaking different languages could not reason about the same thing, but "a Frenchman and a German can reason about the same things, despite the fact that the words they think of are completely different" (1985, 2:126). Second, and more important, if Hobbes is right, then "when he concludes that the mind is a motion he might just as well conclude that the earth is the sky, or anything else he likes" (ibid.). If the meaning of language is a function of "arbitrary conventions," Descartes argues, then if we reason with words, truth is arbitrary as well. This is exactly the problem Leibniz aimed to solve.

The underlying theme in Descartes' discussions of language is that language is wholly parasitic on thought and that mind is wholly independent of language. This approach is preserved and developed in the *Port-Royal Grammar* (1660) and *Logic* (1662). The *Grammar*, coauthored by Antoine Arnauld and Claude Lancelot, who most likely was the principal author, assumes a sharp divide between mind and language. Language is simply using physical signs to explain one's thoughts (Arnauld and Lancelot 1975, 41). Moreover, "what occurs in our minds is necessary for understanding the foundations of grammar," but there is not even the remotest suggestion that what occurs in language is necessary for understanding the mind (1975, 65–8). Needless to say, the turn to language is also not motivated by the desire to achieve a better understanding of mind or to find solutions to philosophical problems. The primary concern of the *Grammar* is to show how grammatical distinctions common to diverse languages (mostly French and Latin) are a necessary consequence of the basic operations of the mind: conceiving, judging, and reasoning.[22]

The nature of these three operations, plus a fourth, namely ordering or method, is the subject of the *Port-Royal Logic*, whose full title is *Logic or the Art of Thinking* and which was coauthored by Arnauld and Pierre Nicole. The *Logic* is even more explicit than the *Grammar* in its Cartesian submission of language to thought. Language is needed only for communication, and if we did not have to communicate, "it would be enough to examine [thoughts] in themselves, unclothed in words or other signs" (Arnauld and Nicole 1996, 23).[23] Arguing that

---

[22] The primary focus of the *Grammar* is on judgment. Reasoning is considered to be only an extension of judgment, and conception is treated only insofar as it plays a role in judgment (Arnauld and Lancelot 1975, 67).

[23] Arnauld and Nicole go on to claim that because in communication we must associate ideas and words, "this habit is so strong that even when we think to ourselves, things are presented to the mind only in the words in which we usually clothe them in speaking to others" (Arnauld and Nicole 1996, 23–4). This, however, is treated only as a habit, and the conclusion they draw is that they need to examine how ideas and words are joined, and not how words are presented to the mind and play a role in reasoning.

there is a sharp divide between imagination and pure intellection and that ideas are not "images painted in the fantasy, but... anything in the mind when we can truthfully say that we are conceiving something, however we conceive it," Arnauld and Nicole conclude:

> It follows that we can express nothing by our words when we understand what we are saying unless, by the same token, it were certain that we had in us the idea of the thing we were signifying by our words.... For there would be a contradiction in maintaining that I know what I am saying in uttering a word, and yet that I am conceiving nothing in uttering it except the sound itself of the word. (1996, 26)

Arnauld and Nicole use this conclusion right away against Hobbes's objection to Descartes that "reasoning will depend on words" (1996, 27). What bothers them the most about this claim is the consequence Hobbes draws that the soul is not immortal, but they also have a more interesting argument against Hobbes. They argue that Hobbes appeals to the conventionality of names, but if there are no ideas of things independent of the conventional names of things, conventions cannot be established (1996, 28). This problem resurfaces famously in Rousseau's *Discourse on the Origins and Foundations of Inequality among Men* (1964, 3:151), and it becomes a defining task for Condillac.

A Cartesian treatment of language devoted primarily to language is Géraud de Cordemoy's *A Philosophical Discourse Concerning Speech* (*Discours physique de la parole*) of 1668. Because speech, following Descartes, is the standard of rationality, Cordemoy aims to examine speech more closely in order to understand better which aspects of language use can be attributed to the body only and which require a rational soul. Armed with that knowledge, Cordemoy maintains that he has a more secure knowledge of other minds, because on his view we know other minds primarily on the basis of speech. Moreover, this knowledge will also allow him to distinguish human beings more precisely from other animals and strengthen the Cartesian distinction between mind and body.

Cordemoy distinguishes between natural signs – for example, cries, gestures, and facial expressions – and "*signs* of *Institution*" or natural language. The former do not require a soul, Cordemoy argues, because they can be rooted wholly in the body (1972, 19–20). "Brutes need no Soul to cry, or be moved by cries," he writes (1972, 69). The arbitrary signs of natural language, however, do require a soul, and so in others they are the proper sign of the presence of a mind. The soul is needed not for articulating sounds – animals and machines without souls can pronounce words – but signification requires a soul (1972, 76–7). Speech's function is to signify thoughts, and because thoughts cannot be identified with words or any other motion of the body, they require a soul.

An interesting feature of Cordemoy's argument is that he relies on the conventionality and arbitrariness of language to show that language requires a mind distinct from the body. "*Institution* necessarily supposeth reason and thoughts in those, that are capable to agree about it" (1972, 15). Such an agreement requires the use of the will, and the will, Cordemoy maintains, is obviously located in the soul (1972, 75). Moreover, he argues that thoughts are distinct from words because, first, different signs, in the same language and also different languages, can be used to signify the same object; second, there are signs that we do not comprehend upon hearing; and, third, typically we remember what a person said without remembering what words were used (1972, 39–40). In fact, Cordemoy claims that all this shows that thoughts are distinct from any motion of the body and that mind and body are distinct.

In some ways Cordemoy's treatise comes close to looking like a possible rival to Locke's *Essay* as a wellspring for modern philosophy of language. Cordemoy turns to language in order to achieve philosophical insight regarding the mind-body problem. Facts about language are used to support Cartesian dualism, and Cordemoy's discourse is devoted wholly to language. However, Cordemoy has next to nothing to say about linguistic meaning or its structure, and even his discussion of the grammatical or syntactic structure of language is very meager. Moreover, Cordemoy's sharp distinction between language and mind keeps him from finding a significant or even interesting role for natural language in human reasoning and cognition. The discourse is primarily about the physiology of sound production, as indicated by the French title and glossed over by the English title (even considering its seventeenth-century context).

Finally, Cordemoy's influence certainly does not come close to Locke's. But his *Discours* does provide a good context for understanding Condillac's *Essai*. Where Cordemoy draws a sharp line between natural and conventional signs and uses this border to bolster Cartesian dualism, Condillac sees significant overlaps and points of contact, because for him natural languages develop out of instinctive cries and gestures. At the same time, Condillac continues certain Cartesian traditions. First, Condillac is an avowed dualist. He even rejects Locke's concession to materialism that it is possible that the faculty of thinking is "superadd[ed]" to matter (Locke 1975, 540–1, IV.3.6). Condillac simply affirms Descartes' argument that because a mind "must be *one*" whereas matter is divisible, matter cannot be given the power of thought (1947, 1:7; 2001, 13). Second, Condillac is an occasionalist about the Cartesian mind-body problem: changes in the body are the occasion for changes in the mind and vice versa. Although occasionalism is a departure from Descartes' position that mind and body causally interact, it is part of the development of Cartesian thought in the writings of Cordemoy as well as Malebranche. Finally and most significantly, Condillac follows Descartes in giving volition a central role to play in the human understanding.[24] Voluntary self-control is what distinguishes human beings from other animals, and it is at the heart of the evolution of human language.

Mind, Will, and Sign

In the *Essai*, Condillac distinguishes between three types of signs: accidental signs, natural signs, and instituted signs (1947, 1:19; 2001, 36). Accidental signs are objects that happen to be associated with certain ideas. For instance, the perception of hunger can be an accidental sign for the idea of a tree loaded with fruit that at some earlier time satisfied one's hunger (1947, 1:60; 2001, 114). Although in this case the perception of hunger produces the idea of that tree, by itself the connection is "no more than the effect of . . . circumstances" and not under the control of the person having these perceptions and ideas (ibid.). On another occasion the perception of hunger might revive some other object that satisfied hunger and thus function as an accidental sign for that object.

Natural signs have a more constant connection with states of the mind. He believes that nature has established that certain cries are regularly linked to certain passions or emotions, such as joy, fear, or grief (ibid.). The same holds for certain gestures or facial grimaces, and due to the regular connections between cries and gestures and their associated mental states, cries and gestures are natural signs for inner mental states.

For Condillac, both accidental and natural signs play a role in the mental lives of human beings as well as other animals that perceive

---

[24] On the role of volition in Descartes' philosophy, see Losonsky 2001, 12–41.

and imagine. Animal instincts depend on these signs because they allow animals quickly to respond to objects and cooperate with other animals. That the perception of an object automatically produces other relevant ideas makes quick reactions possible, and the instinctive behavioral expression of fear or joy allows animals to respond appropriately. But in these cases the mind is not being directed or controlled by the animal. For example, the presence of hunger is needed to recall an idea of food, and this idea cannot be revived at will. Similarly, a creature with only accidental or natural signs can express the behavioral expressions of emotion only when the emotions are actually present.

Consequently, Condillac argues, creatures with only accidental or natural signs will not have a memory. Such beings will have sensation, perception, attention, and consciousness, but they will not have "the ability to recall the signs of our ideas, or the circumstances that attended them," which is how Condillac defines memory (1947, 1:19; 2001, 37). A key feature of this account of memory and, for that matter, Condillac's account of human reason in general is that memory involves not just the ability to have certain ideas revived as a consequence of the presence of some objects, but it is having the power to revive these ideas when we want to have them (1947, 1:15; 2001, 27–8).

This power, as well as the power to control the imagination, comes only with instituted signs, that is, signs "we have chosen ourselves" (1947, 1:19 and 21; 2001, 36 and 40). Condillac maintains that by connecting ideas to signs, a person can use these signs to recall at will ideas connected to them, and this technique is how the mind is raised from its dependency on surrounding objects (1947, 1:21–2; 2001, 41). This is also the source of the human capacity to reflect on its own mental states. Reflection is the ability to control one's attention, and only with instituted signs is a being able to choose to focus on only one aspect of our mental states. All animals can perceive a variety of objects at once, and typically temperament, passion, or condition of life will produce an increased awareness of only some of those objects (1947, 1:3; 2001, 24). But without instituted signs, attention is guided automatically by the interplay of the environment and inner conditions.

With instituted signs, a human being can decide to favor one perception over another, continue it at will even after the object of perception is not present anymore, and revive specific perceptions. By being able to reflect, human beings acquire the capacity to distinguish, abstract, compare, compose, and decompose the mind's ideas (1947, 1:23–4; 2001, 44–5). These capacities, particularly the ability to compose and decompose ideas, are essential to analysis, and therefore analysis requires instituted signs. This is the basis of what Condillac later comes to express succinctly as "every language is an analytic method and every analytic method is a language" (1947, 2:419).

Of course, this essential connection between analysis and language reverberates through Condillac's account of human cognition. The only way to discover truth, Condillac maintains, is by analyzing the ideas we have, that is, by composing and decomposing the ideas we get from sensation and reflection (1947, 1:105–6; also 114; 2001, 199 and 213–14). Because analysis is the only method for acquiring knowledge, instituted signs are needed for cognition, including scientific knowledge. As Condillac writes a few years after the *Essai*, a science is nothing but a well-made system of instituted signs, and consequently if "you wish to learn the sciences easily...[b]egin by learning your language" (1947, 1:216–17).

Circles, Cries, and Gestures

Raising the constitutive role of language in human cognition raises a significant problem of circularity for Condillac. If reflective human reasoning depends on language, then how could human beings institute a language before they had the capacity to reflect? "It seems that one would not know how to make use of instituted signs, unless one were previously capable of sufficient reflection to choose them, and attach ideas to them," Condillac observes (1947, 1:22; 2001, 42). This is Arnauld and Nicole's objection to Hobbes.[25]

Condillac does not answer immediately: "I shall solve this difficulty, when I come to treat the history of language" (ibid.). However, this answer highlights a central feature of Condillac's approach to language. Condillac does not see this problem as conceptual or theoretical; rather, he sees an empirical problem that can be solved by looking more closely at the actual evolution of human language. Of course, Condillac's history is going to be conjectural, but nevertheless in his mind it is a plausible empirical conjecture about the evolution of language.

His basic idea is that human beings transformed natural cries and gestures into a "language of action," which in turn evolved into natural language (1947, 1:61; 2001, 114–15). Fears and pains come naturally with certain cries and facial grimaces, and laughter and pleasure are also

---

[25] Compare Quine's (1936) critique of conventionalism.

regularly connected. Human beings also show their interests or desires for certain objects by automatic, instinctual head and limb movements toward the object, and observers will have their attention directed to the same objects. In this manner, cries and gestures came to be associated with emotions and perceptions. This pattern of connections between external behavior and inner mental states stimulated various mental operations such as imagination and attention, but these cries and gestures were not instituted signs. They were wholly involuntary and do not involve any deliberation or reflection, such as thinking that these particular motions will express my desire (ibid.).

Because the connections between cries and gestures and mental states were frequently repeated, however, human beings became very familiar with them, and "the more familiar they became with those [natural] signs, the more readily they were able to recall them at will" (ibid.).[26] Somehow "insensibly," Condillac asserts, this regular pattern of natural signs gave human beings the ability to "themselves command their imagination as they pleased" and "do by reflection what they had formerly done only by instinct" (ibid.).

Once cries and gestures are used voluntarily to revive certain mental states – for instance, mimicking the cries and gestures of fear without actually being frightened to warn someone of possible danger (ibid.) – we have a language of action. Of course, this is still a long way off from explaining the emergence of natural language with a constitutive structure that cries and gestures do not have. Although in a language parts can be put together in various rule-governed ways to yield new complex signs, cries typically do not have such a structure. Still, Condillac attempts to weave a story of how such structure can emerge from a simple language of action.

He speculates that by analogy to cries and gestures human beings develop a language of articulate sounds, and Condillac suggests that dance may have played an intermediate role in this development. Gestures and cries were divided into various parts, which were used to

[26] It is a telling fact about Herder's case against Condillac in his prize essay that although this passage is a major exhibit in Herder's case, it is quoted while omitting, without ellipses, the phrase "at will" (Herder 1960, 13). Throughout his discussion, Herder completely ignores that voluntary control over mind and language is a cornerstone of Condillac's philosophy. For instance, consider Herder's objection that "however one builds and refines and organizes this cry [of nature], if understanding does not come along to use this tone with intent, then I do not see how... human, arbitrary language could ever originate" (Herder 1960, 12).

revive various parts of a complex experience. For instance, the diverse agitations of a gesture can express degrees of urgency, and these signs can then be used to analyze the understanding and distinguish sequentially what initially was given in experience simultaneously. By having distinct signs for fear and its degrees, a person can decompose this emotion into its qualitative and quantitative aspects and attend to them separately. Eventually cries and gestures became rule-governed sequences of sounds and movements of the body, much like a dance (1947, 1:63; 2001, 118). Due to their outstanding usefulness for disambiguating gestures, the articulate sounds that were mixed with the language of action grew in number and systematicity. Finally, articulate sounds used voluntarily to control or direct one's own and other's minds outnumbered cries and gestures, and thus the language of action turned into natural language.

Needless to say, the linguistic structure that emerges is impoverished. It is unclear how he can generate the distinction between names, sentences, and syncategorematic terms on the basis of cries, gestures, and other movements without begging the question by assuming that the introduced sounds he mentions do not already have specific grammatical or logical functions. Condillac struggles to locate sufficient form in linguistic behavior, and this struggle characterizes perspectives that give primacy to linguistic behavior.

But structure is not Condillac's primary concern. His main concern is to show how external symbols are constitutive parts of human reasoning. For Condillac, the sign itself is a proper part of the reasoning process. Condillac explicitly endorses what was only implicit or vague in Hobbes, Locke, and Leibniz, namely that chains of reasoning include words. Thus, in addition to the connection of ideas, human reasoning, according to Condillac, involves a connection between signs and ideas (Ricken 1994, 80). What enables the voluntary control over the mind's operations is the ability to produce *signs* voluntarily, and not simply the ability to produce *ideas of signs*. This distinction is crucial to Condillac's attempt to escape the circle that he mentions at the outset of the *Essai*. Voluntary mental control, which is the essence of reflection, depends on the voluntary production of signs. By voluntarily producing signs, we can remember, reflect, and ultimately reason. But the voluntary production of signs, on Condillac's account, does not require reflection or voluntary control over one's ideas. The voluntary production of a sign is a physical action, not a mental action, and Condillac assumes that the ability to produce external signs is more basic than the ability to exercise control over one's understanding. The human understanding needs the external crutch of voluntary bodily behavior – using physical symbols – in order to transcend automatic operations, exercise voluntary control over the understanding, and begin to reason.

Nature, Action, and Mind

Although Condillac is not a materialist, it is easy to see why his philosophy has a role in the evolution of naturalism, particularly French materialism (Yolton 1991; Ricken 1994). By making physical behavior a basic building block of human reasoning and by finding the roots of natural language in the instinctive behavioral patterns shared by many different kinds of animals, Condillac blurs the line between mind and body, persons and animals. The same holds for his sensualism. Locke's aim to reduce all ideas to sensations and reflection was already seen as too sympathetic to materialism, and Condillac pushed this reduction even further by placing the origins of the operations of the mind in sensation as well. In the *Essai*, Condillac announces that his aim is "to see how they are all generated from but one primary and simple perception" (1947, 1:10; 2001, 19). Although the *Essai* is not wholly clear about what this means for the operations of the understanding, Condillac is clear about this in his later writings. The introduction to the *Treatise on Sensation* states that all the operations of the understanding, including reflection, are nothing but "sensation itself transformed in different ways" (1947, 1:222).

Condillac's contribution to the evolution of materialism is a consequence of his explicit desire to avoid metaphysical or speculative theories of the human understanding and instead to contribute to empirical and scientific perspectives on the mind. Although Condillac is not a materialist, he is, philosophically speaking, a naturalist in the sense that he seeks to expand the scope of the natural sciences. Although Condillac's account is by today's standards completely speculative, it is nevertheless unquestionably informed by an overarching commitment to develop an empirical account of human cognition without relying on introspection. That is why Condillac has a place in the history of psychology. Similarly, as we will see in the next chapter, the emergence of linguistics as an empirical science in the work of Wilhelm von Humboldt is also rooted in what has been described as "the tradition of Condillac" (Aarsleff 1982, 335).

As we have seen, the focus on linguistic activity is a central feature of Condillac's philosophy, and this perspective dovetails with his naturalism. Condillac focuses on action and the public use of physical signs because these, at least at a first glance, are straightforward, observable events. Besides naturalism and the primacy of linguistic behavior, Condillac explicitly articulates the view that natural language determines how human beings think – that is, linguistic determinism. For Condillac, the idea that language is a constitutive part of reasoning naturally leads to the idea that language shapes the way human beings think. Linguistic determinism, however, should not be confused with its close ally, linguistic relativism. Although linguistic determinism and relativism come to cohabitate, perhaps most famously in the work of Benjamin Whorf (1956, 212–14), they are distinct. Linguistic relativity combines linguistic determinism with the diversity of natural languages and the assumption that natural languages have structures that are incommensurate. Because language determines thought, people who think with these radically distinct languages think in radically different ways. Although Condillac discusses the "genius of languages," how it differs between peoples, and how some languages aid the understanding more than others (1947, 1:98–104; 2001, 185–95), he does not draw or even suggest the conclusion that languages are radically distinct or incommensurate.

Conclusion

Leibniz and Condillac, then, develop Locke's linguistic turn in decisively different ways. Although both continue the strategy of tying language tightly to mind and relying on linguistic studies to achieve insight into the human understanding, they develop distinct perspectives on natural language.

Whereas Leibniz develops what might be called the "system perspective" on natural language, Condillac, as we saw, develops a "use perspective" on language.[27] Leibniz laments that Locke shares the widely held opinion that the "forms of the logicians are of little use" (1962, 6.6:9), and he, being "of quite another opinion," zeroes in on the underlying logical form of language. Condillac shows little interest in logical form, and he adopts Locke's disdain for traditional logic. "What the logicians have said [about reasoning] in a good many volumes seems to

---

[27] "System perspective " and "use perspective" is borrowed from Stainton 1996.

me to be entirely superfluous and of no use" (1947, 1:27; 2001, 51). When Condillac turns to logic in his *Logic; or, The First Developments of the Art of Thinking*, posthumously published in 1792, it is, as Condillac himself writes, a "logic like no other" (1947, 2:371). Instead of an account of entailment and validity, it relates how human beings come to use the physical signs of language intentionally to think, to analyze, and to acquire knowledge. For Condillac, language is primarily action, something people do – not an abstract formal system.

The naturalism of Condillac also distinguishes him from Leibniz, at least in terms of emphasis. Leibniz, as we saw, does not deny the relevance of empirical investigations into the grammatical structures of diverse languages, but this is not the focal point of his philosophy of language. The empirical work on language is only to serve the discovery of the underlying formal features of all natural languages, and it is this formal system shared by "angels and men" that Leibniz seeks to uncover. In the pursuit of this structure, Leibniz contributes to the development of formal systems; consequently, the idea that the study of language is at its core a formal discipline related more to mathematics and logic than to history or anthropology will find its roots in Leibniz's philosophy of language.

Just as naturalism dovetails with Condillac's use perspective, Leibniz's system perspective on natural language is more comfortable with philosophies opposed to naturalism. The system perspective is not as amenable to observation on account of its appeal to formal systems and its commitment to underlying formal structures. Formal systems even as simple as arithmetic have properties – for instance, their infinite size, which plausibly can be thought of as something that cannot be grasped by observation but requires the intellect. Moreover, the very idea that there is a deeper structure that underlies the apparent structure is in tension with the primacy of observation. Accordingly, in traditional histories of philosophy, Leibniz, along with Descartes and Spinoza, is a pillar of rationalism, and there is something right about Condillac's claim that Leibniz is an ambitious metaphysician seeking the most general and abstract principles and seeking to penetrate hidden causes (Condillac 1947, 1:3 and 121; 2001, 3–4)

These two different approaches to language – language as a structure behind the surface and language as the voluntary human activity – will remain very stable in the subsequent evolution of the philosophy of language.

FOUR

◆

The Form of a Language
Wilhelm von Humboldt

Wilhelm von Humboldt's (1767–1835) major work, *On the Diversity of Human Language Construction and Its Influence on the Mental Development of the Human Species* (*Über die Verschiedenheit des menschlichen Sprachbaues und ihren Einfluss auf die geistige Entwicklung des Menschengeschlechts*), labeled the "Kawi Introduction" by his editor, has been called "the first great book in general linguistics" (Bloomfield 1933, 133). It anticipates contemporary generative linguistics and, at the same time, is considered a precursor to linguistic relativism as developed early in the twentieth century by the anthropologists Edward Sapir (1884–1939) and Benjamin Whorf (1897–1941). It is even seen as anticipating the later philosophy of Ludwig Wittgenstein.[1]

That Humboldt appears to fit generativism as well as relativism is striking because, strictly speaking, generativism and relativism in linguistics are incompatible. Whereas generativism looks for the universal linguistic and mental structures rooted in human nature, relativism denies such shared structures common to all human beings. Instead, relativism focuses on the diversity of linguistic structures and how these structures determine the way in which human beings see and know the world. But it should not be surprising that both of these trends have been located in Humboldt's work on language because his work is a crossroads of the directions set out by Leibniz and Condillac. Humboldt attempts to meld together the system and use perspectives on language,

---

[1] The locus classicus that ties Humboldt to generative linguistics is Chomsky 1966, but also see Pinker 1994, 84. Chomsky (1966, 30–1), Aarsleff (1982, 335), Lyons (1984, 303–5), Trabant (1990), and Crystal (1997, 15) all tie Humboldt either to Wittgenstein or the so-called Sapir-Whorf hypothesis.

as well as the angelic and the earthly, into a synoptic empirical and philosophical theory of human language.

The Biological Turn

Humboldt kept detailed diaries throughout his life, including his illegal journey as a young man in 1789 to Paris and Switzerland.[2] The diary the twenty-two-year-old Humboldt kept during this visit documents that Humboldt had already arrived at a biological perspective that will characterize his thinking throughout the rest of his intellectual life. Humboldt reports that in Bern, Switzerland, he visited Johann Samuel Ith, a professor of philosophy who had published an *Anthropology or Philosophy of the Human Being according to His Corporal Dispositions*, which, according to Humboldt, attempts to describe first what is "corporal, physiological, then the spiritual, psychological, and then the human being in relation to external objects around him" (1968, 14:210). Humboldt was particularly eager to visit the author of this work, and Ith was to impress him more than anyone else on his trip so far, particularly because Ith kept returning to the topic of the nature of human reasoning (ibid.).

Nevertheless, Humboldt noted an important difference of opinion they had. Ith "separated the physiological and the psychological too much" (1968, 14:211). Even in thought the physiological and the psychological cannot be separated very well "without detriment" (*ohne nachtheil*; ibid.). Such separation ignores the fact that human beings are integrated beings. Anthropology lags significantly behind because it does not see the human being "as a whole, recognizing all his diverse aspects – the spirit, the heart, the body – in relation to each other." These different aspects are not distinct parts of a human being, but they are various modifications of a single whole. As long as the unity of a human being is not recognized, "the study of character – the purpose of all anthropology... – can never become a science." The scientific study of human character, that is, the scientific study of human nature and dispositions, must include "detailed investigations... of what we call feeling and thinking, [and] moreover how the corporeal and incorporeal are related to each other" (ibid.).

---

[2] Prussians could not travel abroad without permission, and Humboldt certainly would not have received permission from the Prussian monarchy to travel to revolutionary France.

This entry expresses four commitments that will remain stable features of Humboldt's thinking. First, he is committed to naturalism in the sense of a commitment to expanding the domain of science. The study of human psychology – that is, the dispositions, emotions, and thoughts human beings have – can and should be studied scientifically, Humboldt believes. Second, his naturalism, unlike that of Condillac, includes a commitment to "detailed investigations." Humboldt cared about empirical data and traveled throughout his life to collect data for his linguistic studies, which is the major reason why in Humboldt's work philosophy of language begins to be transformed into a science. Third, Humboldt by nature is a holist about human beings. Human beings are unified beings in such a way that their parts or aspects cannot be understood without knowing how these are interconnected.

But the most striking commitment expressed in Humboldt's assessment of Ith is that human biology is essential to understanding the integrated human being, including the scientific understanding of human psychology. When Humboldt refers to the unity of the physiological and the psychological, he is not just thinking about physiology as the science of the basic activities of the cells and tissues of living organisms, but in the broader eighteenth-century sense as the science of the normal functions and phenomena of living things.[3]

Humboldt was not just an armchair biologist. Humboldt's younger brother by two years, the explorer and scientist Alexander von Humboldt, wrote in 1795 when Wilhelm was studying human anatomy at the University of Göttingen that "Wilhelm lives and breathes in cadavers. He procured himself a whole beggar and (as Goethe wrote him) eats human brains" (Jahn and Lange 1973, 433; quoted in Müller-Sievers 1993, 17). Later Humboldt assisted his younger brother in 3,000 experiments in which they were generating and studying galvanic currents in muscle and nerve tissue (Müller-Sievers 1993, 19). They were interested in the nature of physiological irritability and sensibility, properties that Humboldt discusses in an essay he wrote during this period. It is called *On Sexual Difference and Its Influence on Organic Nature* (*Über den Geschlechtsunterschied und seinen Einfluss auf die organische Natur*, 1795), and in it Humboldt tries to use sex and

---

[3] James Harris in 1704 writes: "*Physiology*...teaches the Constitution of the Body so far as it is sound, or in its Natural State; and endeavors to find Reasons for its Functions and Operations." Quoted in *The Compact Edition of the Oxford English Dictionary* (1971), 2:811.

gender differences as a general model for understanding human nature. Sensibility is feminine, whereas irritability and desire are male, and human thought is an offspring of feminine sensibility and reason's masculine drive to create – namely, reason's genius (Humboldt 1968, 1:316 and 336).[4]

This biological perspective persists in Humboldt's philosophy of language. He compares language development to crystallization, which in the eighteenth century was considered a biological phenomenon (1999, 148), and to the flowering of a tree (1968, 6:226). For Humboldt, language is not just a collection words and rules of grammar but a "noble work of nature" that has an "organic nature, and that must be treated as such" (1968, 4:10). What "the growth of muscle tissue and nerves or blood circulation are to the body, the functions of language are to the mind" (1968, 4:249). Humboldt expresses this biological turn in the study of language in the Kawi Introduction: "*[L]anguage* and *life* are inseparable concepts" (1999, 93). For example, the vocabulary of a language is not an "*inert completed mass*," but "a continuous *generation* and regeneration of the *word-making capacity*" (ibid.). This applies not only to the creation of new words in a language but the learning of words by children and in daily usage. Using a word is not simply recalling a word stored in memory, Humboldt claims, but involves the forces that are necessary for the initial generation of words.

Language "arises from a depth of human nature" (Humboldt 1999, 24) and "the power of speech" is a universal human capacity (1999, 26). "The *bringing-forth of language* is an *inner need* of a human being... a thing lying in his own nature, indispensable for the development of his mental powers" (1999, 27). It is not an instrument created in order to facilitate human communication and cooperation. For this reason, Humboldt denies that language is a human artifact. Because language is tied to human nature, it is a mistake "to regard it as a true product and creation of peoples." It is "an involuntary emanation..., no work of nations but a gift fallen to them by their inner destiny" (1999, 24). It is involuntary because linguistic activity is not intentional: language does not emerge because people have some goal in mind for which language is a means (1999, 115).

---

[4] Schiller sent one of these essays to Kant who, needless to say, was not impressed (Zweig 1967, 221). Kant refers to earlier attempts to use such models, which he says were criticized for being enthusiastic (*Schwärmerei*).

Perhaps Humboldt's most famous claim is that "language is the formative organ of thought" (1999, 54; also see 21). As an organ responsible for the growth and development of thought, language "is an element of the whole human organism" (1999, 54.) He also describes language itself as an organism. "Language, in direct conjunction with mental power is a fully-fashioned *organism*," and consequently, language "not only [has] *parts*, but also *laws* of procedure, or rather... *directions* and *endeavours*," which can be compared to physiological laws (1999, 90). Elsewhere Humboldt explicitly contrasts anatomical and physiological perspectives, and he writes that languages must be treated physiologically, not anatomically (1968, 6:146). Anatomy is concerned with the static structure of an organism, but language is a living and dynamic organism that needs to be characterized as such. This means that a proper theory of language cannot limit itself to an anatomical characterization of vocabulary and grammar, which can at best be compared with the "dead skeleton" of a language (1968, 6:147). A proper physiological characterization will determine the functions and principles of the generation of language.

In fact, the Kawi Introduction is driven by a biological problem, namely to account for "the division of humanity into peoples and races," which for him are physiological categories that are "directly linked" to the diversity of languages and dialects (1999, 21–2). Specifically, he is concerned with the racial classification of the Malayan populations, and he believes that the classification of their languages will shed light on their racial identity (1999, 15). His overarching strategy is to explain the diversity of languages and peoples in terms of "a... higher phenomenon, the *growth of human mental powers*" (1999, 21), and uses the principles of this growth to classify languages and so to contribute to the classification of races. He develops this theme in the Kawi Introduction.

What follows this theoretical and philosophical introduction is a massive three-volume case study, namely *On the Kawi Language on the Island of Java* (*Über die Kawi Sprache auf der Insel von Java*), in which Humboldt relies on a wealth of empirical linguistic and cultural data to develop a theory of the formal differences between the Indic language family and what today would be characterized as the Western and Central Austronesian languages, which include Malagasy, Malayan, and the ancient Javanese courtly language Kawi. Humboldt was particularly interested in Kawi because it was not clear how to classify it due to the fact that it mixed elements of Sanskrit and Javanese, which belong to two distinct language families. Humboldt believed that his theory of language led to the proper classification of this language in terms of its function and principles of generation, unlike superficial comparisons of vocabularies and grammatical structure.

Divinity and Infinity

Although Humboldt's philosophy was biologically informed, it would be wrong to characterize him as a materialist. While taking a biological turn, Humboldt preserves and develops the Leibnizian system perspective on language. For Humboldt, although human language is rooted in human needs, this human "neediness" is also "intimately joined" (*trauliches Anschmiegen*) with the "divinity of the nature of language" (1968, 4:249).

The divinity of human language lies in the origins of human language. According to Humboldt, there is a mental power (*Geisteskraft*) that is responsible for language, the diversity of languages, as well as culture and cultural diversity (1968, 7:45–7; 1999, 48–9). The appearance of language is part of the spiritual development of human beings, and "all spiritual progress can only proceed from an internal emission of force" (1968, 7:26; 1999, 31). This mental power responsible for language or any other human activity is inexplicable. According to Humboldt, our attempts to explain cultural phenomena will "run from time to time…into knots, so to speak, which resist further resolution." This untiable knot is "that mental power, which can neither be wholly penetrated in its nature, nor calculated beforehand in its effect" (1968, 7:15; 1999, 23).

This mental power sets the limits of Humboldt's naturalism. There will always be a dimension to language that escapes scientific understanding. Although Humboldt affirms that language is subject to scientific scrutiny, he also believes that what is understood by science is a "dead contraption" or an "abstraction" (1968, 7:46–7; 1999, 49–50). What science understands is the finished product – the completed work – but language, in Humboldt's famous words, is "no product (*Ergon*), but an activity (*Energeia*)" (1968, 7:46; 1999, 49). The *Energeia* is the activity of the language-generating power, and for this reason Humboldt also characterizes language as a kind of human action (1968, 7:15; 1999, 23) or a kind of human labor (1968, 46–7; 1999, 49–50), although, as we saw previously, it is important to keep in mind that this is not an intentional or voluntary activity.

A central feature of this power responsible for language is that it is free because, as Humboldt writes, it is an "independent and original *cause*" and is not "conditioned" by other causes. An "inner life-principle," it allows human beings to break the "quasi-mechanical advancement of human activity." It can make "sudden and unforeseen intrusions" into an "evidently cause-and-effect governed path" (1968, 7:18–19; 1999, 26). This is not true just of language but of all mental development. According to Humboldt, "all spiritual progress can only proceed from an internal emission of force, and to that extent has always a hidden, and because it is autonomous, an inexplicable basis" (1999, 31).[5]

Linguistic freedom is the reason why language, at least partially, escapes scientific explanation. The mental power that generates language "creates of its own accord" – that is, is independent of prior causes. Thus "all possibility of explanation automatically ceases" (1968, 7:26; 1999, 31). Human language is always a "mental exhalation," and so no matter how much "we may fix and embody, dismember and dissect, there always remains something unknown left over in it, and precisely this which escapes [scientific] treatment is that wherein the unity and breath" of language resides (1968, 7:48; 1999, 51). On account of the essential role in natural language of human freedom, and the attendant role of consciousness, human language development cannot be explained "on merely physiological grounds" (1968, 7:250; 1999, 214).

In sum, for Humboldt, human language is "divinely free" (1999, 24). An important dimension of linguistic freedom is that language involves what Humboldt calls a "*creative principle*" and even an "*artistically* creative principle" (1999, 214 and 91). The linguistic freedom human beings have consists in the "*mental labour* of making the *articulated* sound capable of expressing *thought*" (1999, 49). Human beings, according to Humboldt, must "transform sounds into *articulate* sounds," and this "symbolizing activity" involves relating sounds to each other to form a system or structure capable of expressing thought (1999, 214). Humboldt compares this transformation of sound into language to musical activity because "concepts are conveyed in language by tones" (1968, 7:98; 1999, 91). This aesthetic dimension of language is not a "casual adornment" of language, but it is "an essentially necessary consequence of the rest of its nature" (ibid.).

But human linguistic creativity, in Humboldt's philosophy of language, has a specific task to accomplish. Because language is the "*mental labour* of making *articulated* sound capable of expressing *thought*," language must be rich enough to express human thought. Any human

---

[5] See Chapter 8 for a parallel emphasis on force in Derrida's philosophy of language.

language has the capacity to express "the totality of sense-impressions and spontaneous mental activity" (1999, 52), and consequently "the language of every people, however uncultivated," is capable of expressing any thought human beings are capable of, "without alien assistance" (1999, 33). This is true at the very genesis of linguistic development. The linguistic sense that drives the development of language "must...include...another thing that we cannot explain in detail, an instinctive presentiment of the entire system that language will have need of" (1999, 69).

Language, then, must be able to express thought, which, according to Humboldt, "at its most human is a yearning...from confinement into the infinite" (1999, 55). Thus language at its very base is infused with the "mind's effort to give language as many distinctive *forms* as are needed to fetter the infinite variety of fleeting *thoughts*" (1999, 78). In sum, because the capacity for thought is infinite or boundless, "language is quite peculiarly confronted by an unending and truly boundless domain, the essence of all that can be thought" (1968, 7:99; 1999, 91).

However, all natural phenomena are finite, and the natural elements available for language – the sounds human beings are capable of making, for instance – are finite. Consequently, language "must...make infinite employment of finite means" (ibid.). This observation – that language must have an infinite or boundless capacity, but that it must have this using finite means – is the main reason Humboldt has found a place in the history of generative linguistics (Chomsky 1966, 20, and Pinker 1994, 84). The way generative linguists develop this observation is by adapting certain features of formal axiomatic systems.[6] They suggest that a human language is a kind of formal system in which an infinite or at least boundless set of sentences is generated from a finite vocabulary together with a finite set of recursive rules for this vocabulary – that is, rules that can be repeatedly applied to their own products or outputs.

There is some doubt that Humboldt's idea that language must "make an infinite employment of finite means" significantly overlaps with the generative grammars of contemporary linguistics (Coseriu 1971 and Borsche 1981). Clearly Humboldt did not have in mind a generative grammar in the sense of a set of recursive rules operating on a finite

---

[6] Chomsky 1957 refers to Shannon and Weaver 1949, who extend formal metamathematical techniques to communications theory or what also came to be known as information theory.

vocabulary, and he was not specifically thinking of sentences when he refers to language's "unending and truly boundless domain." But the problem Humboldt defines is the same problem generative grammars aim to solve. Language has infinite or boundless capacities, but this capacity must be based on a finite repertoire. True, the capacity Humboldt has in mind is the capacity to express the "essence of all that can be thought," whereas Chomsky was interested in developing an account of the generation of all possible syntactic or grammatical forms of a language. But this is only a difference in degree of specificity. The "essence of all that can be thought" includes much more than syntactic structures, but it includes those as well.[7]

Thus Humboldt's philosophy of language is formed under the same pressure that is found in Leibniz, namely to account for what, as we saw in the previous chapter, Leibniz called "the very form or possibility of those thoughts." What for Leibniz was divine about language, namely that language expressed "possible thoughts" or propositions, persists in Humboldt's thinking about the nature of language. The pressure from propositions drives Humboldt away from a purely empirical and scientific account of language that draws on observed patterns of speech and other linguistic behavior and leads him instead to seek hidden powers that account for the propositional dimension of natural language.

Feedback Loop

A significant difference between Humboldt and Leibniz is that Humboldt seeks to find a place for Leibniz's divine features of language within a biological perspective. For Leibniz the formal dimensions of language still rested on a divine realm of ideas that human minds represent in virtue of being divine creations; Humboldt, however, relies on inexplicable mental powers that can be understood in terms of the principles of life at work in living organisms.

Although there is an inexplicable dimension to human language that is beyond the scope of scientific explanation, Humboldt traces out a place where freedom and science interface. He writes that, although

---

[7] Although Chomsky is not interested in developing theories of meaning for human language and in fact is skeptical about the feasibility of such accounts, generative approaches to syntax have been extended to the semantics of natural language, as we will see in Chapter 6.

"freedom in itself may be indeterminable and inexplicable, its bounds can perhaps be discovered, within a certain sphere reserved to let it alone; and linguistic research must recognize and respect the phenomenon of freedom, but also be equally careful in tracing its limits" (1968, 7:65; 1999, 64).

The node where freedom and necessity interact is described in the same passage in which Humboldt discusses the infinite employment of language:

> It must therefore make infinite employment of finite means, and is able to do so through the identity of the thought and language-producing power [*durch die Identität der Gedanken- und Sprache-erzeugenden Kraft*].[8] But this also necessarily implies that language has an effect in two directions at once, in that it first proceeds outwards to the utterance, but then also back again to the powers that engender it. (1968, 7:99; 1999, 91)

The very same power that brings about thought also brings about language, and this power enables language to express, using finite means, the infinite domain of thought. Moreover, this power is such that language has two effects. First, it brings about the utterance, but second, this effect feeds back into the speaker to transform the very powers that produced language.

This feedback loop is why Humboldt believes that thought and language depend on each other. "*Intellectual activity*, entirely mental, entirely internal, and to some extent passing without trace, becomes through *sound*, externalized in speech and perceptible to the senses. Thought and language are therefore one and inseparable from each other" (1968, 7:53; 1999, 54). Thought and language are inseparable because thought has to be externalized in verbal sound, which in turn affects the mind in virtue of the mind's perception of the sound. Let us look at this loop more closely.

The first leg of this loop is the mind's externalization in sound. Without sound human thinking "cannot...achieve clarity, nor representation [*Vorstellung*] become a concept [*Begriff*]." External sounds are needed by the mind to "compare, separate and combine" the objects in "external nature" it experiences, and the mental activities of comparing, distinguishing, and combining or classifying objects are essential to clear

---

[8] The first edition of the Kawi Introduction published in 1836 omits the hyphens, but it is still clear that the identity is a relation between the language and thought-producing powers. Compare the mistaken translation in Humboldt 1999, 91.

and conceptual thinking (1968, 7:54; 1999, 55). Humboldt describes the process as follows. The mind's representations are a product of a synthesis of the passive reception of the senses and inner mental activity. From "this combination a representation tears itself away," becomes an object for the mind, and, "perceived anew as such, returns back" to the mind. The sound of language, Humboldt asserts, is needed to tear the representation away from the mind and turn it into an object. The active mental power emits a sound, which returns back to the speaker's ear. In this manner, the mental representation, which is subjective, is "transformed into real objectivity" (1968, 7:55; 1999, 56).

The second leg of the loop involves the perception of the sound and completes the process of concept formation. A concept, in Humboldt's view, is the internal representation of a heard linguistic sound emitted by a speaker. This internal representation makes comparison, distinction, and classification possible, which is necessary to "true thinking." Thinking requires "the collection of the *manifold into unity*," and articulation makes this possible of sounds (1968, 7:66; 1999, 66). So, although there is mental activity without language, what might be called cognitive thinking or thinking involving judgment as well as awareness depends on speech. Even the solitary or quiet human being relies on language to form concepts, Humboldt believes.

The reason the sound makes classification and the other mental activities central to human cognition is that the sound that is turned into a concept is a "designating impression" (1968, 7:54; 1999, 55). The impression is used in place of objects, and in this way the impression can be used to unify diverse objects. However, Humboldt emphasizes that although language designates objects, the designated objects are not simply given; the objects we experience are in some sense made possible by language. "Just as no concept is possible without language, so also there can be no object for the mind" (1968, 7:59; 1999, 59). Human beings can become conscious of objects only with the help of concepts, and language, as we just saw, is necessary for the existence of concepts.

Because language is involved in structuring human cognition, and languages are diverse in their structure, "there resides in every language a characteristic world view [*Weltansicht*]." Human beings represent the world around them conceptually through the public language they have acquired as children, and to learn a new language is "to acquire a new standpoint," although it is a new point of view within the world view of the old language (1968, 7:60; 1999, 60).

Although language structures a world view, Humboldt does not believe that language falsifies or veils the world in which human beings live. Language, particularly the sound of spoken language, does "stand between" human beings and nature, but human beings surround themselves "with a world of sounds in order to take up and process internally the world of objects" (ibid.). In other words, language makes cognition of the world possible, and consequently by surrounding ourselves by a world of linguistic sounds "we do not abandon the world that really surrounds us" (1968, 7:61; 1999, 61). The law-governed structure of language is related to the regularity of nature, and the more human beings exercise their power of speech, the closer they come to understanding nature.

Why Humboldt believes that sound in particular, rather than other sensible objects such as inscriptions, is indispensable for the externalization of mental representations and the possibility of cognition is not clear, but it seems that Humboldt believes that there is a particularly close "agreement of sound and thought [that] is...plain to see" but cannot be explained (1968, 7:53; 1999, 55). He believes that sound has a "penetrating power" that distinguishes it from all other sense impressions, and it is this power that is needed to externalize mental representations and turn them into concepts.

Form and Freedom

The two poles on a feedback loop – inner subjectivity and outer objectivity – constitute the linguistic form that Humboldt uses to characterize and classify human languages. Language consists of an external sound form and an internal or intellectual form (1968, 7:52ff. and 86ff.; 1999, 54ff. and 81ff.), and the unity of these two forms, particularly their "mutual interpenetration, constitute the individual form of a language" (1968, 7:52; 1999, 54).

The sound form, according to Humboldt, is "the truly constitutive and guiding principle of the diversity of languages" (ibid.). It consists of the way a language organizes sound into grammatical and meaningful units, particularly the sentence. Giving the sound form for a language involves presenting its root words, the various classes that words fall into (nouns, pronouns, adjectives, verbs, etc.), the grammatical forms the language has (e.g., person, number, gender, mood, case, etc.), how the classes of words and grammatical forms are marked out by sound, and how the basic and complex words are put together to form complete sentences. In sum, the sound form of a language consists of what Chomsky describes as the language's syntactic structures.[9] But it is important to highlight that, unlike Chomsky, Humboldt believes that semantic properties are needed to characterize linguistic structure. For Humboldt, the sound form of a language rests on the semantic task of designating concepts: the word units and forms of a language cannot be recognized without understanding what concepts the sound form designates (1968, 7:72–6 and 89; 1999, 70–3 and 83).

The concepts as well as the relations of concepts belong to the "inner, intellectual part of language" (Humboldt 1968, 7:89; 1999, 83). The inner part of language appears to consist of two broad components. On the one hand, there is what we might call "the inner conceptual form." Although not a label Humboldt uses, it is a component that Humboldt clearly distinguishes. The human mind forms a rule-governed system, and the rules that order this system are "the laws of intuiting, thinking and feeling as such," or what he also describes as "the universal *forms of intuition* and in the logical ordering of concepts" (1968, 7:87 and 90; 1999, 81 and 84).

The laws of intuition and thinking are universal and form the basis for all laws of language (1968, 7:52; 1999, 54). The forms of intuition are the ways in which human perception is structured and formed into concepts, and the laws of thinking are the fundamental ways in which concepts are related. Humboldt does not refer to these laws of intuition and thought in any systematic manner, but he does refer to diverse examples: spatial and temporal relations (1968, 7:87, 90, and 104; 1999, 82, 84, and 95), personhood and gender (1968, 7:90 and 111; 1999, 84 and 101), predication or attribution (1968, 7:214; 1999, 185), conjunction (1968, 7:233; 1999, 200), and modality (1968, 7:87; 1999, 82).

The inner linguistic form consists of the laws for expressing in language the mind's concepts and its inner conceptual form. "Those laws," Humboldt writes, "are nothing but the paths on which mental activity moves in producing language, or to use another metaphor, the *forms* in which it mints out the *sounds*" (1968, 7:86; 1999, 81). These laws are "based on the requirements that *thinking* imposes on language," and they are also, at least in their "original tendency," shared by all human

---

[9] Chomsky (1960) highlights the affinity between his own generative linguistics and Humboldt's conception of language. For a critical assessment and a defense, see Aarsleff 1982, 101–19, and my introduction to Humboldt 1999.

beings (1968, 7:52; 1999, 54). Finally, these laws are powerful enough to make anything human beings can think expressible in language. "Nothing within a human being is so deep, so rare or so wide-ranging that it may not pass over into language and be recognizable there" (1968, 7:86; 1999, 81).

Although the inner conceptual and linguistic forms are universal, this universality is compatible with great linguistic diversity. Specifically, the original linguistic tendency is universal, but subsequent developments will diverge on account of the interaction between the sound form of language and the internal dimensions of mind. As we just saw, the sound form has a "retro-active effect" on the intellectual capacities of speakers because the sound "modifies in its turn the outlook and procedure of the inner linguistic sense" (1968, 7:250–2; 1999, 214–15), and in this way language changes the very "powers that engender it" (1968, 7:99; 1999, 91). For instance, words can further or impede the recognition of relationships among concepts, and conceptual nuances can be lost if a language does not reflect them in its sound form. On the other hand, within certain limits (1968, 7:166; 1999, 149), an "ever-greater *refinement* of language" will enrich the mind and enhance the overall development of thoughts (1968, 7:100 and 120; 1999, 92 and 109).

Freedom and the strength with which this freedom is exercised are responsible for the diversity of human language (1968, 7:19 and 52; 1999, 26 and 54). On account of freedom, human language appears suddenly and unpredictably. Humboldt believes that the appearance of language at different times in different regions is a rupture in the steady and predictable causal pattern of physical events, and the freedom of the language-making power is responsible for that. Moreover, freedom is exercised in varying degrees according to the confidence and commitment of individuals exercising their power (1968, 7:16; 1999, 23). The appearance of language as well as linguistic change is due to "the unpredictable, immediately creative advance of human mental power" – namely, the "effects of genius, which is no less displayed at particular moments in peoples than it is in individuals" (1999, 32).

Freedom is also a work of the imagination and emotion, which "engender individual shapings, in which the individual character... emerges, and where, as in everything individual, the variety of ways in which the thing in question can be represented in ever-differing guises, extends to infinity" (1968, 7:87; 1999, 82). Language is rule-governed for Humboldt, but it is also like a work of art, and this dimension of language "cannot be measured out by the understanding" and is "the deepest and inexplicable part" of language (1968, 7:87 and 96; 1999, 81 and 89).

Finally, there is also the simple matter of the sheer mental strength available to speakers. The "*energy* of the force" that transforms a sound into "living expression of thought...cannot everywhere be the same, cannot everywhere display a like intensity, veracity, and regularity" (1968, 7:252; 1999, 215). For instance, speakers may have a clear distinction in mind between the subjunctive and future moods, but their language-making power may be too weak to mint out the corresponding sounds.

Classification and Quality

Although Humboldt believes that the classification of languages is very difficult, given "the present state of...knowledge," and that the required knowledge may never be attained (1968, 7:278; 1999, 235), he does have a general strategy for classifying languages. Humboldt characterizes languages in terms of their individual form, and he classifies languages in terms of how close they are to what he takes to be the ideal form of language.

That all languages aim to designate the mind's universal inner conceptual form – the universal laws of intuition and thought – and that they aim to do this without ambiguity, reserving distinct sound forms for distinct conceptual relations, is a core belief of Humboldt's philosophy of language. The goal of all languages is to have "the total structure of sound-form and inner shaping...fused together with equal firmness and simultaneity" (1968, 7:94; 1999, 88). Of course, languages achieve this goal only in varying degrees, but they all approximate this ideal, which constitutes the form of all languages (1968, 7:252–3; 1999, 216).

He specifically focuses on these syntactic categories: the verb, the conjunction, and the relative pronoun. He pays particular attention to the verb that in his view has the role of conjoining the subject and predicate into a complete thought expressible in a sentence. On Humboldt's account, some languages have a clear syllable or sound change to mark out the verb in the sound form, while others do not. For example, he believes that Burmese has no way of distinguishing by sound the syntactic difference between a noun and a verb. This difference, Humboldt maintains, is something Burmese speakers have in mind, and so it is preserved in the meanings of Burmese root words, but they are not reflected in the sound form of Burmese (1968, 7:280–2; 1999, 237–9). On the other hand, the sound form of Sanskrit clearly demarcates nouns and verbs. None of the endings used to mark out the various moods, tenses, and conjugations of verbs are used to mark out noun forms, and none of the sounds used to mark out noun forms are used to express verb forms, according to Humboldt (1968, 7:215; 1999, 186).

He distinguishes three general ways in which the sound form of a language can demarcate syntactic categories: isolation, inflection, and agglutination. Isolating languages do not have special sound units or sound changes to designate grammatical forms. Sentences consist of strings of words, and word order is used to mark out grammatical relationships. Humboldt highlights Chinese as a paradigm case of an isolating language, but English has many examples where word order and not inflection is used to designate relationships – for instance, "Simba hits the ball" and "The ball hits Simba." Agglutinating languages such as Japanese, Swahili, and Finnish compound words to show grammatical form. English also has examples of agglutination: changing a noun into an adjective by compounding it with the word "like," as in "lifelike." Inflecting languages demarcate grammatical forms by changing words, either by changing the sound of the word itself, as in "flew," which is the past tense of the verb "to fly," or by adding prefixes or suffixes that by themselves are not words, as when "s" is added to form the plural of a noun. Indo-European languages as well as Semitic languages, including Hebrew and Arabic, are inflecting languages, but Humboldt's favorite example of inflecting languages is Sanskrit.

Humboldt believes that there is a qualitative difference between these types of languages. The quality of a language is a function of how well it contributes to the mental development of people, and a language that fuses "sound-form and inner shaping" the most contributes the most to mental development. Humboldt believes (along with most of his contemporaries) that in this respect inflectional languages are superior to noninflectional ones.

The reason inflecting languages contribute more to mental development than isolating languages do is that they exhibit grammatical form with sounds whereas isolating languages "consign all *grammatical form...to the work of the mind.*" This calls for "inner effort" to compensate for what is missing in the language (1968, 7:271; 1999, 230). What is missing, Humboldt asserts, is a proper expression of a closed or completed thought that the speaker has in mind. A complete thought involves a concept that is the subject of the thought and a concept that is a predicate of the subject. Moreover, on Humboldt's view, this attribution involves a commitment about the way things are. In thinking that lightning is striking, we are judging that lightning is really striking (1968, 7:214; 1999, 185). By not demarcating the parts of a completed thought and their relations to each other with special sounds – for example, by not distinguishing subjects and predicates with special sounds – isolating languages fail to exhibit the complete thought with clarity and vigor. Humboldt believes that exhibiting these relations with sentence order only, that is, by "soundless" means, is "too feeble in conveying the feeling of sentential unity" (1968, 7:143; 1999, 128). Consequently, an isolating language, in and of itself, does not contribute to or reinforce strongly enough the development of thought.

Nevertheless, Humboldt is very conflicted about Chinese, his paradigm example of an isolating language. On the one hand, it has the defects of isolating languages and does not guide the mind "to the true centre, from which poetry and philosophy, scientific research and eloquent discourse, spring forth with equal readiness" (1968, 7:255–6; 1999, 218). On the other hand, Chinese has a "high degree of excellence" precisely because it designates soundlessly formal relations (1968, 7:271; 1999, 230). On account of this, Chinese contributed to a stricter attention to formal relations and enhanced the mind's capacity to understand the distinction between concepts and how concepts are related.

Inflecting languages are better than agglutinating languages because they express and contribute to conceptual unity. According to Humboldt, when human beings think, they categorize or classify the concepts that constitute the thought. For example, when a person thinks of an object, she has a concept of that object in mind, and at the same time this concept is classified, for example, as a concept of a living creature or as a concept of a particular gender (1968, 7:109–11; 1999, 100–1). Although Humboldt does not address this issue in much detail, he clearly has the categories of both inner conceptual form and inner linguistic form in mind because he refers to categories of animation, gender, person, pronoun, verb, causality, and mood, among others.

This classification of concepts is not the compounding of two concepts. Instead, it involves placing the concept in "a class whose concept runs through many things in nature" (1968, 7:111; 1999, 102). Consequently, the unity of the concept is not affected by this classification. Now, the function of a word is to *designate* a concept, to *indicate* its classification, and to do this with a "sound-unity" that symbolizes the conceptual unity of its meaning (1968, 7:111 and 121; 1999, 102 and 110). Agglutination achieves this by compounding distinct words, whereas inflection achieves this by keeping in one word but changing it. Thus, on Humboldt's view, agglutination does not capture the conceptual unity as well as inflection does. Agglutination symbolizes one concept with two words compounded together, whereas inflection symbolizes one concept with just one word.

Accordingly, Humboldt believes that only

> the *method* of inflection in all its completeness ... imparts true inner fixity to the word for both mind and ear, and likewise separates with certainty the parts of the sentence, in keeping with the necessary ordering of thought and this method harbours the sure principle of language-construction. (1968, 7:162; 1999, 145)

Although Humboldt evaluates languages on this basis, it is important to highlight two caveats that Humboldt offers. First, no matter what method a human language uses to designate concepts, indicate categories, and express thoughts, "every language is produced by the original tendency or 'original talent' shared by all human beings. Every language has a structure worthy of study and every language has the infinite resources to assimilate the richest and loftiest ideas" (1968, 7:256; 1999, 218). Second, Humboldt is careful to distinguish the quality of a language from the quality of mind of its speakers (1968, 7:163 and 255; 1999, 145 and 217). An imperfect language by itself, is only evidence for the claim that less energy has been devoted to language. As was the case with Chinese speakers, a less than perfect language can be compensated for in other ways. No language is "an absolute restraint" on the human capacity for mental development. Finally, no human language is perfect, according to Humboldt. Inflectional, isolating, and agglutinative languages are only abstract models, and human languages are always a mix of inflection, isolation, and agglutination, although some languages fit one model better than others.

Nation and Alienation

The feedback loop of language that has inner central power and the articulated sound for its two foci is an example of what Humboldt takes to be a more "general law of human existence in the world," namely that a human "can project nothing from himself that does not at once become a thing that reacts upon him and conditions his further creation" (1968, 7:251; 1999, 214). Consequently, this loop also limits human freedom, particularly the freedom exercised by human beings in language. Although language is an expression of freedom and autonomy in that it is generated by a free and autonomous mental power, it is at the very same time "truly an alien power" (1968, 7:63; 1999, 62).

Humboldt writes that "however internal language may altogether be, it yet has at the same time an independent outer existence that exerts power against humanity itself" (1968, 7:21–2; 1999, 28). In fact, language is not only an independent power, but its power greatly exceeds the power of individual human beings. The source of the independence of language is its external existence after articulation. "The representation transformed into language is no longer the exclusive possession of a single subject" (1968, 7:56; 1999, 56). The articulated sound – that is, the meaningful sound generated by the language-making power – is "necessarily...a joint possession...and is in truth the property of the whole human species" (1968, 7:63; 1999, 62).

When a person speaks, the articulated sound is a product of the mental power and form of the speaker, but the hearer transforms this sound. First, the hearer transforms the heard, articulated sound into a mental representation that is shaped by the hearer's mental power, including the hearer's own language-making power. Second, when the hearer begins to speak, even if it is the same word she heard, it is now infused with the power and form of the hearer. In this way, language grows and becomes a crosscurrent of all the individual mental powers of its speakers. This process includes not only contemporary speakers but also speakers across time, as language is passed from generation to generation.

What happens in such exchanges is that the sound form or sound system of a language changes, even if the change is very slight. As human beings communicate, they transform the sound form of a language, each language user imposing her own individuality on language. Consequently, the sound form is constantly being altered by other people, which is one reason why language is not only an expression of individual human creativity but also something alien to the individual.

The alien dimension of language is not just a function of the fact that language is shared by a community of speakers but also depends on the very fact that language involves sound. "The construction of language must be seen as a production in which the inner idea, to manifest itself, has to overcome a difficulty" (1968, 7:82; 1999, 77). This obstacle is the very making of sound, a physical activity. The vocal chords have to be able to make sounds and the different kinds of sounds that are needed to express distinct concepts, and this can be done with varying degrees of success.

The sound form, in short, is alien when there is a conflict or tension between the thoughts the speaker is trying to express and the available phonological and syntactic structures of the speaker's language. Speakers attempt to manifest their thoughts in language by using words and word complexes to designate their concepts, but this project can run into problems when the appropriate sounds are not available. For instance, the speaker may in his mind distinguish between the future and subjunctive moods, but the sound system of his language (e.g., Sanskrit, according to Humboldt) may lack a corresponding distinction (1968, 7:82–4 and 87–9; 1999, 77–9 and 82–3). So when the speaker is trying to express that something will happen and his thought that something might happen, he either needs to modify the sound system, however slightly, or suppress the manifestation of this mental distinction. In the latter case, the sound form becomes the master of the speaker's mind.

Another reason Humboldt has for believing that language changes internal structure is tied to his holism. Humboldt believes that "language resides in every human being in its whole range" (1968, 7:57; 1999, 57). In articulating a sound, Humboldt believes, a speaker not only expresses the word's meaning but presents the word as having a certain place in the whole language, which is infinitely large. Consequently, language is not built up atomistically out of individual words, where the totality of language is a product of the individual words compounded into a language, but "words, on the contrary, emerge from the totality of speech" (1968, 7:72; 1999, 70).

As human beings communicate, they transform the sound form, and thus hearers must develop their linguistic capacity to understand the newly transformed language. In order to do this, the "listener...is bidden, as it were,...in his own mind to supply the missing element in harmony with what is given" (1968, 7:180; 1999, 159). The articulated word that is heard is characterized in terms of its place in a whole language, and the hearer must, upon understanding the word, incorporate the pattern that characterizes the word into her own linguistic structure.

An important consequence of Humboldt's holism is that languages are very fluid for him. Humboldt characterizes languages in terms of their forms, and each part of language is characterized in terms of the total language to which it belongs. But forms change as language develops in communication, each speaker and hearer imposing his or her own individuality on language. Consequently, language is in a constant flux; moreover, in a sense each language user has her own language (1968, 7:51; 1999, 53).

At the very same time, he affirms that "we may say with equal correctness that the whole of human species has but one language" (ibid.). Because the identity of languages rests on their form, and a universal form exists for all languages, in a sense there is only one language. The general laws of language, at least in its general tendency, are the same in all human beings; and in that sense all human beings have the same language, even though their original tendency can subsequently develop in diverse ways.

These diverse developments are, on Humboldt's account, primarily the products of nationality. Throughout most of his Kawi Introduction, Humboldt attributes language to something larger than individual human beings, particularly nations. "Languages," he writes, are "bound and dependent on the nations to which they belong" (1968, 7:17; 1999, 24). Language is shaped by "the mental individuality of a people" (1968, 7:42; 1999, 46), the form of language is "the individual urge whereby a nation gives validity to thought and feeling in language," and "language . . . is always the spiritual exhalation of a nationally individual life" (1968, 7:47–8; 1999, 50–1). This is not just a manner of speaking; for Humboldt, nations, as well as persons, must be regarded as a "human *individuality*, which pursues an inner spiritual path of its own" (1968, 7:37; 1999, 41). This nationalist point of view appears to predominate throughout the text, which is concerned primarily about the mental development of nations, not about individual human beings.

Nevertheless, in a section explicitly addressing the relationship between individuals and nations, Humboldt presents a more complex picture, maintaining that languages are "spiritual creations which in no way whatever pass out from a single individual to the remainder" (1968, 7:38; 1999, 42). He adds, "So although languages are thus the work of *nations*, . . . they still remain the self-creations of *individuals*, in that they can be produced solely in each individual" (1968, 7:40; 1999, 44). Part of his reason for this belief is surely his view that nothing can be in the human mind that wasn't put there by its "own activity" (1968, 7:56; 1999, 57). How can this be? How can language belong to both individuals and nations?

Humboldt's answer is that it is a "mystery" (1968, 7:33; 1999, 38). Language is first an activity of individual speakers – people begin to speak because they must speak. Human beings need to speak because they must cooperate and communicate; more important, however, they need to speak in order to think and cultivate their minds. But just as one person begins to speak because she must, so does everyone else, and language then emerges from the "simultaneous self-activity of all" (1968, 7:38; 1999, 42). In this process, the language of the individual is in some sense broken off from the individual and is united with the language of his group. How this happens is, for Humboldt, a mystery that inspires "reverential awe."

Hamann, Herder, and Humboldt

The appeal to mystery and the inexplicable poetic dimensions of language lend Humboldt's philosophy of language a hue that has been used to tie Humboldt's work to the post-Kantian German Counter-Enlightenment, particularly the philosophies of Johann Georg Hamann (1730–88) and his student Johann Gottfried Herder (1744–1803). Both Hamann and Herder were reacting to the primary role assigned to formal and systematic features in the philosophy of Kant.

Without oversimplifying too much, Kant can be characterized as attempting to develop in the *Critique of Pure Reason* a synthesis of Locke's focus on the actual and observed properties of the human understanding – our actual thoughts and experiences – and Leibniz's focus on the mind's propositional structures: the domain of all possible thoughts, to use Leibniz's terminology. The synthesis Kant develops is that actual human cognition is a product of given sensible intuitions and conceptual forms that order the sensible intuitions. The conceptual forms or categories are universal for rational creatures who must judge and infer in order to acquire knowledge, and they set the boundaries of all possible cognition for such discursive creatures. But without sensible intuitions, the concepts are empty, and the goal of traditional metaphysics to extend cognition to objects of which human beings do not have sense experience leads to the illusions, fallacies, and other confusions of traditional metaphysics, according to Kant.

In his philosophy, Kant thoroughly ignores language, and the Counter-Enlightenment reaction to Kant's synthesis seeks to take advantage of this deficit. Kant's earliest critic and contemporary, Hamann, argues in his *Metacritique: Concerning the Purism of Reason* (1784) that reason cannot be pure because it cannot be abstracted from custom and tradition, from experience, and from ordinary language (1993, 206–7). The pursuit of purity is driven, Hamann continues, by a "*gnostic* hate of matter or also a *mystical* love of form" and is nothing more than a "cold prejudice for mathematics" (1993, 207–8). In reality, Kant's apparently systematic inventory of the pure forms or categories of the human understanding is just an abstract recapitulation of ordinary linguistic usage. Echoing Renaissance humanist critiques of Scholasticism, Hamann writes in 1784 that language is "the only, the first, and the last organon and criterion of reason," and the only authority language has is "custom and usage [*Usum*]" (1993, 207).

Language, Hamann observes with characteristic irony, is prior to the "holy functions of the propositions and inferences of logic" (1993, 208). The "whole capacity to think rests on language" and "sounds and letters are... the pure forms *a priori*" (1993, 208–9). Accordingly, philosophical analysis is analysis of linguistic usage, and thus "analysis is nothing more than cutting to a pattern of fashion" (1993, 212). But language is not just a source of clarity. Departure from custom, tradition, established linguistic usage, and experience is the root of bad philosophy. He writes that "metaphysics misuses all the words and phrases of our empirical knowledge," and this "learned mischief transforms the probity of language into such a senseless, whirling, unsteady, indeterminate something = x, that nothing remains but a windy whooshing, a magical shadow-play,... the talisman and rosary of a transcendental superstition..., empty bags and scat [*Losung*]"[10] (1993, 208).

Thus Hamann agrees with Kant that metaphysics falls into various illusions that constitute what Kant calls the paralogisms, antinomies, and ideals of reason, except that Hamann believes that these confusions are not, as Kant thinks, due to reason's intrinsic striving for totality and completeness, but due to using words that are removed from "the tree of life" (1993, 215). In fact, and this is the brunt of Hamann's criticism of Kant, the very idea of pure reason is an ideal derived from the misuse of language. Moreover, the concept of reason is itself a construction based on the illegitimate idealization of pure reason: "According to my *Metacritique*, without the *ideal of pure reason*, there would be no *angelic, let alone human reason*" (ibid.).

This assessment of form and reason sharply distinguishes Humboldt from Hamann. Reason and its general laws and forms, including the laws of logic, have a central role in Humboldt's philosophy, and he does not reject what I have called the Leibnizian systems perspective

---

[10] Hamann plays on the double meaning of the German *Losung*, which is the singular for slogan and the distributive noun for scat, or droppings. The distributive noun is the primary word in the context of this sentence.

on language. Humboldt's philosophy of language is an attempt to validate the angelic (i.e., the formal and propositional) dimensions of mind and language, while at the very same time carving out a significant place for the lived, concrete experience that Hamann fights for in the face of eighteenth-century intellectualism. In other words, Humboldt attempts to synthesize the system and use perspectives on language, whereas Hamann, at best, presents a radical restatement of the humanist use of perspective on language, emphasizing the resistance of linguistic action to formal treatment.

Herder is a much more systematic philosopher than Hamann, but he shares Hamann's negative assessment of form in mind and language. Herder's major work on language is his *Essay Concerning the Origins of Language* (1772), which won the Prussian Royal Academy of Science's essay contest in 1770.[11] The topic was "Supposing that human beings were left to their natural faculties, are they in a position to invent language? And by which means will they achieve this invention on their own?" and Herder's general answer was simple: "*The invention of language is as natural to* [*a human being*] *as it is to be a human*" (1967, 5:34), and human beings invent language when they use reason, particularly reflection and abstraction, with which they are naturally endowed (1967, 5:39).

By making language an essential aspect of human rationality, and rationality a proper part of human nature, Herder, with an additional assumption, circumvents the origin-of-language problem. The additional assumption is that explaining the origin of humanity is not within the scope of philosophy. Because for Herder the origin of humanity is not subject to philosophical and presumably scientific explanation, the origin of human rationality and, ipso facto, the origin of human language are off limits to theory. Philosophical explanation must take for

---

[11] The Berlin Academy of Science was originally founded in 1700 by Leibniz but declined soon after his death. It was reactivated by Frederick the Great, who in 1746 appointed the French scientist Pierre Louis Moreau de Maupertuis (1698–1759) president of the academy. Maupertuis published his *Reflections on the Origins of Language and the Signification of Words* in 1748, two years after Condillac's *Essais*, and he infused his linguistic interests into the academy. He read various papers on linguistic topics to the academy and in 1757 formulated the academy's first linguistic topic for its essay contest: "What is the reciprocal influence of the opinions of a people on language and of language on opinions?" This question is taken up by Condillac, referring to Maupertuis and the Berlin Academy, and the winner of the 1757 contest suggested the topic for the 1770 contest that Herder entered (Aarsleff 1982, 183 and 185–9).

granted the human being in a "condition of free activity" and with the "full feeling of his healthy existence" (1967, 5:95). This redirection of linguistic interest away from the origins of language to the mechanisms of linguistic activity is Herder's most notable achievement.

The diminutive role assigned to form in Herder's theory of mind and language is expressed most clearly by the claim that, for Herder, human beings in their "condition of free activity" and "full feeling of... healthy existence" can have language without grammar. In fact, for Herder language begins completely without grammar. "The more primal a language is, the less grammar it must have," Herder maintains, "and the oldest one is just... the dictionary of nature" without any grammatical forms or rules (1967, 5:82–3). This is Herder's recognition of the tension between linguistic activity and the formal features of language.

The lack of attention to form is also evident in Herder's explanation of the basis of this dictionary of nature. Human beings have a language simply in virtue of being rational because rationality requires reflection, and reflection is the capacity to use a particular idea as a sign (*Merkmal*) for an experienced object. Human beings are overwhelmed by an "ocean of impressions" and, in order to be able to reflect on some of these and not others, they abstract individual ideas. Herder illustrates this with the example of a person perceiving a lamb, which involves many impressions, including of something white, soft, wooly, and making a bleating sound, among others, but in order to dwell on this sheep and reflect on it, the person will abstract the idea of bleating and use it as a sign for the whole sheep. This internal mental sign or representation, Herder maintains, is just a word, and "what is the whole of human language but a collection of such words?" (1967, 5:25).[12] For Herder, language at its basis is simply a list of representations for things, or what Saussure called "a nomenclature" (Saussure 1955, 97), without any constitutive role assigned to forms, structures, or rules.

The lack of interest in form also explains another peculiarity of Herder's account. Herder's explanation of language is, strictly speaking, a sleight of hand. He assumes without argument that the internal signs of the human understanding constitute a language and that the existence

---

[12] It is not a coincidence that Herder chooses an idea of sound to illustrate his theory. According to him, all experienced objects are initially tied to either ideas of sounds they make or ideas of sounds that the emotions evoke in human beings when they experience an object. For Herder, auditory ideas are uniquely fitted to serve as mental representations (1967, 5:43).

of spoken or written language automatically follows from the existence of this dictionary of mental representations. He makes this assumption because, for him, language is simply a collection of representations, without any regard for how the representations are structured and how they can be related to each other. With such a minimalist conception of language, it is not very puzzling that a list of internal signs should generate a parallel list of spoken words. It only becomes puzzling if one begins to think about the relation between mental structures and the grammatical structure of language.

Herder's assessment of form is a stable part of his philosophy and plays a role in his own metacritique: *Understanding and Experience: A Metacritique for the Critique of Pure Reason* (1799). The categories or forms of thought are not rules or forms that make experience or cognition possible. Instead, they are simply drawn from given experience (1960, 204). For example, arithmetic truths are not constructions or products of the understanding, but recognition or grasping of a given fact. "That $4 + 3 = 7$ is not a product of the understanding, but it is a recognition that in $4 + 3$ contains one seven times" (ibid.). More generally, "the activity of the understanding is recognizing the one in the many" (ibid.).

Inner forms of thought without objects, Herder writes, are empty schemes that do not even have understandable verbal counterparts (1960, 204–5). To think is simply to have impressions of objects whose unity and difference are simply recognized. The organization of our impressions is produced by the impressions themselves (1960, 205). Thus the mind's "gift to schematize, that is, create nebulous forms" must not be seen as "a ladder" that is required for experience (1960, 211). "The human understanding has a much higher power than to schematize darkly," Herder claims; "it can express its apprehended signs [*Merkmale*] through words, it can speak, so that the things are seen and it is understood" (ibid.).

This assessment of form and structure in Hamann and Herder creates a sharp divide between them and Humboldt. As we saw, diverse forms, including general laws of reason, have a central role in Humboldt's account of mind and language. In this important respect, Humboldt is closer to Kant than the critics of the Counter-Enlightenment. Of course, there are important points of convergence. Hamann, Herder, and Humboldt all place natural language at center stage in the workings and development of the human understanding. Moreover, for Herder, power (*Kraft*) is one of the fundamental categories that reason apprehends in experience, and it plays a pivotal role in Herder's philosophy of mind, as it does for Humboldt's. Moreover, force is a feature of language in action – linguistic performance – and for both this eludes scientific explanation. Finally, both Herder and Humboldt make language essential to human rationality and the drive to speak a constitutive part of human nature. As we will see in the next section, however, it is unlikely that these points of convergence between Hamann and Herder on the one hand and Humboldt on the other are lines of influence, as is often assumed.

Humboldt and the Enlightenment

By December 1799 Humboldt had made his linguistic turn. During his travels in Spain he wrote to a friend: "I feel that from now on I will devote myself more exclusively to the study of language, and that a thorough and philosophically based comparison of several languages is a task I might be able to shoulder after several years of serious study" (1988, 5:214). A little over a year later Humboldt returned to Spain to study Basque. It seems clear that the path that brought Humboldt to this turn begins with the Enlightenment, and not its critics.[13]

Humboldt was educated by popular tutors of the Berlin Enlightenment and attended the *Mittwochsgesellschaft*, which included important figures of the German Enlightenment such as Moses Mendelssohn. One of Humboldt's private tutors in 1785 was Johann Jakob Engel, who was a published philosopher and also a tutor in Frederick the Great's household. Humboldt admired Engel very much and, after each lecture, would go home to write a summary. What is striking about Engel's lectures is that the philosopher mentioned most often and always with approval is Leibniz. Engel's lectures were a Leibnizian introduction to philosophy, complete with a summary of Leibniz's monadology. Consequently, the notion of power plays an important role in Engel's account: substances *are* forces, minds are substances, and the essential force of a mind is to produce representations (Humboldt 1968, 15:411–18 and 427–8). Because mental power plays a key role in Humboldt's philosophy, it is very likely that these lectures left a lasting impression on his thinking.

---

[13] This confirms the thesis that early German romanticism, to which Humboldt is often assigned, is not tied to the Counter-Enlightenment but represents a return to the principles of the Enlightenment. I owe this point to Jane Kneller.

In 1788 Humboldt begins to show an interest in Kant, particularly the Kantian problem of the relation of reason and sensibility. Humboldt refers to this problem first in a draft of an essay on religion, written between August 1788 and July 1789, that discusses Kant's position on the relation between faith and reason. Humboldt argues that in human beings sensibility and reason are united and that consequently the cultivation of sensibility must play a role in morality (1968, 1:53–7). Humboldt wrote this essay during the time he came to know Friedrich Heinrich Jacobi, who felt that Kant did not properly understand the relation between reason and sensibility and assigned too little significance to feeling, sensibility, and imagination. Humboldt visited Jacobi at his estate for five days in November 1788, and they spent a good part of this time discussing Kant and the relation between reason, sensibility, and the sources of certainty (1968, 14:57–62).

Humboldt returns to this theme again in 1793 and begins to search for a solution in a draft on the education of human beings. In this draft he contrasts the receptivity of sensibility and the spontaneity of human reason and worries about the need human beings have to unite these. He claims that what a human being needs is an object that will make this interaction of the mind's receptivity and spontaneity possible (1968, 1:285). He asserts that this object has to be the world, or what is viewed as the world. A few years later in 1795 he addresses this problem again in the essay on *Sexual Differences*, mentioned earlier (1968, 1:316 and 336).

During this early period Humboldt also exhibits some interest in language. He studies classical Greek language at the University of Göttingen, and in an essay he drafts in 1793 on the study of ancient civilizations, he writes that language is evidence for the spirit and character of a people, or what he also describes as their individuality (1968, 1:263 and 265). Ancient Greek is a good source of evidence about the character and spirit of ancient Greeks because it contains very few deviations from the original. It has few foreign words and foreign inflections and constructions, he maintains. In this essay, he explicitly ties "syntax and grammar" to the individuality of a speaker. He also uses the term "philosophy of language," arguing that the philosophy of language appears very late in Greek culture, which is good, because reflecting on the nature of language leads to deviations from ordinary formations (1968, 1:265).

What appears to be missing in these essays from 1788 to 1795, two years before the death of his mother and an extended trip to Paris, is a unification of his interest in language and his Kantian concern for the nature of the unity between reason and sensibility. Soon, however, Humboldt comes to combine these two concerns. In a three-page draft entitled "On Thinking and Speaking" that was written sometime between 1795 and 1800, Humboldt brings together his concern about the constitution of human thinking and language. He writes that thinking is essentially reflection, which involves distinguishing the thinking self from what is thought. In order to accomplish this, the thinker has to hold on to what is being thought as a unified object set against the thinker. So the essence of thinking is for the mind "to construct unities out of certain portions of its activity" and present these constructions together as objects to the thinking subject (Humboldt 1968, 1:581). But this cannot be achieved without help from the "general forms of our sensibility," and the sensible signs of language provide this unity. Consequently, language is essentially tied to human thinking. The theme appears again, perhaps even more distinctly, in a letter to Schiller from 1800. He describes language as something sensible that is both a human product and an expression of the world. As such, language has the capacity to unite inner thoughts, sensations, and external objects (Seidel 1962, 2:207–9).

Since Humboldt's base of operation from 1797 to 1801 was Paris, it makes sense to look to this sojourn for evidence that there he comes to combine his Kantian concern and his interest in language. And, as a matter of fact, there is a French connection in Humboldt's development.[14]

Humboldt's diaries show that in Paris he studied Condillac's works, while at the same time he struggled on many occasions to present and defend Kantian philosophy to the French *idéologues*. The first serious discussion he has about Kantian philosophy is with Destutt de Tracy in May 1798, where Humboldt tries to understand the differences between French and German philosophy in order to facilitate a possible union of these two trends (1968, 14:466–8). Humboldt was not happy with the outcome of this discussion, but nevertheless Tracy organized a meeting ten days later at the Office of Public Instruction devoted to current developments in German philosophy.

Humboldt organized his presentation around three points. First, metaphysics is a science that investigates the nature of our intellectual capacities in order to determine its limits and the sources of certainty. Second, metaphysics must explain the origins or sources of mental

---

[14] The case for Humboldt's French connection has been made eloquently by Aarsleff 1982. However, Aarsleff ignores the role Kant's philosophy plays in this relationship.

representations (*Vorstellung*). Third, representations involve passive impressions as well as a reaction, namely an activity of the self. These activities of the self are the conditions that make representation possible (Humboldt 1968, 14:484).

Humboldt again was not happy with the discussion. Humboldt maintains that his audience was not convinced that the mind's reaction and its laws can or need to be investigated. They did not have an adequate notion of the self and its activity. This complaint surfaces in his reading notes on Condillac. Humboldt writes that in the *Essai* Condillac wants to "pursue the production of concepts, but he does not even come close" because Condillac does not distinguish what is received in our concepts and what is a product of "self-activity" or spontaneity (1968, 14:445). About the *Treatise on Systems*, Humboldt writes that Condillac does not understand true synthesis, that is, bringing something under a concept. "In a word, he is missing the capstone of metaphysics, namely the feeling or better yet the activity of the I" (1968, 14:479). The same comment is made about Condillac's *Treatise on Sensations*, which Humboldt judges to be boring and empty of content (1968, 14:504–5). The treatise aims to explain the nature of phenomena, but does not recognize the original power of the self. The only activity Condillac mentions is the recalling of sensations, and the imagination is just a kind of recalling of sensations.

In short, Humboldt believes that Condillac does not appreciate the Kantian problem of how reason and sensibility are synthesized or brought together and does not have a rich enough notion of the mental activity that contributes to the construction of what we think and experience. Nevertheless, his comments on Condillac's *Essai* conclude with the following remarks:

> Results. In Condillac still lies the source of all contemporary metaphysics in France. Two things are characteristic about it. 1. they do not assume any innate ideas, and this with justification. That is why they discount everything *a priori* because they know of no other manner [of knowing *a priori*] than through such ideas.... 2. because they do not assume this, their metaphysics is mere rational psychology. 3. they place an infinite amount of weight on the relation between concepts and signs, and that is why universal grammar seems to them to be an essential part of metaphysics. (1968, 14:449)

It is not completely clear what Humboldt's attitude is toward the third result about concepts and signs, but it seems significant that he mentions this as a fundamental feature of Condillac's and contemporary French philosophy.

This suggests the following hypothesis about the development of Humboldt's philosophy of language. Humboldt comes to Paris with a Kantian view that the human mind actively constitutes experience and a concern for the Kantian problem of how reason and sensibility, that is, the mind's spontaneity and receptivity, are unified. He also comes to Paris with an interest in language. He then brings these two concerns together. Either the *idéologues*' emphasis on the connection between language and concepts suggests this to him or it confirms something that he had already been thinking about.

It is unlikely that he was directly motivated to bring these two concerns together by the work of Hamann or Herder. Humboldt knew about these thinkers before 1795, but he did not bring his linguistic and Kantian interests together at that time. In 1795 he was still relying on sex as a model for understanding the unity of reason and sensibility. Moreover, if his published diaries, references, and autobiographical entries are any evidence for Humboldt's intellectual development (1968, 15:517–31), then Hamann has no role in Humboldt's development.[15] The case for Herder is stronger. According to Humboldt's notes, Engel discusses language, and in his notes Humboldt writes "Herder's Prize Essay." But this is the only time Humboldt mentions Herder on language, and in general Humboldt makes surprisingly few references to Herder, mentioning him just six times in his published diaries, only in passing, and never on language. One of the entries suggests that Humboldt had a low opinion of Herder (1916, 14:385).

The hypothesis that Humboldt's stay in Paris spurred him to combine his Kantian and linguistic interests is corroborated by Humboldt's relation to the *idéologue* Pierre Laromiguière, whom he met on several occasions, at meetings and privately. Laromiguière is the only *idéologue* about whom Humboldt writes that in their discussion they arrived at "very good and pure results" (1968, 14:551). Humboldt, who criticizes philosophers who are too fast, careless, and impatient, likes Laromiguière, who is "perhaps...slow" but with whom discussions are

---

[15] Perhaps when Humboldt visited Jacobi, they discussed Hamann, but none of this is mentioned in Humboldt's diaries. In fact, it seems that the only time they come close to discussing language is when they discuss geometry. Humboldt reports that Jacobi asserted that propositions about space are necessary because in this case "signs and concepts are identical" (1968, 14:58–9).

good because he is "a logical thinker who always proceeds one step at a time."

Laromiguière was a student of Condillac, and today he is remembered for his critique that Condillac attributed too much passivity to the human mind. Ideas are not simply passive modifications of the mind that are then combined in various ways by an active mind with other ideas. Instead, an idea already involves mental activity – namely attending to it, comparing it, and reasoning with it, as well as desiring it, preferring it, and freely choosing whether to act on it. These critiques were published in 1805.

In May 1798, when Humboldt and Laromiguière first met, Laromiguière still believed that the human mind is passive with respect to its representations, and Humboldt addressed this issue in their discussion (1968, 14:485). But a month later in June when Humboldt visited him, Laromiguière was very interested in Kant. He had been reading Kant in Latin and had started translating Kant's preface to the *Critique of Pure Reason*, where Kant writes about the mind's contributions to our knowledge of objects (1968, 14:524). In July Laromiguière visited Humboldt, and they had a long discussion about metaphysics and the difference between analytic and synthetic propositions. This discussion almost certainly had to cover Kant's views about synthesis, mental activity, and the relation between concepts and intuitions or reason and sensibility. This discussion, Humboldt claims, arrived at "good results."

This chain of events strongly suggests that Laromiguière was encouraged by these encounters to focus on the role of mental activity in the production of ideas. Similarly, this suggests that these encounters encouraged Humboldt to look at language to resolve his Kantian concerns, or if he was already thinking about this strategy, he was encouraged to pursue this strategy with greater intensity. Perhaps it is this new focus that Humboldt had in mind when in November 1798 he writes to a friend that "my stay in Paris is making a [new] epoch in my thinking" (1965, 62; quoted in Aarsleff 1982, 336) and why, as we saw, by December 1799 he had completed his linguistic turn.

Conclusion

Just as Kant's philosophy was an attempt to combine rationalist and empiricist insights into the nature of human cognition, Humboldt's philosophy of language brings together Leibniz's concern for the form of natural language and Condillac's concern for linguistic activity.

Language is an observable and diversified human activity that takes shape in diverse human cultures. But at the same time, this activity is a product of the mind's universal structures so that the observable diversity is also informed by an underlying structure shared by all speakers.

While language as a completed system is subject to scientific study and formalization, language as an activity escapes the net of science. For Humboldt, language has dual aspects – a "two-fold *Silence*," to adapt Poe's words from his sonnet that serve as a motto for this book. It is a rule-determined system, and it is also a human activity responding to specific human needs, whims, and contexts. The former is subject to the methods of science, but the latter is not. I contend that the way philosophy of language evolves from Humboldt into the twentieth century confirms this duality of linguistic form and action.

Although Humboldt does indeed highlight the form of language, his target is the sound form of language, "the truly constitutive and guiding principle of the diversity of languages." Although Humboldt clearly emphasizes that the external form of language aims to express the inner conceptual form and that the form of a language is the "interpenetration" of its external and internal forms, the overwhelming weight of his work is on the syntactic structures of language, including the phonological and morphological structure of language. The semantics of natural languages had to wait for the revival of logical form in the work of Mill.

FIVE

◆

The Import of Propositions
John Stuart Mill

John Stuart Mill (1806–73) liked to use mottoes in his works that captured guiding themes of his overall philosophy. The mottoes he chose for his two major works on logic and politics, *A System of Logic* and *On Liberty*, are no exception and shed light on Mill's philosophy of language. Book I of his *System of Logic*, called "Of Names and Propositions," is headed by two passages praising Scholastic contributions to philosophy. The first is by the French mathematician, philosopher, and revolutionary Marquis de Condorcet (1743–94); The second is from *Discussions in Philosophy* by the Scottish philosopher and logician William Hamilton (1788–1865):

> Scholasticism, which produced in logic, also in ethics, and in a part of metaphysics an acuteness and precision of ideas, a custom unknown to the ancients, contributed more than one might think to the progress of good philosophy.
>
> To the schoolmen the vulgar languages are principally indebted for what precision and analytic subtlety they possess. (Mill 1974, 7:18)

These passages express Mill's esteem for formal logic. Mill writes in the preface to the *System of Logic* that he does not share "the contempt entertained by many modern philosophers for the syllogistic art," and he announces that in book I he will revive "many useful principles and distinctions which were contained in the old Logic" (1974, 7:cxi–cxii). For this reason he worries that this discussion of "Of Names and Propositions" will "appear, to some readers, needlessly...scholastic" (1974, 7:cxii).

Mill combines this commitment to formal reason with a commitment to the ideals of romanticism. In the nineteenth century, the scientific study of human nature came to be associated with the idea of the uniformity and stability of human nature and opposed to romanticism's commitment to individuality, freedom, and creativity (Skorupski 1989, 249–50). Mill captures this commitment in a quotation by Humboldt that serves as the motto for Mill's *On Liberty*:

> The grand, leading principle, towards which every argument unfolded in these pages directly converges, is the absolute and essential importance of human development in its richest diversity. (Mill 1974, 17:215)

The "free development of individuality," Mill maintains in his discussion of political liberty, "is one of the leading essentials of well-being." Mill again cites Humboldt's view that the object "towards which every human being must ceaselessly direct his efforts... is the individuality of power and development," and that "freedom, and variety of situations" are necessary for "originality," "individual vigour and manifold diversity" (1974, 17:261).

Mill's philosophy of language is an attempt to bring both of these perspectives together. It picks up the threads of the logical perspective on human language spun by Scholasticism and developed by Leibniz, but at the same time it affirms the creative aspects of human language use and the perspective on language as a human action.

Logic and Science

Mill's study of language serves his quest to show that the human mind and society are natural phenomena subject to scientific inquiry and explanation. The logic of induction, the centerpiece of the *System of Logic*, not only serves to exhibit more clearly the structure of explanation and inquiry in the physical sciences but applies to the moral and social sciences as well. Moral and social phenomena are also natural phenomena and the "backward state of the Moral Sciences can only be remedied by applying to the methods of Physical Science" (1974, 8:833; also 7:cxiii). As Condorcet writes in the motto Mill chooses for book 6 of the *System of Logic* "On the Logic of the Moral Sciences":

> If man can, with almost complete assurance, predict phenomena when he knows their laws and... with great expectation of success, forecast the future on the basis of his experience of the past, why, then, should it be regarded as a fantastic undertaking to sketch, with some pretense to truth, the future destiny of man on the basis of history? The sole foundation for belief in the natural sciences, is this idea, that the general laws directing

the phenomena of the universe, known or unknown, are necessary and constant. Why should this principle be any less true for the development of the intellectual and moral faculties of man than for the operations of nature? (Condorcet 1955, 173)

The reason why it was important to extend the scientific method to mind and society, according to Condorcet, was that it would shed light on practical issues: "our hopes for the future condition of the human race" (ibid.).

Mill shares this practical, that is, moral and political, perspective. He writes that the concluding book of the *System of Logic,* "On the Logic of the Moral Sciences," was intended to "contribute towards the solution of a question, which the decay of old opinions, and the agitation which disturbs European society to its innermost depths, render as important in the present day to the practical interests of human life, as it must at all times be to the completeness of our speculative knowledge" (1974, 7:cxiii). Applying the scientific method, whose "conscious observance" led to the "achievements of science" in the past, to human agency is necessary for further human progress. The social and behavioral sciences will give human beings a better understanding of the causal connections among mental and social phenomena and thus be more secure in the attainment of human ends (1974, 8:943–50).[1]

Mill affirms that a system of logic is necessary for understanding, improving, and extending the scope of the sciences. Logic, as understood by Scholastic logicians, had three parts: the study of terms, the study of propositions, and the study of arguments. Mill maintained that these studies can all be brought under one heading, namely, "the science which treats of the operations of the human understanding in the pursuit of truth" (1974, 7:6). Defining terms, making judgments, and drawing conclusions from premises are all operations that are "subsidiary" and

---

[1] It must be mentioned that Mill's scientific image of the study of human beings has significant limits. For Mill, science will "only show that certain consequences follow from certain causes, and that to obtain certain ends, certain means are the most effectual," but "whether the ends themselves are such as ought to be pursued, and if so, in what cases and to how great a length, it is no part of" science (1974, 8:950). It is tempting, Mill believes, to those who treat human nature and society scientifically to believe that science will yield results about not only "what is, but what ought to be," but this is a mistake (ibid.). In the *System of Logic,* however, Mill does not commit himself to how human beings arrive at their ultimate ends and how they can be justified. He only declares that the promotion of happiness is the ultimate principle of human practice and refers the reader to "the little volume entitled *Utilitarianism*" (1974, 8:951).

"contrivances for enabling a person to know the truths which are needful to him" (ibid.). Because all science simply "consists of data and conclusions from those data, of proofs and what they prove," and if there is a difference between concluding justly and making false inferences, then science observes or conforms to the relations and laws logic studies (1974, 7:10–11). For this reason, Mill affirms Bacon's claim that logic is the science of science itself (*ars artium*).

Universal Grammar

What stands out in Mill's *System of Logic*, however, is not only that logic serves all the sciences, including the sciences of mind and society, but that Mill also reconnects logic and the study of natural language. This reunification of the study of logic and language in the philosophy of Mill comes on the heels of what has been called the universal grammar tradition in Britain, an evolution that culminates in the work of Jeremy Bentham (1743–1832).[2] In 1816 Bentham declares that "a demand exists for an entirely new system of *Logic*, in which shall be comprehended a *theory of language*, considered in the most general point of view." He continues: "For the construction of such an edifice, a considerable proportion of the *materials* employed in the construction of the *Aristotelian* system of logic, would be indispensably necessary" (1962, 8:120). Although Aristotelian logic cannot be adopted uncritically and requires "*taking to pieces* the whole mass of" this system, still for Bentham it is a "justly admired and venerated monument of human industry and genius" (ibid.).

Plato, on the other hand, is the "spoiled child of Socrates" who produced a "wilderness of words" in "which so many wits, beginning with those of Cicero, have been lost" (ibid.). Of course, the reference to Cicero in this context is also a reference to the rhetorical tradition that not only aimed to divorce logic and philosophy but also logic and the study of language.

The reason that a system of logic should include a theory of language, according to Bentham, is that "the faculty of *discourse*, including the

---

[2] Two important earlier figures in this tradition are John Wilkins (1614–72), author of *Essay towards a Real Character and a Philosophical Language* (1668), which was written independently of the *Port-Royal Grammar* (1660); and James Harris (1709–80), author of *Hermes; or, a Philosophical Inquiry Concerning Language and Universal Grammar* (1751), which also does not mention the *Port-Royal Grammar*.

faculty of *speech*," is the "grand instrument of thought" (1962, 8:230). For Bentham, human language is not only an instrument of communication, but "an instrument by which... ideas are formed" (1962, 8:231). Echoing Hobbes, Bentham writes that without language "thoughts are but dreams: like shifting clouds of the sky, they float in the mind one moment, and vanish out of it the next" (1962, 8:228–9; for Hobbes, see Chapter 2).

Specifically, language plays a role in the retention of ideas, drawing inferences, and inventing new ideas (1962, 8:224–7). Moreover, using the capacity to designate individual objects and to denominate collections or classes of things, the mind can arrange ideas according to a method; following Condillac, Bentham maintains that language renders "indispensable assistance" to this operation (1962, 8:227) because "it is only by means of names... that things are susceptible of arrangement" (1962, 8:262). This operation, or what Bentham calls "methodization," is particularly important because it plays some role in all the other operations of the mind. It is for this reason that Bentham calls methodization the "master-operation" (1962, 8:227); in fact, if "Logic were to be termed a *queen* [of the mind's operations], methodization, method, might be termed her *prime-minister*" (1962, 8:261).

Bentham stresses the role of designation – that is, using a sign such as a proper name to refer to or pick out single objects (1962, 8:226). Designation is central to methodization and also communication. Communication is possible because human beings are able to designate as well as express, literally "press out," its ideas (1962, 8:227). Although designation can take place without discourse or language, "without *designation*, discoursing... could not have taken place," and language is "indebted for its existence" to designation (1962, 8:228). Bentham also highlights the fact that designating signs have been labeled "proper names" by grammarians (1962, 8:226).

Now the signs of discourse – language – can be organized in various ways into parts of speech, and some of these parts, according to Bentham, are the same in all languages, and these universal parts of speech are the subject of universal grammar (1962, 8:187). But a theory of universal grammar needs an "exposition of... the principles of Logic (1962, 8:185). Universal grammarians like Bentham believe that the universal parts of speech are rooted in the categories of logic. Accordingly, "[c]onsiderations of the logical cast, form... all along the basis of... considerations of the grammatical cast" (ibid.). Elsewhere he writes, "logic in which, when taken in its most extended sense, grammar, even universal grammar, has its foundation" and so expertise in logic is necessary for success in the project of finding the universal grammar. Unfortunately, success has eluded this project because "no professed Grammarian seems, as yet, to have given himself this qualification" (1962, 8:188).

An important insight Bentham has that Mill preserves in his discussion of language is that the fundamental unit of analysis is the proposition.

> But by anything less than an entire proposition, *i.e.* the import of an entire proposition, no communication can have a place. In language, therefore, the *integer* to be looked for is an entire proposition, – that what Logicians mean by the term logical proposition. Of this integer, no one part of speech, not even that which is most significant, is anything more than a fragment; and in this respect, in the many-worded appelative, part of speech, the word *part* is instructive. By it, an intimation to look out for the integer, of which it is a part, may be considered as conveyed. A word is to a *proposition* what a *letter* is to a word. (ibid.)

Not only do we analyze language ultimately in terms of logical categories, but the unit of analysis is the complete proposition. More specifically, the unit of analysis is the import or meaning of a complete proposition. Words are to be understood and analyzed in terms of the contribution they make to the meanings of propositions.[3]

Bentham's analogy between letters and words, and words and propositions is apt.[4] Just as letters or phonemes are identified in terms of the contribution they make to meaningful words, words are identified in terms of the contribution they make to meaningful propositions. For instance, in English the letter "l" or the phoneme /l/ in the English words "clear" and "pool" are identical, although the actual pronunciation of "l" is different in these two words. The "l" in "clear" is sharp and clear whereas the "l" in "pool" is soft and dark. In English, these phonetic differences do not make a difference to the meanings of words – that is, these phonetic differences are not phonological differences. When

---

[3] Thus it is false that no philosopher before Frege understood that the unit of significance is the sentence, not the word, in the sense that the meaning of a word is to be understood in terms of the contribution it makes to the meaning of a proposition (Dummett 1973, 3–7).

[4] *Pace* Dummett (1973, 3), who claims that this analogy is nonsensical.

someone speaking English pronounces "clear" with a soft and dark "l," she is not articulating a new word but only a variant pronunciation. However, in many Slavic languages this is not the case. What in English are two variant pronunciations of the same letter, in Russian, for example, are distinct letters marking out different words.

In addition to recognizing the proposition as the primary unit of linguistic analysis, Bentham realizes that because the project of universal grammar maps one set of linguistic structures onto another, there needs to be some mechanism or specific relation that connects the two structures. For example, if we are going to say that two apparently distinct structures really have the same underlying part of speech in universal grammar, there needs to be some specific tie that connects the apparent structure to the real underlying structure. This is a simple problem whose solution ultimately flourishes in the idea of a transformational rule in generative linguistics, that is, a rule for transforming one type of structure into another. Although obviously Bentham did not have the notion of a transformational rule as defined by generative linguistics, without a doubt Bentham recognizes that if one is going to make a claim that there are universal structures that diverse languages share despite appearances, there needs to be a mechanism that relates the apparent diversity to the real, underlying unity.

Bentham borrows this insight from John Horne Tooke (1736–1812), as Bentham freely acknowledges. According to Bentham, Tooke's discovery was to show the "identity" of certain parts of speech "with other parts of speech" (1962, 8:185). This discovery gave an "hitherto unprecedented advantage" to the study of universal grammar (1962, 185). In fact, Bentham goes even further, writing that "[w]ithout ... the discoveries made by Horne Tooke, no ... universal grammar ... could have been formed," and adds: "By him the way has been prepared for a work of this sort" (1962, 8:188).

Tooke infused the universal grammar tradition with the Lockean perspective on mind and language. Tooke, like Locke, looks to language to clarify philosophical issues, believes that the purpose of language is to "communicate our thoughts," and maintains that there is an "inseparable connexion between words and language" (Tooke 1806, 14 and 27). But he denies Locke's claim that words only signify ideas or things. Some words, he argues, are "merely *abbreviations* employed for dispatch, and are the signs of other words" (1806, 21). Human thought is much faster than language, he maintains, and therefore such abbreviations improve the capacity of language to communicate human thoughts. Parts of speech, then, are identical to each other in virtue of being abbreviations of each other.[5]

Applying the idea that some words signify other words to Locke's *Essay*, Tooke claims that "the *whole* of Mr. Locke's essay is a philosophical account of the ... abbreviations of language" (1806, 24). Tooke believes this because on his view, strictly speaking, there are no complex ideas. Complex ideas are really words that signify other words that ultimately signify simple ideas, and so all abstract and general words only signify other words, not abstract or general ideas (1806, 30). Accordingly, Tooke also denies that there are operations of the mind such as abstraction or composition. What Locke takes to be operations of the mind are only "operations of language" (1806, 41). On Tooke's view, "the mind ... extends no farther than to receive impressions, that is, to have sensation or feeling" (ibid.) and these are all of particular things (1806, 55–6). Consequently, all commonality is due to language.

Tooke also takes Locke to task for devoting only a "vague chapter ... comprized in *two pages* and a half" to particles or syncategorematic words, even though Locke himself maintains that these are all marks of the operations of the human understanding (1806, 34). Tooke believes that this is evidence that Locke "had not settled his own opinion concerning the manner of signification of words" (1806, 35) and that eventually he would have seen that his whole *Essay*, not just book III, is really about language.

With that in mind, Tooke turns to developing his universal grammar, which has only two parts of speech – nouns and verbs – and all other parts of speech are abbreviations for various combinations of words. However, Tooke's account is not as clean as advertised, because he immediately runs into an exception in the case of articles, whose function or "business it is ... to enable us to employ *general* terms for *particulars*" (1806, 57). Although all words other than nouns and verbs are supposed to be abbreviations for other words, articles are not abbreviations in that sense. Instead, an article "supplies the place of words which *are not* in the language," presumably words that would uniquely describe the particular object. Moreover, strictly speaking a general term also falls outside of Tooke's parts of speech. Because there are no general ideas, it is not a sign of a general idea, but it is also not an abbreviation. Instead, it is the name of several distinct ideas at once (1806, 42).

---

[5] Tooke makes a brief appearance in Quine's celebrated essay "Two Dogmas of Empiricism" (1953, 38–9).

Presumably the general term "human" refers to various ideas of particular human beings, but Tooke does not explain how a term can come to refer to various distinct ideas and how those distinct ideas come to be grouped together under a single name.

Mind, Logic, and Language

Following Bentham's lead on the relationship between logic and language, Mill devotes the first chapter of his *System of Logic* to "the Necessity of Commencing with an Analysis of Language." Mill argues that starting point is necessary because language is the "principal instrument that helps thought"; language is to the thinker what optical instruments are to the astronomer (1974, 7:19). For instance, reasoning or the drawing of inferences usually takes place by means of words, and "in complicated cases can take place in no other way" (ibid.). So language is only an aid to thinking in some cases, but in other cases it is essential to thinking.

But there is still another novel reason Mill has for beginning logic with an analysis of language. Mill believes that language, logic, and belief are tied together by propositions. A proposition, for Mill, is an item of language; it is an "assertion" (1974, 7:20) or a "portion of discourse" (1974, 7:78). Mill does not use the term "proposition" in the sense it was used later by Frege, Russell, and Moore – namely, to refer to the objects of belief and the meaning of declarative sentences. However, there is an essential connection between beliefs and propositions. "Whatever can be an object of belief, or even disbelief, must, when put into words, assume the form of a proposition." So "to know the import of all possible propositions, would be to know all questions which can be raised, all matters which are susceptible of being either believed or disbelieved" (1974, 7:20).

The inference that knowledge of the meanings of all possible propositions is to know everything that can be believed rests on several important assumptions. Not only must it be true that the objects of belief, when put into words, will have the form of a proposition, but Mill must also assume that everything that can be believed can in fact be expressed in language. Moreover, the objects of belief need to be expressible in language completely and without remainder. Finally, Mill must also assume that the "import of all possible propositions" is not larger than the set of all things that can be believed. Without this assumption, it is possible that the import of some proposition is not susceptible of being believed or disbelieved.

It seems that Mill attempts to capture these assumptions with the following statement: "How many kind of inquiries can be propounded; how many kinds of judgments can be made; and how many kinds of propositions it is possible to frame with a meaning; are but different forms of one and the same question" (ibid.). This statement is rich in ambiguity, but it at least means that the number of possible beliefs is identical to the number of possible meaningful propositions. It also seems to mean that the *types* of possible beliefs are identical to the *types* of meaningful propositions.

Mill's reasons for these assumptions are not clear, but the way Mill continues his argument suggests an explanation.

> Since, then, the objects of all Belief and of all Inquiry express themselves in propositions; a sufficient scrutiny of Propositions and of their varieties will apprize us what questions mankind have actually asked of themselves, and what, in the nature of answers to those questions, they have actually thought they had grounds to believe. (ibid.)

He then immediately begins with a definition of a proposition as "*discourse, in which something is affirmed or denied of something*" and an analysis of its parts. This suggests that Mill assumes that, in some sense, propositions and the objects of belief are identical. By analyzing propositions, we ipso facto analyze the objects of belief. For this reason, propositions give us an insight into not only what human beings in fact believe, but everything they could believe.

It is tempting to conclude from this that for Mill belief, and hence knowledge, is of propositions, and so an analysis of propositions is an analysis of what human beings can believe and know. But this would not be quite right. First, Mill never writes that propositions are the objects of belief. As argued earlier, Mill only writes all possible objects of belief, "when put into words, assume the form of a proposition." Moreover, this would gloss Mill's distinction between propositions and the *import* of propositions. For Mill, what beliefs and propositions share is the imports of propositions. The objects of belief are the imports of propositions.

This conclusion is clear from Mill's discussion of the nature of objects of belief and the import of propositions. Mill distinguished a belief, which is a "state of mind" or an "act, as a phenomenon of mind," from what is believed or the object of a belief (1974, 7:87). He is also emphatic that objects of belief are not mental entities. He rejects what he takes to be the received view "from Descartes downwards, and especially from the era of Leibniz and Locke," according to which "Ideas, or

Conceptions, or whatever other term the writer preferred as a name for mental representations generally, constituted essentially the subject matter and substance" of mental operations such as belief or judgment (ibid.). In order to believe that gold is yellow, Mill argues, a person must indeed have an idea of gold and an idea of yellow, but these ideas are not the objects of this belief. "What I believe is a fact relating to the outward thing, gold, ... not a fact relating to my conception of gold, which would be a fact in my mental history, not a fact of external nature" (1974, 7:88).

Mill illustrates his point with a metaphor. The intentional digging of a hole in the ground involves the ideas of the ground, digging, and a hole, but "it would be a very ridiculous description of digging the ground to say that it is putting one idea into another." He continues: "Digging is an operation which is performed upon the things themselves." Similarly, "believing is an act which has for its subject the facts themselves" (ibid.).

Mill intended this discussion of the distinction between beliefs and the objects of belief to explain the nature of the import of a proposition. This discussion stands at the beginning of the chapter entitled "Of the Import of Propositions," and Mill moves easily back and forth between beliefs and propositions. Just as the objects of beliefs are not ideas or conceptions, the imports of propositions are not mental states or acts. Whatever happens when we conjoin ideas in a belief or judgment, "it can have nothing whatever to do with the import of propositions." Propositions "are not assertions respecting our ideas of things, but assertions respecting the things themselves" (ibid.). So, for example, the statement that fire causes heat does not mean that an idea of fire causes an idea of heat, but "that the natural phenomenon, fire, causes the natural phenomenon, heat" (1974, 7:89).

So matters of fact, or things themselves, are both objects of belief and imports of propositions. This identity clearly is at work in the consequences for the study of logic Mill draws from his discussion. Mill's inquiry in the *System of Logic* is "not into the act of believing, but into the thing believed" (ibid.). In the very same breath, he poses this set of questions defining his subject matter:

> What is the immediate object of belief in a Proposition? What is the matter of fact signified by it? What is it to which, when I assert the proposition, I give my assent, and call upon others to give theirs? What is that which is expressed by the form of discourse called a Proposition? (1974, 7:89–90)

Because Mill regularly uses "import," "signification," and "meaning" as synonyms,[6] and if we assume that the pronoun "it" in the second question refers to "a Proposition," Mill here nearly explicitly states that the objects of beliefs are identical to the imports of propositions, namely things themselves or, more specifically, matters of facts.

Due to this identity, an analysis of the imports or meanings of propositions is also an analysis of what can be believed. This is why Mill believes that "how many kind of inquiries can be propounded; how many kinds of judgments can be made; and how many kinds of propositions it is possible to frame *with a meaning*; are but different forms of one and the same question" (1974, 7:20; emphasis added). An analysis of language, then, is relevant to understanding belief not because the meaning of language resides in the mind of the speaker, but because the meanings of language, specifically of the propositions of language, are identical to the objects of human belief.

Mill's meanings, then, have a double duty. As objects of belief, they have a cognitive function and as meanings of propositions, they have a semantic function. It is this double duty that brings Mill to language. For Mill, all possible objects of belief are identical to the meanings of language, and thus an understanding of the meaning of language sheds direct light on the nature of the human mind. For this reason, in Mill's philosophy the understanding of language remains a critical part of philosophy, and in this respect Mill stands in the tradition of Locke and Leibniz.

But at the same time it is important to recognize that Mill departs from this tradition. For Locke and Leibniz, language is important for philosophy because it is both an instrument of thought and a mirror. Language mirrors the mind, and thus the human understanding can be studied as a reflection in this mirror. Language also is an instrument we use to organize our reasoning, especially complex reasoning, and hence studying language allows human beings to know the structure of human reasoning. Strictly speaking, for Mill language is not a mere mirror of the mind. As was the case for Humboldt before him, Mill holds that language has an important degree of autonomy. It can serve as an instrument of thought precisely because it is not a mere mirror of thought. Language and belief are both about the very same thing:

---

[6] For example, see Mill 1974, 7:91, note g-g, where "meaning" and "import" are used synonymously, and Mill 1974, 8:687, where "meaning" and "signification" are variants of each other.

propositions mean what beliefs are about, and neither is about the mind's own states.[7]

Connotation and Denotation

Although Mill rejects the Cartesian approach to the import of propositions according to which propositions are about mental states, Mill also rejects Hobbes's view that propositions consist of two names and that the meaning of a proposition is simply that what is denoted or named by one name is identical to whatever is named or denoted by the other name. In effect, this view treats every proposition as an assertion of identity between the named objects. For example, the proposition "All men are six feet high" would on this view mean that "six feet high" names everything that "man" names, and thus is essentially the same type of proposition as "Tully is Cicero" or "Hyde is Clarendon" (Mill 1974, 7:90–1). Mill believes that while Hobbes's account holds for identities such as "Tully is Cicero," it does not hold for other propositions.

Hobbes's problem, according to Mill, is that he, "in common with other Nominalists, bestowed little or no attention upon the *connotation* of words; and sought for their meaning exclusively in what they *denote*" (1974, 7:91). The meaning of a proposition includes the connotation of the names included in that proposition. Mill gives the example of the proposition "The summit of Chimborazo is white" and explains that the word "white" in this proposition connotes an attribute, and the meaning of the proposition is that the object denoted by "the summit of Chimborazo" has the attribute that "white" connotes (1974, 7:97).

The distinction between the denotation and connotation of names is developed in Mill's discussion of connotative and nonconnotative names, which he calls the "third great division of names" in the *System of Logic*, the first being the distinction between general and individual (or singular) names and the second being the distinction between concrete and abstract names. Mill maintains that the distinction between names that connote and names that do not connote is "one of the most

---

[7] Unless, of course, a person explicitly believes or asserts something about mental states, for example, when people believe or assert that they are hungry or that they believe something.

important distinctions" and "one of those which go deepest into the nature of language" (1974, 7:30–1).[8]

Some names only denote or stand for what they name, without implying that what is named has an attribute. These are nonconnotative names and such names "are attached to objects themselves, and are not dependent on the continuance of any attribute of the object." Proper names are the best examples of such names. For example, if "Dartmouth" is a proper name for the town of Dartmouth located at the mouth of the river Dart in England, it names that town even if "sand should choke up the mouth of the river, or an earthquake change its course, and remove it to a distance form the town" (1974, 7:33). The only thing that "Dartmouth" contributes to the import of propositions that contain this name is the object itself, which in this case is a town.

A connotative term "denotes a subject, and implies an attribute" (1974, 7:31). For example, the general term "man" denotes the class of men,[9] but it also implies that the members of this class have certain attributes. Similarly, "white" denotes the class of white things, but it also connotes the attribute of being white. Mill borrows the term "connote" from the Scholastics, who used *notare* for noting something, as when you note the number of items in a group, and *connotare* to "mark *along with*; to mark one thing *with* or *in addition to* another" (1974, 7:31n).

Several features of the denotation-connotation distinction need to be highlighted. First, when a term has a connotation, the connotation determines its denotation. As Mill puts it, a connotative name applies to its objects "in consequence of an attribute which they are supposed to possess in common.... It is applied to all beings that are considered to possess the connoted attribute; and to none which are not so considered" (1974, 7:31). Because attributes, as we will see shortly, always involve sensations or the possibility of sensations, at least for connotative names, denotation is determined by the content of our experience. So at least for connotative names, Mill preserves Locke's view that the

---

[8] It is tempting to run together the distinction between connotation and denotation and the distinction between names that connote and names that do not connote (Skorupski 1989, 53), but these are distinct. One can grant that names can connote and denote, without granting that some names only denote.

[9] Mill seems to sense an ambiguity about the denotation of the term "men." In his manuscript and the first two editions, he indicates the membership of this class by giving Peter, Paul, and John as examples of members of this class, suggesting that "men" denotes the class of men. In later editions, he replaces Paul with Jane to show that "men," as he uses the term, denotes the class of human beings.

signification of words is limited by the ideas we can have. But it needs to be added that this is not true of all names. In contrast to Locke, Mill believes that some names do not connote and only denote, and this theme is picked up by Bertrand Russell and developed by contemporary direct theories of reference.[10]

Second, with this distinction Mill has enriched the notion of meaning to include two components: connotation and denotation. Mill is not always clear about this. On the one hand, he states that a connotative name "denotes a subject, and implies an attribute" (ibid.), and in discussing universal, particular, and singular propositions, Mill discusses the denotation of general terms, all of which are connotative, in the predicate position of a proposition.[11] On the other hand, he seems to identify meaning and connotation. For instance, he writes that whenever terms "have properly any meaning, the meaning resides not in what they *denote*, but in what they *connote*" (1974, 7:34). He adds that proper names, because they have no connotation, "have, strictly speaking, no signification." We return to this issue when discussing the main topic of the *System of Logic*, the import of propositions.

Objects and Attributes

Mill's distinction between the connotation and the denotation of names relies on a metaphysical distinction, namely the thing-attribute distinction that is introduced with very little fanfare in Mill's discussion of concrete and abstract names. "A concrete name is a name which stands for a thing; an abstract name is one that stands for an attribute of a thing" (1974, 7:29). Fortunately, the distinction between attributes and things receives a bit more attention later on in Mill's discussion of the things denoted by names. According to Mill, things and attributes, along with states of consciousness, are the three classes of nameable things (1974, 7:55).

Things, or substances, are either bodies or minds. Bodies are defined as the external causes of our sensations or the unknown or hidden

---

[10] For introductions to direct theories of reference and relevant references, see Devitt and Sterelny 1999, 76–8 and 82, and Salmon 1991.

[11] For example, in a universal proposition with a general name in the predicate position, the "predicate is affirmed or denied of all and each of the things denoted by the subject" (Mill 1974, 7:84). Similarly, in "No men have wings," the predicate "have wings" is distributed, that is, "it stands for each and every individual which it denotes" (1974, 7:86).

external causes of our sensations (Mill 1974, 7:56 and 63). We are justified in believing in bodies because they explain the lawlike patterns of our sensations, although we have no reason to believe that the sensations in any way resemble their causes. On this issue, Mill sides with Kant, or at least his reading of Kant, and maintains that "of the outward world, we know and can know absolutely nothing, except the sensations which we experience from them" (1974, 7:62).[12] So we do have knowledge of material objects, but it is limited to the causal effects they have on our senses.

While a material object is the "unknown cause of sensations," the mind is "an unknown recipient, or percipient" of sensations as well as all other states of consciousness. "It is the mysterious something which thinks and feels" (1974, 7:63). We are immediately aware of a certain "thread of consciousness" or a "series of feelings, that is, sensations, thoughts, emotions and volitions, more or less numerous and complicated," but not of the mind that has these thoughts and that, Mill believes, can conceivably exist "forever in a state of quiescence, without any thoughts at all" (1974, 7:64). While a body is the cause of our sensations, a mind is "the sentient *subject*" of our sensations, as well as all our other conscious states (ibid.).[13]

As far as attributes are concerned, Mill tries to remain neutral between two alternative views. One is that an attribute is simply a sensation had in the presence of an object or received from an object. For instance, "when we say that snow has the quality whiteness," we assert "[s]imply that when snow is present to our organs, we have a particular sensation, which we are accustomed to call the sensation of white" (1974, 7:65). Mill then also argues that since snow is an object we infer from the fact that we have a group or series of sensations, to assert that snow is white means only, according to Mill, "that of the sensations composing this group or series...the sensation of white colour is one" (ibid.). It is important to highlight that, on this view, the

---

[12] Mill's gloss on Kant is that "there exists an universe of 'Things in Themselves,'" but the "representation of [the thing in itself] in our minds...is all we know of the object: and...the real nature of the Thing is, and by the constitution of our faculties ever must remain, at least in the present state of existence, an impenetrable mystery to us" (1974, 7:59).

[13] In his manuscript and in the first six editions of the *System of Logic*, Mill writes that he is using "subject" in "the German sense of the term" (1974, 7:64n). It is curious that in the seventh and eighth editions of the *System of Logic*, the last two editions to be published in Mill's lifetime, Mill replaced "German" with "scholastic."

attribute is not a mere sensation but a sensation caused by the presence of objects.

On the other view, "when we affirm that snow possesses the attribute of whiteness, we do not merely assert that the presence of snow produces in us that sensation, but that it does so through, and by reason of that power or quality" in the object (ibid.). In other words, the attribute whiteness is not just the sensation of the color white received from the object, but some specific power inherent in the object that is responsible for the received sensation.

Mill's compromise position is that "all the attributes of bodies... are grounded on the sensations which we receive from those bodies, and may be defined, the powers which the bodies have of exciting those sensations" (1974, 7:74). For example, "the quality of whiteness is *grounded* on its exciting in us the sensation of white" or "the sensation of white [is] the foundation of the quality whiteness" (1974, 7:67).

What "grounded" means is not entirely clear, but Mill elucidates this notion in terms of the Scholastic concept of a foundation of a relation (*fundamentum relationis*) (1974, 7:67–9). The foundation of a relation between two objects is a fact in virtue of which the two objects are related. For instance, one object is smaller than another because of the fact that the space occupied by the smaller object cannot contain the larger object. Similarly, the foundation of a quality or attribute of an object is "the fact that a certain sensation or sensations are produced in us by the object" (1974, 7:68). The attribute of an object, then, is characterized in terms of a sensation or pattern of sensations and the relation of these sensations *being produced* or *being caused* by that object.

Mill's theory of denotation and connotation, then, captures his empiricist commitment that whatever we attribute to objects is based on our sensory experience and avoids assuming that there is a specific power inherent in the object responsible for the sensation of white. At the same time, he avoids Berkeley's idealism and captures his naturalist commitment that natural objects are responsible for our experience. Natural objects do have powers to bring about the sensations that we have, but we do not know enough to identify exactly the complex configuration of powers that contribute to our sensations, except to say that the object, when we are in its presence in appropriate circumstances, has the power to produce sensations in us.

The Import of Propositions

The purpose of Mill's theory of terms and their meaning – connotation and denotation – is to prepare the way for his analysis of the meaning or import of propositions. A proposition, as we saw, is "discourse which affirms or denies something of some other thing," and what these things are "can be no other than those signified by the... names, which being joined together by a copula constitute the Proposition" (Mill 1974, 7:46). If we know what names signify, then determining the import of propositions is not an "arduous task," Mill writes (ibid.).

According to Mill's summary statement of the import of propositions, "Every Proposition asserts that some given subject does or does not possess some attribute; or that some attribute is or is not (either in all or in some portion of the subjects in which it is met with) conjoined with some other attribute" (1974, 7:158). However, this does not quite match his own practice because Mill does allow for propositions where both subject and predicate do not connote any attributes, such as "Tully is Cicero" or "Hyde is Clarendon" (1974, 7:90–1). These are the propositions that, according to Mill, Hobbes mistakenly took to be models for all propositions. The meaning of these propositions is that the object denoted by the subject term is identical to the object denoted by the predicate term. The negation of such propositions simply means that the object denoted by the predicate is not identical to the object denoted by the subject.

The other classes of propositions, however, do fit the summary statement. In a proposition in which the subject term does not connote but the predicate term does connote, the meaning of such propositions "is that the individual thing denoted by the subject, has the attribute connoted be the predicate" (1974, 7:97). The denial of such a proposition means that the object denoted by the subject does not possess the attributes connoted by the predicate. If the subject of a proposition is also connotative, then the meaning of the proposition includes the subject term's connotation.

For example, the meaning of the universal and affirmative proposition "All men are mortal" is that whatever objects have the attribute connoted by the subject term also have the attributes connoted by the predicate term (ibid.). Specifically, whatever has the attributes connoted by "man" has the attributes connoted by "mortal" (1974, 7:98). The meaning of a universal negation such as "No horses are web-footed" is that whatever has the attributes connoted by "horse" does not have the attributes connoted by "web-footed" (1974, 7:108). A similar analysis holds for particular propositions. In an affirmative particular proposition such as "Some birds are web-footed," some objects that have the attributes connoted by "bird" have the attributes connoted by "web-footed." In negative particular propositions, some of the objects that have the attributes connoted by the subject do not have the attributes connoted by the predicate.[14]

In these analyses, we see clearly how Mill analyzes the meaning of a proposition in terms of the meanings of its parts – that is, how he preserves the principle of compositionality that characterizes the logical form of language. However, it is important to recognize that Mill also fully embraces Bentham's point that the "integer" or primary unit of linguistic analysis is the proposition, specifically its meaning. For this reason, Mill writes, as was noted earlier, that whenever terms "have properly any meaning, the meaning resides not in what they *denote*, but in what they *connote*" (1974, 7:34). The meaning of a connotative term resides only in what it connotes *in the context of a proposition*. Although such a term may have both a denotation and a connotation, in the predicate position of a proposition only the connotation matters to the import of the proposition: it is the connotation of the term that contributes to the meaning of the whole proposition, not its denotation. In short, the context of the proposition determines what contribution the name makes to the meaning of the whole proposition. Thus Mill combines compositionality with the holism of Humboldt's perspective on human language.[15]

Accordingly, the "analysis of the import conveyed by [propositions]... is the real subject and purpose of this preliminary book," namely book I of the *System of Logic* (1974, 7:78), and the *System of Logic* begins "with a survey and analysis of Propositions" (1974, 7:20). The reason for the primacy of propositions in Mill's account

---

[14] According to Mill, stating the import of propositions in terms of what attributes accompany or do not accompany each other, as was the case in this paragraph, is "a portion of theoretical knowledge" (1974, 7:117). For practical purposes, Mill asserts, we can state the import of propositions in terms of the epistemic relations between attributes. For example, "the proposition All men are mortal, means that the attributes of man are *evidence of*, are a *mark of*, mortality" (ibid.). Mill believes that the practical and the theoretical statements of the import of a proposition are equivalent.

[15] As we will see in the next chapter, this combination will find its full fruition in the philosophy of language that develops under the influence of Frege.

is rooted in Mill's conception of the subject matter of logic. "The province of logic must be restricted to that portion of knowledge which consists of inferences from truths previously known" (1974, 7:9). In other words, logic is concerned to "distinguish between things proved and things not proved" (1974, 7:20). But what is proved or disproved, just as what is believed or disbelieved, is the import of a proposition.

Another way that Mill puts this is that logic is a way of settling or resolving certain questions by means of evidence (ibid). But "the answer to every question which it is possible to frame, must be contained in a Proposition, or Assertion," and what it contains is its import. Consequently, the basic unit of proof is the import of a proposition; we draw inferences from meaningful propositions and seek to prove meaningful propositions. Still another way Mill makes this point is that "all truth and all error lie in a proposition" (ibid.). Because the province of logic is "that portion of knowledge which consists of inferences from truths previously known," logic is, at bottom, concerned with the inferential relationships between meaningful propositions.

Thus the focus of Mill's analysis is what is relevant to understanding inference. Language, under this microscope, appears as a system as much as it was a system for Humboldt. But unlike Humboldt, who was primarily interested in the grammatical and phonological structure of language, Mill isolates its logical structure. Specifically, Mill analyzes those features of language that are essential to understanding logical inference, and thus Mill, like Leibniz before him, is interested in the logical form of natural language.

Now, the properties that are essential to inference are semantic properties, because the concept that plays a key role in logical inference is truth. Mill divides "inference, or reasoning" into two types – induction and ratiocination or deduction (1974, 7:162–3). In both cases, the goal is to "set out from known truths, to arrive at others really distinct from them" (1974, 7:162). So, at a minimum, in both induction and deduction we aim to preserve truth: given true premises, legitimate logical inferences yield true conclusions.

In the case of deduction (which Mill identifies with syllogistic logic), legitimate logical inferences are such that "if the premises are true, the conclusion must necessarily[16] be so" (1974, 7:166). This, of course, is

---

[16] "Necessarily" appears in the manuscript and the first five editions. In the sixth edition (1865) Mill replaces "necessarily" with the less precise term "inevitably."

deductive validity. Inductive inferences are also characterized in terms of truth. Mill writes that induction is "the process by which we conclude that what is true of certain individuals of a class is true of the whole class, or that which is true at certain times will be true in similar circumstances at all times" (1974, 7:288). The warrant or ground for such inferences is the uniformity of nature, which Mill expresses as follows: "[T]he universe, so far as known to us, is so constituted, that whatever is true in any one case, is true in all cases of a certain description" (1974, 7:306). The difficulty in such inferences, as Mill notices, is to find the appropriate description, and this is what Mill sets out to accomplish with his well-known "Four Methods of Experimental Inquiry": Agreement, Difference, Residues, and Concomitant Variations (1974, 7:388–406).

In sum, Mill's turn to language – his linguistic turn – is driven by his logical interests, and this leads him to analyze the semantics of natural language. Mill turns to language because he is interested in logic, and this takes him to the fundamental semantic features of language: meaning and truth. Mill centers on propositions because they are the bearers of truth, and he analyzes propositions into the components and features that contribute to the truth-value of a proposition. For example, Mill does not aim to discuss "the functions of names, considered generally," but instead he treats them only insofar as "they are directly instrumental to the investigation of truth; in other words, to the process of induction" (1974, 8:663). Here Mill highlights induction because he believes that he has shown that deduction rests on induction and that induction is the only kind of inference that can yield real knowledge of matters of fact. But the overall strategy Mill has introduced in his philosophy of language is independent of his inductivism. Mill's main project is to treat the elements of language only insofar as they are relevant to understanding logical inference. In other words, Mill aims to isolate those features that are needed to understand the truth of propositions and the inferences that preserve truth or the likelihood of truth.

Verbal and Real

One of Mill's aims in the *System of Logic* is to show the relevance of logic to the pursuit of truth and, hence, its relevance to science. Because for Mill it is clear that science is about matters of fact and not a matter of ideas or linguistic conventions, logic, if it is relevant, must also yield information about matters of fact. Unfortunately, according to Mill, one of the consequences of "the revolution which dislodged Aristotle from the schools" is that "logicians may almost be divided into those who have looked upon reasoning as essentially an affair of Ideas, and those who have looked upon it as essentially an affair of Names" (1974, 7:95). If we assume that science is not just a mental or linguistic affair, this would make logic irrelevant to science.

Mill's theory of propositions according to which they can be about matters of fact is an important piece in Mill's attempt to shore up logic's role in science. Logic is the science of proof or evidence, and the unit of logical proof or evidence is the proposition. However, if logical inferences do not add any new information to what is already stated in the premises and if the inference only unpacks what is already contained in the ideas or meanings of the premises, then the fact that the premises are about matters of fact does not help logic become more informative. The inference does not add any new information to what is already contained in the propositions from which the inference is drawn.

In order to treat this issue, Mill introduces the distinction between verbal and real propositions. This distinction, however, is also important to Mill for other reasons. As Mill notes (1974, 7:116n), his distinction between verbal and real propositions is his take on Kant's distinction between analytic and synthetic judgments (Kant 1904, 3:B10–B11), which is a successor to Hume's distinction between reasoning about relations of ideas and reasoning about matters of fact (Hume 1996, 4:30–1) and Leibniz's distinction between truths of reason and truths of fact (Leibniz 1960, 612; 1970, 646).

While Leibniz's and Hume's distinctions are actually collections of various distinctions, Kant's distinction is clear. For Leibniz, truths of reason are necessary truths, their denial leads to a contradiction, they can be known by analysis of our ideas, and they are true in virtue of our ideas only. For Hume, judgments about relations of ideas are judgments known by the mere operation of thought, they are known with certainty, they can be demonstrated using logic and definitions only, and the denial of these judgments entails a contradiction. Needless to say, these characterizations of analyticity run together metaphysical, epistemic, and logical principles. For example, the idea that these truths are ones that can be demonstrated using logic and definitions only must not be conflated with the metaphysical idea that these truths are necessary or the psychological idea that these truths are known with certainty. This is not to say that a philosopher cannot believe that these notions are related to each other, but first one needs to be clear to distinguish the concept of analyticity from its related concepts.

Kant succeeds in introducing a relatively univocal notion of analyticity. Building on Leibniz's characterization of truths of reason in terms of analysis, Kant writes:

> In all [affirmative] judgments in which the relation of a subject to the predicate is thought... this relation is possible in two different ways. Either the predicate B belongs to the subject A, as something which is (covertly) contained in this concept A; or B lies outside the concept A, although it does indeed stand in connection with it. In the one case I entitle the judgment analytic, in the other synthetic. (1904, 3:B10)

Kant borrows from Leibniz the idea that concepts can be contained within each other, and specifies that in affirmative analytic judgments the predicate concept is contained in the subject concept. Unfortunately, strictly speaking Kant characterizes only *true* affirmative analytic judgments. Presumably, in a false affirmative analytic judgment, it is judged that the predicate concept is part of the subject concept, but in fact this is not so. Be that as it may, Kant's fundamental idea is that the truth of analytic judgments is determined solely by conceptual relationships.

From this Kant draws certain conclusions about the properties of analytic judgments. First, "[a]nalytic judgments (affirmative) are therefore those in which the connection of the predicate with the subject is thought through identity" (ibid.). That is, the predicate concept in the judgment is identical to part of the subject concept in affirmative analytic judgments. Second, due to this identity, analytic judgments are not informative, but only "explicative." The affirmative analytic judgment, when true, is "merely breaking [the subject concept] up into those constituent concepts that have all along been thought in it" (1904, 3:B11). Third, because the truth of analytic judgments is determined by conceptual relations only, Kant believes it follows that they can be known a priori, that is, without any evidence from experience. Finally, the fact that the predicate concept is identical to some part of the subject concept entails, Kant seems to believe, that "*if the judgment is analytic*, whether negative or affirmative, its truth can always be adequately known in accordance with the principle of contradiction" (1904, 3:B190).

Mill's concept of verbal propositions fastens onto Kant's idea that true analytic judgments are ones in which the predicate is contained in the subject, but transforms this idea into a linguistic notion. A verbal proposition, Mill writes, "asserts of a thing under a particular name, only what is asserted of it in the fact of calling it by that name"

(1974, 7:115). Mill, like Kant, draws the conclusion from this definition of a verbal proposition that it "either gives no information, or gives it respecting the name, not the thing" (ibid.). It would be more accurate to say that such propositions contain no information about "any matter of fact, in the proper sense of the term" (1974, 7:109). Consequently, they are also neither true nor false because truth is defined by Mill in terms of matters of fact: a true proposition is one that "is in accordance with the facts" or "a proposition is true, if the fact asserted is true" (1974, 8:971).

Real propositions are about matters of fact, and they are true in virtue of matters of fact. Mill does not attempt to give a general characterization of matters of fact except to tie them to his characterization of the import of propositions. As we have seen, Mill believes that except for identities, the meaning of a proposition is that its subject does or does not possess some attribute or that some attribute is or is not conjoined with some other attribute (1974, 7:158). But "every attribute is *grounded* on some fact or phenomenon...and that to *possess* an attribute is another phrase for being the cause of, or forming part of, the fact or phenomenon upon which the attribute is grounded" (1974, 7:98). This means, Mill believes, that the meaning of propositions really needs to be analyzed one more step.

For example, the universal affirmative proposition "All men are mortal" was analyzed as meaning that whatever objects have the attribute connoted by the subject term also have the attributes connoted by the predicate term. Given the grounding of attributes in phenomena, this and similar propositions mean "that one phenomenon always accompanies another phenomenon" (ibid.). The attributes that the term "man" connotes are grounded in certain phenomena men exhibit, that is, the experiences we have and can have of men. These phenomena – the appearance of men – are understood "by any one to whom the meaning of the word is known" (ibid.). The same holds for the attribute connoted by the predicate "mortal." So the proposition "All men are mortal" means "that wherever these various...phenomena are all found," namely the phenomena in which the attributes connoted by "man" are found, "there we have the assurance that the other...phenomenon, called death, will not fail to take place" (ibid.).

The kind of matter of fact that is the meaning of the proposition "All men are mortal" is described by Mill as either coexistence or sequence: the two phenomena either coexist in the same place or follow each other in time. According to Mill, there are five types of matters of fact that propositions can be about – existence, order in place, order in time, causation, and resemblance – and he asserts that this is an exhaustive list (1974, 7:99–108). Verbal propositions, Mill maintains, are not about any of these things. They do not assert or deny that some phenomena exist, coexist in space, temporally succeed each other, or resemble or cause each other (1974, 7:104); they assert nothing more "than the meaning of words" (1974, 7:99) or, in other words, they "do not relate to any matters of fact, in the proper sense of the term, at all, but to the meaning of names" (1974, 7:109).

Although Mill is not precise about the content of verbal propositions, the general idea has sufficiently clear contours. When an object is called by a name that connotes an attribute or a set of attributes, we assume or implicitly assert that the object has the attributes connoted by that name (1974, 7:223 and 115). A connotative name is applied to a set of objects "because they possess, and to signify that they possess," the connoted attributes (1974, 7:31), and a verbal proposition simply makes explicit what we assume or already assert by naming an object with a connotative name. Propositions involving nonconnotative names can also be verbal. For instance, propositions of identity, such as "Tully is Cicero" are all verbal propositions because they do not carry any information about matters of fact, but only information about how human beings conventionally have assigned names. In the case of "Tully is Cicero," the information conveyed is that the names "Cicero" and "Tully" denote the same individual, and this gives us no information about Cicero.

Strictly speaking, however, Mill's doctrine of verbal propositions, namely that verbal propositions are not about matters of fact, in the proper sense of the term, but about the meanings of words, cannot be true. Given Mill's commitment to naturalism, names are things, and that a name denotes an object or connotes an attribute has to be a matter of fact. What a term denotes or connotes is completely a matter of usage and convention, Mill maintains, but usage and convention are matters of fact as much as are plant growth or animal life. Baptisms and conventions for using names are part of the world of matters of fact, and thus are resolvable into facts of existence, spatial order, temporal order, causation, and resemblance. So verbal propositions are about matters of fact, *pace* Mill, but a special class of matters of fact, namely linguistic facts. More specifically, they are about semantic matters of fact about the denotation and connotation of human language.

Thus Mill's account of verbal propositions should be stated as follows. There are two classes of matters of fact: the facts about the semantic feature of language and all other facts.[17] Verbal propositions are about the former facts and real propositions are about all other facts. So Mill's treatment of analyticity depends on his ability to draw this distinction between two classes of facts. Mill transforms Kant's realm of ideas into a realm of meaning – the import of propositions – and characterizes analyticity in terms of this new realm. This change in the notion of analyticity is important, but the common core must not be overlooked. Mill follows Kant in preserving a realm that is distinct from the realm of "matters of fact, in the proper sense of the term," and thus, as Kant does with judgments, Mill can divide propositions into two classes, one of which is the class of verbal or analytic propositions. As long as there is such a realm that can be neatly separated from other matters of fact, the notion of analytic statements will be preserved.[18]

In general, just as the notion of a domain of ideas or concepts with a structure of its own lays the foundation for the concept of a judgment about this realm and is true or false in virtue of this realm (Kant's analytic judgment), the notion of an independent and identifiable domain of meaning for language with a structure of its own that can be the proper subject of theoretical discourse makes the idea of analytic propositions possible. Of course, for Mill knowledge of this domain of the meaning of language is a posteriori or empirical. No special mode of knowledge is required to know the truth of verbal propositions; only knowledge of linguistic usage and convention is required (1974, 7:109). On this epistemic issue, Mill differed sharply from Kant, who argued that analytic judgments were known a priori because our knowledge of concepts was not known on the basis of experience but through rational reflection on the structure of our concepts.

---

[17] Mill's initial claim that there are only two classes of propositions, verbal and real, is modified in the last chapter of the *System of Logic*, called "Of the Logic of Practice, or Art; Including Morality and Policy." There Mill introduces propositions in "a class by themselves," namely propositions that "do not assert that anything is, but enjoin or recommend that something should be" (1974, 8:949). A proposition with "the words *ought* or *should be*, is generically different" from propositions with "*is* or *will be*" (ibid.). Mill begins by characterizing these propositions as not asserting any matters of fact, but then – anticipating twentieth-century moral philosophy in the analytic tradition (Hare 1952) – he struggles with the relation between the meaning of moral propositions and matters of fact.

[18] Compare Quine's "Two Dogmas of Empiricism" (1953, 20–46).

Diversity and Freedom

There is a point in Mill's discussion of language where he begins to worry about the sharp distinction between semantic issues, which for him are questions about linguistic usage and convention, on the one hand, and questions of nonlinguistic matters of fact, on the other. This worry appears in his chapter on definitions, in a section where Mill argues that although all definitions are always of names only, not things, they nevertheless are "grounded in knowledge of the corresponding things" (1974, 7:150). For instance, when Plato through Socrates in the *Republic* asks "What is justice?" he is not, Mill claims, just asking about the meaning of the term "justice" and investigating linguistic conventions regarding that term. Plato is really asking the practical question what *should* this term mean – what should the usage and convention for the term "justice" be – and those questions do take us "into the properties not merely of names but of the things named" (ibid.).

In general, the conventions for abstract terms typically do not determine a clear set of attributes. In other words, Mill claims, there is "no precise agreement" on what attribute people mean when using terms such as "justice" (1974, 7:152). In such cases, four questions must be asked to understand the meaning of a term. First, is there agreement regarding the denotation of the term – namely, is there sufficient agreement regarding what actions are called "just"? Second, if there is sufficient agreement about the denotation, do those actions all have a common set of attributes, that is, does the denotation form a class? Third, if they do, what are they? Fourth, if they do not, what should the class be that forms the denotation of the term, that is, what is the best way of reforming the usage and convention for "just"? The first question, Mill maintains, is purely linguistic: it is "an inquiry into usage and convention," but the other questions lead to "inquiries into matters of fact" (ibid.).

But those who wish to reform language must be very careful. Natural languages are not the product of deliberate human artifice. "Language is not made but grows" and "the study of the spontaneous growth of languages is of the utmost importance to those who would logically remodel them" (Mill 1974, 7:151–2 and 153). General terms are introduced on the basis of resemblances between objects, and people extend the use of general terms on the basis of "gross and general" resemblances. Over time, even these gross resemblances do not exist as the usage of a term combines early conventions as well as later uses.

The logician, Mill maintains, cannot simply adopt these unscientific "classifications rudely made by established languages," but he suggests that these linguistic classifications nevertheless *contain* useful information (1974, 7:153).

Mill illustrates this point with an analogy to customary law and Roman or Napoleonic law. The classifications of natural language are like "the customary law of a country, which has grown up as it were spontaneously, compared with laws [such as Roman or Napoleonic law] methodized and digested into a code." Although customary law is not the product of scientific and systematic reflection, it is the "result of a long...course of experience," and on account of this experience, customary laws "*contain* a mass of materials which may be made very usefully available in the formation of the systematic body of written law" (ibid.; emphasis added). Similarly, the fact that a wide range of objects is classified under a general name by a language is "evidence," Mill argues, "that the resemblance [between these objects] is obvious, and therefore considerable" and that "it is a resemblance which has struck a great number of persons during a series of years and ages" (ibid.). Thus these rude classifications of natural language are evidence for real resemblances that need to be recognized by those who wish to "remodel" or "retouch" natural language to make it more useful for science.

The rude classifications of natural language are important even where such a resemblance is missing because "a name, by successive extensions, has come to be applied to things among which there does not exist this gross resemblance common to them all." At every step in these extensions of the name's usage, there is a resemblance, Mill maintains, "[a]nd these transitions of the meaning of words are often an index to real connexions between the things denoted by them, which might otherwise escape the notice of even philosophers" (ibid.).

It is striking that in the case of law Mill uses the term "contain" to say that customary law contains information, whereas in the case of natural language Mill avoids "contain" and instead uses "evidence" and "index," thus keeping verbal information neatly distinct from information about classification. If Mill had transferred the word "contain" from law to language in his analogy, then instead of writing that usage and custom are *evidence* or an *index* for real resemblances or connections, he would have written that the usage and custom of natural language *contain* information about real resemblances or connections. This would have undermined the sharp line Mill draws between verbal and real propositions, and the claim that verbal propositions contain no information about matters of fact, in the proper sense of the term.

So by very carefully managing the terms of his analogy, Mill is able, at least in theory, to maintain a clear domain for analytic propositions, sharply divided from propositions that convey information about the world. However, he does go so far as to admit that it is difficult to maintain this in practice. In a very revealing footnote to this discussion, Mill cites a book review he did for the reform-minded weekly *Examiner*.

> Few people ... have reflected how great a knowledge of Things is required to enable a man to affirm that any given argument turns wholly upon words. There is, perhaps, not one of the leading terms of philosophy which is not used in almost innumerable shades of meaning, to express ideas more or less widely different from one another. Between two of these ideas a sagacious and penetrating mind will discern, as it were intuitively, an unobvious link of connexion, upon which, though perhaps unable to give a logical account of it, he will found a perfectly valid argument, which his critic, not having so keen an insight into Things, will mistake for a fallacy turning on the double meaning of a term. And the greater the genius of him who thus safely leaps over the chasm, the greater will probably be the crowing and vain-glory of the mere logician, who, hobbling after him, evinces his own superior wisdom by pausing on its brink, and giving up as desperate his proper business of bridging it over. (1974, 7:153–4n)

Is the penetrating mind using terms univocally or equivocally, as the "mere logician" and "critic" maintains? The answer to this question turns on the distinction between verbal and real propositions for the term that is in dispute. Do the penetrating mind and mere logician merely differ in the verbal propositions they affirm or do they actually have different beliefs about matters of fact? Mill clearly senses that this is not an easy question to answer, and his unease anticipates the drama of the analytic-synthetic distinction in twentieth-century philosophy of language, to be discussed in Chapter 7.

There is another important aspect to this discussion. The problem of drawing the line between verbal and factual disputes arises for Mill because languages, as he and Humboldt before him wrote, are not deliberate artifacts but grow in response to human experience. A name is not "imposed at once and by a previous purpose upon a *class* of objects, but is first applied to one thing, and then extended by a series of transitions to another and another" (1974, 7:152). In each of those applications and extensions, individuals are guided by resemblances they notice. Resemblance, according to Mill, is a basic, unanalyzable and felt relation – that is, a sensation, feeling, or state of consciousness of the observer (1974, 7:70). Of course, for Mill it is clear that all sensations are the products of external bodies, but nevertheless all propositions about resemblances are grounded in mental states (1974, 7:71; see 7:850).

But human experiences are never exactly identical. We might say, Mill writes, "that the sight of any object gives me the *same* sensation or emotion today that it did yesterday, or the *same* which it gives to some other person," but strictly speaking this is not correct. Mill argues: "The feeling which I had yesterday is gone, never to return; what I have today is another feeling exactly like the former perhaps, but distinct from it; and it is evident that two different persons cannot be experiencing the same feeling, in the sense in which we say that they are both sitting at the same table" (1974, 7:71–2).

Moreover, human experiences are also deeply dissimilar. In *On Liberty* Mill writes that "it is the privilege and proper condition of a human being, arrived at the maturity of his faculties, to use and interpret experience in his own way" (1974, 18:262). An important source of difference is that human beings differ in their potentialities. "Different minds," Mill maintains, "are susceptible in very different degrees to the action of the same psychological causes" (1974, 8:856). The same object will excite very different degrees of desire in different people, and "the same subject of meditation, presented to different minds, will excite in them very unequal degrees of intellectual action." These are "natural differences which really exist in the mental predispositions or susceptibilities of different persons," and they are in Mill's view due to nature as well as nurture (1974, 8:856–7).

Two natural mechanisms play a role in the diversity of human beings. One is a feedback loop not unlike the one Humboldt discusses between external and internal states. Human beings have causal effects on their external conditions, which in turn affect their internal states. This feedback not only brings about different characters but different cultures and epochs (Mill 1974, 8:913). The other mechanism is internal, namely the association of ideas. Following his father, James Mill, who builds on Hume's empiricism, John Stuart Mill maintains that ideas are associated according to their similarity, intensity, and proximity, and this introduces significant variety in how human beings associate their ideas. For example, differences in human predispositions, either due to their nature or nurture, are responsible for the fact that the intensity of people's experiences differ in the face of the same object, and these differences in intensity lead to diverse associations of ideas. Another interesting difference

Mill mentions is that whereas some people are more inclined to associate ideas that are synchronous, others are more inclined to associate a successive order of ideas. The former association favors the perception of objects, but the latter favors perception of events, particularly causal connections (1974, 8:857–8).[19]

This individuality of associations is one of the reasons for Mill's endorsement of individual liberty. "Human nature is not a machine to be built after a model, and set to do exactly the work prescribed for it," Mill writes in his discussion of individuality in *On Liberty*, "but a tree, which requires to grow and develop itself on all sides, according to the tendency of the inward forces which make it a living being" (1974, 18:263). Our understanding is our own as well as our desires and impulses, and the individuality of these should be encouraged to unfold and be cultivated, and not be pinched, cramped, and dwarfed (1974, 18:264–6). Mill believes that the association of ideas is also partly responsible for the plasticity or changeability of human beings and society (1974, 8:913). Humanity is marked by "change both in the character of the human race, and in their outward circumstances so far as moulded by themselves," and Mill believes that the general tendency of this change is "toward a better and happier state," although this is only a tendency and not a necessity (1974, 8:914; also 790–1). Because the import of language is tied to how individuals associate their ideas, the import of language is also an arena for "human development in its richest diversity" (1974, 17:215).

Conclusion

Mill's philosophy of language is a dramatic mix of anachronistic tendencies: Scholastic formalism and romantic individualism. This fusion also represents a major alternative to Humboldt's linguistic

---

[19] The one who has a strong susceptibility to perceive objects has a "sense of the grand and the beautiful," whereas the other is a "rationative and philosophic intellect" (Mill 1974, 8:858). Moreover, those with strong associations of either kind will "probably be distinguished by fondness for natural history, a relish for the beautiful and great, and moral enthusiasm," but those with only "a mediocrity of sensibility" will result in "a love of science, of abstract truth, with a deficiency of taste and of fervor." In this discussion Mill is quoting at length and with approval from a biographical essay on Joseph Priestley by James Martineau. Mill quotes this passage primarily to make the more general point that once we understand the mind more, we will be able to give detailed explanations of "mental peculiarities."

perspective. Both Humboldt and Mill profile the structural features of natural language, but they focus on different structures. Whereas Humboldt focuses on what we might think of the aesthetic structures of language, for instance, its sound form, Mill is concerned with its logical features. More specifically, Humboldt shepherds the study of the syntactic structures of natural languages, whereas Mill turns to their semantic features. These will remain, as we will see, identifiable, albeit interwoven, tendencies during the prosperous twentieth-century boom for the philosophy of language.

The key concept in Mill's reunification of the study of logic and language is the import or meaning of propositions, and Gilbert Ryle was quite right to note that the opening chapters of Mill's *System of Logic* offer "the first influential discussion of the notion of meaning given by a modern logician" (Ryle 1963, 130). Linguistic meaning is the domain of Mill's linguistic studies, and in this domain Mill introduces a family of issues that will remain alive in subsequent semantic and philosophical studies of language: denotation and connotation, the meaning of proper names, identity, analyticity, necessity, inference, validity, and truth. However, it also needs to be remembered that Mill introduces this domain of linguistic meaning that serves the needs of logical structure without sacrificing diversity, individuality, or liberty. The import of propositions has a logical structure, but the states of mind in this structure are individual human states of mind that are the natural products of our unique characters and conditions.

SIX

The Value of a Function
Gottlob Frege

Gottlob Frege has been called "the founder of modern mathematical logic," "the father of 'linguistic philosophy,'" and "one of the founders of analytic philosophy" (Dummett 1973, 665 and 683; Beaney 1996, 1). Frege, like Leibniz, Humboldt, and Mill before him, focuses on a form of language that runs deeper than its apparent grammatical structure, and he specifically follows Leibniz and Mill in isolating logical form. What distinguishes Frege is his mathematical perspective on language. Drawing on mathematics, Frege constructed a language of logic that he believed also served as a basis for understanding the essential components of all languages, whether natural or artificial. Mill reestablished the tie between logical and linguistic studies, but Frege gave this relation a mathematical character that left a lasting mark in the philosophy and science of logic and language. In doing so, Frege also filtered out what might be thought of as the human dimension of language, namely its psychological properties, and consequently Frege has contributed to the concept of language as an autonomous formal system.

Concept Script

Frege's development began with what is also by far his most significant contribution: his work on the language of logic published in 1879 in "an epoch-making little book" called *Begriffsschrift*, translated as *Concept Script* or *Conceptual Notation* (Kneale and Kneale 1962, 436). It has been compared in significance and scope with Aristotle's contribution to logic. Just as Aristotle's *Prior Analytics* is the foundation of traditional or syllogistic logic – the logic of the categorical three-term syllogism[1] – Frege's *Begriffsschrift* is the keystone of modern or mathematical logic.

Frege is not the first to use symbols to express logical structure. Although Aristotle avoids symbols in the *Categories* and *On Interpretation* (the first two books of Aristotle's *Organon*, which are devoted to terms and propositions, respectively), he introduces symbols without any fanfare in the *Prior Analytics*, the third book of the *Organon*, with these words: "First then take a universal negative with the terms A and B. If no B is A, neither can any B be A" (*Prior Analytics*, 25a). The use of symbols has been a standard part of logic ever since.

Frege is also not the first to express logical relations in mathematical form. Hobbes in part I of *De Corpore*, called "Computation or Logic," already declares that to reason is to compute, and "to compute, is either to collect the sum of many things that are added together, or to know what remains when one thing is taken out of another." He concludes that "*Ratiocination*, therefore, is the same with *addition* and *substraction*" (1839, 1:1.1.2). Hobbes takes only a few steps to work out the details of this declaration, but Leibniz, following his lead, investigates extensively various reductions of logical relations to arithmetic operations, including multiplication and division. Leibniz aimed to treat syllogistic logic mathematically, but unfortunately none of his various very suggestive fragments of systems was powerful enough to capture all of syllogistic logic. This achievement fell to the autodidact George Boole (1815–64), who in his *Mathematical Analysis of Logic, Being an Essay towards a Calculus of Deductive Reasoning*, published 1847, used algebraic notation to express all of traditional syllogistic logic.

Besides capturing the logic of the Aristotelian syllogism, Boole was also able to capture propositional logic, namely the logic of the inferential relationships between propositions that "does not," as Boole puts it, "depend on any consideration which have reference to the terms" that occur in the proposition, but only depend on the meaning of negation and the connectives for propositions – for example, "and," "or," "if . . . , then."[2] Thus Frege cannot be said to be the first

---

[1] This is not to say that Aristotle ignored immediate inferences, but the focus of Aristotle's logical theory is the syllogism with two categorical premises and a categorical conclusion.

[2] Boole 1847, 48. Boole is primarily interested in capturing *modus ponens* and *modus tollens*, and his basic operations and connectives are negation, conjunction of true propositions, conjunction of false propositions, and the inclusive disjunction.

to develop propositional logic or to do so on the basis of a finite set of axioms.[3]

The reasons why Frege's *Begriffsschrift* stands out in the history of logic are that, first, Frege aims to develop his logic as a formal, deductive system. The *Begriffsschrift* begins with a section that introduces the symbols of the system, the formation rules that govern how those symbols can be combined to make new symbols, and the rules of inference or transformation rules that determine what can be inferred from a given proposition. In the next section Frege lists the axioms of the system and derives important theorems. The second reason the *Begriffsschrift* is a major landmark is that it is more general than any logical system developed before him. Frege captures the logic of propositions, syllogistic logic, as well as the logic of relations and identity. These areas had been studied by Frege's predecessors – Augustus DeMorgan and Charles Sanders Peirce, for example, developed the logic of relations – but none had integrated them into one system. Even Boole's treatment of syllogistic and propositional logic is not integrated because he develops these logics as two distinct systems that cannot be combined because they are different interpretations of the very same set of symbols.[4]

Finally, and most important, Frege introduces a powerful analysis of quantification that is the foundation of what is known as the predicate calculus, namely the logic of quantification and predication. Frege's insight has two basic components: he uses the mathematical notion of a function to analyze propositions, and he includes variables in quantifiers so that the quantifier, to use later terminology, *binds* that variable in the functions that follow the quantifier. Function-argument analyses will be examined more closely later, but one thing can already be made

---

[3] Because the second book of Aristotle's *Organon*, *On Interpretation*, was devoted to propositions, traditional logic always consisted of a logic of propositions. However, Aristotle himself focused on the relations between propositions that are determined by their constituent terms, and it was not until the Stoics that logicians studied the logical relations between propositions that did not depend on the constituent terms (Lukasiewicz 1935).

[4] Boole notices that he can capture the proposition "All the inhabitants of a particular island are either Europeans or Asiatics" in his logic of syllogisms and that he can capture the disjunction "Either all the inhabitants are Europeans, or they are Asiatics" in his logic of propositions, and he recognizes that he cannot combine them since in the first case the algebraic notation is used to represent classes and the combination of classes, whereas in the case of propositional logic the very same symbols stand for something else, namely propositions and propositional connectives (1847, 58–9). Unfortunately, he did not recognize that, as a consequence of this lack of integration, he could not express in his system the logical relationships between these propositions.

clear. The traditional universal affirmative propositions of the form *All F are G*, which consists of a quantifier and two predicates, is symbolized so that there is a single variable for the quantifier and the two predicates (1879, 23). Frege's symbolism is cumbersome, but in Bertrand Russell and Alfred North Whitehead's *Principia Mathematica* (1910) it received its more recognizable expression: (x)(Fx ⊃ Gx), which informally can be read as "For all x, if x is F, then x is G."

There are many important consequences of this new notation for quantification and predication, including that it makes it easy to express propositions with nested quantifiers, for example, "Every natural number has some successor" or "No one loves everyone," which posed difficulties for syllogistic logic. However, a consequence that will play an important role in the philosophy of language is that it signifies a departure from the traditional subject-predicate analysis of propositions. In traditional syllogistic logic, "All F are G" and "Some F are G" have the same subject-predicate structure: "All F" and "Some F" are subjects, and "are G" is a predicate. In Frege's logic, universal and particular affirmative propositions have very distinct structures. The first is symbolized as we saw as "(x)(Fx ⊃ Gx)," the second as "∃x(Fx & Gx)," which informally can be read as "There is an x such that x is F and x is G." Not only are their structures distinct, but they do not have the traditional subject-predicate form anymore.

For these reasons it is widely held by philosophers trained in the analytic tradition that "post-Aristotelian logic begins only with Frege" (Sluga 1980, 65), that he is "the initiator of the modern period in the study of logic" (Dummett 1973, xiii), or that Frege "laid the groundwork for...mathematical logic" (Burge 1992, 7). It is also for these reasons that a significant number would agree with the opening statement of Willard van Orman Quine's *Methods of Logic*: "Logic is an old subject, and since 1879 it has been a great one" (1949, vii). Of course, all of these claims are, strictly speaking, false. But it is accurate to describe Frege as the keystone in the development of modern mathematical logic. There are many stones in the arch that leads to modern mathematical logic, but due to its scope and power, Frege's *Begriffsschrift* is the keystone.

From the perspective of a philosopher, Frege's *Begriffsschrift* also stands out because it is motivated by philosophical concerns.[5] Not only does Frege argue that his *Concept Script* can become a useful tool for

---

[5] Baker and Hacker (1984, 6–7) underestimate Frege's education in and familiarity with philosophy.

philosophers (1879, vi–vii), but the work is motivated by epistemological concerns. "The recognition of scientific truth," he writes in the opening sentence, "as a rule passes through several stages of certainty" (1879, iii). Universal propositions "are gradually more firmly established by being connected with other truths through chains of inferences," and Frege immediately distinguishes between two kinds of propositions that need justification. There are propositions "whose proof can proceed purely logically and those whose proof must rest on facts of experience" (ibid.). The "firmest" and "most perfect proof" for Frege "is obviously the purely logical one" because it "disregard[s] the particular conditions of things" (ibid.), and Frege writes that he had asked himself the question whether the judgments of arithmetic rest on purely logical proofs or on proofs that involve empirical judgments. "In considering the question of to which of those two kinds arithmetical judgments belonged," Frege writes, "I first had to see how far one could get in arithmetic by inferences alone, supported only by the laws of thought that transcend all particulars" (1879, iv). He adds: "The course I took was first to seek to reduce the concept of ordering in a series to that of *logical* consequence, in order then to progress to the concept of number" (ibid.).[6]

In short, Frege is concerned with the degree of epistemic certainty and the kind of justification available for judgments in arithmetic. It should also be noticed that Frege transforms this epistemological worry into a metaphysical concern about the relation between logic and arithmetic. Frege begins with the issue of whether the proofs of arithmetic are purely logical proofs, but transforms this issue about the nature of proofs in arithmetic into a much broader issue of how much of arithmetic can be generated using logic alone. The first project is limited to the question of whether there are proof procedures in arithmetic that are not logical deductions and is aimed at showing that all proof procedures in arithmetic are purely logical proofs. If successful, this would be an argument against Mill, who argued that all proofs that yield knowledge of matters of fact, including proofs of arithmetic, rest on empirical induction. The second project involves trying to identify not only the proofs of arithmetic but its objects as well – for example, numbers and arithmetic functions – with the concepts and operations of logic. This project of trying to reduce all or some portion of mathematics to logic

---

[6] Frege does not get to numbers in the *Begriffsschrift*. This is the topic of his second major work, *The Foundations of Arithmetic/Die Grundlagen der Arithmetik* (1884).

came to be known as "logicism" and occupied Frege throughout his life.[7]

The Language of Life and Conceptual Content

Frege's contributions to logic, though great, do not automatically confer special status in the history of the philosophy of language. In fact, the full title of the *Begriffsschrift* does not suggest that it is relevant to the philosophy of language: *Concept Script: A Formula Language of Pure Thought Modelled on That of Arithmetic* (*Begriffsschrift, Eine der Arithmetischen Nachgebildete Formelsprache des Reinen Denkens*). This announces a book about a new language for the expression of pure thought, and as such it appears to be irrelevant to human natural language. The phrase "pure thought" suggests that this is going to be an artificial language for thoughts that are not soiled by natural language. The union of logic and natural language forged by Mill appears to be severed again. For this reason, some have argued that Frege is not concerned with natural language and so is not a philosopher of language (Baker and Hacker 1984, 66–7). A closer reading of the *Begriffsschrift*, however, reveals a different picture.

In the preface Frege writes that while he was trying to reduce the concept of a numeric series to the concept of logical consequence, he "found an obstacle in the inadequacy of language" (1879, iv). Language did not have the precision he needed to express more-complex relationships, and "out of this need came the idea of the present *Begriffsschrift*." It would forgo "the expression of anything that is without significance for logical inference," and, Frege continues immediately, "I have called...that which solely mattered to me conceptual content [*begrifflicher Inhalt*]" (ibid.). Conceptual content contains only what is relevant to deductive validity, and it is the pure thought mentioned in the full title to this book.

Distinct judgments, according to Frege, can have the same conceptual contents. For instance the grammatically active judgment, "The Greeks defeated the Persians at Plataea," and the passive judgment, "The Persians were defeated by the Greeks at Plataea," have slight differences

---

[7] The conflation of these two projects is especially dramatic in the third and final section of the *Begriffsschrift* (1879, 55–87), where Frege combines these two issues: showing that mathematical or recursive induction is really a special case of a purely logical inference, and showing that the number series and the successor relation can be defined in the terms of deductive logic alone.

in sense or content, Frege grants, but they also have a common core and this is their conceptual content (1879, 3). Conceptual content is not subjective and is not the "result of an inner process or a product of human mental activity." For Frege, it is as objective as the sun (1983, 7).

The most important feature of conceptual content is its essential tie to deductive validity. Conceptual content consists of only what "influences possible [logical] consequences" and it is "everything that is necessary for a valid inference" (1879, 3). This suggests that for Frege two propositions are identical just in case they have exactly the same logical consequences.[8] This is precisely the idea of logical form (*forme logique*) that we encountered in the philosophy of Leibniz (1962, 6.6:480).

The unit of conceptual content with which Frege begins the *Begriffsschrift* is the "judgable content" (1879, 2). The first symbol Frege introduces is a horizontal line with a vertical line on its left end, which indicates a judgment or affirmation and its content:

⊢——

So for instance,

⊢—— Opposite magnetic poles attract one another

is the judgment or affirmation that opposite magnetic poles attract one another. Frege then analyzes this sign into two parts, which allows him to distinguish something that he believes was ignored in traditional logic, namely judgment and the content of the judgment (1983, 11n).

Traditional logic analyzed judgments into three components: subject, predicate, and a copula that unites them. The role of the copula is to unite the subject and predicate into a judgment of affirmation or rejection. For instance, Mill writes that the word "is" is "the sign denoting that there is an affirmation or denial ... the word *is* ... serves as the connecting mark between subject and predicate, to show that one of them is affirmed of the other" (1974, 7:1.1.2). Accordingly, Mill defines a proposition, as we saw in the preceding chapter, as "*discourse, in which something is affirmed or denied of something* (1974, 7:20). Because "is" is assigned this role of forming an affirmation, it was not clear how to

---

[8] See Beaney 1996, 57. Beaney frames this discussion in terms of the conditions when "two propositions have the same *conceptual content*." This is not quite accurate. As we saw, for Frege in the *Begriffsschrift* propositions *are* conceptual contents, and so they cannot have conceptual contents. Judgments and sentences are the entities that *have* conceptual contents for Frege.

make the distinction that Mill also wants to draw "between assent and what is assented to" (1974, 7:1.5.1).

To mark out this distinction, Frege maintains that the horizontal line by itself without the vertical line is the *content stroke* and what follows the content stroke expresses content without any assertion. So

———Opposite magnetic poles attract one another

only expresses the "representation of the mutual attraction of opposite magnetic poles,...[and] [w]e *paraphrase* in this case using the words "*the circumstance that*" or "*the proposition that*" (1879, 2). Note that Frege's use of the term "proposition" (*Satz*) here differs significantly from Mill's use, which always meant a linguistic item – either a declarative sentence or a statement. Frege's use is also distinct from Humboldt's use of the word *Satz*, which also referred to a linguistic item and suffered from the same ambiguity between declarative sentence and statement that characterizes Mill's use of "proposition" (Humboldt 1999, 128). Frege's use of "proposition" initiates the standard way this term is used in the analytic tradition, namely to denote the contents of sentences or the objects of beliefs.[9]

The vertical line is the *judgment stroke*, and it expresses that the content is affirmed. It should be noted that the judgment stroke does not add any content to the original proposition. It only converts the content into a judgment. Because it converts the content that follows the content stroke into a judgment, the content has to be "judgable content," that is, something that is capable of being affirmed in a judgment. Consequently, not every content can be expressed after the content stroke – for example, the concept of a house – although the proposition that there are houses is a "judgable content" (1879, 2).

Although conceptual content is tied to deductive validity, Frege believes conceptual content is relevant to natural language. After introducing the notion of conceptual content in his preface, Frege writes:

> I believe I can make the relationship of my *Begriffsschrift* to the language of life clearest if I compare it to that of the microscope to the eye. The latter, due to the range of its applicability, due to the flexibility with which

---

[9] The German *Satz* is ambiguous, as Frege notes in a letter to Bertrand Russell, written October 1902. Frege writes that German logicians use *Satz* to refer to the linguistic *expressions* of thoughts, whereas mathematicians use the term to refer to the thought, and Frege adds that he prefers to side with the logicians (1976, 2:231). The logicians' use prevails in Frege's later writings, particularly in *Foundations of Arithmetic* and "On Sense and Reference."

it is able to adapt to the most diverse circumstances, has great superiority over the microscope. Considered as an optical instrument, it of course has many imperfections, which usually remain unnoticed only because of its intimate connection with mental life. But as soon as scientific purposes place great demands on sharpness of resolution, the eye turns out to be unsatisfactory. The microscope, on the other hand, is perfectly suited for just such purposes, but precisely because of this is useless for all others. (1879, v)

It is significant that the microscope and eye can focus on the same object but with different powers of resolution. Similarly, natural language and the language of logic can also express the same thing, namely conceptual content, but with different powers of resolution. Just as the microscope reveals details hidden from the naked eye, the language of logic can express details and distinctions that ordinary language cannot express.[10]

Frege repeats this perspective on the relationship between the language of logic and natural language in an essay he wrote in 1880 comparing his *Begriffsschrift* to Boole's logic, an essay that was rejected twice and never published in Frege's lifetime. The purpose of the *Begriffsschrift* is to "express content," and it is supposed to "render content more precisely than ordinary language" (1983, 13). Ordinary language "corresponds only imperfectly to the structure of concepts" and much is left up to guesswork, whereas a *Begriffsschrift* should "express completely what language only indicates" (ibid.). In sum, the language of logic and natural language both express content. The difference lies in the precision with which they express content.[11]

It is not surprising that Frege also develops a critique of natural language that is characteristic of the logical perspective on natural language. Not only does natural language often lack the means to express certain relations of concepts, but it is also a source of error and illusion. Frege thought the *Begriffsschrift* can become a "useful tool for philosophers" because it can "break the rule of words over the human mind, by uncovering illusions about the relations of concepts that often almost unavoidably arise through the use of language" (1879, vi–vii). The *Begriffsschrift* can achieve this by "liberating thoughts from" the

---

[10] Mill uses similar optical metaphors to compare natural language and logic. See 1974 7:1.1.1.

[11] Elsewhere Frege compares natural language to the human hand and his language of logic to a tool we use for purposes for which the human hand by itself is inadequate (1882, 52).

limitations of expression of natural language (ibid.). The subject-predicate structure of natural language is one of the sources of confusion, and Frege writes that it had confused him in the early stages of developing the *Begriffsschrift* (1879, 4).

In 1882, in a very short popular summary of the *Begriffsschrift*, Frege distinguishes between the grammatical or linguistic form (*sprachliche Form*) of natural language and logical form (*logische Form*) (1882, 50–2). The problem with natural language is that the linguistic form does not track the logical form. For instance, Frege writes, Euclid's demonstration in *The Elements* of the Nineteenth Theorem, namely that in every triangle, the largest angle lies opposite the largest side, is perfectly grammatical; as far as the linguistic form is concerned, there are no gaps in the demonstrations. Nevertheless, the proof as written relies on three missing premises, and so the linguistic form of natural language does not track the logical form. Natural language, Frege writes, usually only hints at logical relations but does not actually express them (1882, 51).

So for Frege, the grammatical form of natural language is not identical to the structure of conceptual content, at least not in every respect. But this does not mean that in the *Begriffsschrift* there is no connection between logic and the language of life. First, as we already saw, natural language and the language of logic both express conceptual content. What natural language fails to do sometimes is express this content accurately, just as the eye and the microscope are aimed at the same object but with different powers to resolve the details of the object. So what the *Begriffsschrift* can do is express more accurately part of the content of natural language. For example, when Frege's language of logic departs from the subject-predicate structure of natural language, he is not severing logic's ties to language. The subject-predicate structure is part of the *grammar* of language, while the function-argument structure of the *Begriffsschrift* expresses the *conceptual content* of natural language.

Frege is explicitly committed to the view that the function-argument structure is not just the structure of thought, but it is also part of the *content* of natural language (1879, xiii). He maintains that the *Begriffsschrift* expresses something "about the meanings of the words: if, and, not, or, there is, some, all, and so forth" (ibid.). Accordingly, the discussion of quantifiers and propositional connectives and operators in the *Begriffsschrift* is not just about the logical structure of pure thought; it is also about "the meanings of…words." Conceptual content is the content of human judgments as well as human language.

This notion of content will later be distilled by Frege into two components, but it must be noted that already in the *Begriffsschrift* Frege senses that conceptual content has various elements. He argues that names in identity statements acquire two distinct meanings. Names when flanked by the sign for identity do not represent their content only, which is what symbols usually represent. An identity sentence "denotes [*bezeichnet*] the circumstance that two names have the same content" (1879, 13). Consequently, "with the introduction of a symbol for identity of content a bifurcation in the meaning of every symbol is necessarily effected, the symbols standing one moment for their content, the next moment for themselves" (1879, 13–14). The reason a symbol for identity is needed is because "the same content can be fully determined in different ways" (1879, 14). For instance, a point can have several distinct "modes of determination" – for example, it can be determined as the intersection of two lines or "immediately through intuition" – and these modes of determination will be attached to distinct names (ibid.). The sign for identity allows us to state that two different modes of determination determine the very same object.

Distilling Content

Frege refines his theory of content in what is his major and most influential contribution to the philosophy of language, namely his essay "Über Sinn und Bedeutung" (1892). There is quite a bit of discussion about how to translate this title into English, particularly Frege's use of *Bedeutung*. In ordinary German, *Sinn* (sense), *Bedeutung* (meaning), and *Inhalt* (content) are used interchangeably, as are their ordinary English translations. So in German the title "Über Sinn und Bedeutung" is redundant and thus seems a bit odd to the ordinary reader, as would "Of Sense and Meaning" in English. Because Frege aims to draw a distinction using German words that ordinarily are used synonymously, his use of those terms in the essay itself is bound to be odd, as would be the case when using the synonymous English terms "sense" and "meaning" to draw a distinction. These are all reasons for translating this essay as "On Sense and Meaning."[12]

---

[12] "Meaning" and *Bedeutung* also share similar ambiguities. For example, "meaning" can be used to discuss linguistic meaning as well as the significance or importance of something, and the same holds for *Bedeutung*. For a good discussion and evaluation of the controversy over translating *Bedeutung*, see Beaney's introduction to Frege 1997, 36–46.

The translations that have prevailed, however, are ones that aim to render the meaning of Frege's technical uses of these terms; that is, they do not try to capture what Frege is splitting or bifurcating but the result of this split.[13] This is the approach of Bertrand Russell, the first philosopher to mention Frege's work in English. Russell (1903) first used "indication" for *Bedeutung*, but in 1905 in his own landmark essay in the philosophy of language "On Denoting," he writes that Frege "distinguishes... two elements, which we may call the *meaning* and the *denotation*," where *Sinn* is meaning while *Bedeutung* is denotation (1905). Russell goes on to write that when phrases have meaning and denotation, they "*express* a meaning and *denote* a denotation: (ibid.).[14] The title "On Sense and Reference" (Frege 1952, 56–7) continues this approach and follows Russell's identification of *Bedeutung* and denotation. "On Sense and Reference" has become the standard title for this essay, and these terms have become widely accepted as the terms that capture the distinction that Frege is making in this essay.[15] I continue this practice, but I also argue here that the more accurate translation is "On Sense and Denotation," as Russell indicates with his use of "denotation" for *Bedeutung*.

There are important reasons to believe that Mill had some role to play in Frege's thinking about meaning. Frege's main work between *Begriffsschrift* and "On Sense and Reference" was *The Foundations of Arithmetic: A Logico-Mathematical Inquiry into the Concept of Number* (*Die Grundlagen der Arithmetik: Eine logisch mathematische Untersuchung über den Begriff der Zahl*, 1884). In this book Frege addresses the second step of the project he began in the *Begriffsschrift* of trying to see how much of arithmetic he can generate from logic alone. Whereas in the *Begriffsschrift* he wanted to show that mathematical proofs are logical ones, here he aims to show that the concept of a number can also be reduced to the concepts of logic. To motivate his theory of

---

[13] I borrow the term "splitting" from Beaney's apt phrase "The Splitting of 'Content'" (1996, 151–2).

[14] Using "denotation" and its cognates for Frege's technical use of *Bedeutung* is also followed by Church 1951 and Carnap 1947. Carnap changes his mind in the second edition (1956, 97n).

[15] Following P. Long and R. White's translation of volume 1 of Frege 1976 (Frege 1979), Geach and Black change the title to "Sense and Meaning" in the third edition. An alternative translation is "On Sense and Nominatum" by Hebert Feigl in Feigl and Sellars 1949. Feigl follows the terminology used by Rudolf Carnap in *Meaning and Necessity* (1947).

number, Frege examines the views of his predecessors and Mill's empiricist account of number is a primary target.[16]

Because for Mill all truths about matters of fact were synthetic truths known empirically or a posteriori and arithmetic was a source of truths about matters of fact, Mill believed that arithmetic consisted of synthetic, a posteriori truths. Accordingly, the concept of number had to be defined empirically. Mill believed that we repeatedly recognize groups of objects – say three pebbles or three trees – and "we term all such parcels Threes" (1974, 7:257). Moreover, we recognize that these groups can be separated into parts – for instance, three pebbles can be separated into a group of two pebbles and a single pebble – and this is the basis of the arithmetic operations. Frege is particularly critical of this account. Already in the preface, Frege describes this as "gingerbread or pebble arithmetic" and that "the only thing missing is to ascribe to the flavor of the case a special meaning for the concept of number" (1978, vii); later he responds to Mill's text sentence by sentence (1978, 9–11).

The section Frege critiques includes this sentence:

> The expression, "two pebbles and one pebble," and the expression, "three pebbles," stand for the same physical fact. They are names of the same objects, but of those objects in two different states: though they *de*note the same things, their *con*notation is different. (Mill 1974, 7:256).

Frege must have read this passage (Beaney 1996, 308n51). Mill returns to counting pebbles in his discussion of the laws of nature, where he writes that each name of a number "denotes physical phenomena, and connotes a physical property of those phenomena" (1974, 7:610). A bit later Mill summarizes the ensuing discussion:

> What, then, is that which is connoted by a name of a number? Of course, some property belonging to the agglomeration of things which we call by the name; and that property is, the characteristic manner in which the agglomeration is made up of, and may be separated into, parts. (1974, 7:611)

---

[16] In the introduction and parts I–III, the historical and critical discussion prior to Frege's presentation of his own theory in part IV, Mill's name is used more than anyone else's name, including that of Leibniz. Mill's name is used thirty-one times while Leibniz's name is used twenty-five times. There is a large gap between the number of occurrences of Mill's and Leibniz's names and the next most frequently used names, which belong to Stanley Jevons (nine times) and Kant (eight times).

Taking some liberties by transforming Mill's question into an answer, Frege quotes this text as follows:

> The name of a number connotes [*bezeichnet*] some property belonging to the agglomeration of things which we call by the name; and that property is, the characteristic manner in which the agglomeration is made up of, and may be separated into, parts. (1978, 29–30)

In reading this passage, Frege must have at least had some awareness of Mill's distinction between denotation and connotation.

Nevertheless, Frege's choice of words for Mill's "connotation" in his paraphrase ignores this distinction. The German translation by J. Schiel of Mill's *System of Logic* that Frege read and cited clearly distinguishes between connotation and denotation. Schiel consistently used *Bezeichnung* for denotation and *Mitbezeichnung* for connotation, preserving in German the fact that in English "connotation" and "denotation" have "notation" as a common root (Mill 1863, 1:35). So Schiel very appropriately uses *mitbezeichnet* when translating "connoted" in Mill's question "What, then, is that which is connoted by a name of a number?" while Frege ignores this in his paraphrase. Frege, as noted in the text just quoted, uses *bezeichnet* instead.

This could be taken to mean that in the *Foundations of Arithmetic* Frege was still completely confused about the components of meaning and that he did not distinguish denotation from other components of meaning, as he does eight years later in "On Sense and Reference." Perhaps this attributes more confusion to Frege than is warranted. A more plausible interpretation is that Frege simply ignored Mill's concept of connotation, a concept that was too closely tied to subjectivity to be useful for Frege, and instead focused on denotation and assimilated Mill's connotation to denotation. The view Frege is considering in this passage is that number terms denote properties of objects.

In German, it would be natural to suppose that connotation (*Mitbezeichnung*) is just a kind of denotation (*Bezeichnung*): one can denote only an object and nothing else, or one can *also* denote along with it other things, such as its properties. Mill himself suggests this interpretation by how he uses italics, for example, when he writes, as we saw in the previously cited quotation, that "though [the expressions 'two pebbles and one pebble' and 'three pebbles'] *de*note the same things, their *con*notation is different."

The opening sentence of the *Foundations of Arithmetic* clearly shows that here Frege is concerned with the denotation of number terms: "To the question, What is the number one, or what does the sign 1 mean [*bedeuten*], one usually gets the answer: a thing" (1978, i). The question "What is the number one?" is paraphrased in terms of the second question, which is about the relationship between a sign and an object. That is, Frege is asking what is it that a number term stands for or names, and this is precisely the relation that the verbs "denote" in Mill's English and *bezeichnen* in the German translation of Mill signify.

That denotation is what Frege had in mind in this opening sentence is made clear in a discussion of the *Foundations* in an unpublished draft written in the years 1891 and 1892 and called "On the Concept of Number." Clearly smarting from the fact that the *Foundations* was being ignored, he chastises an author who writes about the basic concepts of arithmetic "as if the third section of my *Foundations* had never been written" (1983, 82). In the course of this acerbic critique, Frege repeats his opening question from the *Foundations*: "One could ask: what does the word 'one' actually mean [*bedeutet*]? Does it denote [*bezeichnet*] a number?" (ibid.). Similarly, in a summary of his life's work that Frege wrote in July 1919, six years before his death, he asks "Is arithmetic a game or a science?" and ties this question to the problem of what number terms denote. "Is the visible the thing arithmetic is concerned with," he asks, "or is the visible only a sign for it . . . ? Is the denotation [*das Bezeichnete*] a number and if not, what is it?" (1983, 277).[17]

The verb "denote" (*bezeichnen*) also appears in a key paragraph of the *Foundations* (§62), which has been described as "arguably the most pregnant philosophical paragraph ever written" (Dummett 1991a, 111). This paragraph lays out the general strategy Frege will use for defining number terms, and it is the opening paragraph of a section Frege calls "*To obtain the concept of number, the sense* [Sinn] *of a numerical equation must be determined*" (1978, 73). As the use of "sense" (*Sinn*) in this title indicates, it is also in this text that Frege distills content into two components.

Frege arrives at sense as the semantic companion to denotation as follows. Earlier Frege had concluded that numbers are neither physical

---

[17] Frege identifies a "mathematical sickness of the times" and a "widespread mathematicians' sickness" as the inability to "distinguish between the sign [*Zeichen*] and the denotation [*Bezeichnete*]" (1983, 172 and 241). A letter Frege wrote to Husserl in 1891 also shows that denotation is the primary topic of the *Foundations*. He writes that in many places in the *Foundations* he should have used *Bedeutung* in the technical sense he develops in "On Sense and Reference," where, as we will see, *Bedeutung* and *Bezeichnung* are explicitly identified (1976, 96).

things, physical properties of things, nor subjective entities such as mental representations (1978, 58). But if a number "is neither something sensible nor a property of an external thing," we cannot mentally represent numbers as such (1978, 70).[18] Moreover, if we cannot mentally represent numbers, which are the denotations of number terms, and denotation is all there is to the meaning of a word, it follows that we do not have mental representations of the meanings of number terms. This raises a problem for Frege that opens paragraph 62 and the section on "*the sense of a numerical equation*": "How, then, shall a number be given to us, when we cannot have any representations or intuitions of it?" (1978, 73). This central question leads Frege to a notion of linguistic sense in addition to denotation.

The pivot that gets Frege from denotation to sense is what has come to be called Frege's "context principle" (Dummett 1973). Frege maintains that the lack of a mental representation for the meaning of a number word can suggest that number terms do not have meanings, but Frege believes this is a mistake. The fact that no representation can be formed of the meaning of a word "is...no reason for denying it any meaning [*Bedeutung*]" (1978, 71). We might be inclined to deny such words meaning if we look at words in isolation, but this is a mistake. "Only in a complete sentence[19] do words really have meaning [*Bedeutung*]," Frege writes, appealing to a principle he already highlighted in the introduction to the *Foundations of Arithmetic* as one of the three "fundamental principles" of his inquiry into the nature of number (1978, x and 71).

Given how Frege elucidates this principle, it is clear that he had denotation in mind. Frege first points out very briefly that this principle "throws light on quite a number of difficult concepts.... and its

---

[18] Given Frege's Platonism, it is easy to forget that Frege believes that thinking requires sensible perceptions, including sensible signs (1879, ix; 1882, 48–9). Frege maintains that sensible signs such as language allow us to use what is sensible "to free ourselves from its constraint." He adds that "signs have the same importance for thought that discovering how to use the wind to sail against the wind had for navigation" (1882, 49).

[19] The word Frege uses here is *Satz*. Because Frege mentions words in the context of a *Satz* and later, in "On Sense and Reference," he writes about the *Satz* and the thought [*Gedanke*] that it expresses, it is clear that with *Satz* Frege has linguistic items in mind and not conceptual contents, as was the case in the *Begriffsschrift*. For Frege, as we will see, *Gedanke* is usually translated as proposition in the sense of the meaning or content of a declarative sentence.

scope is certainly not restricted to mathematics" (1978, 71). Then he concludes the introduction of this principle with the following words: "The independence that I am claiming for number is not to be taken to mean that a number word denotes [*bezeichnen*] something when removed from the context of a sentence" (1978, 72). Frege is concerned with the apparent conflict between his view that a number is an "independent object" (*selbstständiger Gegenstand*) (1978, 68) and the context principle, which might suggest that a number term has meaning by itself in isolation from a complete sentence. This is not so, Frege believes. Although numbers are independent objects – and not properties of objects, for example – the context principle still holds for number terms. Frege's use of "denotes" (*bezeichnen*) to make this clarification regarding the context principle shows he had denotation in mind when he used *Bedeutung* in the context principle.

It is now clear how the context principle allows Frege to answer his question about how numbers are given to us. Although we have no mental representations or intuitions of numbers, they are given to us by means of number terms in the context of whole sentences. Hence, understanding how numbers are given to us "depends on defining the sense of a sentence in which a number word occurs" (1978, 73). Frege argues that the sentences we must look for in this inquiry are ones that "express recognition" of the number. "[I]f the sign *a* is supposed to denote [*bezeichnen*] an object for us, then we must have a criterion [*Kennzeichen*] that decides in all cases whether *b* is the same as *a*," and sentences of identity will yield such a criterion (ibid.). "Our aim is to construct the content of a judgment that can be understood as an equation on each side of which is a number" (1978, 74). In other words, we will understand how numbers are given to us if we understand the sense of identity sentences involving number terms, for example, "$7 + 5 = 12$." Frege takes for granted that we have a general concept of identity that is expressed in statements of identity and, "by means of this already known concept of identity, obtain that which is to be regarded as identical" (ibid.).

This analysis of the content of identity sentences leads Frege to a notion of meaning in addition to denotation. It is not the case that "an object can be given in one single way" and the "versatile and meaningful use of identities rests... on the fact that something can be reidentified even though it is given in a different way" (1978, 79). So although in an identity statement there is only one denotation, nevertheless the identity statement expresses distinct ways in which the object is given, and the way an object is given is another component of meaning besides denotation.

I believe that in writing the *Foundations of Arithmetic* Frege began to distill the raw concept of meaning or content into two components. Moreover, the space and effort Frege devotes to presenting and responding to Mill's views about the nature of numbers and the meaning of number terms as well as his use of *Bezeichnung*, the standard German translation of Mill's term "denotation," strongly suggest that Mill's *System of Logic* played a key role in this distillation process. In reading and responding to Mill, Frege narrows his concept of meaning to denotation or *Bezeichnung*, but this leaves Frege with a remainder that he isolates in his study of identity statements: how objects are given to us. Thus Frege is left at the brink of the distinction he draws in his essay "On Sense and Reference."

Sense and Denotation

In "On Sense and Reference," the distinction between denotation and what he called the "modes of determination" in the *Begriffsschrift* or how "an object can be given" in the *Foundations* is now made explicitly and clearly. In this essay, Frege explicitly introduces a technical sense for the word *Bedeutung* that ties it down to *Bezeichnung* and uses *Sinn* for the other component of content, which he still describes as the "way in which an object is given" (*Art des Gegebenseins*) (1892, 26). Moreover, whereas Frege's discussion in the *Foundations of Arithmetic* is understandably preoccupied with the language of arithmetic, in "On Sense and Reference" he applies his distillation of content to natural language as well. For these reasons, this essay is indeed one of the "landmarks in linguistic thought" (Harris and Taylor 1997).

Following his strategy in the *Foundations*, Frege establishes the distinction between sense and denotation by an analysis of identity sentences. Frege's argument has become famous and it is worth repeating. He begins with two alternative views: identity is a "relation between objects, or between names or signs of objects" (1892, 25). As we saw earlier, Mill endorses the former view, whereas Frege in the *Begriffsschrift* endorses the latter. But both views are inadequate. The first view has the following problem. Sentences of the form $a = a$ and $a = b$ obviously have different cognitive values as can be seen from the fact that the first "holds *a priori* and, according to Kant, is to be labeled analytic, while sentences of the form $a = b$ often contain very valuable extensions of our knowledge and cannot be established *a priori*." Frege adds: "The discovery that the rising sun is not new every morning, but always the same, was one of the most fertile astronomical discoveries" (ibid.). But if identity is a relation between objects, that is, "a relation between that which the names 'a' and 'b' denote [*bedeuten*]" and it is true that $a = b$, there would be no difference in cognitive value of $a = a$ and $a = b$. Both $a = a$ and $a = b$ would "express" the same thing (1892, 26).

So it seems that "what one wishes to state [*sagen*] by $a = b$ is that signs or names denote [*bedeuten*] the same thing, and then we would be discussing those signs; a relation between them would be asserted" (ibid.). But those signs or names are related in this manner only if they "name or denote [*bezeichnen*] something" and if the two signs are connected "with the same denotation [*Bezeichneten*]." This connection, however, "is arbitrary [and] [n]obody can be forbidden to use any arbitrarily[20] producible event or object as a sign for something." Consequently, "the sentence $a = b$ would no longer be concerned with the object itself but only with our manner of denotation [*Bezeichnungsweise*]." This sentence would not "express genuine knowledge," but as a matter of fact such sentences, to use Frege's words, express valuable extensions of our knowledge (ibid.).

Frege's solution is to ignore the signs as objects, for example, the physical shape or "a," but instead to consider the "difference in the way the object is given [*Art des Gegebenseins*]" that is associated with the difference in signs.[21] To illustrate this difference in the way an object is given, Frege gives a geometric example reminiscent of the example in the *Begriffsschrift* discussed previously – namely, how the very same point can be the intersection of two different pairs of line segments. Later Frege suggests an astronomical example that has achieved canonical status in analytic philosophy of language. Venus has two distinct ways in which it is given: as morning star and as evening star. So what makes an identity sentence of the form "$a = b$" cognitively significant is that it

---

[20] The German word used here is *willkürlich*, which explicitly expresses that something depends on individual choice, decision, or discretion. Frege is referring to events or objects produced by human will.

[21] *Art des Gegebenseins* was translated by Max Black in Frege 1952 as "mode of presentation," and that phrase has found its way into the philosophical literature. Unfortunately, this obscures the important fact that in the *Foundations*, as discussed in the previous section, Frege uses the same words to discuss this topic: "Wie soll uns denn eine Zahl gegeben sein?" (1884, 73). Also see the last sentence of §68 (1884, 79).

expresses the identity of objects by means of distinct ways in which that object is given. So the sentence "The Morning Star is identical with the Evening Star" is cognitively significant because it expresses two distinct ways in which an object is given and expresses that the same object is given in these two distinct ways.

With this distinction in place, Frege bifurcates the concept of content:

> It is now plausible to think that connected with a sign (name, combination of words, written mark), besides its denotation [*dem Bezeichneten*], which may be called the *Bedeutung* of the sign, is also what I should like to call the sense of the sign, wherein the way the object is given is contained. (1892, 26–7)

Accordingly, the *Bedeutung* of "Morning Star" and "Evening Star" would be the same, but not the sense. Frege then makes clear that he is now only considering singular terms, that is, signs whose denotation is a single object, and calls all such signs "proper names," with the proviso that proper names can also be a phrase such as a definite description.

A bit later he formally introduces his new terminology:

> In order to make brief and precise expression possible, may the following phraseology be established:
>
> > A proper name (word, sign, combination of signs, expression) expresses its sense, means [*bedeutet*] or denotes [*bezeichnet*] its *Bedeutung*. With a sign we express its sense and denote its *Bedeutung*. (1892, 31)

The term *Bedeutung* is now a new technical term that is synonymous with *Bezeichnung* and accordingly the technical sense of *Bedeutung* is best preserved by the English word "denotation." The terms "designation" or "reference"[22] are also acceptable, but "denotation" is the better translation because it preserves the historical tie – *Bezeichnung* – to Mill's "denotation."[23]

---

[22] "Reference" is problematic only because Strawson (1950) has tied reference with a human action. He maintains that words do not refer to objects, but people refer to objects using language. For this reason also "denotation" would be better than "reference," but I don't think this is a decisive advantage because for most analytic philosophers "reference" does not have the meaning that Strawson assigns to it.

[23] There are numerous places in Frege's letters and posthumously published writings where he explicitly uses its cognates *Bedeutung* and *Bezeichnung* synonymously. For instance, to the mathematician E. V. Huntington, Frege writes: "Es liegt hier... eine Vermischung zweier Verschiedener Arten von Zeichen vor, nämlich der bezeichnenden (oder bedeutenden) und der nur andeutenden, wie ich sage. Die Zeichen '2', '3' nenne

While the term *Bedeutung* defined in Frege's "On Sense and Reference" is precisely what Mill meant with "denotation," Frege's "sense" (*Sinn*) is very different from Mill's psychological concept of connotation. These differences are highlighted in the next section, but it is also important to underscore their similarities. A meaningful sign is connected to its sense, which in turn corresponds to a denotation – that is, the sense of a word determines its denotation (1892, 27).[24] While a sense determines a unique denotation, it is not the case that a "denotation (an object) belongs only to a single sign" (ibid.). Objects can be given in many ways and thus correspond to many distinct senses, which in turn can tie them to many different signs. Similarly, the same sense can be expressed by different signs in different languages and even in the same language. Ideally, distinct signs in a language would express distinct senses, but natural languages usually do not fulfill this requirement, and "one must be satisfied if in the same context a word has the same sense" (ibid.). Moreover, that a sign has sense does not guarantee that it has a denotation. As Frege illustrates, the expression "the least rapidly convergent series" has a sense, but it is provable that it does not have a denotation.

Finally, Frege's sense as a way in which an object is given and Mill's connotation both have epistemic features. As we saw, for Mill a connotation is the attribute a name implies (Mill 1974, 7:31), and attributes of bodies "are grounded on the sensations which we receive from those bodies, and may be defined, [as] the powers which the bodies have of exciting those sensations" (1974, 7:74). Thus attributes involve ways in which objects are known by us. Similarly, the way objects are given is an epistemic relation. This is particularly clear if we recall the discussion of how numbers are given in the *Foundations* and the different "modes of determination" in the *Begriffsschrift*. The mode of determination in the *Begriffsschrift* is the way an object – for instance, an intersection – is

---

ich Eigennamen; jedes von ihnen bezeichnet oder bedeutet eine bestimmte Zahl" (This presents . . . a conflation of two distinct kinds of signs, namely, as I say, the denoting [or *bedeutenden*] and the only indicating ones. I call the signs "2," "3" proper names; each one of these denotes or *bedeutet* a specific number) (1976, 90). Also see 1976, 172, 241, 268, and 280; and 1983, 119–20, 240, and 246. This passage to Huntington also suggests one reason why Frege settles on *Bedeutung* instead of *Bezeichnen*. Frege likes to contrast *bedeuten* with *andeuten*, which he uses synonymously with "express," that is, the relationship between the sign and its sense. The usual translation for *andeuten* is "indicate."

[24] Also 1976, 96, and 1983, 135.

picked out or individuated, whereas in the *Foundations* the way numbers are given to us is by means of a "a criterion [*Kennzeichen*] that decides in all cases whether" two numbers are identical.[25]

Although the general distinction between the sense and denotation of linguistic signs cannot be said to be Frege's discovery – it is not only a successor to Mill's distinction between the connotation-denotation of words, but also the distinction between the comprehension and extension of terms of the *Port-Royal Logic* and the doctrine of supposition of Scholastic logic – Frege's argument for it and its strength are novel. The greatest importance, however, of "On Sense and Reference" lies in the application of this distinction, particularly its application to difficult cases, and thus in carving out canonical problems in analytic philosophy of language.

In addition to the analysis of the meanings of singular terms, Frege applies this distinction to explain the meaning of words in the context of quotation marks, thus addressing one of his favorite grievances, namely the inability to distinguish between the use and mention of words. He also uses it to analyze the meaning of whole sentences as well as subordinate clauses. In the case of whole sentences, Frege notoriously maintains that they are singular terms that express a sense, namely a complete thought or propositions, and denote an object, namely a truth-value, either "the True" or "the False" (1892, 34). He also addresses the meaning of complex sentences, paying attention to the sense and denotation of various kinds of subordinate clauses, including noun, adjective, and adverbial clauses. Throughout this analysis, however, he is not interested in the grammatical categories for their own sake but intends to "group together what is logically of the same kind" (1892, 36).

Frege's special interest is in isolating clauses where the denotation of the clause becomes a sense instead of its usual denotation. One such example is indirect discourse, where we aim to convey what someone said without quoting their actual words. Frege maintains that in such sentences words denote their customary sense, not what they normally denote, and accordingly in this context they also have a different sense. When an expression denotes what ordinarily is its sense, Frege calls the sense the "indirect denotation" of the expression, whereas its usual denotation is "customary denotation," and its sense in these contexts

---

[25] The epistemic nature of sense is also expressed in following passage: "Different signs for the same thing are unavoidable because one can be led to it by different paths" (Frege 1983, 95).

is the "indirect sense" as opposed to its "customary sense" (1892, 28). Typically, in indirect discourse, the sense of what was said is denoted by a "that" clause that includes a complete sentence, for example, the clause "that the Earth moves" in the sentence "Galileo said that the Earth moves" contains the sentence "The Earth moves." According to Frege, the proper analysis is that, in the context of this complex sentence, the sentence "The Earth moves" does not denote its customary denotation but instead denotes its customary sense, which in this case is the thought or proposition that the Earth moves.

Sentences with verbs such as "to believe," "to think," "to regret," "to approve," "to blame," "to hope," and "to fear," are treated in the same way by Frege. Frege argues that they need special treatment because Leibniz's law or the principle of the substitutivity of identity does not appear to apply to these sentences. This principle, as understood by Frege, states that the truth-value of a sentence remains unchanged when an expression in it is replaced by another with the same denotation (1892, 35 and 36),[26] but this does not seem to hold for such sentences. For example, it is possible that the sentence "Copernicus believes that the Morning Star is illuminated by the Sun" is true while "Copernicus believes that the Evening Star is illuminated by the Sun" is false even though "Morning Star" and "Evening Star" have identical denotations. Frege's solution is to maintain that, in the context of "believes that," words do not have their customary denotations. Instead, they have indirect denotations, which are their customary sense. Accordingly, the sentences "The Morning Star is illuminated by the Sun" and "The Evening Star is illuminated by the Sun" in the context of "believes that" denote different propositions even though customarily they both have exactly the same denotation.

Following Frege's analysis, these kinds of sentences have come to be known as expressing *intensional contexts* – that is, complex sentences that have subordinate clauses that do not denote what they ordinarily denote, but denote their senses instead. The term "intension" is rooted in the work of William Hamilton, who used it instead of "comprehension"

---

[26] Frege gives the following citation: "Eadem sunt, quae sibi mutuo substitui possunt, salva veritate" (Those things are identical that can be mutually substituted while preserving truth) (1892, 35). Leibniz gives several formulations of this principle and the one that comes closest to Frege's quotation in "On Sense and Reference" has *ubique* (everywhere) instead of *mutuo* (mutually) (Leibniz 1988, 264). In the *Foundations* (1978, 76), Frege quotes another formulation (Leibniz 1988, 259).

of the *Port-Royal Logic*, and since Carnap (1947, 119), Frege's senses have come also to be called "intensions." Such contexts are also known as "referentially opaque" contexts because the principle of the subsitutivity of identity does not hold in these contexts. The latter term was preferred by philosophers such as Quine who wished to avoid Fregean commitments to senses (1960). The desire to avoid senses received some inspiration from Mill's belief that there are proper names whose only meaning is their denotation.

No Further Discussion

There is a deep divide between Frege's and Mill's notion of sense, a divide that stems from Frege's militant opposition to empiricist accounts of logic and arithmetic and their languages. According to these accounts, for example, numbers and arithmetic functions are either psychological entities and processes (psychologism) or signs and rules for the computation of signs (formalism), and it is these views Frege argues against in the *Foundations*. Empiricism was broadly allied with nineteenth-century German naturalism, which maintained that only natural processes and objects existed and accordingly aimed to explain the objects of the more abstract subjects – ethics, logic, and mathematics, for instance – in terms of the methods of the natural sciences.

Nineteenth-century German naturalism was part of the critique of Hegel (1770–1831) and, more generally, the philosophical idealism that dominated the first third of the nineteenth century in Germany (Sluga 1980, 17–19).[27] Mill's sympathy for explanations of mental functions in terms of natural processes and the reliance on feeling and sensation in Mill's epistemology and philosophy of mind resonated in a period that had as one of its slogans Feuerbach's declaration:

> Food becomes blood, blood becomes heart and brain, thoughts and sentiments. Human fare is the foundation of human culture and mind. Would

---

[27] Well-known figures who are part of the naturalist response to Hegel are Ludwig Feuerbach (1804–72) and Karl Marx (1818–83), but they also include the philosopher of language Otto Friedrich Gruppe; Hermann Helmholtz (1821–94), who is remembered most for his contributions to the psychology of vision, although he also made contributions to physics; the chemist Justus Liebig (1803–73); and the brothers Georg Büchner (1813–37), author, and Ludwig Büchner (1824–99), philosopher. Ludwig Büchner is perhaps one of the first philosophers to argue for philosophical materialism on the basis of empirical evidence.

you improve a nation? Give it better food instead of declamations against sin. A human being is what he eats [*Der Mensch ist, was er isst*]. (1975, 4:263)[28]

For this reason Germany in the mid-nineteenth century was receptive to Mill's philosophy, and his *System of Logic* enjoyed two different translations, each of which was published in several editions.

So while Mill endorses the subjective and psychological dimensions of logic and language, Frege believes that there is a domain of linguistic meaning that can be purged of human subjectivity and that constitutes the cognitive content of language and determines the nature of logically valid reasoning.

"The denotation and sense of a sign," Frege declares, "are to be distinguished from the associated representations" (1892, 29).[29] Representations as well as what Frege also calls "intuitions" (1892, 30) are subjective, psychological states, and as such they are not only tied to sense impressions, but they are also "often saturated with feeling" (1892, 29). These subjective states also include the "coloring and lighting which poetry and eloquence seek to give to sense," and these, of course, are also "not objective, but each hearer or reader must himself provide these according to the hints of the poet or speaker" (Frege 1892, 31).

Frege believes that senses stand between the subjective representation and the objective denotation, and he illustrates this relationship with the following metaphor. When looking through a telescope at the moon, the denotation can be compared to the moon. The retinal image is the subjective mental representation, but the real optical image projected by the lens – or, in the case of a reflecting telescope, the image on the

---

[28] This is a consequence Feuerbach draws in a book review published in 1850 of Moleschott's *The Theory of Nutrition* (*Die Lehre der Nahrungsmittel*) (1975, 4:243–65).

[29] Max Black uses "idea" instead of "representation" to translate the German word *Vorstellung* (Frege 1952). H. Feigl (Frege 1949) uses the word "image." Although Feigl's translation is more accurate, both translations illustrate the ahistorical character of early English translations of Frege from analytic philosophy's ahistorical period. Kant turned the term *Vorstellung* into a term of art in German philosophy, and no German philosopher after Kant can use this term without positioning himself with respect to Kant, including Frege. See Frege's discussion and critique in *Grundlagen* of Kant's use of the term *Vorstellung* (Frege 1978, 37). The best available English term for the philosophical use of *Vorstellung* is "representation."

mirror – is the sense. The optical image is the same for all observers, whereas the retinal image is different for every observer. Similarly, all mental representations, that is, sense impressions, intuitions, feelings, and other "items in the stream of consciousness" (Dummett 1995, 7), vary from individual to individual and "this essentially distinguishes the representation and the sense of a sign, which can be the common property of many and accordingly not a part or a mode of the individual mind" (Frege 1892, 30). For this reason, Frege declares that there will be "no further discussion of representations and intuitions" (1892, 32). He mentions them, he concludes, only to "ensure that the idea aroused in the hearer by a word shall not be confused with its sense or its denotation" (ibid.).

The sense of a declarative sentence is a *Gedanke* (thought); just as a name expresses its sense, a "sentence *expresses* a thought" (Frege 1892, 32–4; 1918, 61). A thought is not a "subjective act but its objective content," and, as is the case for all sense, it is "capable of being common property of several thinkers" (1892, 32n). In a later essay called "The Thought" (*Der Gedanke*), Frege sharply distinguishes thoughts from anything psychological. Thoughts are "imperceptible by the senses," and the sentence is only "the perceptible garb" that clothes a thought (1918, 61). Thoughts, in fact, are independent of any subjective psychological properties and could exist and be true if there were no human beings (1918, 69). Consequently, strictly speaking human beings do not have thoughts the way they have sensations or representations. When thinking, however, human beings can "grasp" thoughts, although the thought remains distinct from the thinking of the thought (1918, 74). In grasping a thought, human beings think of something that is objective and independent of their or anyone else's psychological state. Moreover, insofar as objective, nonpsychological thoughts are the senses of declarative sentences, Frege removes the meaning of natural language from the realm of psychology.

Since Frege, it has become a common practice to use the English term "proposition" to refer to the objects of thoughts as well as the sense of a declarative sentence – that is, what Frege called a "thought" (Chierchia and McConnell-Ginet 1990, 58). An important advantage that the term "proposition" has over the English word "thought" is it avoids the strong psychological connotations that "thought" has. However, as Frege points out in his correspondence, his contemporaries still appear to use "proposition" ambiguously, either as a thought or the linguistic expression of a thought (1976, 118, 130, and 232).[30]

Frege also distinguishes thoughts or propositions from judgments. A person can have or express a thought without affirming it – for example, when asking a question. Hence the thought and what came to be called the various attitudes toward it, such as affirmation, questioning, or doubt, need to be distinguished, and for Frege a judgment is the affirmation or acknowledgment of a thought (1918, 62).[31] The linguistic expression of a judgment is an assertion or statement, in which a declarative sentence is used to state or assert the proposition that the sentence expresses. Frege laments the fact that in ordinary language there is no special sign that distinguishes the declarative sentence from the statement (1918, 62–3 and 62n). Such a sign would be like the judgment stroke in the *Begriffsschrift*, adding the "assertoric force" to the declarative sentence and turning it into a statement (1918, 63).

Function-Argument Structure

An extremely important feature of Frege's theory of propositions is his account of the structure of propositions, namely what has come to be known as the "function-argument structure" (Partee 1997, 27). Frege's insight was to use the mathematical notion of a function to analyze the structure of propositions and hence the meanings of sentences.

For Frege, a proposition is a structure of concepts, and following a suggestion made by Hermann Lotze in 1874, Frege develops the idea that concepts are like mathematical functions.[32] Although Frege used the idea of a function in his *Begriffsschrift*, there it is not clear whether functions in logic are supposed to be symbolic notations or what symbolic notations express. This confusion vanishes in a lecture

---

[30] The correspondence reveals an interesting misunderstanding between Frege and Russell. Russell failed to understand that for Frege thoughts were not subjective psychological entities (1976, 250–1), while Frege assumed that for Russell propositions are linguistic items because Russell understood propositions to be complexes that included what he called "terms" (1976, 118).

[31] Corresponding to a judgment that affirms content, one might suppose that there are also judgments that deny content. But Frege does not make such a distinction between affirmations and denials. To deny a proposition is simply to affirm its negation, according to Frege.

[32] Sluga (1980, 33 and 56–7) highlights the similarities on this issue, as well as others, between Lotze and Frege.

that Frege published in 1891 called "Function and Concept" (*Funktion und Begriff*), a year before "On Sense and Reference" appeared. In this lecture, Frege rigorously distinguishes between the expression of a function – Frege gives the example "$2 \cdot x^3 + x$" – and the function itself.

The function itself is a "law of correlation" (*Zuordnung*) that correlates or assigns objects to each other. In the simplest case – namely, a function of one argument – for every object that is the argument of the function, the function correlates with it a unique object (Frege 1904, 662). Of course, in the ordinary case functions are mathematical functions that correlate numbers. For example, the function x^2 correlates for every number the square of that number – for example, this function assigns the number 9 to the number 3. This function can be expressed as an equation, $y = x^2$, that makes the correlation explicit. The variable x is a placeholder for the names of numbers that can be arguments of the function, and y is the variable for the names of numbers that the function assigns to the argument. This latter assignment is the value of the function, so that we can speak of the value of a function for a given argument. Moreover, a function always correlates sets of numbers, for example, the set of real numbers, and so it can also be said that a function is a function from a set X to a set Y, where X consists of the arguments and Y of the values.

While Frege uses "*x*-range" and the "*y*-range" to refer to the sets of objects that can be the arguments and values of a function, today it is standard to refer to what Frege called the "*x*-range" as the *domain* of the function and the term "range" is limited to the set consisting of the values of the function.

Frege argues that there is no reason to limit functions only to numbers. He writes that it was found to be necessary to extend functions beyond the real numbers to include complex numbers, and he will go even further: "Not merely numbers, but objects in general, are now admissible; and here persons must assuredly be counted as objects" (1891, 17; also 137 and 1904, 661). "We have thus admitted objects without restriction as arguments and values of functions" (1891, 18).

Accordingly, a concept is a function that correlates sets of objects. Consider the sentence, taken from Frege, "Caesar conquered Gaul,"[33] and treat it as consisting of two parts: the name of an argument and a

---

[33] Frege treats this as a sentence with a one-place predicate whereas strictly speaking it should be treated as a relational sentence – that is, "conquered" should be treated as a two-place predicate. I follow Frege in order not to stray too far from his own account.

functional expression or, more simply, the name of a function (1891, 17–18). "Caesar" names the argument, namely the Roman general, and the predicate "conquered Gaul" is a functional expression. Thus the concept of *conquered Gaul* – that is, the meaning of the predicate "conquered Gaul" – is a function, according to Frege. This concept is a law of correlation that assigns to objects certain objects as values. The values that Frege takes to be the assignments in this case are peculiar. He assumes that truth-values are individual objects, so that True and False are objects that are assigned to objects by functions. In this example, the value of the function *conquered Gaul* for the argument Caesar is True. For the argument George Washington, the value is False, and so on.[34]

With these pieces in place, Frege is in a position to give an analysis of the meaning of predicates or what he also calls concept words. Predicates, such as the expression "conquered Gaul," are like proper names in that they have senses and denotations. The denotation is the concept *conquered Gaul*, which is a function, and the sense of the expression is the way in which this function is given. The complex of the function together with the argument – or what Frege also calls the "saturated function (1891; 1983, 129) – is a proposition or thought, and propositions, as we have seen, are the senses of declarative sentences. The denotations of declarative sentences, then, are the values of these functions, namely truth-values. "That is to say, if we complete the name of a concept with a proper name, we obtain a sentence whose sense is a thought; and this sentence has a truth-value as its denotation" (ibid.).

An important feature of Frege's use of functions is how he combines them with quantification. To yield a value, a function needs to be completed by an argument and a functional expression represents this with a variable – for instance, "x is mortal." This by itself is not a sentence, but it becomes a sentence, as we just saw, when the variable is substituted by a proper name, for example, "Socrates is mortal." It also becomes a sentence when the variable is bound by a quantifier, for example, "For all x (x is mortal)," that is, "Everything is mortal." Using the *Principia* notation already mentioned, this can be symbolized as "$(x)(Mx)$."

---

[34] It must be mentioned that for Frege some functions that are concepts do not assign truth-values to arguments – for example, the function named by the functional expression "the capital of x" assigns cities as values to arguments, such as "If we take the German Empire as the argument, we get Berlin as the value of the function" (1891, 18).

Function-Argument Analyses in Semantics

The function-argument analysis that Frege develops has played an important role in the development of semantics and theories of linguistic meaning in the twentieth century. A prominent early extension is Bertrand Russell's use of the function-argument analysis in his celebrated treatment of definite descriptions, which has been called "a paradigm of philosophy" (Ramsey 1931, 263n) and has certainly become a war horse in analytic philosophy of language.

A key component of Russell's account is a propositional function, which is like a Fregean function except that its value is not a truth-value. Instead, for Russell the values of propositional functions are propositions. Accordingly, the value of the function "x is mortal" for the argument Socrates is not the value True, as Frege believed, but the proposition that Socrates is mortal. Russell's views about the nature of propositions are not constant, but in a famous letter to Frege on this topic Russell maintains that the proposition that Mont Blanc is higher than 4,000 meters is a complex object of which "Mont Blanc itself is a constituent part" (Frege 1976, 250–1). It follows that the denotation of a declarative sentence is not a truth-value but a proposition, and it is the proposition that is either true or false. For Russell, this account has the advantage of avoiding the consequence of Frege's view that all true sentences denote the same thing.

Russell uses propositional functions to analyze the meaning of sentences with definite descriptions, such as "The author of *Waverly* was Scotch," as follows (Russell 1905; Russell and Whitehead 1910, 1:30–32). Although the surface structure of such sentences suggests that definite descriptions are names or what Russell calls "denoting phrases," in the logical structure of the propositions that these sentences denote, definite descriptions are not identifiable units. Definite descriptions disappear in the whole proposition. Let us use the language that Russell used in his original Theory of Descriptions:

1. The propositional function "x wrote *Waverly*" is not always false.
2. The propositional function "if x and y wrote *Waverly*, x and y are identical" is always true.
3. The propositional function "if x wrote *Waverly*, x was Scotch" is always true.

This terminology is cumbersome, and it also has the false consequence that someone who states "The author of *Waverly* was Scotch" is stating something about propositional functions, but Russell avoids this later in the *Principia Mathematica* with the use of quantifiers. With quantifiers, the analysis is expressed as follows:

> There is an x such that x wrote *Waverly*, for all y, if y wrote *Waverly*, $y = x$, and x was Scotch.

According to Russell, this expresses the proposition that the declarative sentence "The author of *Waverly* was Scotch" denotes. One advantage of this analysis, according to Russell, is evident when it is applied to meaningful declarative sentences that contain definite descriptions that do not have a denotation, for example, "the present king of France is bald." Russell's analysis of this sentence has the consequence that it is false because it is not the case that there is something that is now king of France.

Russell also uses the function-argument analysis in his treatment of classes. For instance, instead of characterizing the class of human beings extensionally simply in terms of its members, Russell characterizes it as the set of objects that, as arguments of the propositional function x is human (i.e., the function named by the propositional expression "x is human"), yield a true proposition. If we follow Frege and let truth-values instead of propositions be the values of propositional functions, then Russell's view can be stated very simply: the set of humans is the set of objects that as arguments of the function x is human yield the value True.

This suggested a way of extending the argument-function analysis to the semantic interpretation of language. An important contribution to this development is Alfred Tarski's definition of the concept of truth that allowed for formal treatments of the semantics of formal languages.[35] Tarski introduces the notion of a *sentential function*, namely an expression such as "x is white" or "x is greater than y" that turns into a sentence when the variables are replaced by names (1944, 352).[36] As Tarski points out, he is really not using the notion of a function in its mathematical sense because his sentential functions are not mappings

---

[35] Tarski's contributions to semantics were first presented by J. Łukasiewicz to the Warsaw Scientific Society in 1931. This was published in Tarski 1933 and translated into German with a postscript in Tarski 1936. The influential German translation was translated into English in Tarski 1956. Tarski acknowledges his debt to his teacher and dissertation adviser at the University of Warsaw, S. Leśniewski. An informal summary of Tarski's results is in Tarski 1944.

[36] Tarski treats sentences themselves as limit cases of sentential functions.

from argument values (1994, 5–6 and 95).[37] However, Tarski develops his definition of truth by introducing the concept of satisfaction, which is a relation between sequences of objects and sentential functions. Tarski pairs the variables of a language that occur in sentential functions as well as the objects that occur in sequences in such a way that each variable is assigned a unique object. Relative to an assignment of variables to objects, a sentential function – say, "x is white" – is satisfied by a sequence of objects just in case the object paired with the same integer as the variable x in the sentential function "x is white" is white. This is then generalized to sentences of a language. Roughly speaking, a sentence of a language – that is, a sentential function with no free variables – is true just in case it is satisfied by some sequence of objects.

The assignment of objects to variables of a language can be treated as a function from variables to objects. Accordingly, Tarski's treatment of satisfaction can be revised so that functions satisfy sentential functions. For instance, let there be a function V from variables to objects; then a sentential function "x is white" is satisfied by $V(x)$ just in case $V(x)$ is white.

Treating the assignment of objects to variables as a function suggests a more general strategy of treating the semantic interpretation of a language as a function from the grammatical expressions of that language to semantic values. In the simplest case, the sentences of a language are the arguments of this interpretation function, and truth-values are its values. Given an assignment of values to the atomic or simple sentences of a language $\mathfrak{L}$, the values of complex sentences can be generated. For instance, letting V be the functional expression for the interpretation function for $\mathfrak{L}$ and letting p be a variable for the sentences of $\mathfrak{L}$, we can define negation or $\sim$ as follows:

For any p of $\mathfrak{L}$, $V(\sim p)$ = TRUE just in case $V(p)$ = FALSE.

Rudolf Carnap's work on the semantics, published in 1947, suggested for the modal phrases such as "is necessary" and "is possible" further extensions of function-argument analysis. Carnap introduces the notion of a *state description*, that is "a complete description of a possible state of the universe" (1947, 9). More precisely, it is a set of sentences such that for every sentence of a language, it contains either the sentence or

---

[37] Accordingly, Carnap (1947, 5) uses the term "sentential matrix" instead of "sentential function."

its negation, but not both. This yields various distinct state descriptions and Carnap characterizes the *range* of a sentence as the set of state descriptions in which the sentence is true, and this range is the meaning of a sentence. A sentence is necessary, according to Carnap, just in case it is true in every state description. Because state descriptions are, in effect, models of a language, Carnap's account of necessity can be characterized as truth in all models for a language.

In the following decade, this procedure was generalized and enriched by extending the domain of function-argument analyses, primarily in the work of Saul Kripke (1959) and Stig Kanger (1957). State descriptions were replaced with possible worlds, or different ways things might have been, and these possible worlds are understood as elements of the models used in interpreting language. Grammatical sentences of a language are correlated with propositions, and a proposition is a function from possible worlds to truth-values. A necessary proposition, then, is one that is true in all possible worlds. Thus an interpretation for a language is a function that maps grammatical sentences of a language onto propositions, which in turn are functions from possible worlds to truth-values.

Tarski, Carnap, Kripke, and others who contributed to the development of formal semantics were primarily interested in formal, not natural, languages. Tarski in particular was emphatic that natural languages are not capable of being given a formal semantics. Nevertheless, his discussions as well as those of the other contributors to formal semantics, are filled with examples from ordinary languages, and a reader cannot help but think about trying to apply these formal approaches to natural languages. Donald Davidson and Richard Montague actually make this leap from formal semantics to natural languages. Davidson (1967) argues that Tarski's strategy for providing formal definitions of truth for a language can be extended to natural languages and developed as a theory of meaning for human language.[38] Montague (1970b and 1973) treats English as an interpreted formal system to influence and inspire work in linguistics as well as philosophy (Dowty, Wall, and Peters 1981; Chierchia and McConnell-Ginet 1990).[39]

---

[38] This is the programmatic underpinning of two important anthologies in the philosophy of language: Davidson and Harman 1972 and 1975.

[39] Montague (1968 and 1970a) was also instrumental in applying the function-argument analysis to the pragmatic aspects of natural language, making the contexts of the use of a sentence into arguments of functions into truth-values.

Davidson and Montague represent two diverging strategies for extending the formal treatment of natural language. Davidson is part of a tradition to naturalize the formal features of natural language. An important step in this naturalization is to embody formal structure in empirical linguistic phenomena, typically the sentence in use, rather than the proposition. Montague, on the other hand, belongs to a line that remains true to Frege's Platonism (see Church 1951). On this view, natural language is itself an abstract object – an interpreted formal system – that cannot be identified with the empirical manifestations of language in linguistic performances. Just as Frege's conceptual structure is an abstract object to be studied using a priori methods, as in mathematics, natural language is an abstract structure discovered by reason and intuition, not perception and induction (Katz 1985, 174). Whereas the Platonist approach preserves structure at the cost of separating it from actual linguistic activity, naturalism, as I argue in Chapter 7, fails to sustain the semantic structure of natural language.

Frege and Chomsky

The influence of function-argument analysis is not limited to semantics. A key strategy of formal approaches to semantics is to tie meaning to syntax in such a way that complex meanings are built out of simpler parts and the structure of meaning tracks the structure of the expressions that have the meaning. This is the principle of compositionality, which Frege in his later writings expressed as follows:

> If, then, we look upon thoughts as composed of simple parts, and take these in turn, to correspond to the simple parts of sentences, we can understand how a few parts of sentences can go to make up a great multitude of sentences. (1984, 390)

But if the meaning of a complex linguistic expression is a function of the meanings of its parts and the way these parts are combined, then semantics must rest on an account of how the expressions are combined to form more-complex expressions – that is, it will depend on the language's syntax. The syntactic rules for combining expressions must have enough order to map onto the semantic functions, and thus the syntactic rules themselves can be treated as functions.

Consequently, the strategy of treating a natural language as an interpreted formal system depends on natural language having sufficient structure to be treated syntactically as a formal system. This is the essence of Noam Chomsky's early contribution to linguistics. Building on Zellig Harris's insight that language is a set of sentences and a grammar "a set of instructions which generates the sentences of a language" (1954, 260), Chomsky develops the idea that the syntax of natural languages can be described as a formal system in much the same way that the syntax of artificial languages of mathematical logic was described.[40] The basic idea is simple. Treat the complex expressions of a language as values of functions that have simpler expressions for their arguments. These functions are syntactic operations, typically the concatenation of expressions. For instance, given two well-formed sentences p and q, a new well-formed sentence is formed when they are concatenated with *and* placed between them.

Chomsky describes the grammar of a language as a phrase structure [Σ, F], where Σ is a finite set of "initial strings" of a language and F is a finite set of "instruction formulas" of the form $X \rightarrow Y$, which is to be read as "rewrite X as Y" (1957, 29). The following is Chomsky's well-known simple example of such a set of formulas:

(i) *Sentence* → NP + VP
(ii) NP → T + N
(iii) VP → Verb + NP
(iv) T → *the*
(v) N → *man, ball*, etc.
(vi) V → *hit, took*, etc.

Using these rules, Chomsky "derives" a sentence from the repeated application of these instruction formulas and the initial strings, which include the words "*man*," "*ball*," "*hit*," and so on. Chomsky goes on to argue that such a phrase-structure grammar is inadequate and needs to be supplemented by transformational rules, but the function-argument analysis remains the same. Whereas the phrase-structure rules take strings as inputs to yield new strings, transformational rules take strings that are derivations as inputs.

An important feature of these functions is that they are recursive: their values can themselves be arguments of this function yielding new values. This recursive application of syntactic functions allows the generation of an infinite set of sentences on the basis of a finite base of sentences and

---

[40] Bach's (1989) contrast between the Chomsky thesis, namely that natural languages can be described as formal systems, and the Montague thesis, namely that they can also be described as interpreted formal systems, is very helpful.

rules. For Chomsky, recursive syntactic functions explain the "creativity of language," that is, a language user's competence to understand and produce new sentences – potentially an infinite number of sentences – on the basis of finite input (1957, 18–24; 1966, 29). In this way Chomsky unites the Fregean mathematical perspective on language with psychology. Whereas Frege's function-argument analysis primarily contributed to the view that language could be treated as a formal structure that was independent of human psychology, Chomsky showed how functions could be incorporated in psychology. The human mind, on this view, is not simply a causal structure of associated ideas but a formal system.

The difference between Frege and Chomsky is not as great as it first appears (Moravcsik 1981). Frege denies that the mind's only properties are natural or causal properties that are subject to investigation by the empirical sciences (Sluga 1980, 104–5). In addition to the mind's causal structure, the human mind is capable of grasping abstract objects, such as concepts and propositions, which are mind-independent. Once grasped, human beings are then able to think with concepts and propositions and also represent them sensibly, for example, in language. Once human beings think in terms of concepts and propositions, however, they are thinking in terms of objects that are not governed by natural or causal laws but by logical relations, such as entailment. It is also in this respect that the mind is independent of causal laws and subjective associations, and the study of these abstract objects is a formal study facilitated by the mind's intellectual capacity to grasp abstract objects and be guided by them.

This is what makes Frege an intellectualist in addition to a Platonist. Human thinking is not always subject to causal laws because sometimes human thinking is guided by abstract systems of rational rules that are not causal laws. But the same is true of Chomsky's conception of language (D'Agostino 1986, 114). Language is a "system of rules and principles that determine the formal and semantic properties of sentences" that "are not laws of nature" or causal laws but are subject to "purely formal investigation" (Chomsky 1976, 28; 1971, 33; and 1957, 12). As we just saw, these rules are functions, just as Frege understood the rules of formal systems. Moreover, this formal system is sharply distinguished from observable linguistic phenomena, namely linguistic performance. For Chomsky, language as a system of rules constitutes a speaker's "ideal...competence" that is quite distinct from the fragmented and unsystematic performance of human speech (1965, 4). "[I]t is obvious that the set of grammatical sentences" cannot be identified with any particular corpus of [observable] utterances obtained by the linguist in his field work" (1957, 15). What language users do is project fragmentary observed linguistic performances onto the system of grammatical sentences that defines their competence.

The primary difference is that whereas Frege is a Platonist for whom the system of concepts is an abstract object that exists independently of mind or any material object, for Chomsky language is one of the "abstract properties of brain mechanisms" (1988, 8). So, if Frege is a Platonist in that there are abstract systems that transcend nature, including the human brain, Chomsky is Aristotelian in that there are abstract systems but they are immanent in nature, that is, the human brain.[41]

An important dimension of Chomsky's position is that it is not clear how to "assimilate" the study of these abstract properties "to the mainstream of the natural sciences," but "it may turn out that these fundamental sciences must be modified to provide foundations for the abstract theories of complex systems, such as the human mind" (1988, 145–6). So far, "there is no definite concept of body" that allows us to formulate appropriate hypotheses that would allow us to assimilate the study of language to the study of the brain. For example, we do not know enough about the brain yet to be able to understand exactly what mechanisms of the brain exhibit or represent the abstract structures of language (1988, 144–5). A related problem is that language is "free from control of external stimuli or internal states" (1966, 29; 1988, 5 and 138). Unlike machines that are "compelled to act in a certain way under fixed environmental conditions," human beings, particularly in their linguistic behavior, are not compelled, but are "merely being *incited and inclined*" (1988, 139). We know from introspection and experiment, according to Chomsky, that our actions are "free and undetermined," but we do not know and it is possible that we are physically not able to know how this property is instantiated by material bodies (1988, 139 and 147). So for Chomsky, as for Frege, the study of abstract structures is autonomous of "the mainstream of the natural sciences."

From Leibniz to Frege

Major strategies for studying the formal structure of natural language, then, are developments of Frege's concept of the function-argument

---

[41] I am relying on the distinction between Platonic or transcendent realism and Aristotelian or immanent realism as drawn by Armstrong 1978.

analysis. But if we look backward from the milestone set by Frege's philosophy of language, we see that his work belongs to the tradition of Leibniz, namely the line of thought rooted in Scholasticism that sees language as a system structured by the categories of logic. Frege himself isolates Leibniz for praise, stating that "Leibniz in his writings strew such an abundance of seeds of ideas that in this respect hardly any other can measure up to him" (1983, 9). He characterizes his own *Begriffsschrift* as a revival of Leibniz's project of a *lingua characteristica* [*universalis*], that is, a language that can explicitly and precisely represent the structure of all possible conceptual content (1983, 10–12). But as Frege notes in his preface to the *Begriffsschrift*, his own project is much more modest. Whereas Leibniz tried to design a language that would express all possible content, Frege limits himself to logical form, that is, the content that is relevant for logical validity.

Providing a link between Frege and Leibniz were German writers on logic who belonged to the generation of Frege's professors. This group included August Trendelenburg, whose main work was called *Logical Investigations*, and who wrote an essay "On Leibniz's Project of a Universal Characteristic," which is Frege's only reference for the discussion of Leibniz in the preface to the *Begriffsschrift*. In fact, the term "conceptual script" (*Begriffsschrift*) is drawn from Trendelenburg, and it is noteworthy that in this preface he refers to his conceptual script as one among many. For instance, he writes that "the *Begriffsschrift* offered here adds a new" realization to "the Leibnizian conception," the languages of arithmetic, geometry and chemistry being older realizations (1874, vi). Also, Frege's discussion of Leibniz repeats Trendelenburg's claim that Leibniz's project in its complete generality is too ambitious for now, but that a more gradual and limited approach that first pays attention only to the "formal side of thinking" can come closer to achieving Leibniz's aims (Trendelenburg 1867, 26).

Another important link between Leibniz and Frege is the philosopher Rudolph Hermann Lotze (1817–81), whose *Logik* (1874) Frege read and commented on early in his career before he wrote the *Begriffsschrift* (Dummett 1991b, 65–78) and who also taught at the University of Göttingen where he was one of Frege's professors. Frege's colleague at Jena, Bruno Bauch,[42] in an essay called "Lotze's Logic and Its Significance in German Idealism" (1918), includes Frege in the circle of people influenced by Lotze. Bauch's essay was published in the first issue of the

---

[42] Bauch (1877–1942) is a neo-Kantian who became professor of philosophy in Jena in 1911 and was Rudolf Carnap's thesis adviser.

journal *Contributions to the Philosophy of German Idealism*, and it was immediately followed by Frege's essay "The Thought," suggesting that the essay was intended as an introductory essay setting the context for Frege's contribution (Sluga 1980, 192n47). Bauch highlights Lotze's critique of psychologism, particularly his view that logic is independent of psychology; the tie between logic and mathematics, particularly Lotze's suggestion that concepts are functions; and Lotze's sharp distinctions between thought and experience and between the objective content or meaning of thought and the subjective thinking.

Such comparisons between Frege and Lotze, one of the most widely discussed philosophers in Germany during the decades prior to World War I but who has become the most "pillaged" philosopher of the nineteenth century (Passmore 1966, 49), have been subject to harsh criticism. Although it is granted that there might be some relevant points of contact, any claims that Frege was aware of and encouraged or stimulated by these points of contact early in his own development are treated as immodest. The reasons for this are as follows. Although Frege read and commented on Lotze's *Logik* early in his career before he wrote the *Begriffsschrift*, Frege does not refer to Lotze, and Lotze's writing is not rigorous enough to have influenced Frege (Dummett 1991b, 77–8). That Frege attended a course Lotze taught in Göttingen is completely irrelevant because this was a course on the philosophy of religion (Baker and Hacker 1984, 6–7). Finally, Bauch's essay in *Contributions to the Philosophy of German Idealism* in which Bauch ties Frege to Lotze is not useful evidence because Bauch "may well have exaggerated the extent of Lotze's influence on Frege," Frege "can hardly have been sympathetic to the goals of the new journal," and he probably was not familiar with its intended readership (Beaney 1996, 306n34).

These criticisms are not convincing. First, with the exception of Leibniz, it is Frege's practice to mention people primarily for criticism. He does find some praise for Kant, but it is really only an afterthought in order to avoid "the reproach of picking petty quarrels" (1978, 101). Second, there is no reason to assume that only rigorous writing could have influenced Frege. Clearly, Lotze's *Logik* was rigorous enough for Frege to read and comment on. It is also important to note that Frege appears to be a very selective reader who sought out the ideas in a work that related to his specific interests. So given that Lotze was one of his professors and one of the well-known contemporary philosophers writing on logic, it is likely that Frege read Lotze's *Logik* as a textbook to get an overview of contemporary tendencies and for the "big ideas" rather than for the full details of Lotze's system.

Third, it was certainly Lotze's general outlook that attracted Frege to Lotze's lectures, most likely Lotze's commitment to the natural and exact sciences combined with a rejection of materialism, and not the particular topic Lotze was covering in his courses during Frege's time in Göttingen. The typical German university student often chose to attend lectures on account of the person giving the lectures rather than the specific topic on which this person happened to be working. Moreover, Lotze's lectures could have included a substantial methodological discussion, including an extensive critique of empiricism and psychologism. This might also have covered some of the formal issues associated with the concept of God, such as infinity and necessity, as well as the nature of our knowledge of abstract objects. Of course, without knowing anything about the contents of Lotze's course, all this is a matter of speculation, but this is equally true of the argument that Lotze's course was completely irrelevant to Frege's development.

Fortunately, the content of Lotze's lectures on the philosophy of religion were captured in the notes of the mathematician Aurel Voss, who attended Lotze's course in 1867, a few years before Frege, and is credited with first discovering in 1880 the so-called Bianchi Identities that Einstein used to develop the field equations of general relativity. As Voss's notes show, Lotze's course on the philosophy of religion attracted mathematicians because Lotze focused on formal topics in the philosophy of religion. He limits the philosophy of religion to those topics that can be treated rationally and scientifically and begins his course with a discussion of the ontological, cosmological, and teleological arguments for God's existence.

Finally, it certainly is possible that Bauch exaggerated the extent of Lotze's influence on Frege, but there is no direct evidence that he did. It is more likely that Bauch had the insight into Frege's thought that is available to a colleague, and it is certain that Frege never publicly repudiated the claims Bauch made about Lotze's influence. It is also very unreasonable to think that Frege did not know the intended readership of the new journal. This journal was the official publication of the new German Philosophical Society (Deutsche Philosophische Gesellschaft), cofounded in 1917 by Bauch and of which Frege requested to become a member in 1919. Frege then corresponded with Bauch, as well as the other founder of the society, Arthur Hoffman, sending Bauch several manuscripts. In addition to "The Thought," Frege published two more studies in this journal, "The Negation" (1918) and "Compounded Thoughts" (1923), and apparently asked about the possible publication of Wittgenstein's *Tractatus* in the *Contributions to the Philosophy of German Idealism*! Incidentally, the aims of the journal – "the cultivation, deepening, and preservation of ... philosophy ... in the spirit of the German idealism that was founded by Kant and continued by Fichte" – were clearly stated in the first issue of the journal, and these did not stop Frege from continued collaboration with the journal and its editors. Clearly, Frege had some basic sympathies with the aims of this journal.

The term "idealism" is a source of confusion for English-speaking and analytically trained philosophers who usually do not clearly distinguish German idealism from other forms of idealism, a distinction that is very clearly made in the traditional philosophical curriculum at a German university. Sluga (1980) is quite right that it is a fundamental mistake to associate idealism in Germany with psychologism. German idealism explicitly distinguished itself from other forms of idealism, such as Berkeley's subjective idealism or even Kant's own version of transcendental idealism, and tied itself to what came to be known, following Hegel, as absolute idealism (Guyer 2000). This form of idealism was revived in Germany in the latter third of the nineteenth century as a reaction to the naturalism, empiricism, and materialism of German philosophy in the period that immediately followed Hegel's death. As Sluga argues, Frege is part of this reaction, and Frege himself shows clear awareness in the ambiguity of the term "idealism." He qualifies the term when he is referring to the various forms of subjective or psychologistic idealism. The idealism he rejects is "the idealism of Berkeley" (Frege 1983, 115), "epistemological idealism" (*erkenntnistheoretische Idealismus*) (1983, 141, 155, and 250), and "extreme idealism" (1983, 156).[43]

Frege, then, stands in the tradition of Leibniz not only on the basis of overlapping aims but on the basis of influence. That there was some degree of influence from Lotze, who after all was one of the two philosophy professors Frege had and the only one who had written explicitly on logic, does not in the least bit detract from the significance or originality of Frege's contributions. It only detracts from the romantic ideal of Frege as the lonely genius creating his philosophy ex nihilo without any historical context. This is not how people work and think. The

---

[43] For more discussion on Frege and Lotze, see Gabriel 2002.

greatness of a work, in any case, does not consist of the occasional insight, no matter how deep, but in the clarity of vision informed by sufficient detail. Even if it were the case that Frege was directly inspired by Lotze's idea to treat concepts as functions, it was Frege, not Lotze, who gave that idea the content it needed to become a useful and lasting tool in logic, philosophy of language, and linguistics.

SEVEN

◆

From Silence to Assent
Wittgenstein, Carnap, and Quine

Frege, who was turning sixty-three in November 1911, was visited that fall by a twenty-two-year-old Austrian who was neglecting his studies in aeronautical engineering at the University of Manchester. While studying aeronautics, Ludwig Wittgenstein had become interested in the nature of mathematical proof, which led him to Russell's *Principles of Mathematics*. In this book Russell aimed to popularize the project he and Whitehead pursued in the *Principia Mathematica*, namely to show that mathematics is reducible to a few logical principles. The *Principles* also contained something new, namely an appendix devoted to "The Logical and Arithmetical Doctrines of Frege" (Russell 1903). While the *Principles* were being prepared for print, Russell discovered that Frege had already devoted a lifetime of work to the project of logicism, and so he decided quickly to study Frege's work and write an appendix for the book. This appendix brought Frege's neglected work into the limelight and to the attention of Wittgenstein.

Little is known about Wittgenstein's visit in Jena except Wittgenstein's comment that Frege "wiped the floor" with him. Frege recommended that Wittgenstein return to England and study with Russell at Cambridge University, which he did. Nevertheless, Frege and his works left a lasting impression on Wittgenstein, as Wittgenstein himself suggests in the preface to the *Tractatus Logico-Philosophicus*, published ten years after his meeting with Frege, when he writes, "I am indebted to Frege's magnificent [*Großartig*] works."[1]

---

[1] Dummett does not exaggerate when he writes that "Wittgenstein was soaked in Frege's writings and Frege's thoughts," and "Frege is very nearly the only one whom he quotes with approval" (1991b, 237).

Wittgenstein is indeed indebted to Frege's work, particularly his first published work – and the only book to be published during his lifetime – the *Tractatus*. Relying on the methods of mathematical logic and function-argument analysis, Wittgenstein develops first the view that language is a system of representations with a compositional structure such that the meaning of the whole is a function of the meaning of its simpler parts. Moreover, like Frege, Wittgenstein aims to divest his studies from anything psychological, and accordingly the meaning of language is not something psychological but a relationship between language and reality. Third, Wittgenstein also distinguishes the logical form of language, which he is aiming to exhibit in the *Tractatus*, and its surface or "outward form of the clothing," which "is not designed to reveal the form of the body" (Wittgenstein 1922, 4.002). Finally, for Wittgenstein, an understanding of logical form also serves a larger purpose – namely, to solve, or rather dissolve, philosophical problems because "the reasons why these problems are posed is that the logic of our language is misunderstood" (1922, preface).[2]

Yet the *Tractatus* also breaks with the tradition of Frege. Wittgenstein breaks with Frege's Platonism. First, for Wittgenstein there is no realm of logical objects or facts that are named or described by the propositions of logic. Instead the truths of logic are tied to the syntax of propositions. Second, Wittgenstein transforms Frege's thoughts or propositions understood as abstract, disembodied objects that are independent of language into significant sentences in a language. Third, Wittgenstein sets out on a path that undermines the very thing he appears to be doing in the *Tractatus*, namely presenting a theory of the form and content of human language. Wittgenstein's rejection of theory in the *Tractatus* anticipates the fractured conception of language that marks the work of Quine and Davidson, as well as the mature Wittgenstein's work in the *Philosophical Investigations* and the postmodernism of Derrida. This fracturing, I argue, is endemic to naturalizing logical form.

Whereof One Cannot Speak

The *Tractatus* is a formidable and austere work of numbered sentences that appear to describe the structure of any proposition. At the same

---

[2] For a discussion of how Wittgenstein aims to dissolve philosophical problems in the *Tractatus* and whether he aims to state or exhibit anything in the *Tractatus*, see the essays on the *Tractatus* in Crary and Read 2000, including Hacker's (2000, 353–88) more traditional reading of the *Tractatus*.

time, what the *Tractatus* appears to describe is something that according to Wittgenstein in the *Tractatus* "*cannot* be said" using language but only "shown" (1922, 4.1212). It is one of the paradoxical theses of the *Tractatus* that "anyone who understands me eventually recognizes them as nonsensical" (1922, 6.54). Language itself is one of the things Wittgenstein has in mind when he writes in the final sentence of the *Tractatus* "Whereof one cannot speak, thereof one must be silent" (1922, 7).

The central feature of language about which no theory is possible, according to the *Tractatus*, is logical form. "A proposition can represent the whole of reality ... but it cannot represent logical form" (1922, 4.12). A proposition can "mirror," "show," "display," and "reflect" the logical form of propositions, but this is not the same thing as stating what the logical form is (1922, 4.121–4.1212). Thus even apparent formal facts, such as that two propositions contradict each other or that one proposition follows from another, are not capable of being described but only are shown or exhibited by propositions (1922, 4.1211). A proposition shows its logical form without stating what its form is, just as a person can manifest or display happiness without making a statement that one is happy. Of course, in the case of happiness, a person could also express happiness by making the statement that one is happy, but in the case of logical form, according to Wittgenstein, there are no propositions about logical form.

Wittgenstein first introduces the notion of logical form in the ontological section of the *Tractatus*, namely propositions 1 through 2.063, where Wittgenstein outlines an ontology of simple, individual, and independent objects that can be combined or configured into various states of affairs. In the *Tractatus* form is tied to possibility, and the different ways in which an object can be combined with other objects to form different states of affairs is the logical form of an object (1922, 2.0141–2.0233). So logical form is not something that belongs only to language. In fact, according to Wittgenstein logical form is something that language and reality have in common, and it is in virtue of this shared form that language can represent reality (1922, 4.12).

A guiding idea of the *Tractatus* is that a proposition is a picture and a picture is a state of affairs in which the elements of the picture are arranged or concatenated in a certain way. Each element of the picture represents an object and the fact that the elements of the picture are arranged in a certain way represents or means that those objects for which the elements stand are combined in a specific way (1922, 2.15). In the *Notebooks, 1914–1916*, which Wittgenstein kept before writing the *Tractatus*, he gives an example of various blocks representing different cars, and the fact that the blocks are arranged in a certain way represents the way the cars were arranged at a scene of an accident (1961, 7). The arrangement of blocks is a state of affairs with a certain structure (e.g., that one block is behind another one) and the state of affairs also has a certain structure (e.g., that one car is behind another), and the one state of affairs represents the other.

It represents the other in virtue of this common structure. For Wittgenstein, a picture must have something "in common with reality in order to be able to represent it" (1922, 4.12). What a picture and what is depicted have in common is not simply the actual arrangement or structure of the elements in each but a form. The elements of the picture could be arranged in different ways – for example, one block can be next to another or on top of another – and these various ways in which the elements of a picture could be arranged is the "pictorial form of the picture" (1922, 2.15). Similarly, the elements of reality also have a form because there are various possible ways in which they could be arranged, and for Wittgenstein the pictorial form is also "the possibility that things are related to one another in the same way as the elements of the picture" (1922, 2.151). Consequently, the pictorial form also includes what Wittgenstein calls the "pictorial relationship," namely the correlation between the individual elements of the picture (e.g., the blocks) and the depicted objects (e.g., the cars).

Ordinary pictures are iconic. For instance, the blocks of wood arranged to depict an accident is an iconic picture of the accident because the picture and the accident share spatial characteristics. Moreover, the various ways in which the blocks can be arranged in space correspond to various ways in which cars can be arranged in space. According to Wittgenstein, all pictures are logical pictures, but some pictures, such as propositions, are purely logical pictures. The only characteristic that a purely logical picture and what it depicts have in common is that they are both states of affairs in which objects are combined together and form a unity. Accordingly, logical form is the limit case of pictorial form where what the shared form of a picture and what is depicted have in common is that the various ways in which the elements of the picture can be arranged correspond to the various ways in which the elements of states of affairs can be arranged. No other shared properties are required in a logical picture.

A logical picture of facts is a thought,[3] a thought is a proposition (*Satz*) with a sense, and the totality of propositions is a language (1922, 3, 4 and 4.001).[4] A *Satz* in ordinary German discourse is a sentence or statement, and Wittgenstein's use of this term does not depart sharply from this ordinary usage. As it was for Mill and Humboldt, for Wittgenstein a proposition is a linguistic entity. "[A] proposition," he writes in the *Tractatus*, "is a propositional sign in its projective relation to the world" (1922, 3.12). A propositional sign, in turn, is the "perceptible sign of a proposition (spoken or written, etc.)" and "[w]hat constitutes a propositional sign is that in it its elements (the words) stand in a determinate relation to one another" (1922, 3.14). Accordingly, to have a thought is to have a proposition, which includes a propositional sign, which in turn consists of elements arranged in a determinate manner. Consequently, something that thinks is a composite. A thinker needs to have or include the elements out of which propositions are composed. Wittgenstein is well aware of this consequence; he explicitly recognizes that on his view there is no such thing as a simple, noncomposite Cartesian soul (1922, 5.5421).

These elements are essential because "a proposition is a picture of reality" (1922, 4.01, 4.021), and as such it needs to have elements that are arranged in a such a way that it can depict or, in this case, describe a state of affairs. Specific configurations of elements in a proposition represent specific states of affairs. Wittgenstein illustrates his view as follows: "Instead of, 'The complex sign "*aRb*" says that *a* stands to *b* in relation *R*' we ought to put '*That* "*a*" stands to "*b*" in a certain relation says *that aRb*'" (1922, 3.1432). For instance, the sentence "Aristotle tutored Alexander" is not to be treated as a complex name that represents that Aristotle stands to Alexander in the relation of *tutoring*.

---

[3] "Thought" (*Gedanke*) in the *Tractatus* is not a psychological term. Wittgenstein is following Frege's use of the term in "The Thought" (1918), where thoughts are distinguished from psychological states.

[4] Max Black juxtaposes these propositions and emphasizes that "it was one of Wittgenstein's distinctive innovations to consider thoughts only as embodied in what he calls the 'significant proposition [*der sinnvolle Satz*]'" (1964, 7; also see 100 and 159). It should be noted, however, that Wittgenstein also writes that "[i]n a proposition a thought finds an expression that can be perceived by the senses" (1921, 3.1). This suggests that a proposition is only a species of thought, and also that there may be logical pictures that are not perceived by the senses. Also, compare this statement to Frege's statement that "The thought, in itself, is immaterial, clothes itself in the material garment of a sentence and thereby becomes comprehensible to us" (1918, 60).

Instead, the syntactic *fact* that the name "Aristotle" is to the left of "tutored" and "Alexander" is to the right of "tutored" represents the *fact* that Aristotle tutored Alexander, and the syntactic fact represents the other in virtue of a form that both facts have in common.

Wittgenstein's reasons why pictures cannot depict pictorial form are that a "picture represents its subject from a position outside it" and a picture's "standpoint is its pictorial form" (1922, 2.173). In other words, a picture and its subject must be distinct, and what makes a picture into a picture is that it has a pictorial form, that is, the pictorial form is an essential part of the picture. This means that if a picture were to depict its pictorial form, the picture would have to be able to depict itself, but this is impossible on account of the assumption that a picture represents its subject from a position external to its subject.

Because propositions are also pictures of reality, the argument extends to propositions: "Propositions can represent the whole of reality, but they cannot represent what they must have in common with reality in order to be able to represent it – logical form" (1922, 4.12). Propositions "reflect," "mirror," "show," or "display" their logical form, but they cannot "represent" or "express" it (1922, 4.121). "What *can* be shown, *cannot* be said," Wittgenstein writes (1922, 4.1212). The reason Wittgenstein gives parallels the argument he gave for pictures. "In order to be able to represent logical form," he argues, "we should be able to station ourselves with propositions somewhere outside logic, that is to say outside the world" (1922, 4.12). Because logical form is a structure that propositions have in common with reality or the world, to represent this structure, Wittgenstein maintains, a proposition would have to be outside of or distinct from logical form. Because logical form is also the form of the world – "logic pervades the world," he writes (1922, 5.61) – this would also mean that propositions about logical form would be outside of or distinct from the world, and this is not possible. "The world," as Wittgenstein asserts at the beginning of the *Tractatus*, "is all that is the case" (1922, 1).

Saying Nothing

Wittgenstein's argument about the inability of pictures and propositions to depict pictorial and logical form involves an ambiguity. The fact that a proposition p cannot describe its own logical form does not entail that no proposition can describe the logical form of p. More generally, as Russell argues in the concluding paragraph of his preface to the first

English translation of the *Tractatus*, even though "every language has, as Mr Wittgenstein says, a structure concerning which, *in the language*, nothing can be said... there may be another language dealing with the structure of the first language" (Wittgenstein 1922, xxii). This distinction between object language and metalanguage, developed by Tarski (1933) and Carnap (1942), is a foundation of contemporary semantic theory.

However, Wittgenstein has reasons for rejecting this strategy. One argument he seems to suggest is that a description of the logical form of a language will itself rely on the very same logical form that is to be described. For example, descriptions of the predicate form "x is F" will themselves rely on this form (1922, 3.333, 4.041, 4.1211, and 6.123).[5] A key assumption of this argument is that forms cannot be stratified so that, for example, the form "x is F" in the object language is distinguished from the form "x is F" in the metalanguage.

Another reason in the *Tractatus* for rejecting this strategy relies on its key assumption that propositions are possible only because there are objects and names for those objects (1922, 4.0312). All propositions can be analyzed into simple or elementary propositions, and every elementary proposition is a configuration or concatenation of names (1922, 3.202–3.21 and 4.22–4.221). But "[a] name means [*bedeutet*] an object" and there is no other kind of meaning for names (1922, 3.203, 3.3). So if there were no objects, there would be no meaningful names, and without meaningful names, there would be no propositions.

A proposition by definition represents something – that is, it has sense (*Sinn*) (1922, 3.1–3.12). What an elementary proposition represents is completely determined by the concatenation of names that make up the simple proposition, and this concatenation corresponds to or represents something (1922, 3.21–3.23). A proposition is not just "a blend of words," Wittgenstein writes, "[j]ust as a theme in music is not a blend of notes," but instead it is a fact, namely that the names in a proposition are combined as they are, and this fact expresses the sense of a proposition (1922, 3.14–3.142). What these concatenations of names represent are possible states of affairs. The sense of an elementary proposition, in Wittgenstein's words, is "a projection of a possible situation," that is, a representation of a possible state of affairs (1922, 3.11). This account of the sense of a simple proposition exactly parallels his account of the sense of a picture. A picture represents "a possibility of existence and

---

[5] For this interpretation, see Pears 1987, 143, and Carruthers 1989, 61–4.

Saying Nothing 197

non-existence of states of affairs" (1922, 2.201), it represents this possibility "by means of its pictorial form," and "[w]hat a picture represents is its sense [*Sinn*]" (1922, 2.22–2.221).

The possibility of states of affairs, however, depends on the existence of objects. For Wittgenstein, "objects make up the substance of the world," and one thing this means is that "[o]bjects contain the possibility of all situations," that is, states of affairs (1922, 2.021 and 2.014). Wittgenstein is very vague about how objects contain possibilities, but he does write that the "possibility of its occurring in states of affairs is the form of an object," suggesting that the way in which an object can be combined or configured with other objects constitutes the nature of an object (1922, 2.0141). These objects, by the way, are not ordinary physical objects. For instance, on their own these objects do not have any material properties. Space, time, color, and all other material properties are configurations of objects, that is, states of affairs (1922, 2.0231–2 and 2.0251). What objects are in themselves are simply bundles or loci of possibility.

In sum, objects constitute all possible states of affairs, and the sense of all propositions depends on the fact that they can be analyzed into simple propositions that depict or describe these states of affairs in virtue of the fact that they are combinations of names of these objects. In the *Tractatus*, the root of the problem with semantic theory is that "there are no 'logical objects' or 'logical constants'" (1922, 4.441). In fact, Wittgenstein describes it as the "fundamental idea" of the *Tractatus* that logical constants such as "and," "or," "not," "for all," and "some" are not names of objects (1922, 4.0312).[6] Accordingly, there can be no propositions about logical facts. *Pace* Russell and Frege, who believed that there was a realm of logical objects and facts described by logic, for Wittgenstein propositions of logic do not describe any states of affairs. General logical propositions, such as the laws of non-contradiction ($\sim(p$ *and* $\sim p)$) or excluded middle (p *or* $\sim p$) and particular applications of the laws of logic such as "Either it is raining or it is not raining," do not describe anything.

Accordingly, "logic is not a body of doctrine" and "the propositions of logic say nothing" and "lack sense" (1921, 6.13, 6.11, and 4.461). Any theory that makes it appear that these propositions have content

---

[6] Wittgenstein gives only one explicit argument for this claim. He argues that the various equivalencies of logical constants – for example, $p \leftrightarrow \sim\sim p$ and $p \rightarrow q \leftrightarrow \sim p \vee q$ – show that they cannot be names of objects (1921, 5.4–5.441).

and are about something in the way that the propositions of natural science are about something, Wittgenstein maintains, is false (1922, 6.11–6.111). So, for instance, Frege's philosophy of logic, according to which "not" is the name of a function from truth-values of propositions to truth-values, or Russell's view according to which logic is a science of the most abstract forms of reality, are both false.

Instead, all logical propositions are tautologies and tautologies are not really combinations of names that determine the meaning of propositions (1922, 6.1 and 4.66). Either they are combinations of variables and logical constants, as in the case of *p or ~p*, or they are combinations of names where the meaning and sense of the combination is irrelevant to the truth of the proposition. For example, in the tautology "Either it is raining or it is not raining," the meaning of the individual signs in "It is raining" as well as the sense of the whole combination of signs "It is raining" plays no role in the tautology. Consequently, tautologies do not correspond to "determinate combinations of objects" and "are not pictures of reality" (1922, 4.66 and 4.462).

"It is the peculiar mark of logical propositions that one can recognize that they are true from the symbol alone, and this fact contains in itself the whole philosophy of logic," and Wittgenstein outlines a method for calculating just on the basis of the proposition's structural properties whether or not it is a tautology (1922, 6.113, 6.1203, and 6.126). Nonlogical propositions, like the propositions of natural science, do not have this mark: their truth or falsity "*cannot* be recognized from the proposition alone" (1921, 6.113). To recognize their truth or falsity requires a comparison with reality in order to see whether they agree with it or not.

No Expressible Syntax

If logic deals with the structural properties of propositions, then perhaps the fact that there are no special logical objects and states of affairs need not be an obstacle to describing logical form after all. Perhaps logic does describe states of affairs. It describes the syntactic structures of propositions: the names and their configurations that constitute propositions. Consequently, a metalanguage that can describe the structure of an object language will capture its logical form because there is nothing more to logical form than the structure of propositions. However, this strategy is also unavailable to Wittgenstein in the *Tractatus*. In order to describe propositional structure, a metalanguage would have to contain propositions about the syntax of the object language, but, as Carnap put it, for Wittgenstein "there is no expressible syntax" (1934, 208; 1937, 282).

Propositions about the structure of language must contain predicates that designate the formal properties of language. At the very least, it must have predicates such as "x is a proposition," "x is a name," "x is a variable," "x is a logical constant," "x is a predicate," and so on. But these sorts of predicates are not proper predicates, and so propositions of this sort are, like the propositions of logic, nonsense. However, they are worse off than logical propositions because, while logical propositions at least show or exhibit an appropriate structure, propositions about formal structure "neither say nor show anything" (Hacker 1989, 25). This is the fate not only of propositions that aim to describe the structure of language but of propositions about the logical structure of the world as well. Propositions with predicates such as "x is an object," "x is a number," "x is a function," or "x is a state of affairs" also neither say nor show anything, which has devastating consequences for philosophy.

A proper predicate, such as "x is red" is a propositional function whose values are all the propositions that are formed when the variable x is replaced with a name.[7] Accordingly, that some object satisfies this predicate, say the tomato on the counter, can be described with the proposition "The tomato on the counter is red." But that something satisfies a formal predicate cannot be expressed in a proposition because a formal predicate is not a propositional function.[8] For example, there

---

[7] This does not mean that a proposition consists of a single name, which would conflict with Wittgenstein's claim that every elementary proposition is "a concatenation of names" (1921, 4.22). The function "x is red" can also be treated as a name of an object, and hence an elementary proposition that is the value of this function can be seen as a concatenation of two names of objects. There is significant debate about what objects are in the *Tractatus*. Some argue that properties and relations are objects for the early Wittgenstein (Hacker 1989, 67–71), some deny this (Carruthers 1989, 108–19), while others claim he remains neutral (Pears 1987, 137–9).

[8] I depart from Wittgenstein's actual terminology here because it is more complex than necessary. In this discussion, he introduces the term "formal concept," which otherwise does not play a role in the *Tractatus*. So at this point in the discussion Wittgenstein is discussing formal properties, formal concepts of those properties, and the propositional functions that express formal properties. Accordingly, Wittgenstein writes, "[w]hen something falls under a formal concept,... this cannot be expressed by means of a proposition," because "formal concepts cannot be represented by means of a function, as concepts proper can" (1921, 4.126).

are no names that can replace the variables in "x is a proposition" or "x is an object" and form a well-formed proposition.

To understand why Wittgenstein believes this, it helps to dwell on his notion of a formal property. Wittgenstein maintains that all objects and states of affairs have certain formal properties, which he also calls "internal properties" and "structural properties" (1922, 4.122). These are the features of objects or states of affairs that are necessary or essential to it: "A property is internal if it is unthinkable that its object should not possess it" (1922, 4.123). In the case of objects, the formal property is simply its form, which is, as we saw earlier, "[t]he possibility of its occurring in states of affairs" (1922, 2.0141).

These formal properties, however, cannot be depicted or described by propositions, and although Wittgenstein does not argue for this claim, it seems that he is assuming that the form of an object or state of affairs is itself not an object or state of affairs. For instance, the possibility that an object can be combined with another object is not itself an object or state of affairs that can be named or described. Instead, this formal property is exhibited by parallel formal or structural properties of propositions (1922, 4.124). "The expression for a formal property is a feature of certain symbols" (1922, 4.126). For example, the formal feature of objects that only in combination with other objects form states of affairs is shown by the fact that only in combination with other names does a name form a proposition. But these formal properties of propositions – the ways in which names and propositions can be combined – are also not capable of being described, according to Wittgenstein. After all, propositions are states of affairs, and so the formal property of a proposition is itself the formal property of a state of affairs.

An example Wittgenstein discusses in the *Tractatus* is the predicate "x is an object." What shows or exhibits what this predicate attempts to express is simply the individual variable: "[T]he variable name 'x' is the proper sign for the pseudo-concept *object*" (1922, 4.1271). So the proposition "There is an object on the table" does not mean that there is something that has the property of being an object and being on the table, but instead "is an object" in "There is an object" has the very same meaning as "is something" in "There is something," and this just is a variable expression that can be expressed as "There is an x." In the symbolism of mathematical logic, this is made explicit by symbolizing "There is an object" or "There is something" as "x."

Similarly, "x is a proposition" aims to express a property, but actually is nonsense, according to Wittgenstein (1922, 5.5351). What this predicate aims to express is actually shown or exhibited by the propositional variable p, for example, when stating propositions of logic such as $\sim p \ v \ p$. This is also all there is to being a proposition, namely a value of propositional variables, and to be the value of a propositional variable is neither an object nor a state of affairs.

So although it is exhibited whenever a proposition is used as the value of a propositional variable,[9] the form of a proposition can neither be named nor represented. Any attempt to speak about propositions and their formal structure, then, is doomed to being nonsense, and for this reason Wittgenstein believes there is no ascent to a metalanguage that will permit a description of formal structure. Formal structure in Wittgenstein's *Tractatus* is among the things that "cannot be articulated." He adds: "These *manifest* themselves; they are what is mystical" (1922, 6.522).

Because the *Tractatus* is devoted to the topic of the logical form of language, it aims to articulate what cannot be articulated. This is the fate not just of the *Tractatus* but of all of philosophy. Only the natural sciences describe the world, and "[p]hilosophy is not one of the natural sciences" (1922, 4.11–4.111). Philosophy shares the fate of logic: it too "is not a body of doctrine" and it "does not result in 'philosophical propositions'" (1922, 4.112). Instead, it is an activity. "The correct method in philosophy," Wittgenstein writes at the end of the *Tractatus*, "would really be ... to say nothing except what can be said, i.e., propositions of natural science – i.e., something that has nothing to do with philosophy – and then, whenever someone else wanted to say something metaphysical, to demonstrate to him that he had failed to give a meaning to certain signs in his propositions" (1922, 6.53). Philosophy, then, is limited to a critique of language, but it has to perform this critique without saying anything about the logical form of language!

Philosophy as Syntax

Wittgenstein's account of logical propositions in terms of the formal properties of language and the extension of this approach to all propositions that contain formal concepts had a tremendous influence on the

---

[9] In general, for Wittgenstein a "formal concept is given immediately any object falling under it is given" (1921, 4.12721). Here "object" (*Gegenstand*) is used loosely and not in the technical sense. What Wittgenstein has in mind, I believe, is that once a variable and its values are given, then ipso facto the formal concept is given.

logical positivists and subsequent analytic philosophy. Moritz Schlick in his manifesto "Die Wende der Philosophie" (The Turning Point in Philosophy) writes that "Wittgenstein (in his *Tractatus Logico-Philosophicus*...) is the first to have pushed forward to the decisive turning point" (1930, 5). The turning point for Schlick is an "insight into the nature of logic itself," that is, recognizing "the nature of pure forms" of logic. Forms belong to "the nature of expression" (1930, 6–7). Carnap, who has been described as "the embodiment of logical positivism, logical empiricism, the Vienna Circle" (Quine and Carnap 1990, 464), writes in his preface to *The Logical Syntax of Language*, "I have much for which to thank Wittgenstein in my reflections concerning the relations between syntax and the logic of science" (Carnap 1934, vi; 1937, xvi) and, subsequently, "I owe a great deal to his ideas" (1934, 208; 1937, 282).[10] Years later in his "Intellectual Autobiography," Carnap writes that the "most important insight" he "gained from Wittgenstein's work in the *Tractatus* was the conception that the truth of logical statements is based only on their logical structure and on the meanings of the terms" (Schilpp 1963, 25).

Carnap's *Logical Syntax of Language*, described as "the definitive work at the center, from which waves of tracts and popularizations issued in ever widening circles" (Quine and Carnap 1990, 464), is devoted to presenting and developing "the view that logic...is concerned with the *formal* treatment of sentences."[11] Logical relations, for instance, such as the deducibility of one proposition from another, Carnap argues, "are solely dependent upon the syntactic structure of sentences" (1934, 2; 1937, 1–2). Moreover, Carnap develops with care and detail the further idea that other formal properties are also properties of the logical syntax of language. In particular, he is interested in the "logical analysis of the concepts and sentences of the sciences," and this "logic of science" is "nothing other than the logical syntax of the language of science" (1934, iii–iv; 1937, xiii) or, as he puts it later in a lecture, "the *syntactical analysis of scientific language*" (1935, 7).

---

[10] References are to the German edition (1934) as well as the English translation by Amethe Smeaton, the Countess von Zeppelin (1937).

[11] In his first major work, *The Logical Construction of the World*, Carnap, in the words of Quine, "undertook the task in earnest" of doing something Russell merely "talked" about, namely logically constructing the world from the elements of experience (Quine and Carnap 1990, 463). Similarly, *Logical Syntax* actually does the work of showing what Wittgenstein suggests in the *Tractatus*, namely that "it is the peculiar mark of logical propositions that one can recognize that they are true from the symbol alone" (Wittgenstein 1921, 6.113).

For Carnap, this is all there is to philosophy: "[O]nce philosophy is purified of all its unscientific elements, only the logic of science remains" (1934, 205; 1937, 279). The unscientific elements include pseudoproblems, that is, apparent problems that turn out to be unproblematic when subject to proper logical analysis, and problems that properly belong to the domain of the empirical sciences, not philosophy. Metaphysical claims about the nature of reality are the primary sources of pseudoproblems and psychological questions about the nature of the mind – for example, about the nature of perception and belief – are misplaced in philosophy. All that remains is "Philosophy as syntax," to borrow the apt slogan Quine used in a lecture to introduce Carnap's philosophy in the United States at Harvard University in November 1934 (Quine and Carnap 1990, 87).

So although Carnap accepts Wittgenstein's conception of logical and philosophical propositions as tied to the formal structure of language, he rejects Wittgenstein's claim that the "correct formulation of syntactical sentences [is not] possible" (1937, 296). On Carnap's view, Wittgenstein's claim in the *Tractatus* that "1 is a number" aims to express "formal (in our terminology: syntactical) concepts," but these concepts are genuine ones and can indeed be expressed by the language of logical analysis. The syntax of philosophy and science can be formulated "in perfectly correct sentences" (1934, 209; 1937, 283). A fundamental reason for this difference is that while for Wittgenstein linguistic form is not itself a state of affairs, for Carnap this is not so: "Syntax... is nothing more than the mathematics and physics of language" (1934, 210; 1937, 284). The syntax of language is as much a physical fact as the mass of a substance.

Carnap's logical analysis relies on two tools. One is a substantive thesis about the nature of meaning, namely that every proposition is either an empirical proposition that properly belongs to one of the natural sciences, or it is a proposition that is true or false simply in virtue of the syntactic structure of the language to which it belongs. The former are synthetic propositions, whereas the latter are analytic. This view was a prominent fixture of logical positivism, and it famously entails that Kant was wrong to believe that there are propositions that are neither empirical nor analytic, namely Kant's synthetic a priori propositions.[12]

---

[12] This view about the bipolar nature of all propositions is often coupled with a view about the meaning of empirical propositions – namely, that their meaning is the empirical method of verification used by which their truth or falsity is determined

Relying on this tool, Carnap can then argue, for instance, that the traditional metaphysical issue about the existence of matter, for example, is a pseudoproblem. The idealist's claim that all of reality is mental, as well as the denial of that claim, is neither empirical nor analytic, and therefore both idealism and its denial are species of literal nonsense. Similarly, arguments about the existence of God are nonsensical because both "There is a God" and "There is no God" strictly are without sense (Carnap 1934, 237; 1937, 309–10).

The second important tool is a pair of distinctions: between "object-sentences" and "syntactical sentences" (1934; 1937) and between what Carnap calls "the material mode of speech" and the "formal mode of speech" (1934, 180–2; 1937, 237–9).

Object sentences are about states of affairs – that is, they describe objects and their properties and relations, excluding sentences about a language's formal structure. The sentences of the empirical sciences are object sentences, and for Carnap they are the only real object sentences. Syntactical sentences (namely the propositions Wittgenstein declared to be senseless) contain terms for the various structural features of languages, including logical terms such as "is deducible from" or "contradicts," and philosophy, when meaningful and properly formulated, consists wholly of syntactical sentences. The problem is that some sentences appear to be object sentences but in fact are covert syntactical sentences. These are "pseudo-object sentences" and much of philosophy consists of such propositions (1934, 211; 1937, 284–5).

The distinction between material and formal modes of speech applies to pseudo-object sentences. Consider Carnap's examples of such sentences "The rose is a thing" and "Five is not a thing but a number" (1934, 224; 1937, 286). Both appear to be object sentences along with "The rose is red" or "Lions are mammals" in which an ordinary property is attributed to an object. But such sentences are not object sentences; instead they attribute syntactical properties to words. The syntactical sentence that expresses the actual content of "The rose is a thing" is "The word 'rose' is a thing word," whereas the content of "Five is not a thing but a number" is "The word 'five' is not a thing word, but a number word." When syntactical facts are expressed as apparently nonsyntactical object sentences, as in the case of "The rose

---

or discovered. Carnap avails himself of this principle in Carnap 1935 and his famous essay "The Elimination of Metaphysics through Logical Analysis of Language" (1931). However, it does not play a role in *The Logical Syntax of Language*.

is a thing," they are expressed in the *material mode of speech*. When these syntactical facts are expressed explicitly, they are in the *formal mode of speech*.

An important task of logical analysis in philosophy is translating pseudo-object sentences of philosophy in the material mode of speech into sentences in the formal mode of speech. Carnap suggests various such translations, as shown in the following selection:

Material Mode of Speech	*Formal Mode of Speech*
1a. *Time* is one-dimensional; *space* is three dimensional.	1b. A time-designation consists of one coordinate; a space-designation consists of three coordinates.
2a. Identity is not a relation between objects.	2b. The symbol "=" is not a descriptive symbol.
3a. Philosophical questions are sometimes concerned with objects which do not occur in the object-domain of the empirical sciences.	3b. In philosophical questions expressions sometimes occur which do not occur in the languages of the sciences.
4a. The word "daystar" *designates* the sun.	4b. The word "daystar" is synonymous with "sun."

The last example illustrates the view Carnap held in the *Logical Syntax of Language* that all propositions about meaning – for example, propositions with the words "speaks about," "means," "names," or "signifies" – are really syntactical sentences. In this period, Carnap embraces Wittgenstein's rejection of semantics and treats all apparently semantic predicates as syntactic predicates. For example, the "interpretation of a language is translation and therefore something which can be *formally represented*; the construction and examination of interpretations belong to formal syntax" (1934 171; 1937, 228).

Although often it is easier, according to Carnap, to express syntactical facts with sentences in the material mode, this mode of speech is a source of philosophical confusion. It can "mislead us into thinking that we are dealing with extra-linguistic objects such as numbers, things, properties,... and so on; and the fact that, in reality, it is a case of language and its connections... is disguised from us in the material mode of speech" (1934, 225; 1937, 298–9). But the most significant error caused by the material mode of speech leads "to a disregard of the relativity to language of philosophical sentences; it is responsible for an *erroneous conception of philosophical sentences as absolute*" (1934,

226; 1937, 299). Although the sentence in the material mode "Five is a number" does not suggest that it needs to be relativized to a language, "The word 'five' is a number word" clearly needs to be indexed to a language. In English "five" is a number word, but in another language "five" might not be a number word.

Linguistic Frameworks

It bears repeating that for Carnap the linguistic relativity of philosophy is a major insight. According to his lecture at the University of London outlining the major points of *The Logical Syntax of Language*,

> *The relativity of all philosophical theses in regard to language*, that is, the need of reference to one or several particular language-systems, is a very essential point to keep in mind. It is on account of the general use of the material mode of speech that this relativity is nearly always left unnoticed. (1935, 78)

In the material mode of speech it is easy to suppose that a dispute is about extralinguistic facts and that an issue needs to be resolved in the same way that other factual disputes are resolved. Because these disputes cannot be resolved in that way, what ensues is the "chaos of subjectivist philosophical problems" (1934, 261; 1937, 332). But in the formal mode of speech, attention is diverted to exact syntactical problems, and clarity is achieved.

The formal mode of speech, however, does not circumvent subjectivity altogether. A language is a calculus, that is, a set of symbols as well as a system of syntactic rules for manipulating the symbols: formation rules for constructing sentences out of given symbols and transformation rules that govern how one sentence can be transformed into another (1934, 4; 1937, 4; 1935, 41–7).[13] Language, then, is a system that is distinct from language use or performance, for example, from the act of speaking. Language itself is not a human action and appears independent of human subjectivity. Yet, for Carnap human action and choice do play a role in what language or system of rules is adopted by human beings. Language is a system of symbols and rules, but these rules are human conventions – that is, "a matter of free choice" (1934, 260; 1937, 332). "[W]e have in every respect complete liberty with regard

---

[13] The transformation Carnap has in mind is the logical consequence relation, which in the early 1930s he conceives of as a purely syntactic relation.

to the forms of language," and both the formation and transformation rules are subject to choice (1934, v; 1937, xv). Human action, then, is external to language; it is one of the background conditions, but not internal to the system of language.

Accordingly, many philosophical theses, including Carnap's own work, really are not theses or assertions at all, but suggestions or proposals for using language in a new way or for adopting a new language (1934, 226; 1937, 299–300). As such, it is a mistake to argue about its truth or falsity because proposals are neither true nor false. Proposals recommend certain choices, and what should be discussed are the consequences and the utility of these choices.

When it comes to choosing between languages, Carnap promotes a "Principle of Tolerance in Syntax," or what he later calls "the principle of conventionality" (1942, 247), which states that "*It is not our business to set up prohibitions, but to arrive at conventions*" (1934, 44–5; 1937, 51). Moreover, "*In logic, there are no morals*," Carnap asserts, adding: "Everyone is at liberty to build up his own logic, i.e., his own form of language, as he wishes." Of course, Carnap does endorse certain prohibitions by limiting object sentences to those that belong to the empirical sciences, but this prohibition is due to his choice of syntax and not an a priori or absolute prohibition on any possible language.

This freedom does not mean that there are no empirical constraints on this choice. For example, "all questions about the structure of space and time are *syntactical* questions, that is, questions about the structure of the language, and especially of the formation and transformation rules concerning space- and time-coordinates" (1935, 86). Similarly, questions about the nature of causality – for example, whether the fundamental physical laws are statistical or deterministic – are questions about what form of language to choose. The choice of syntax will be informed by empirical experiments and observation, yet the empirical results at which scientists arrive "by no means *dictate their choice*" of language. "The form in which a law is to be stated has to be decided by an act of volition. This decision, it is true, depends upon the empirical results, but not logically, only practically" (1935, 87). So, in addition to empirical results, issues about usefulness, fruitfulness, and even taste will play a role in what rules are adopted (1934, 260; 1937, 332; 1935, 97).[14] Within a system of language, we are guided by logic and empirical

---

[14] Accordingly, the construction of the language of science is "co-operative work... of... various investigators" (Carnap 1934, 261; 1937, 333). Scientists as well as

results, but the choice to use a language is not determined by logic or evidence.

The development of Carnap's philosophy itself reflects his commitment to his principle of tolerance. Soon after writing the *Logical Syntax of Language*, Carnap relaxes his syntactic austerity and turns to semantics (Carnap 1942). Carnap was convinced, primarily by Tarski, that logical deduction or the consequence relation cannot be treated only as a syntactic relation and that semantic features of language, such as designation and truth, can be stated with as much rigor as a language's syntactic structure. Philosophy is not limited to syntax anymore, and now many problems require logical analyses that consider the meanings of expressions (1942, 245). A few years later, Carnap deepens his semantic studies and develops modal concepts in *Meaning and Necessity* (1947). Here Carnap introduces intensional entities such as properties and propositions, understood as neither linguistic nor psychological entities. This turn away from sentences and propositions (in Mill's sense of this term) to Fregean thoughts or propositions is a significant departure from the asceticism of Wittgenstein's *Tractatus* and Carnap's *Logical Syntax of Language*.

But Carnap defends this departure on old grounds, namely tolerance and conventionality, in a celebrated essay, "Empiricism, Semantics, and Ontology," first published in 1950 and republished as the first essay in a supplement to the second edition of *Meaning and Necessity* (1956). Carnap announces that in this essay he addresses "[t]he problem of the nature and admissibility of propositions and other entities," such as properties (1956, v), but the primary significance of this essay is that it is a concise statement of the idea of linguistic frameworks and the linguistic relativity of philosophical problems.

An important part of philosophy involves questions about the existence of certain types of entities: minds, material objects, properties, classes, numbers, propositions, causal powers, values, God, and so on. These are typically the questions of metaphysics or, more specifically, ontology, and they are usually seen as questions about nonlinguistic matters of fact, namely questions about what there is. Carnap, however, continues with the strategy suggested in *The Logical Syntax of*

philosophers, that is, logicians of science, must take part in these discussions about the language of science. "A satisfactory solution can only be found," Carnap insists, "if both points of view, the empirical view [of science]...and the formal one of syntax, are taken into consideration" (1935, 87–8).

Language to treat philosophical sentences, insofar as they make sense, not as matters of fact, but as expressions concerned with language.

In order to be able to discuss a new kind of object not discussed before, a person must "introduce a system of new ways of speaking, subject to new rules" (1956, 206). To introduce a system of new ways of speaking is to introduce a new "linguistic *framework*," that is, a "framework of new forms of expressions to be used according to a new set of rules" (1956, 206 and 213). For example, a semantic theory that explains linguistic meaning in terms of propositions will have to introduce the predicate "p is a proposition" and allow the formulation of new sentences such as "There is a p such that p is a proposition," "For every p, either p or not-p," and "There is a p such that distinct sentences express p," and so on. With this linguistic framework that includes "proposition" and the rules governing its usage, propositions can be discussed and referred to in explanations of linguistic meaning.

Questions about linguistic frameworks are "external questions" (1956, 206). For Carnap, questions about the existence of propositions or any new kind of entity are really questions about linguistic frameworks. Strictly speaking, they are not about propositions but about "propositions." Once such a framework that includes the predicate "p is a proposition" is introduced and accepted, questions about propositions can be formulated and answered, and these will be "internal questions," that is, questions that are raised within the structure provided for by the framework (ibid.). Although Carnap does not dwell on this, parallel to the distinction between external and internal questions, there must be a distinction between external and internal answers. External questions have external answers whereas internal questions have internal answers. When the sentence "There are propositions" is a response to an internal question, then it is formulated from within a framework that already includes "proposition" and the appropriate rules governing its usage. In fact, from within such a framework, "There is a proposition" is an analytic truth. When this sentence is formulated as an answer to an external question, it is formulated in a context where there is no established system for using the predicate "p is a proposition," and hence its status is problematic.

Internal and external questions and answers do not have the same cognitive status for Carnap. Internal questions are cognitive questions whose answers have a truth-value. The methods used for answering internal questions are either empirical or logical, and they lead to beliefs or assertions. For example, the internal assertion "Red is a color" is established by logical means appealing to definitions and rules, whereas the assertion "Some apples are red" is established by empirical means. In contrast, external questions and answers are "non-cognitive" (1956, 210 and 215). An external question is a "practical, not a theoretical" question about "whether or not to accept... new linguistic forms" and an "acceptance cannot be judged as either true or false because it is not an assertion" (1956, 214). The acceptance of a framework does not entail any sort of "belief or assertion or assumption" about the reality of the objects of this framework. Accordingly, "the acceptance of a linguistic framework must not be regarded as implying a metaphysical doctrine concerning the reality of the entities in question" (ibid.).

As a practical question, an external question is "a matter of a practical decision concerning the structure of... language," and this involves "a choice" (1956, 207). This choice will "usually be influenced by theoretical knowledge, just like any other deliberate decision," but practical factors such as "efficiency, fruitfulness and simplicity" will also play a role (1956, 208). In the concluding paragraph of the essay Carnap writes: "The acceptance or rejection of... any... linguistic forms in any branch of science will finally be decided by their efficience as instruments, the ratio of the results achieved to the amount of complexity of the efforts required" (1956, 221). It is important to emphasize that for Carnap this evaluation as well as the acceptance or rejection of a linguistic framework does not involve a belief in the existence or nonexistence of the objects to which the framework refers. For Carnap, the efficiency, fruitfulness, and simplicity of the framework of spatiotemporally ordered physical objects, for example, is not evidence for the existence of physical objects but is a motivation for accepting the *language* of physical objects. Once the language with the appropriate expressions and their rules is accepted, then one can use those terms to assert something and formulate beliefs about those objects. However, before the language of physical objects is accepted, only the *language* of physical objects and the utility of such a language with respect to some set of goals can be discussed. Moreover, the acceptance itself of the language does not involve any commitments to the existence of physical objects. Carnap draws a sharp distinction between the acceptance of a framework and the employment of it after acceptance. The acceptance of a linguistic framework – the choice to use henceforth a certain language – is not itself part of the framework.

Linguistic Frameworks 211

Carnap's bifurcation of language into a framework defined by a vocabulary and rules, and an external choice of frameworks is precisely what Humboldt aimed to express with his distinction between language as a product (*Ergon*) and language as an activity (*Energeia*) (see Chapter 4). The linguistic framework is the product subject to scientific inquiry – the mathematics and physics of language, in Carnap's words – but the choice of framework is an action alienated from the framework but free of its commitments. The system and action of language remain unintegrated dual aspects of language.

Of course, not all linguistic frameworks are deliberately chosen. For instance, the language of physical objects or things is acquired in childhood. However, for Carnap "we may regard it as a matter of choice in this sense: we are free to choose to continue using the thing language or not." There are alternatives, Carnap adds. We could restrict ourselves to a language of sense-data, construct still another language, "or, finally,... refrain from speaking" (1956, 207). Presumably this is a choice available only after a certain degree of maturity – when a person is able to decide to continue using one's language. Because silence is an option for the mature person, it seems that Carnap believes that it is possible for the adult to refrain from accepting any framework whatsoever. So not only is the acceptance or rejection of "*any*... linguistic forms in *any* branch of science" a decision motivated by practical concerns, but we are also free, at least in principle, to refrain from choosing a linguistic framework.

The choice still is governed by tolerance. Carnap denounces "dogmatic prohibitions of certain linguistic forms instead of testing them by their success or failure in practical use" (1956, 221). Such prohibitions are not only futile but are "positively harmful" because they may "obstruct scientific progress." He maintains that in the past "such prohibitions based on religious, mythological, metaphysical, or other irrational sources" have been detrimental to scientific progress, and that kind of mistake should not be repeated – for example, by banning the Fregean linguistic framework of propositions and properties simply because they are abstract objects.

> Let us grant to those who work in any special field of investigation the freedom to use any form of expression which seems useful to them; the work in the field will sooner of later lead to the elimination of those forms which have no useful function. *Let us be cautious in making assertions and critical in examining them, but tolerant in permitting linguistic forms.* (ibid.)

Here perhaps is the crux of the difference between Wittgenstein and Carnap. Carnap's rejection of Wittgenstein's prohibition against theorizing about the syntactic and semantic features of language comes with a view about the sources of these features of language. The syntax and semantics of language are human conventions – products of human choice – and Carnap advocates tolerance regarding these conventions. Because linguistic conventions are also frameworks for human knowledge and because all knowledge, and not just philosophy, is subject to linguistic relativity, human knowledge itself is subject to conventionality. Knowledge is always formulated within a framework, and frameworks are chosen by human beings who evaluate them on practical grounds, such as efficiency, fruitfulness, and simplicity. Human beings choose, construct, and evaluate linguistic frameworks from within which they pursue their quest for knowledge.

Wittgenstein, on the other hand, not only denies the possibility of describing linguistic frameworks but leaves the sources of language shrouded in mystery. Wittgenstein does agree that human usage is a source of linguistic structure, and this is an important feature of the *Tractatus* that is easily overlooked. Linguistic signs acquire their logical form through "use" (*Gebrauch*) and "employment" (*Verwendung*), and human beings "construct languages capable of expressing every sense" (1921, 3.326–3.327 and 4.002). However, the construction, use, and employment are cognitively blind in the *Tractatus*. Human beings construct languages "without having any idea how each word has meaning or what its meaning is – just as people speak without knowing how the individual sounds are produced" (1921, 4.002). So language is also conventional for Wittgenstein, but these conventions are not subject to description and theoretical reflection. The conventions show themselves in the use of language, but they cannot be stated.[15]

The form of language, then, as Wittgenstein puts it in the *Tractatus*, is "transcendental" (1921, 6.13). It is a condition or limit of everything that can be known and described, but it itself cannot be known or described.[16] Linguistic form is a framework for all scientific knowledge

---

[15] For a discussion on the differences between Wittgenstein and Carnap, see Witherspoon 2000.

[16] Wittgenstein actually writes that "Logic is transcendental" (1921, 6.13), but logic is the form of language. Regarding the term "transcendental," Wittgenstein uses this term in the sense familiar from Kant's and post-Kantian philosophy: as something that is a necessary condition of any possible experience but itself is not experienced,

and theory, but this framework can only be shown, not described or captured by a theory. Moreover, because for Wittgenstein "[t]*he limits of my language* mean the limits of my world" (1921, 5.6), "the limits of my world" are also transcendental for Wittgenstein in the *Tractatus*. Although Wittgenstein says very little to explain the phrase "my world," he does write that "[t]he world and life are one," followed by "I am my world" (1921, 5.621–5.63), which suggests that at the very least he is referring to the world as lived and experienced.[17] This means that for Wittgenstein in the *Tractatus* the form of this lived and experienced world, and hence the limits of this world, cannot be described. The form and limits of the lived world are not subject to propositional knowledge, reflection, and theory.

Thus the form and limits of this world are not subject to rational human control and construction. "The world is independent of my will," Wittgenstein writes (1921, 6.373). He believes that "the good or bad exercise of the will...can alter only the limits of the world, not the facts – not what can be expressed by means of language" (1921, 6.43).[18] Accordingly "even when all *possible* scientific questions have been answered, the problems of life remain completely untouched" (1921, 6.52). The problems of life lie at the limits of the world and hence they are not cognitive problems and cannot be articulated meaningfully. But if they cannot be articulated, they also cannot have answers or solutions, and that itself is Wittgenstein's "solution to the problem of life" (1921, 6.521). Wittgenstein's "metaphysics of silence" (McGuinness 2002, 81) is the solution to the problems of life.

A very different spirit infuses Carnap's philosophy. Our frameworks lay down the form and limits of our lived and experienced world, and these are subject to our knowledge, deliberation, choice, and control. The form and limits of our lived and experienced world can be known and changed, and it is one of the goals of science and philosophy to

---

except that Wittgenstein is not concerned with experience but with the conditions of language. Anscombe's (1967, 166) gloss on "transcendental" in this passage is useful: it "pervades everything sayable and is itself unsayable." It must be added that for Wittgenstein, what is transcendental is not just the condition of language but the world itself.

[17] Wittgenstein's concept of world bears a strong resemblance to existential concepts of the world, particularly Heidegger's concept of "being-in-the-world" (Friedlander 2001, 164 and 164n3).

[18] Ethics "cannot be put into words" and itself is "transcendental" (Wittgenstein 1921, 6.421).

exercise and enhance this knowledge and control. Carnap affirms this in the first preface to his first major work, *The Logical Construction of the World* (*Der logische Aufbau der Welt*, 1928) and again almost forty years later in his preface to the Czech translation of his major essays:

> As a matter of fact, strictly scientific and exact methods are now beginning to be used by those scientific disciplines that study human beings and society. Such applications are beginning to be more and more essential given the goal of developing a rational and reasonable organization of society, namely a society that makes it impossible for one nation to exploit another, for one class to exploit another, and that in the end encompasses all humanity. This is still a distant goal but today we are living in critical times. All thinking, including philosophical thinking has to help promote this major humanitarian goal. (Carnap 1966)

This includes Carnap's own philosophical thinking, including his conception of linguistic frameworks as constructed by human beings and subject to their knowledge, deliberation, and choice. Practical decisions are bifurcated from cognition, in Carnap's philosophy, in that the latter is internal to frameworks whereas the former is not, but practice is not a mystery of which we cannot speak.[19]

Semantic Ascent

While in Prague in spring 1933, finishing the final draft of *The Logical Syntax of Language*, the forty-one-year-old Carnap was visited by "an unknown young foreigner of 23," who just a few months earlier had received his Ph.D. (Quine and Carnap 1990, 465). This was Willard Van Orman Quine, who later described Carnap as a "towering figure" comparable to Wittgenstein as well as "my old and valued friend, ... the greatest of my teachers" (1990, 457, 462, and 463). Quine also became Carnap's greatest critic. In fact, Quine's philosophy is best seen as an evolving reaction to Carnap's most central assumptions.

---

[19] Carnap's view of linguistic frameworks, unlike Wittgenstein's mysticism, is an heir to the Enlightenment project of improving the human understanding. From Descartes and Locke through Kant, philosophers were seeking methods for such improvement, including ways to improve the material conditions that enable human beings to improve their minds (Losonsky 2001). A key assumption of this project is that the way human beings think and process information is an artifact of human deliberation and choice.

In a footnote to "Empiricism, Semantics and Ontology," (1950; 1956, 205–21), Carnap gives a succinct summary of the distinctions that pervade Carnap's philosophy and that Quine subjected to profound criticism:

> [A]ccording to [Quine's] general conception there are no sharp boundary lines between logical and factual truth, between questions of meaning and questions of fact, between acceptance of a language structure and the acceptance of an assertion formulated in the language. (1956, 215n5)

The rejection of these distinctions, which amounts to the rejection of the analytic-synthetic distinction and the distinction between internal and external questions, together with his irrealism about meaning, remained the core features of Quine's philosophy. They also portended an end to the heyday of the philosophy of language and the twentieth-century linguistic turn of analytic philosophy.

Quine begins his critique of Carnap early in 1936 with an examination of the suggestion that a proposition is "true by convention" (1936/1983). Quine's target is the claim that logical truths are true simply in virtue of the conventions of language – the formation and transformation rules of a linguistic framework. In response, Quine argues that this claim runs aground on "the infinitude of the truths of logic" (1936/1983, 353).[20] In order to generate an infinite set of sentences, Quine maintains, the conventions have to rely on logical connectives, such as the conditional. The basic number of conventions will be finite, but they will yield an infinite set of sentences on the basis of *inferences* from instances of these conventions. These inferences, however, will be logical ones. Consequently, "logic is needed for inferring logic from conventions" (1936/1983, 352).

This criticism rests on the assumption that the linguistic conventions of a language are deliberately and explicitly formulated by the users of that language. Of course, not all conventions are explicit and deliberate agreements on a set of conventions. Some conventions are adopted by observing or conforming to a pattern of behavior for various independent reasons without formulating and agreeing to observe the conventional code. Fashions are a matter of convention, but in most

---

[20] Page references are to the reprint in Benacerraf and Putnam 1983.

cases this is not the result of an explicitly and deliberately formulated dress code.[21] Quine grants this but argues:

> In dropping the attributes of deliberateness and explicitness from the notion of linguistic conventions we risk depriving the latter of any explanatory force and reducing it to an idle label. We may wonder what one adds to the bare statement that the truths of logic and mathematics are *a priori*, or to the still barer statement that they are firmly accepted, when he characterizes them as true by convention in such a sense. (1936/1986, 353–4)

Quine's critique is vulnerable at several points, especially as a response to Carnap. Carnap pursues neither of the two alternatives Quine presents. In "Empiricism, Semantics, and Ontology" as we saw, Carnap recognizes that not all linguistic conventions are deliberately chosen, but he has more to say about them than that we simply adopt conventions through behavior. For Carnap these behaviors are still "a matter of choice in this sense: we are free to choose to continue using" the the acquired language. Carnap's account is intended for speakers who have the capacity to reflect on their acquired languages and deliberate about alternatives. This is an ongoing theme in Carnap's work. *The Logical Syntax of Language* is explicitly limited to contexts in which we are at "liberty with regard to forms of language," and we are engaged "in constructing a language" (1934, v; 1937, xv), and it continues into his later replies to Quine on the analytic-synthetic distinction.

But Quine's major objection is to reject the suggestion that we can isolate and stand apart from linguistic frameworks in order to evaluate them and compare them with alternatives. In Quine's hands, the distinction between external and internal points of view turns into just a difference internal to a conceptual scheme. Quine characterizes the shift from internal discussions about the existence of objects to external discussions about linguistic frameworks as "semantic ascent" (1960, 271). It is "the shift from talk of miles to talk of 'mile'" (ibid.). Quine agrees that such a shift contributes to the resolution of disputes in science as well as philosophy, because this maneuver "carries the discussion into a domain where both parties are better agreed on the objects

---

[21] David Lewis's landmark theory of conventions in 1969 and 1983 (1:164–6) is a fairly stringent conception of conventions – they require that people who participate in conventions have mutual knowledge and intentions about other people's beliefs and intentions. Still, deliberate and explicit formulation of the conventions is not required by Lewis's theory.

(viz. words) and on the main terms concerning them" (1960, 272). However, for Quine to discuss words and their meanings about the meanings of words is as much a discussion about what there is as are scientific discussions about quarks and quartz or commonsense debates about unicorns or brick houses. Similarly, apparently internal questions and statements about quarks or bricks are also implicitly about the conceptual frameworks with the words "quarks" or "bricks." To change one's views about quarks is to change the conceptual framework and the ways in which words are used as much as a new definition or formation rule changes a framework.

Consequently, the philosopher who focuses on language, theories, linguistic frameworks, and the like is as much concerned with factual matters about the way the world is as is the scientist who uses rather than mentions theories and linguistic frameworks. At the same time, the scientist is also involved in an ongoing process of evaluating and revising the language scientists use by evaluating and revising their theories. Philosophers' and scientists' tasks differ not in kind, but "in detail" (1960, 275). While scientists are concerned with the "reasonable construction" of special parts of conceptual schemes, for example, "the biological or the physical part," philosophers are concerned with "a reasonable construction of the whole" conceptual framework, and the same interplay of language and reality plays a role in both activities (1953, 17). This seamless fabric that ties scientists and philosophers together constitutes Quine's naturalism.

The reliance on pragmatic considerations about the simplicity or efficiency of a system of language does not mark out a difference between external and internal questions.

> For it is not as though considerations of systematic efficacy, broadly pragmatic considerations, were operative only when we make a semantic ascent and talk of theory and factual considerations of the behavior of objects in the world were operative only when we avoid semantic ascent and talk within theory. Considerations of systematic efficacy are equally essential in both cases; it is just that in the one case we voice them and in the other we are tacitly guided by them. (Quine 1960, 274)

At the same time, factual issues about the behavior of objects in the world, including how we perceive this behavior, are relevant at both levels.

Human beings are also not able to pry apart how much of our knowledge "is merely contributed by language and how much is a genuine reflection of reality" (1953, 78). In order to pry these apart, "we must talk about the world as well as about language, and to talk about the world we must already impose upon the world some conceptual scheme peculiar to our own special language" (ibid.). In other words, there is no "cosmic exile" or "vantage point" from which we are able to separate language from the world (1960, 275). The philosopher "cannot study and revise the fundamental conceptual scheme of science and common sense without having some conceptual scheme, whether the same or another no less in need of philosophical scrutiny, in which to work" (1960, 275–6).

Quine's argument is subject to a similar ambiguity that threatened Wittgenstein's argument about the inability of pictures and propositions to depict pictorial and logical form. The fact that external questions and statements about a linguistic framework will rely on a linguistic framework does not mean there is no distinction between external and internal questions. Questions that are internal to one framework can be external to another. Just because there is no cosmic exile from frameworks entirely does not mean there is no exile: we can emigrate from one framework and become immigrants in another.

We can emigrate between frameworks and distinguish external and internal questions, however, only if it is possible to identify distinct linguistic frameworks. Without this possibility, it makes no sense to maintain that it is possible to use one framework to discuss another. But in order to identify distinct frameworks, it must be possible to identify the meanings of different frameworks. Consequently, at the very least we must be able to draw a distinction between analytic sentences – that is, between ones that are true in virtue of meaning alone and ones that are also true in virtue of nonlinguistic facts, or synthetic sentences. The external-internal distinction rests on the analytic-synthetic distinction, and the denial of this distinction is the centerpiece of Quine's philosophy of language and critique of Carnap.[22]

Ascent without Dogma

Quine's most widely read essay is "Two Dogmas of Empiricism" (1953). The two dogmas Quine attacks are that there is a distinction between analytic and synthetic truths and a collection of positions Quine gathers

---

[22] See Quine 1976, 210. Bird 1995 and Yablo 1998, 235–7, deny that Carnap's external-internal distinction rests on the analytic-synthetic distinction.

under the label "reductionism," whose common feature is that a synthetic statement "taken in isolation from its fellows, can admit of confirmation or infirmation at all" (1953, 41). Quine's alternative is that the "totality of our so-called knowledge or beliefs, from the most casual matters of geography and history to the profoundest laws of atomic physics or even of pure mathematics and logic is a man-made fabric" and the "[r]eëvaluation of some statements entails reëvaluation of others, because of their logical interconnections" (1953, 42). There is only a distinction of degree in this seamless fabric. Although there are always competing ways of accommodating recalcitrant experiences and all truths can in principle be revised, some statements are more likely to be revised or dropped than others. Those most resistant to revision in light of experience are logical and analytic truths, whereas the rest are synthetic truths (1953, 43).

The central argument Quine directs against the analytic-synthetic distinction is that analyticity cannot be defined without reliance on intensional concepts, but this is circular.[23] For example, we may try to characterize analytic statements as those which can be reduced to logical truths by substituting its terms with synonyms. So, the analytic truth "All triangles are three-sided figures" can be turned into the logical truth "All three-sided figures are three-sided figures" simply by replacing "triangles" with the synonymous term "three-sided figures." But synonymy, Quine maintains, "is no less in need of clarification than analyticity" (1953, 23). One way to remedy this problem is to define synonymy in terms of Leibniz's principle of the substitutivity of identity, which we encountered in Chapter 6 because Frege uses it to identify what have come to be known as intensional contexts. Two terms are synonymous just in case they can be substituted for each other in any statement without changing the truth-value of the statement. So the suggestion is that "triangles" and "three-sided figures" are synonymous because they can be interchanged with each other in any statement without turning truths into falsehoods or falsehoods into truths.

---

[23] Burge (1992) argues that Quine as well as respondents to him run together two notions of analyticity: analyticity as truth in virtue of meaning alone and analyticity as true in virtue of logic and definitions. Burge maintains correctly that Quine's argument runs in a different direction. His target is the thesis that there are statements true in virtue of meaning alone, and he aims at this target by substituting the notion of meaning for other notions. So one of the steps of his argument is to replace the notion of *true in virtue of meaning* with the notion *true in virtue of logical truths and definitions*.

But as Quine points out, this remedy only works if we are able to rely on intensional contexts, such as statements about beliefs or ones that include the modal adverb "necessarily." For instance, if we assume that "creatures with a heart" and "creatures with a kidney" refer to exactly the same class of creatures, that is, they are coextensional, then these two terms can be replaced in all extensional contexts without changing truth-values, but these terms are not synonymous. Coextensional terms may have distinct meanings, but they can be interchanged in purely extensional statements. The difference in meaning appears when we try to replace them in intensional contexts. For example, "Jonah believes that creatures with hearts have hearts" is true, while "Jonah believes the creatures with kidneys have hearts" is false. Similarly, "Necessarily, creatures with hearts have hearts" is true, but the statement "Necessarily, creatures with kidneys have hearts" is false. However, Quine asserts that we are able to understand the intensional adverb "necessarily" only if "the notion of analyticity is already understood in advance" (1953, 31).

Similarly, analytic statements can be characterized as the statements that are true simply in virtue of logic and the semantical rules of a language. But for Quine "semantical rule" is an "unexplained phrase" and "meaningless" (1960, 34). In short, for Quine there is a family of concepts – "analytic," "synonymous," "necessarily," "meaning," "intension," "semantical rule," and so on – that are all equally suspect and none of them can be understood without a prior understanding of analyticity itself.

Quine's second argument, one that he adds to the revised version of "Two Dogmas of Empiricism" (1953, 35n14), is directed against the suggestion that analyticity is to be understood in terms of meaning postulates (Martin 1952; also see Carnap 1947, 198, and 1956, 222). Meaning postulates belong to artificial languages, and they are sentences in the language that determine the meanings of the terms they contain. For instance, a language system might contain the predicates "raven" and "black," and the meanings of these predicates will be determined by meaning postulates, such as "For any x, if x is a raven, then x is black." Thus, "No ravens are not black" will be an analytic truth, namely a sentence true in virtue of logic and this meaning postulate. What postulates to include in the construction of a language, Carnap emphasizes in accordance with his principle of tolerance, is "not a matter of knowledge, but decision." Again, language builders are "free to choose their postulates, guided not by their beliefs concerning facts of the [extra-linguistic] world but by their intentions with respect to the meanings, i.e., the ways of use of the descriptive constants" (1956, 225).

The argument against this strategy for defining analyticity is that meaning postulates are chosen by the researcher constructing a language, and thus what the meaning postulates are is a selection of statements "relative to an act of inquiry" (Quine 1953, 35). But "any finite (or effectively specifiable infinite) selection of statements ... is as much *a* set of postulates as any other" (ibid.). Two linguistic systems can consist of exactly the same sentences, but in one system "All ravens are black" is a meaning postulate whereas in the other it is a synthetic statement. Quine generalizes his point to all languages, natural and artificial. Meaning postulates are chosen for the purpose of "schooling unconversant persons in ... some natural or artificial language *L*," but there are various ways of doing this, and no subset of sentences of *L* is "intrinsically" more a meaning postulate (or semantical rule) than another.

Quine's illustrative metaphor is instructive: it is "as meaningless as asking which points in Ohio are starting points for traveling through Ohio" (ibid.). Any point in Ohio can serve as a starting point and no set of geographical points in Ohio is privileged over others as *the* set of starting points. What serves as a starting point for a traveler depends on the interests and decisions of the traveler.

Both arguments rest on a refusal to countenance a serious role for linguistic meaning. In "Two Dogmas of Empiricism," Quine simply assumes that "meanings as obscure intermediary entities, may well be abandoned" (1953, 22). The only way to understand linguistic meaning is in terms of synonymy and analyticity, neither of which are sufficiently clear to yield a robust notion of meaning, he assumes. This assumption is explicitly at work in the first argument, but it also plays a supporting role in the second argument. Quine assumes that the choice of statements that serve as meaning postulates cannot be determined by any facts about meaning.

A closer look at Quine's metaphor about starting points in Ohio makes it clear that there are indeed limitations on starting points depending on how one travels. If traveling overland from outside of Ohio's borders, the privileged set of starting points is the set of points that constitute the borders of Ohio and can serve as entry points for overland travelers. Points in central Ohio, for example, Centerburg, Ohio, cannot be starting points for overland travelers entering the state. Similarly, seaborne travelers are limited to entering the state from Lake Erie and cannot start their journey in Centerburg. Airborne travelers, of course, can choose a starting point in central Ohio, but they too have a limited set of starting points. They cannot begin where underground travelers can start their journey through Ohio. So just as the set of starting points in Ohio is determined by where one is coming from, the proper subset of sentences of a linguistic framework that serves as meaning postulates is a function of what those who have to learn the language – the "unconversant persons" we encountered earlier – already *have in mind*, and what speakers are thinking is a traditional locus of linguistic meaning. But meaning, especially meaning that is in the mind, Quine rejects.

Indeterminacy and Assent

Quine turns to a direct attack on meaning in his celebrated argument for the indeterminacy of translation. By establishing the thesis that radical translation is not determinate, Quine believes he has shown that meaning itself is indeterminate and that there is no principle of individuation or standard of identity for linguistic meaning. Quine assumes that if a purported entity does not have some standard that distinguishes it from other things, then there is no such entity, that is, "No entity without identity" (1969, 23).

Radical translation is the project of translating an alien language without making any assumptions about the meaning or syntax of the alien language, or what the alien speakers have in mind when speaking. The only evidence the radical translator can use to decipher the alien tongue is her observation of the use of language – that is, what Quine describes as the alien speaker's "current dispositions to respond verbally to current stimulations" (1960, 28). What motivates this requirement is Quine's "philosophical anthropology" (Glock 2003, 36), namely that human behavior is the touchstone for understanding language and mind and that language is fundamentally to be identified with linguistic behavior or "the observable mouthing of words under conspicuously intersubjective circumstances" (Quine 1960, 1).

Quine glosses his argument in terms of a newly discovered tribe a radical translator is attempting to understand by observing "what the natives say under observed circumstances" (ibid.).[24] Observing the linguistic behavior of her subject, the radical translator "may establish inductively, beyond a reasonable doubt, that a certain heathen

---

[24] Quine in the end modified his views (1987, 1989, 1990); here I only consider the original argument.

Indeterminacy and Assent   223

expression is one to which natives can be prompted to assent by the presence of a rabbit, or a reasonable *facsimile*, and not otherwise" (1969, 2).[25] For example, if the expression to be translated is *Gavagai*, the radical linguist lists the conditions under which the subject assents, dissents, or neither to the use of *Gavagai* (1960, 29).

But this evidence is not sufficient to support the identification of the native term with the English word "rabbit" – that is, it does not support that the native expression and "rabbit" are synonymous. All the available behavioral evidence is compatible with competing hypotheses, for example, that the subject meant "various temporal segments of rabbits," "integral or undetached rabbit parts," or even "just 'Rabbiteth,' like 'Raineth,'" that is, the presence of abstract rabbithood rather than a particular rabbit (1969, 2–3; 1960, 52–3).

In fact, there is no observable evidence that would support one hypothesis over another. In order to choose between hypotheses, the radical linguist needs to be able to ask questions using concepts of identity and quantification. For instance, to determine if the subject's expression means a temporal rabbit stage or rabbit, we would need to be able to ask him: "Is this [pointing to the rabbit at one time] identical to that [pointing to the same rabbit a few moments later]?" or "Is this one rabbit or many rabbits?" But the linguist is not in a position to rely on these concepts because they have not been translated (1969, 2). Moreover, any attempt to radically translate "identity," "there is," or any other logical constants will fail. For instance, translating "identity" is subject to the same indeterminacy as translating the expression the subject uses in the presence of rabbits (1960, 71–2). Logical constants suffer because they are "learned only in sentential contexts," and to have translations of some sentential contexts in the subject's language, the radical linguist needs to have translated some terms. But as we just saw, the translation of terms is indeterminate.[26]

> English general terms and singular terms, identity, quantification, and the whole bag of ontological tricks may be correlated with elements of the native language in any of various mutually incompatible ways,

---

[25] In *Word and Object*, this is the "stimulus meaning" of the subject's expression because we are correlating the native expression with visual stimulations occasioned by the presence of rabbits (Quine 1960, 31).
[26] The radical translation of any formal term suffers from the same problem. For example, the radical translator is not in a position to distinguish between the subject's terms and sentences.

each compatible with all possible linguistic data, and none preferable to another save as favored by a rationalization of the *native* language that is simple and natural to *us*. (1969, 4–5)

The radical translator can get beyond correlating the subject's expressions and visual stimuli in the environment of the subject by "catapulting" herself into the subject's language and imposing the categories of her language. But this imposition will "exceed anything implicit in any native's disposition to speech behavior" (1960, 70).

Quine's argument is subject to various important challenges, the most significant is that Quine's translation project relies on "closet hermeneutics" that violate his own behavioral restrictions (Glock 2003, 170–82).[27] Even to get started, the radical translator needs to distinguish between assent and dissent, but observable behavior stripped of any psychological assumptions does not support attributions of assent or dissent. In fact, it is not clear how behavior by itself, without relying on any supplementary presuppositions, categories, or mental maps about other creatures' psychological states, supports the assumption that the radical translator has encountered a linguistic being. Quine begins his discussion with the proposal: "Imagine a newly discovered tribe whose language is without known affinities" (1969, 1). But clearly there are some known affinities – this is a tribe with language – and Quine does not discuss the grounds for attributing language to an entity.

But all these challenges reject Quine's starting point of linguistic behavior stripped of semantic assumptions and grant themselves a stock of evidence that includes semantic facts and conceptual contents. Thus Quine's point remains that linguistic behavior does not determine a semantic structure. So Quine exemplifies the historical tendency of theories of language that give primacy to linguistic activity to have difficulties sustaining the idea of natural language as an identifiable and determinate semantic structure. Both Locke and Condillac suffer from this difficulty, and Quine's work follows suit. The best they can do is make semantic structure a matter of imposition or interpretation.

Radical Interpretation

This is particularly clear in the work of Davidson. As we saw in the previous chapter, Davidson (1967) argues that Tarski's formal definitions

---

[27] For other influential objections, see Chomsky 1969, Evans 1975, and Fodor 1981.

of truth for a language can be adapted to natural languages and used as a theory of meaning for human language.[28] A theory of truth for a natural language gives the necessary and sufficient conditions for the truth of every sentence of this language, and "to give truth conditions is a way of giving the meaning of a sentence" (1967; 1984, 24). But such a theory of truth, and hence meaning, for natural languages will assign a recursive structure to language so that a "natural language can be seen as a formal system" (1984, 55).[29]

This assignment of structure, though, is in Davidson's philosophy of language a projection or interpretation and not an intrinsic feature of language. Davidson follows Quine in maintaining that "an important degree of indeterminacy will remain after all the evidence is in; a number of significantly different theories of truth will fit the evidence equally well" (1984, 62). For both Quine and Davidson this is not just an epistemic problem resting on insufficient evidence. Even if all the available evidence is in and we are theorizing from an omniscient point of view, the indeterminacy will remain. "When all the evidence is in," Davidson maintains, "there will remain, as Quine has emphasized, the trade-offs between the beliefs we attribute to a speaker and the interpretations we give his words" (1984, 139).

According to Davidson, linguistic meaning cannot be interpreted without determining what speakers believe and intend, but speakers' beliefs and intentions cannot be determined without determining the meaning of the language speakers use. This is not just a practical dependence but a "principled" dependence. A theory of meaning requires a theory of truth, and a theory of truth needs to specify under what conditions a speaker holds a sentence to be true. Davidson assumes that we can determine when speakers hold sentences to be true without making any assumptions about what the sentences mean, what the speakers think the sentences mean, or what their beliefs are about whatever the subject matter of the sentences might be.[30] However, we cannot interpret a sentence that is held true without knowing what the speaker believes, and we cannot know what the speaker believes without interpreting the

---

[28] This is the programmatic underpinning of two important anthologies in the philosophy of language: Davidson and Harman 1972 and 1975.
[29] Moreover, Davidson writes, "insofar as we make the construction of such a theory our aim, we can think of linguists and analytic philosophers as co-workers" (1984, 55–6).
[30] For a critical discussion of this assumption, see Heal 1997, 184.

meaning of the sentence. Therefore, Davidson concludes, "in interpreting utterances from scratch – in *radical* interpretation – we must somehow deliver simultaneously a theory of belief and a theory of meaning" (1984, 143–4).

> The problem, then, is this: we suppose we know what sentences a speaker holds true, and when, and we want to know what he means and believes. Perhaps we could crack the case if we knew enough about his beliefs and intentions, but there is no chance of this without prior access to a theory of interpretation. Given the interpretations, we could read off beliefs from the evidential basis, but this assumes what we want to know. (1984, 145)

The solution Davidson proposes is inspired by a strategy in decision theory for determining subjective probabilities. The problem in decision theory is that a wager is also a function of two unknown factors: the subjective probability a bettor assigns to the possible outcomes, and the value or utility the bettor assigns to an outcome. A person might refuse a bet because of his assessment of the probabilities of the outcomes or because of her valuation of the outcome. The strategy in decision theory is to keep subjective probabilities constant by finding an event where the bettor is indifferent as to whether the event occurs or not, although the outcomes are different. For example, if the bettor is indifferent between "winning if E occurs and losing if E does not occur" and "losing if E occurs and winning if E does not occur," then the bettor assigns the occurrence and nonoccurrence of E the same subjective probability.

On the basis of this indifference, numeric values are assigned to the bettor's values and subjective probability of these indifferent bets, and then the bettor's values and subjective probabilities are comparatively rank-ordered on the basis of the preferences the bettor expresses for various bets. There are various ways in which numeric values can be assigned to subjective probabilities and values, and there is no unique assignment that will preserve the comparative rank ordering. "The same facts," Davidson writes, "may be represented by quite a different assignment of numbers" (1984, 147). The situation here is similar to the case of temperature, where the assignment of "0" and the numeric scale used to represent temperature is arbitrary. Just as there are only comparative and no absolute magnitudes of temperature – the freezing point of water at sea level may be assigned "0" or "32" – there are no absolute magnitudes for bettors' values and subjective probabilities.

The interpretation of the sentences a speaker holds true are also a function of two unknowns, namely meaning and belief, and Davidson suggests that the assignment of propositions is as indeterminate as the assignment of numeric values in decision theory. Davidson suggests that we cannot only determine when a speaker holds a sentence to be true without making assumptions about meaning and belief, but that we can also choose "preferences that one sentence rather than another be true" without making assumptions about meaning or belief (1984, 148; 1990). Propositions are assigned so that the comparative preferences for truth are preserved, but there is no unique assignment. As in decision theory, the same facts may be represented by quite a different assignment of propositions to what the speaker means and believes. Moreover, in interpretation there also are no absolute assignments of propositions, but only relative assignments that preserve a speaker's comparative preferences.

More specifically, because for Davidson meanings are given by truth-conditions, the same set of preferences for the truth of sentences can be represented by different assignments of truth-conditions. In assigning truth-conditions to the speaker's sentences, interpreters can help themselves with various principles, such as the principle of charity, according to which the interpreter aims to optimize agreement between the speaker and the interpreter (1984, 136–7 and 152–3).[31] But for Davidson, this is the bottom line: "Broadly stated, my theme is that we should think of meanings and beliefs as interrelated constructs of a single theory just as we already view subjective values and probabilities as interrelated constructs of decision theory" (1984, 146). There is no fact of the matter regarding meaning and belief apart from a theory constrained by the empirically determined speakers' preferences for truth and the task of constructing a Tarski-style theory of truth. Meanings as well as beliefs are theoretical constructs.

In addition to this indeterminacy of meaning and belief, both Quine and Davidson see a similar problem for the reference of names, namely the "inscrutability of reference," and in fact it seems that for Quine the indeterminacy of translation, and hence irrealism about meaning, follows from the inscrutability of reference (Quine 1969; Davidson 1984). Although the terms "rabbit," "undetached rabbit part," and "rabbit stage" are true of different objects, their reference "proves behaviorally

---

[31] Also see Ramberg 1989. Some have rejected Davidson's principle of charity and proposed a principle of humanity, according to which interpreters should interpret speakers so that they have beliefs that the interpreter would have when in the same position as the speaker (Grandy 1973; also see McDowell 1976 and Lewis 1983, 1:112).

inscrutable" (Quine 1969, 35). Consequently, the available behavioral evidence is not only compatible with competing translations of *Gavagai* but with competing referents – "extension itself goes inscrutable" (ibid.). Thus limiting language to linguistic behavior undermines the determinacy of even the most basic relation between word and object.

Conclusion

In the *Tractatus*, Wittgenstein attempts to divorce sentences from propositions conceived of as abstract objects and, in doing so, undermines the project of presenting a theory of the form and content of human language. Of form and content we cannot speak. Wittgenstein's rejection of theory in the *Tractatus* anticipates the fractured conception of language that we find in the philosophies of Quine and Davidson. Actual sentences as they occur in linguistic behavior cannot by themselves support a conception of language as a system with a determinate and identifiable semantic structure. It cannot even support a determinate notion of reference.

EIGHT

✦

The Whimsy of Language
Wittgenstein, Derrida, and Davidson

While linguistic performance – the actual use of language in speech and writing – is the most natural and empirical manifestation of human language, performance does not sustain the conception of language as a system. Wittgenstein's mature work in the *Philosophical Investigations*, Jacques Derrida's poststructuralist deconstructions, and Davidson's skepticism about language itself are dramatic instances of the pull of linguistic performance away from the idea of language as a determinant system that can be caught by the net of linguistic theory. In fact, these most recent linguistic turns to language are turns away from linguistic theory altogether. Performance is used to foil the work of theory.

Language Games

The style of Wittgenstein's *Investigations* already exemplifies the philosophy of language Wittgenstein recommends in this work. Whereas the *Tractatus* appears as a systematic formal treatise with hierarchically ordered propositions and new symbols, the *Investigations* consists of, according to Wittgenstein himself, "*remarks*, short paragraphs," sometimes "jumping from one topic to another" (1953, ix). Instead of a scientific or scholarly essay, he offers "a number of sketches of landscapes, . . . really only an album" (ibid.). Accordingly, the *Investigations* is driven by what might be considered case studies.

Wittgenstein begins his *Investigations* not with his own words but with a passage from Augustine's *Confessions* where he recalls how he learned language.[1] "When they (my elders) named some objects,"

---

[1] For a stimulating discussion of the significance of how Wittgenstein begins the *Investigations*, see Cavell 1996.

Wittgenstein quotes Augustine, "and accordingly moved toward something, I saw this and grasped that the thing was called by the sound they uttered since they wanted to point it out" (1953, §1). After noting that Augustine is primarily thinking of names of objects and ignoring names of actions and properties, Wittgenstein offers a contrasting example:

> I send someone shopping, I give him a slip marked "five red apples." He takes the slip to the shopkeeper, who opens the drawer marked "apples"; then he looks up the word "red" in a table and finds a colour sample opposite it; then he says the series of cardinal numbers – I assume that he knows them by heart – up to the word "five" and for each number he takes an apple of the same colour as the sample out of the drawer. – It is in this and similar ways that one operates with words. (1953, §1)

This juxtaposition of examples anticipates key positions Wittgenstein advances in the *Investigations*.

One of these is the view that there is no "*essence* of language" – no set of necessary and sufficient conditions that would answer to "What is language?" or "What is a statement?" once and for all (1953, §92). Instead, human language, just like the *Investigations*, is a patchwork. Early in the *Investigations*, Wittgenstein compares language to "an ancient city: a maze of little streets and squares, of old and new houses, and of houses with additions from various periods; and this surrounded by a multitude of new suburbs with straight rectangular streets and uniform houses" (1953, §18). The various formal languages of mathematical logic that have been proposed as better instruments for representing or showing the logical form of natural languages – for example, by Frege, Russell, or Wittgenstein in the *Tractatus* – are only highly regimented suburbs of a city. Just as suburban developments do not express the essence or form of an old city, neither do these regimented languages of logic express the form of language, according to Wittgenstein.

Later in the *Investigations* he writes that in the "actual use of expressions" we do not follow a "straight highway," but "we make detours, we go by sideroads." The straight highway is the vision of human language as having an underlying logical form, but on it we cannot travel "because it is permanently closed" (1953, §426).

Logic, Wittgenstein maintains, "does not treat of language – or thought – in the sense in which a natural science treats of a natural phenomenon, and the most that can be said is that we *construct* ideal languages" (1953, §81). Wittgenstein is quick to point out that "ideal" in this case does not mean "better, more perfect, than our everyday language" and that it is not the case that the translation of a sentence in a natural language into a sentence of formal logic will "show people at last what a proper sentence looked like." Using a natural language, according to Wittgenstein, typically is not "operating a calculus according to definite rules" (ibid.).

Wittgenstein compares language with games. He writes that we can think of "the whole process of using words" as Augustine described – to name objects – as a language game (1953, §7). There are various uses of words – the example of sending someone shopping for red apples is another – and these various "processes...might also be called language games." He adds that he will "also call the whole, consisting of language and the actions into which it is woven, the 'language-game'" (ibid.). But the whole of language, for Wittgenstein, is a "multiplicity of language-games," and he gives a list of examples, including commanding, describing, reporting, storytelling, joking as well as "Asking, thanking, cursing, greeting, praying" (1953, §23). However, even this list is too abstract and general. For example, there is no overarching language game of asking questions. "If you do not keep the multiplicity of language-games in view," Wittgenstein writes, "you will perhaps be inclined to ask questions like: 'What is a question?'" (1953, §24). But there is no unity to what can be done with a question, according to Wittgenstein. People can ask questions in order to request information, to state that they do not know something, to express doubt, to cry for help, and so on.

A reason for using the term "game" to describe language, according to Wittgenstein, is that it brings "to prominence the fact that the *speaking* of language is part of an activity" (1953, §23), but this activity cannot be defined. There are no necessary and sufficient conditions for being a game. One might begin by suggesting that a game consists in moving objects about on a surface according to certain rules, but Wittgenstein retorts: "You seem to be thinking of board games, but there are others" (1953, §3). There are board games, card games, ball games, Olympic games, and so on (1953, §66). Not even the property of *doing something according to a rule* captures all games. Children can play with a ball making up rules and changing them as they go along, and "in between throwing the ball aimlessly into the air, chasing and throwing a ball at one another for fun, etc." (1953, §83).

Instead of there being features common to all games and that would distinguish games from nongames, the set of games is "a complicated network of similarities overlapping and criss-crossing," much like the similarities of "family resemblances," where "the various resemblances between members of a family: build, color of eyes, gait, temperament, etc. overlap and criss-cross in the same way" (1953, §§66 and 67). Games form a family tied by family resemblances but without a single property shared by all games and similarly language and its parts – for example, a sentence is a "family of structures more or less related to one another" (1953, §108).

> Instead of producing something common to all that we call language, I am saying that these phenomena have no one thing in common which makes us use the same word for all, – but that they are *related* to one another in many different ways. And it is because of this relationship, or these relationships, that we call them all "language." (1953, §65)

Family resemblances do not only account for the commonality of languages and games, but such things as numbers (1953, §§67–8), colors, and shapes (§§72–3), and this has suggested an account of universals according to which commonality is characterized by family resemblances (Bambrough 1960). It has also suggested a more modest but very influential psychological theory of concepts according to which most human concepts do not have necessary and sufficient conditions and instead have analog and prototype structures that rely on "networks of overlapping attributes" (Rosch and Mervis 1996, 443).

Wittgenstein specifically targets the view that using natural language is to be characterized in terms of "operating a calculus according to definite rules" (1953, §81). Wittgenstein suggests various reasons against this view including that observation of linguistic behavior "does not enable us to see any clear rule" and it is not clear how someone is supposed "to determine the rule" according to which a person is using language (1953, §82; also §§151–2). He also argues that rules are like signposts on a road and that by themselves do not determine a unique interpretation (1953, §85). Suppose a sign uses a finger to point in a direction. "But where is it said," Wittgenstein asks, "which way I am to follow it; whether in the direction of its finger or (e.g.) in the opposite one?" Moreover, once it is determined that it points in the direction of the finger, exactly in which direction does it point: "along the road or the footpath or cross-country?" (ibid.).[2]

---

[2] Exit signs on a highway in a foreign country can be ambiguous in the same way.

Wittgenstein's main point is that "no course of action could be determined by a rule, because every course of action can be made out to accord with the rule" (1953, §201). Wittgenstein supports his case with the fact that there is no unique way of continuing a number series. A student may be given the series "2, 4, 6, 8, 10, 12" and asked to continue the series and the pupil continues by counting by twos. If the student continues the series "beyond 1000 – and he writes 1000, 1004, 1008, 1012," then according to Wittgenstein, "We say to him: 'Look what you've done!' – He doesn't understand. We say: 'You were meant to add *two*'" (1953, §185). But the student could be equally baffled and answer "Yes isn't it right? I thought that was how I was *meant* to do it" because perhaps the student continued the series according to the rule "Add 2 up to 1000, 4 up to 2000, 6 up to 3000 and so on" (ibid.).

Accordingly, any series of numbers accords with some rule. Wittgenstein argues that it does not help to appeal to the rule that the teacher meant or had in mind. Every rule is subject to competing interpretations that are equally compatible with the rule. For example, Wittgenstein asks, "So when you gave the order +2 you meant that he was to write 1002 after 1000 – and did you also mean that he should write 1868 after 1866, and 100036 after 100034, and so on – an infinite number of such propositions?" (1953, §186). Wittgenstein suggests that any rule one might offer will be compatible with distinct and incompatible applications of the rule. Accordingly, a rule by itself cannot determine the correct way of determining a series in much the same way that a signpost by itself does not determine the correct way of following the signpost.[3]

What this shows, Wittgenstein argues, is that something else – something other than the rule – must be "exhibited in what we call 'obeying the rule' and 'going against it' in actual cases" (1953, §201). What Wittgenstein offers is use or practice: "And hence also 'obeying a rule' is a practice" (1953, §202). From this he immediately concludes that there cannot be private languages: "Hence it is not possible to obey a rule 'privately': otherwise thinking one was obeying a rule would be the

---

[3] For a full discussion of this part of Wittgenstein's argument and its relation to the Private Language Argument, see Kripke 1982. There is controversy about Kripke's interpretation of Wittgenstein's Private Language Argument, but there is no doubt that Wittgenstein claims that "no course of action could be determined by a rule, because every course of action can be made out to accord with the rule" (1953, §201). It is also clear that, relying on this claim, Wittgenstein concludes "Hence it is not possible to obey a rule 'privately'" (1953, §202).

same thing as obeying it" (ibid.). Earlier he observed "that a person goes by a signpost only in so far as there exists a regular use of sign posts, a custom" (1953, §198) and proceeds to ask rhetorically: "Is what we call 'obeying a rule' something that only *one* human being could do, only *once* his life?" (1953, §199).

For Wittgenstein, "how...words are used" (1953, §180; also §§43 and 432), "regularity" (§208), "common human activity" (§206), and "human action" (§225) are the more basic notions used to explain linguistic rules (§208). Words are taught "by means of *examples* and by *practice*," and "when I do this I do not communicate less...than I know myself" (ibid.). Even in one's own case, a person can do no better than appeal to what one in fact does. Wittgenstein maintains that if I am asked for "the justification for my following the rule the way I do," then the final justification – when "I have reached bedrock, and my spade is turned" – is simply "This is simply what I do" (1953, §217), "*this* is how we play the game" (§71), or "*This is how these words are used*" (§180). "In the beginning was the deed," Wittgenstein quotes Goethe's *Faust* in *On Certainty* on the topic of epistemic justification, and this also captures the fundamental role of action in his philosophy of language (1969, §402).

However, an act is not an atomic event that can be characterized independently of its context. Just as bedrock extends far beyond where one is digging, a linguistic performance for Wittgenstein is essentially tied to a larger context of activity that he indicates with the term "form of life." A language is "woven" into a larger network of actions (1953, §7) – that is, for Wittgenstein, as we saw, "the *speaking* of language is part of an activity," and this activity into which a linguistic performance is woven is "a form of life" (1953, §23). Giving orders, and obeying them, for instance, is a language game that includes the broader but specific social facts that determine who can give orders and who must obey. Accordingly, to "imagine a language game is to imagine a form of life" (1953, §19).

While the elusive term "form of life" (*Lebensform*) easily "becomes a runaway phrase" when reading the *Investigations* (Cavell 1996, 288), Wittgenstein does give it some clear contours. The concept of life already played a key role in the *Tractatus*, where he wrote that "The world and life are one" (1921, 5.621), which is intended to elucidate or develop the claim that "the limits of *language* (of that language which alone I understand) mean the limits of *my* world" (5.62). Life in the *Tractatus* is not to be identified with biological life, although it includes it, and this also applies to a form of life in the *Investigations*. A form of life includes biological factors such as "walking, eating, drinking, playing" (1953, §25; also p. 230) and certainly language use is part of human biology.

But it also includes factors that distinguish human beings from each other and are narrower than biological life.[4] Wittgenstein writes that "To imagine a language means to imagine a form of life" (1953, §19), and the use of the indefinite article "a" for both language and life indicates that he is intending to refer to more than biological factors that apply to all human beings. To imagine a particular language game is to imagine "*a* form of life" (eine *Lebensform*), and Wittgenstein imagines "innumerable" language games, including "a language consisting only of orders and reports in battle" or "a language consisting only of questions and expressions for answering yes and no" (ibid.). Moreover, the multiplicity of language games "is not something fixed, given once and for all; but new types of language, new language games, as we may say, come into existence, and others become obsolete and forgotten" (1953, §23). Wittgenstein immediately follows this observation about the transitory nature of language games with the explanation: "Here the term 'language-*game*' is meant to bring into prominence that the *speaking* of language is a part of an activity, or a form of life" (ibid.). It would make very little sense in this context for Wittgenstein to be claiming that he is using the term "language-game" to highlight the fact that the *speaking* of language is simply part of the general human capacity for language shared by all human beings.[5]

Wittgenstein's focus is on the transiency and variability of human language and the life in which linguistic activity is embedded, and accordingly he follows his observation that the speaking of language is part of a form of life with a "review of the multiplicity of language-games" (ibid.). This suggests that a form of life is a culture (Winch 1958), but Wittgenstein does not use the term "culture" in the *Investigations*, and it would be misleading to assimilate form of life to

---

[4] Cavell (1989, 41) calls the biological sense of "form of life" the "vertical sense" and the cultural or "ethnological sense" of Wittgenstein's term the "horizontal sense." For a defense of the view that Wittgenstein's concept of a "form of life" is the biological concept, see Garver 1994, 239–52.

[5] It should be noted that Wittgenstein does not write that he is bringing into prominence the fact that "the *speaking* of language is part of . . . the [human] form of life." He is bringing into prominence that it is "part of *an* activity [*einer Tätigkeit*], or of *a* form of life [*einer Lebensform*]" (emphasis in English added).

culture.[6] Wittgenstein writes that for human beings "to agree in the *language* they use" is an "agreement... in form of life" (1953, §241). If "language" refers to diverse natural languages, then the concept of a form of life can without much harm be glossed in terms of culture. But, needless to say, this is not what Wittgenstein has in mind. For Wittgenstein, a language is a language game, and language games are narrower than natural languages and can cut across natural languages. A form of life is a network of actual human activity in which specific language games are embedded, and this network includes biological and cultural factors, but it also is fine-grained enough to include the differences in everyday lives of families and communities.[7]

Because the form of life is constitutive of a linguistic performance, Wittgenstein's bedrock of linguistic performance – "This is simply what I do" (1953, §217) – includes a form of life. Wittgenstein states this explicitly: "What has to be accepted, the given – so one could say – is *forms of life*" (1953, 226). But a form of life is "complicated" and a "hurly-burly of human actions," and consequently linguistic performance resists a tractable and unified treatment.

Because his focal point in the *Investigations* is the linguistic performance, Wittgenstein is driven to the conclusion that language is not a system and resists proper theoretical treatment. When Wittgenstein observes that language is a multiplicity of language games, and "this multiplicity is not something fixed, given once and for all," and quite unlike "what logicians have said about the structure of language," he makes it clear that he is thinking about "the *speaking* of language,"

---

[6] The term does appear in the selections in Wittgenstein 1980, but these passages suggest a distinction between culture and life. In 1931 he writes "culture is like a big organization" and describes "an age without culture," which is "fragmented and the power of an individual is used up in overcoming opposing forces and frictional resistance" (1980, 6). Later in 1940 he describes the house he built for his sister as "an expression of great *understanding* (of a culture, etc.)," but adds "*primordial* life, wild life striving to erupt into the open – that is lacking" (1980, 38). In 1950 Wittgenstein writes, "I believe that if one is to enjoy a writer one has to *like* the culture he belongs to as well. If he finds it indifferent or distasteful, one's admiration cools off" (1980, 85). If a shared form of life is a necessary condition for understanding someone's language, then clearly culture, at least as Wittgenstein uses the term here, cannot be identified with life.

[7] Cavell (1989) is right to emphasize the relevance of the concepts of the "everyday" and "home" (Wittgenstein 1953, §§116, 120, and 134) to understanding Wittgenstein's concept of a form of life, but Wittgenstein's concept of home and everyday life cannot be explicated in national or cultural terms. For the important role of marginality in Wittgenstein's philosophy, see Scheman 1996.

which is "part of an activity" (1953, §23). The essence of language, according to Wittgenstein, is not "sublime," "hidden," or "beneath the surface," but it is "something that already lies open before our eyes" (1953, §§89, 92, and 126). What lies open to view is "actual language" (1953, §107), that is, "the spatial and temporal phenomenon of language" (§108). The philosopher should speak of sentences and words "in exactly the sense we speak of them in ordinary life when we say, e.g., 'Here is a Chinese sentence,' or 'No, that only looks like writing; it is actually just an ornament'" (ibid.).

If linguistic performance is bedrock for philosophy, then "[p]hilosophy may in no way interfere with the actual use of language," "it cannot give it any foundation," and "there is nothing to explain" about performance either (1953, §§124 and 126). Philosophy "can in the end only describe" the actual use of language (1953, §124). In fact, Wittgenstein exhorts: "We must do away with all *explanation*, and description alone must take its place" (1953, §109). Accordingly, the proper method of philosophizing is to describe various examples of linguistic use (1953, §133), and, as noted earlier, the assertion that "*This is how these words are used*" (1953, §180) is where justification for why an action counts as following a rule comes to an end (§217).

So Wittgenstein is quite right to state in the *Investigations* that he is "turning our whole examination round" (1953, §108). Rather than beginning with linguistic performance – "the *speaking* of language" (1953, §23) – as the *explanans* that is explained or analyzed in terms of a "*preconceived idea* of crystalline purity," such as the idea of mathematical logic, linguistic performance understood as a particular "spatial and temporal phenomenon" is assigned the role of *explanandum*. But linguistic performance is "a labyrinth of paths" or a "maze" that resists theoretical unity (1953, §§203 and 18). It is possible to describe "how these words are used," but accurate descriptions at best could only duplicate "a complicated network of similarities, overlapping and criss-crossing: sometimes overall similarities, sometimes similarities in detail" (1953, §66), in much the same way that the *Investigations* is an album of a variety of vignettes. Moreover, an accurate description of a linguistic performance would have to capture the form of life of which the performance is a part, but a form of life is not tractable.

There is another source for the fragmentation of discourse on language in Wittgenstein's philosophy. Not only is its subject matter fragmented, but on Wittgenstein's own view, discourses on language are themselves linguistic performances and thus subject to the varieties of performances. Discourse on language, too, is a "multiplicity of language-games" (1953, §23) without an overarching unity. Like language itself, discourse on language will be "a labyrinth of paths" (1953, §203) or like "an ancient city: a maze of little streets and squares" (1953, §18).

Wittgenstein seems to have some recognition of this consequence. He writes that the "work of the philosopher consists in assembling reminders for a particular purpose" without specifying a single purpose (1953, §126). A little later Wittgenstein writes that "[t]here is not *a* philosophical method, though there are indeed methods, like different therapies" (1953, §133). There is no single philosophical method, but it is significant that here he adds "like different therapies," signaling that he actually has a unified conception of philosophy and its purpose as therapy or medical treatment. The "real discovery" is one that "gives philosophy peace, so that it is no longer tormented by questions which bring *itself* in question (ibid.). Statements about the objectivity and reality of facts are not statements that belong to philosophy, but call for "philosophical *treatment*" (1953, §254). A problem of philosophy is a "philosophical disease" caused by a "one-sided diet: one nourishes one's thinking with only one kind of example" (1953, §593). Language has a central role in the etiology of philosophical diseases: "Philosophy is a battle against the bewitchment of our intelligence by means of language" (1953, §109).

The treatment of philosophical disease is simple: "to call in mind the differences between the language games" (1953, §290). For example, the mind-body problem "disappears only if we make a radical break with the idea that language always functions in one way, always serves the same purpose: to convey thoughts – which may be about houses, pains, good and evil, or anything else you please" (1953, §304). If it is not the case that language always functions in one way, then there is no reason to suppose that the philosophy of language or philosophy more generally always functions or functions optimally in only one way. The diversity of language games and forms of life also undercuts Wittgenstein's exclusive conception of philosophy as therapy seeking "*complete* clarity," which for Wittgenstein means that "philosophical problems...*completely* disappear" (1953, §133). Instead of eliminating difficulties, seeking "peace" from the torment of self-undermining questions, or trying to discover something that "makes me capable of stopping doing philosophy when I want to" (ibid.), philosophy can also aim to torment, confuse, undermine, and promote disorder.[8]

Derrida and Structuralism

It falls to Jacques Derrida to develop these aspects of linguistic performance. Whereas Wittgenstein's *Investigations* is a response to the philosophy of language in the tradition of Frege, Derrida's philosophy of language is best seen as a response to structuralism in the tradition of Saussure, particularly structuralist literary criticism.[9]

A central tenet of structuralism in the tradition of the Geneva School is that the relevant structure is not historical or diachronic but exists synchronically or simultaneously at a given time. In his early essay "Force and Signification," Derrida (1967, 1978) responds that the actual reading of a literary work in fact has duration; moreover, any description of the work's structure also is sequential and diachronic, and thus is not presented simultaneously. He writes that "simultaneity" is a "myth... promoted to the status of a regulating ideal" (1978, 24). But this treatment of time "seems to contradict... the most precious and original intention of structuralism" (1978, 26), namely to take seriously the phenomenal form of language – "the form which is visible" (1978, 27) – and not treat it as an incomplete manifestation of an invisible ideal or hidden intention. Structuralism, in other words, is rooted in naturalist commitments, but by abstracting structure from duration, it departs from naturalism. For Derrida structuralism "risks enclosing... becoming – by giving it form," that is, "stifling force under form" (1978, 26) and ceding "force... to *eidos* (i.e., the form which is visible for the metaphorical eye)" (1978, 27).

---

[8] In other words, Wittgenstein's writing and argumentation do seem to express the detours and side roads of actual language use, but *pace* Glendinnig 2004, Wittgenstein does not meander, stroll, or wander but darts about to escape the torments of philosophy.

[9] It is important to highlight the fact that Derrida is responding primarily to the structuralism of the Geneva School and its successors. The structuralists of the Prague Circle, which included Roman Jakobson, Bohuslav Havránek, Vilém Mathesius, Jan Mukařovsk, and Bohumil Trnka, did not believe that there is an "*insurmountable barrier between the synchronic and diachronic methods.*" According to the *Theses* of the Prague Circle, it is not possible that a "*synchronic description absolutely exclude the notion of evolution*, for such a synchronic moment reflects the disappearing, present, and coming stages" (Steiner 1982, 6; also see Merquior 1986).

Although Derrida's philosophy of language is an attempt at the "conceptualization of intensity or force" (ibid.), his concept of force is not easy to decipher, partly because it is informed both by the concept of force in Leibniz's mature metaphysics and Hegel's discussion of force in the *Phenomenology of Mind*. Nevertheless, it is clear that for Derrida force is tied to actual phenomena. Force is "the form which is visible" and "[b]y its very articulation force becomes a phenomenon" (1978, 26–7). Derrida explicitly denies that force should be understood as something distinct that underlies the phenomena, but at the same time "[f]orce is the other of language without which language would not be what it is" (ibid.). At the very least, force involves the temporal duration of the actual linguistic event, whether writing, reading, speaking, or listening. Force "is not hidden under a form" (1978, 28), but instead it belongs to the linguistic event occurring in real time.

But force is not mere temporal duration. Force understood "from within itself" is the sense of creating in writing or speaking. It seems that Derrida's concept of force also includes the actual activity of writing or speaking. Derrida refers to "the moment at which we must decide" to write and states that "writing is the anguish of the Hebrew *ruah*" (Derrida 1978, 4–5 and 9). Writing is "inaugural," and its meaning "is neither before nor after the act of writing" (1978, 11). Force, then, is also the "freedom of speech," "the freedom to augur," or "a freedom of response" (1978, 12). Derrida's use of the term "force" as a contrast to "form" and "structure"[10] is also intended to highlight that he is concerned with the very act of writing or speaking, that is, with speaking or writing as not only an event in time but also a performance of a writer or speaker.[11]

J. L. Austin

It is not surprising, then, that Derrida turns to J. L Austin's 1955 William James Lectures published under the title *How to Do Things with Words*, where Austin develops and criticizes his own distinction between performative and constative sentences. A constative is a sentence that makes a statement that is either true or false, whereas a performative is where "the issuing of the utterance is the performing of an action – it is not

---

[10] Derrida's essay "Force and Signification" is a response to the Swiss structuralist literary critic Jean Rousset's *Form and Signification* (1962).

[11] Note the role of force in Humboldt's philosophy of language, discussed in Chapter 4.

normally thought of as just saying something" (Austin 1975, 6–7). Promising, apologizing, or baptizing are paradigm examples of such linguistic performances. One of Austin's points is that philosophers of language have focused on constatives at the expense of performatives.

In addition to performatives and constatives, Austin distinguishes between locutionary and illocutionary acts. A locutionary act is "the act of 'saying something' in [the] full normal sense" – that is, it includes "the utterance of certain noises, the utterance of certain words in a certain construction, and the utterance of them with a certain 'meaning'..., i.e., with a certain sense and with a certain reference" (1975, 94). An illocutionary act on the other hand, is what is done with a locutionary act. In saying something a speaker can aim to do other things, that is, in performing a locutionary act a speaker can hope to do other things, such as "asking or answering a question, giving some information or an assurance or a warning, announcing a verdict..., making an appointment or an appeal or a criticism, making an identification or giving a description" (1975, 98–9). Whereas a locutionary act has meaning, that is, sense and reference, an illocutionary act has force, for instance "*the force* of a question," of an estimate, an announcement, and so on (1975, 99). For Austin the distinction between the force of an illocutionary act and the sense and reference of a locutionary act, and any careful discussion of the meaning and use of language, need to be clear if the topic of discussion is the sense and reference of a locutionary act or the force of an illocutionary act (1975, 100 and 103).

The distinction between constatives and performatives, however, collapses, according to Austin. When we state something, "we are doing something," and consequently, Austin argues, "to state is every bit as much to perform an illocutionary act as, say, to warn or pronounce" (1975, 133–4). For instance, we can make a statement and insist that we are not warning or protesting but "simply stating the facts." Accordingly, statements are "liable to every kind of infelicity to which performatives are liable" (1975, 134). For example, just as a promise implies sincerity, making a statement implies that the person making the statement believes what is being said. Constatives, then, are kinds of performatives.

Austin draws an important conclusion from the collapse of the constative-performative distinction. If "stating is performing an act" (1975, 139), then stating truly will also be an action as much as arguing soundly, advising well, judging well, or blaming justifiably (1975, 142). Austin points out that "in the case of stating truly or falsely, just as much as in the case of advising well or badly, the intents and purposes of the utterances and its context are important; what is judged true in a school book may not be so judged in a work of historical research" (1975, 143). For example, the statement "France is hexagonal" is a rough description that by itself is neither true nor false, Austin maintains, but it is true or false "for certain intents and purposes" (ibid.). In short, the "truth or falsity of statements depends not merely on the meanings of words but on what act you were performing in what circumstance" (1975, 145). Accordingly, "stating is only one among very numerous speech acts of the illocutionary class" and it has "no unique position" (1975, 147 and 149).

Austin aims to capture this with a new taxonomy of illocutionary acts that includes making statements:

(1) Verdictives
(2) Exercitives
(3) Commissive
(4) Behabatives (a shocker this)
(5) Expositives
    (1975, 151)

Although he is not happy about this taxonomy, it is good "enough to play Old Harry with two fetishes which I admit to an inclination to play Old Harry with, viz. (1) the true/false fetish, (2) the value/fact fetish" (ibid.).

The reason for these dramatic consequences in Austin's philosophy of language is that he takes the unit of linguistic analysis to be the "total speech act in the total speech situation," and according to Austin, this "is the *only actual* phenomenon which, in the last resort, we are engaged in elucidating" (1975, 148). With the actual speech performance of a speaker in the cross hairs of Austin's analysis, it is not surprising that the distinction between constatives and performatives disappears. In his words: "Once we realize that what we have to study is *not* the sentence, but the issuing of an utterance in a speech situation, there can hardly be any longer a possibility of not seeing that stating is performing an act" (1975, 139).

The distinction between locutionary and illocutionary acts is also affected by the primacy of the actual speech situation. "[T]he locutionary act as much as the illocutionary is an abstraction only," Austin writes, because "every genuine speech act is both" (1975, 147). "With the constative utterance, we abstract from the illocutionary ... aspects of the speech act, and we concentrate on the locutionary: moreover, we use an oversimplified notion of correspondence with the facts" (1975, 145–6). On the other hand, "[w]ith the performative utterance, we attend as much as possible to the illocutionary force of the utterance, and abstract from the dimension of correspondence with facts" (1975, 146). In the latter case we attend to the diversity of circumstances in which speakers use language, whereas in the former case the ideal is "what would be right to say in all circumstances, for any purpose, to any audience, etc." Austin adds: "Perhaps it is sometimes realized."

Derrida and Austin

As Derrida points out, he is "in many respects quite close to Austin, both interested in and indebted to his problematic" (1988, 38). Derrida highlights Austin's concern for "the problematic of the *performative*," that he "was obliged to free the analysis of the performative from the authority of the truth *value*," and that Austin turned from truth to the force of a speech act (Derrida 1977a, 186–7). In fact, Derrida calls Austin's "line of thought... nothing less than Nietzschean," which for Derrida is high praise.

The problem with Austin's theory of speech acts, according to Derrida, is that it assumes a determinate context or a set of appropriate circumstances, including intentions and conventions (1977a, 187). The theory of speech acts is, in part, aimed at setting out the rules of this context that determines the force and content of diverse speech acts. Derrida argues that there is no "rigorous and scientific concept of *context*" and that "a context is never absolutely determinable" (1977a, 174). For Derrida, this affects not only Austin's theory of language but any attempt to develop a science of language, in which language is understood in terms of linguistic events or speech acts. Such performances do not allow for the abstraction and idealization that scientific theory requires (Derrida 1988, 69) and therefore there "can be no rigorous analogy between a scientific theory, no matter which, and a theory of language" (1988, 118).

One source of this indeterminacy of speech contexts is that "every sign, linguistic or non-linguistic, spoken or written..., in a small or large unit, can be *cited*, put between quotation marks; in so doing it can break with every given context, engendering an infinity of new contexts in a manner which is absolutely illimitable" (1977a, 185). Strictly speaking, quoted contexts are an instance of a more generic feature of language that according to Derrida is the source of the indeterminacy of contexts, namely "duplication or duplicity, this iterability of the mark" (1977a, 186). In the case of Austin, Derrida highlights that "Austin acknowledges that *all* conventional acts are exposed to failure" in which words, such as "I promise" can be used in contexts where no promises are made (1977a, 188–9). For Austin, these are abnormal, nonserious, or parasitic uses of the words "I promise," whereas using those words to make a promise is the conventional, ordinary, or standard use of those words.

Derrida believes that the possibility of failure is a necessary feature of every speech act, and he understands failure in terms of the "iterability of the mark." What Derrida seems to be maintaining is that every linguistic mark can be repeated and used in a way that undermines the idea that there is a determinate context that defines the meaning of a speech act (1977a, 191). He writes that "No context can entirely enclose it" (1977a, 182).

Part of the problem, according to Derrida, is that a speech act of a certain type, say, an assertion, is "an open corpus," "is not limitable either in the past or in the future," and lacks "the completeness of a set" (1988, 39). Derrida refers to set theory in this context, suggesting that his point is that assertions do not form a set that can be identified or characterized by a rule, formula, or necessary and sufficient conditions that each assertion satisfies. One reason he gives for this claim is that the assertion of such a rule, formula, or set of conditions is itself an assertion, but it cannot satisfy its own conditions. Derrida assumes that assertions of such conditions cannot be self-referential.

The self-referential nature of a theory of speech acts is also a reason why Derrida believes there can be no science of speech acts:

> [T]he language of theory always leaves a residue that is neither formalizable or idealizable in terms of that theory of language. Theoretical utterances are speech acts. Whether this fact is regarded as a privilege or as a limit of speech act theory, it ruins the analogical value (in the strict sense) between speech act theory and other theories. (1988, 70)

While a theory of speech acts has to be self-referential, a scientific theory, say, physics or biology, is not self-referential, and this difference undermines any attempt to assimilate linguistic theory with science, Derrida believes.

At times Derrida also seems to suggest that any attempt to determine a set of speech acts can be refuted by a parody of the theory that, in effect, is also a counterexample to the theory.[12] However, Derrida's main line of argumentation is that the most important features of the context of a speech act that would be relevant to characterizing speech acts are intentions and conventions, but neither can serve to determine the meaning of a speech act or event.

He argues that "no criterion that is simply *inherent* in the manifest utterance is capable of distinguishing an utterance that is serious from the same utterance when it is not" (1988, 68). There is no mark that can determine, to use Austin's terminology, the illocutionary force of a speech act. Any words that one might introduce to identify a sincere and serious assertion or promise – for example, "I really, really mean this" – can also be used by liars and jokers. Of course, no formal features of a mark by itself can indicate seriousness or honesty, but adding a linguistic convention does not help: "[C]onventions are, in fact, never entirely adequate" (1988, 82). Whatever convention that might be introduced to indicate sincerity can also be flaunted. So neither the formal nor conventional features can define different illocutionary forces.

Intentions also cannot serve to determine contexts that define a speech act. First, there are no linguistic marks that are simply the "realizations" of intentions so that the occurrence of the mark guarantees that the speaker has a certain intention (1988, 68). In other words, no linguistic mark is the criterion for a "responsible, deliberate, self-conscious" intention that would be sufficient to distinguish a serious from a non-serious speech act (ibid.). An earnest demeanor or tone is not reserved for serious discourse, and any mark or sign one might try to introduce to signify earnest intentions will be subject to misuse.

Derrida concludes that "solely intention... [that] is not identical with its 'realization'" can differentiate "an utterance when it is serious from the same utterance when it is not" (ibid.). Unfortunately, even an intention that is in some sense "situated 'behind' the phenomenal utterance (in the sense of the 'visible' or 'audible' signs...)," that is, an intention that is not identical with its realization as an utterance or inscription cannot determine the appropriate context (ibid.).

> [G]iven the structure of iteration, the intention animating the utterance will never be through and through present to itself and to its content.... Above all, this essential absence of intending the actuality of

---

[12] For example, see Derrida's discussion of Searle's theory of promising, specifically his critique of Searle's distinction between promises and threats (1988, 74–5).

utterance, this structural unconsciousness, if you like, prohibits any saturation of context. In order for context to be exhaustively determinable, in the sense required by Austin, conscious intention would at the very least have to be totally present and immediately transparent to itself and to others, since it is a determining center of context. The concept of – or the search for – the context thus seems to suffer from the same theoretical and "interested" uncertainty as the concept of the "ordinary." (Derrida 1977a, 192)

Derrida's reasons are not entirely transparent, but two arguments stand out.

First, the "essential absence of intending the actuality of utterance, this structural unconsciousness, if you like, prohibits any saturation of the context" (ibid.). For Derrida, the status and structure of intentions and motivations are undetermined and open-ended. He refers to the "ethical and teleological discourse of consciousness," that is, the various competing accounts of what motivates or drives human beings, which are unsettled, ambiguous, and open-ended (ibid. and 1988, 76). This discourse does not support the assumption that there are determinate and identifiable intentions that have a sufficiently clear structure to serve as a foundation for an account of meaning. Derrida appeals to the possible role of unconscious intentions and raises various skeptical questions about our knowledge of what we or other speakers consciously or unconsciously intend or desire, whether speakers are responsible for their unconscious intentions, and which intentions are decisive in determining the force and content of a speech act (1988, 75). For Derrida, "the identity of an intention" that is supposed to inform a linguistic performance has not been established (ibid.). Derrida ties this to his view that the psychological identity of a person "can never be isolated ideally in its pure identity" (1988, 76).

Second, an actual utterance or inscription used on an occasion in a speech act has an identity or character that a single speaker cannot intend. The identity of an utterance or inscription is a function of the various ways in which it can be iterated or "cited." Another way of stating this, is that the identity of an individual utterance or inscription in part depends on what type or kind of utterance or inscription it is. In Derrida's words, the sameness of a linguistic mark corrupts its singularity and divides it from itself (1977a, 194). For example, what word a speaker utters is a function of what phonological type to which the sounds the speaker makes belongs. For Derrida, however, the type to which the utterance belongs depends on the pattern of iteration, which is open-ended and cannot be determined by anyone's intentions on a particular occasion. So the semantic identity of an utterance is a function of future patterns, and this cannot be intended by the speaker.[13] Consequently, the type to which the speaker's utterance belongs is autonomous of the speaker's intentions. This, I believe, is what Derrida has in mind when he maintains that a linguistic item functions "detached from the present and singular intention of its production" (ibid.). While speakers can intend the singularity of the utterance or inscription they make, they cannot intend its sameness, that is, the way in which their performance will be classified.

What makes Derrida's writing difficult and unsettling, especially his later work, is that he attempts not only to state his position but also to exemplify it. He aims to illustrate the autonomy and indeterminate nature of meaning by developing unintended interpretations and odd contexts for texts that suggest that the text is not univocal and is subject to competing interpretations, including his own writing. At the same time, he aims to demonstrate the freedom of a linguistic performance, namely its time-bound individuality, by performing what resists classification and iteration.

An Epitaph for Language

It is instructive to place Derrida's philosophy of language alongside the dramatic conclusions Davidson reaches in his later work. In "Communication and Convention," Davidson argues that the illocutionary force of a speech act cannot be determined by linguistic conventions: "There is no known, agreed upon, publicly recognizable convention for making assertions" (1984, 270). The same holds for other illocutionary forces, such as giving orders, asking questions, or making promises. This is not to deny that often we succeed in making our intention known to ask a question or make an assertion, but it "was not thanks to a convention we succeeded" (ibid.). Similarly, there is no convention that a speaker is asserting something that she believes because "every liar would use it" (ibid.).

Davidson also argues for the "autonomy of meaning" (1984, 274). The ulterior purposes a speaker has for engaging in a linguistic performance and the literal meaning of the utterance used in the performance

---

[13] See Heal 1997, 193, for a similar gloss of an important premise in Davidson's argument.

are independent of each other. In other words, the literal meaning of language cannot be derived from the nonlinguistic intentions a speaker or writer has. Of course, literal meaning could be derived from the speaker's or writer's intention to use linguistic items with their literal meaning. But this intention assumes that the items already have a literal meaning and hence it cannot be used to explain literal meaning without begging the question (1984, 271–2).

An important reason for the autonomy of meaning, according to Davidson, is that "the criteria for deciding what an utterance literally means... do not decide whether [the speaker] has accomplished his ulterior purpose" (1984, 274). Having determined that a speaker literally said "Eat your eggplant," to use Davidson's example, does not entail that the speaker's ulterior motive was to order the hearer to eat his eggplant. Davidson grants that one may infer that the speaker intends to represent himself as using those words with their literal meanings and force, but representing oneself as giving a verbal order to eat eggplant is not the same as giving an order to eat eggplant or even intending to give an order to eat eggplant.

Derrida's critique of the reliance on normal or standard uses of language to characterize meaning also has a parallel line of thought in Davidson's claim that a literal meaning cannot be derived from standard uses: "Since the literal meaning operates as well when the [standard] use is absent as when it is present, no conventions that operate only in 'standard' situations can give the literal meaning" (1984, 275).

One might reply that even if the literal meaning is autonomous in the sense that it cannot be defined in terms of conventions and nonlinguistic intentions, surely what meanings are assigned to words is a matter of convention. But even this is false, according to Davidson. Conventions require regularity or "rule-governed repetition" (1984, 277 and 279–82), but "[t]he only candidate for recurrence[14] we have is the interpretation of sound patterns: speaker and hearer must repeatedly... interpret relevantly similar sound patterns of the speaker in the same way" (1984, 277). On Davidson's account, this means that speaker and hearer must have coinciding theories for interpreting the speaker and that they use this theory repeatedly. But Davidson denies that coinciding theories are needed to interpret the speaker successfully. Moreover, interpretation depends on "intuition, luck,... skill,... taste and sympathy," and this cannot be formalized or reduced to rules (1984, 278–9).

---

[14] Or iteration, in Derrida's terminology.

Davidson develops this perspective on language by focusing, as did Derrida, on deviant uses of language in the essay "A Nice Derangement of Epitaphs." The title refers to a malapropism – Mrs. Malaprop intended to say "a nice arrangement of epithets" – and Davidson argues that the "widespread existence of malapropisms and their kin" requires that we "modify certain commonly accepted views about what it is to 'know a language,' or about what a natural language is" (1986, 158–9). This is actually an understatement because what Davidson concludes in this essay is the abandonment, and not just the modification, of commonly accepted views. "I conclude," Davidson writes at the end of the essay, "that there is no such thing as language, not if a language is anything like what many philosophers and linguists have supposed" (1986, 174). What does not exist, according to Davidson, is language as a rule-governed structure of system that language users share and that they use to interpret each other's linguistic performances. There is "no learnable common core of consistent behavior, no shared grammar or rules, no portable interpreting machine set to grind out the meaning of an arbitrary utterance" (1986, 173). Of course, if there is no language in this sense, then "[t]here is no such thing to be learned, mastered, or born with" (1986, 174).

The main line of argument for this conclusion is that our capacity to interpret and understand malapropisms undermines the assumption that the person who hears and interprets the malapropism would "share a complex system or theory with the speaker, a system which makes possible the articulation of logical relations between utterances, and explains the ability to interpret novel utterances in an organized way" (1986, 160–1). This is because malapropisms are "expressions that are not covered by prior learning," and hence they are not covered by any system or structure a hearer might have in place when hearing the malapropism. Nevertheless, the hearer interprets and understands the speaker correctly, although "the interpreter did not have a correct theory in advance" (1986, 166). In fact, the hearer needs to alter the theory she might have had in advance in order to accommodate the malapropism.

Davidson maintains that "any general framework, whether conceived as a grammar for English, or as a rule for accepting grammars, or a basic grammar plus rules for modifying or extending it – any such general framework, by virtue of the features that make it general, will be insufficient for interpreting particular utterances" (1986, 171). Linguistic performance eventually outstrips any system language users might have available to them. "There is no word or construction that cannot be converted to a new use by an ingenious or ignorant speaker," not to mention "sheer invention... say in Joyce or Lewis Carroll," Davidson writes, that "we can be... good at interpreting" (1986, 167). I suggest that this is the very same phenomenon that Derrida highlights in terms of the iterability of language and the inability of theory to capture all possible iterations.

The way we interpret such deviant linguistic performances, Davidson suggests, is in terms of a "passing theory" of what a particular utterance on a particular occasion means, no matter how defective. This passing theory, however, is not a rule-generated system, but a constantly changing theory tailored for particular speakers and "every unexpected turn in the conversation" (1986, 173). In constructing this passing theory, an interpreter relies on all kinds of evidence, "character, dress, role, sex... and whatever has been gained by observing the speaker's behavior, linguistic or otherwise" (1986, 167). How interpreters arrive at their passing theories for a particular linguistic performance is a "mysterious process by which a speaker or hearer uses what he knows in advance plus present data" (1986, 172). The process is "mysterious" because "there are no rules for arriving at passing theories, no rules in any strict sense, as opposed to rough maxims and methodological generalities." They are "derived by wit, luck and wisdom" and "there is no more chance of regularizing, or teaching, this process than there is of regularizing or teaching the process of creating new theories to cope with new data in any field" (1986, 173–4). While Davidson focuses on impromptu theory building rather than on art, both he and Derrida agree that deviancy and creativity undermine orthodox conceptions of language.

Conclusion

The focus on linguistic performance – the empirical basis for the study of language – tends to undermine the view that language is a rule-governed system subject to empirical investigation. One might try to stave off this tendency by appealing to first-person knowledge that speakers have of what they have in mind when they speak, relying on the observation that understanding language is not primarily trying to interpret a stranger's utterances but knowing what we have in mind – our "intentional contents" when we perform (Searle 1987, Glock 2003, 206–7). Although this is a viable strategy, it does little to bolster the idea that the study of language is an empirical science in the sense developed after the demise of introspectionism in psychology, namely a science based on a third-person perspective. The turn to first-person knowledge to make sense of linguistic performance only strengthens the suspicion that performance eludes the net of scientific theory.

The history of the study of language suggests that there is a persistent divide in this study. Language is seen either as a systematic, rule-governed structure or it is an empirical object. If it is empirical, its domain and source of evidence are linguistic performance, but performance appears to elude systematic determination. The varieties of linguistic irrealism – whether about form, meaning, or language itself – that we find in the philosophies of Wittgenstein, Quine, Davidson, and Derrida are testimonies to the strength and persistence of this appearance, no matter what one might think about the specific merits of these views.

On the other hand, if language is seen as a system, its study will carve out a domain distinct from performance and empirical investigation. This was Leibniz's response to Locke, and its clearest expression is the work of Frege and his successors, including the linguistic and semantic work of Montague (1974) and Katz (1981). A language itself is or is a representation of an abstract object studied using a priori methods, much like mathematics. A variant approach is followed by Chomsky, for whom language is a psychological object – something that grows in the brain – and not a Platonic object without spatial or temporal location. Nevertheless, language for Chomsky is a formal competence that is distinct from inchoate performance. Moreover, it is an abstract property of the brain subject to formal investigations that can be done independently of empirical research, much like arithmetic is an abstract property of a calculator that can be studied independently of the calculator's physical properties. In other words, for Chomsky as for Frege, language is a structure discovered by reason and intuition, not perception and induction (Katz 1985, 174).

Accordingly, the turn to language in order to answer questions about the nature of the human mind runs into a dilemma. Turns to linguistic performance threaten to spin out of control, turning mind into a mirror, projection, or construction of language, while dissolving the stability and unity of language itself. The mind mirrors something that eludes the grasp of theory. On the other hand, turns to language as an abstract structure distinct from performance have very little spin. The view that language is an abstract structure must come with a set of assumptions about the human mind already so rich that it is hard to see how language could serve as a touchstone for resolving disputes about the nature of the mind. The mind either is or has the capacity to represent an abstract structure of rules that not only guide the mind but can also be known through introspection or rational intuition. Any questions about whether the mind is a causally structured physical object known through perception and induction like any other natural phenomena will not be resolved by the rationalism, mentalism, and intellectualism of such a turn.[15]

Hume maintains that it is "the whimsical condition of mankind" that we must act and reason, but the demands of reason and the demands of action cannot be brought into harmony (1996, 4:182–3). The study of language as exhibited in its history suffers from the same condition. Language seems to us to be both an enduring and determinate formal system, what Humboldt described as *Ergon*, as well as ultimately indeterminate and transitory human action, but the demands of both resist sustainable harmony. The synthesis sought by Kant in the domain of human knowledge still eludes the study of language. The divide between the Renaissance humanist perspective on language as human action and the Scholastic perspectives on language as a formal system – a divide that modern philosophy unsuccessfully tried to overcome – seems to be an enduring and prominent landmark of the study of human language.

---

[15] For a concise discussion of the terms "rationalism," "mentalism," and "intellectualism" in linguistics, see D'Agostino 1986.

Bibliography

Aarsleff, H. 1982. *From Locke to Saussure: Essay on the Study of Language and Intellectual History*. Minneapolis: University of Minnesota Press.
    1994. "Locke's Influence." In *The Cambridge Companion to Locke*, ed. V. Chappell, 252–89. Cambridge: Cambridge University Press.
Abelard, P. 1933. *Peter Abelaerds Philosophische Schriften*. Ed. B. Geyer. *Beiträge zur Geschichte der Philosophie und Theologie des Mittelalters*, vol. 21, nos. 1–4. Münster.
Adams, M. M. 1987. *William Ockham*. Vol. 1. Notre Dame: University of Notre Dame Press.
Anscombe, G. E. M. 1967. *An Introduction to Wittgenstein's Tractatus*. London: Hutchinson.
Anselm of Canterbury. 1998. *The Major Works*. Ed. B. Davies and G. G. Evans. Oxford: Oxford University Press.
Apel, K. O. 1976. "The Transcendental Conception of Language Communication and the Idea of First Philosophy." In Parrett 1976, 32–61.
Arens, H. 1984. *Aristotle's Theory of Language and Its Tradition*. Studies in the History of Linguistics, vol. 29. Amsterdam: John Benjamins.
Aristotle. 1984. *The Complete Works of Aristotle*. Ed. J. Barnes. Princeton: Princeton University Press.
Armstrong, D. M. 1978. *A Theory of Universals*. 2 vols. Cambridge: Cambridge University Press.
Arnauld, A., and C. Lancelot. 1975. *General and Rational Grammar: The Port-Royal Grammar*. Trans. J. Rieux and B. Rollin. The Hague: Mouton.
Arnauld, A., and P. Nicole. 1996. *Logic or the Art of Thinking*. Trans. and ed. J. V. Buroker. Cambridge: Cambridge University Press.
Ashworth, E. J. 1974. *Language and Logic in the Post-Medieval Period*. Dordrecht: D. Reidel.
    1988. "Traditional Logic." In *The Cambridge History of Renaissance Philosophy*, ed. C. Schmitt and Q. Skinner, 143–72. Cambridge: Cambridge University Press.
Austin, J. L. 1975. *How to Do Things with Words*. 2nd ed. Cambridge, MA: Harvard University Press. 1st ed., 1962.

Avramides, A. 1998. "Intention and Convention." In Hale and Wright 1998, 60–86.
Ayer, A. J. 1946. *Language, Truth and Logic*. 2nd ed. London: Victor Gollancz.
Ayers, M. 1993. *Locke: Epistemology and Ontology*. 2 vols. London: Routledge.
Bach, E. 1989. *Informal Lectures on Formal Semantics*. Albany: State University of New York Press.
Bacon, F. 1968. *The Works of Francis Bacon*. Ed. J. Spedding, R. L. Ellis, and D. D. Heath. 14 vols. New York: Garrett Press. Reprint of London: Longmans, 1857–74.
——— 2000. *The New Organon*. Ed. L. Jardine and M. Silverthorne. Cambridge Texts in the History of Philosophy. Cambridge: Cambridge University Press.
——— 2001. *The Advancement of Learning*. Ed. S. J. Gould. New York: Random House.
Baker, G. P., and P. M. S. Hacker. 1984. *Frege: Logical Excavations*. Oxford: Basil Blackwell.
Bambrough, R. 1960. "Universals and Family Resemblances." *Proceedings of the Aristotelian Society* 61: 207–12.
Bauch, B. 1918. "Lotzes Logik und ihre Bedeutung im deutschen Idealismus." *Beiträge zur Philosophie des deutschen Idealismus* 1: 1–57.
Beaney, M. 1996. *Frege: Making Sense*. London: Duckworth.
Benacerraf, P., and H. Putnam (eds.). 1983. *Philosophy of Mathematics: Selected Readings*. 2nd ed. Cambridge: Cambridge University Press. Reprinted 1998.
Bentham, J. 1962. *The Works of Jeremy Bentham*. Ed. J. Bowring. 11 vols. New York: Russell and Russell.
Bird, G. 1995. "Carnap and Quine: Internal and External Questions." *Erkenntnis* 42: 41–64.
Black, M. 1964. *A Companion to Wittgenstein's Tractatus*. Ithaca: Cornell University Press.
Bloomfield, L. 1933. *Language*. New York: Henry Holt.
Boehme, J. 1956. *Sämtliche Schriften*. Ed. Will-Erich Peuckert. 11 vols. Stuttgart: Frommann.
——— 1963. *Die Urschriften*. Ed. Werner Buddecke. 2 vols. Stuttgart: Frommann.
Bonno, G. 1990. "The Diffusion and Influence of Locke's *Essay Concerning Human Understanding* in France before Voltaire's *Lettres Philosophiques*." In *A Locke Miscellany: Locke Biography and Criticism for All*, ed. J. S. Yolton, 75–85. Bristol: Thoemmes Press.
Boole, G. 1847. *The Mathematical Analysis of Logic, Being an Essay toward a Calculas of Deductive Reasoning*. London and Cambridge: Macmillan, Barclay and Macmillan. Reprint, Oxford: Oxford University Press, 1948.
Borsche, T. 1981. *Sprachansichten: Der Begriff der menschlichen Rede in der Sprachphilosophie Wilhelm von Humboldts*. Stuttgart: Klett-Cotta.
Brekle, H. E. 1971. "Die Idee einer Generativen Grammatik in Leibnizens Fragmente zur Logik." *Studia Leibnitiana* 3: 141–9.
Broadie, A. 1987. *Introduction to Medieval Logic*. New York: Oxford University Press.

Bibliography

Burge, T. 1992. "Philosophy of Language and Mind, 1950–90." *Philosophical Review* 101: 3–51. Reprinted in Geirsson and Losonsky 1996, 1–30.

Carnap, R. 1931. "Überwindung der Metaphysik durch logische Analyse der Sprache." *Erkenntnis* 2: 219–41. Trans. A. Pap, "The Elimination of Metaphysics through Logical Analysis of Language," in *Logical Positivism*, ed. A. J. Ayer, 60–81. Glencoe, IL: Free Press, 1959.

   1934. *Logische Syntax der Sprache*. Vienna: Julius Springer. Reprint, Vienna: Springer Verlag, 1968.

   1935. *Philosophy and Logical Syntax*. London: Kegan Paul. Reprint, Bristol: Thoemmes Press, 1996.

   1937. *The Logical Syntax of Language*. Trans. A. Smeaton. London: Kegan Paul. Reprint, Chicago: Open Court, 2002.

   1942. *Introduction to Semantics*. Cambridge, MA: Harvard University Press.

   1947. *Meaning and Necessity: A Study in Semantics and Modal Logic*. Chicago: University of Chicago Press.

   1950. "Empiricism, Semantics, and Ontology." *Revue International de Philosophie* 4: 20–40. Reprinted in Carnap 1956, 205–21.

   1956. *Meaning and Necessity: A Study in Semantics and Modal Logic*. 2nd ed. Chicago: University of Chicago Press.

   1968. *Problémy Jazyka Vědy*. Ed. and trans. L. Tondl and K. Berka. Prague: Nakladatelství Svoboda, 1968. Preface translated from the Czech by M. Losonsky at www.colostate.edu/~losonsky.

Carruthers, P. 1989. *Tractarian Semantics: Finding Sense in Wittgenstein's Tractatus*. Oxford: Basil Blackwell.

Caton, C. E. 1963. *Philosophy and Ordinary Language*. Urbana: University of Illinois Press.

Cavell, S. 1989. *This New Yet Unapproachable America: Lectures after Emerson and Wittgenstein*. Albuquerque: Living Batch Press.

   1996. "Notes and Afterthoughts on the Opening of Wittgenstein's *Investigations*." In Sluga and Stern 1996, 261–95.

Chappell, V. 1994. "Locke's Theory of Ideas." In *The Cambridge Companion to Locke*, ed. V. Chappell, 26–55. Cambridge: Cambridge University Press.

Chierchia, G., and S. McConnell-Ginet. 1990. *Meaning and Grammar: An Introduction to Semantics*. Cambridge, MA: MIT Press.

Chomsky, N. 1957. *Syntactic Structures*. The Hague: Mouton.

   1965. *Aspects of a Theory of Syntax*. Cambridge, MA: MIT Press.

   1966. *Cartesian Linguistics: A Chapter in the History of Rationalist Thought*. New York: Harper and Row.

   1969. "Quine's Empirical Assumptions." In *Words and Objections: Essay on the Work of W. V. O. Quine*, ed. D. Davidson and J. Hintikka, 53–68. Dordrecht: D. Reidel.

   1971. *Problems of Knowledge and Freedom*. New York: Pantheon Books.

   1976. *Reflections on Language*. New York: Pantheon.

   1980. "Rules and Representations." *Behavioral and Brain Sciences* 3: 1–61.

   1988. *Language and the Problems of Knowledge: The Managua Lectures*. Cambridge, MA: MIT Press.

Church, A. 1951. "The Need for Abstract Entities." *American Academy of Arts and Sciences Proceedings* 80: 100–13.
Cohen, L. J. 1954. "On the Project of a Universal Character." *Mind* 63: 49–63.
Condillac, E. B. de. 1947. *Oeuvres philosophiques de Condillac*. Ed. G. Le Roy. 3 vols. Paris: Presses Universitaires de France.
    1971. *An Essay on the Origin of Human Knowledge*. Trans. T. Nugent. Gainesville, FL: Scholars' Facsimiles and Reprints.
    2001. *An Essay on the Origin of Human Knowledge*. Trans. H. Aarselff. Cambridge: Cambridge University Press.
Condorcet, A.-E. de. 1955. *Sketch for a Historical Picture of the Progress of the Human Mind*. New York: Noonday Press.
Conway, G. D. 1989. *Wittgenstein on Foundations*. Atlantic Highlands, NJ: Humanities Press.
Copenhaver, B. P. 1988. "Translation, Terminology, and Style in Philosophical Discouse." In *The Cambridge History of Renaissance Philosophy*, ed. C. B. Schmitt, 77–110. Cambridge: Cambridge University Press.
Copenhaver, B. P., and C. B. Schmitt. 1992. *Renaissance Philosophy*. Oxford: Oxford University.
Copi, I. M. 1949. "Language Analysis and Metaphysical Inquiry." *Philosophy of Science* 16: 65–70. Reprinted in Rorty 1967, 127–34.
Copleston, F. C. 1952. *Medieval Philosophy*. New York: Philosophical Library.
Cordemoy, G. de. 1972. *A Philosophical Discourse Concerning Speech*. Delmar, NY: Scholar's Facsimiles and Reprints. Reprint of London: John Martin, 1668. Translation of *Discours physique de la parole* (Paris: F. Lambert, 1668).
Coseriu, E. 1971. *Sprache: Strukturen und Funktionen*. Tübingen: Tübingen Beiträge zur Linguistik.
Coudert, A. 1978. "Some Theories of Natural Language from the Renaissance to the Seventeenth Century." *Studia Leibnitiana Sonderheft* 7: 106–14.
Courtine, J.-F. 1980. "Leibniz et la langue adamic." *Revue des Science philosophiques et théologiques* 64: 373–91.
Couturat, L. 1901. *La logique de Leibniz d aprés documents inédits*. Paris: J. Vrin.
Crary, A., and R. Read (eds.). 2000. *The New Wittgenstein*. New York: Routledge.
Crystal, D. 1997. *The Cambridge Encyclopedia of Language*. 2nd ed. Cambridge: Cambridge University Press.
D'Agostino, F. 1986. *Chomsky's System of Ideas*. Oxford: Clarendon Press.
Dascal, M. 1987. *Leibniz: Language, Signs and Thought*. Philadelphia: John Benjamins.
    1990. "Leibniz on Particles, Linguistic Form and Comparatism." In *Leibniz, Humboldt, and the Origins of Comparativism*, ed. T. De Mauro and L. Formigari, 31–60. Amsterdam: John Benjamins.
    1993. "The Conventionalization of Language in 17th-Century British Philosophy." *Semiotica* 96: 139–47.
Davidson, D. 1965. "Theories of Meaning and Learnable Languages." In *Logic, Methodology and Philosophy of Science: Proceedings of the 1964 International Congress*, ed. Y. Bar-Hillel, 383–94. Amsterdam: North-Holland.
    1967. "Truth and Meaning." *Synthese* 7: 304–23.
    1984. *Inquiries into Truth and Interpretation*. Oxford: Clarendon Press.

Bibliography

1986. "A Nice Derangement of Epitaphs." In *Philosophical Grounds of Rationality*, ed. R. Grandy and R. Warner, 157–74. Oxford: Clarendon Press.

1990. "The Structure and Content of Truth." *Journal of Philosophy* 87: 279–328.

Davidson, D., and G. Harman. 1972. *The Semantics of Natural Language*. Dordrecht: D. Reidel.

1975. *The Logic of Grammar*. Encino, CA: Dickinson.

Debus, A. G. 1970. *Science and Education in the Seventeenth Century: The Webster-Ward Debate*. New York: American Elsevier.

Derrida, J. 1967. "Force et Signification." In *L'ocriture et lu differance*, 9–49. Paris: Éditions du Seuil. Translated in Derrida 1978, 3–30.

1972. *Marges de la philosophie*. Paris: Editions de Minuit.

1976. *L'archeologie du frivole: Lire Condillac*. Paris: Denoël/Gonthier. English Translation: *Archeology of the Frivolous: Reading Condillac*, trans. J. P. Leavey (Lincoln: University of Nebraska Press, 1987).

1977a. "Signature Event Context." Trans. S. Weber and J. Mehlman. *Glyph* 1: 172–97. First published in Derrida 1972, 367–93, and reprinted in 1988, 1–23.

1977b. "Limited Inc abc..." Trans. S. Weber. *Glyph* 2: 1–79.

1978. *Writing and Difference*. Trans. A. Bass. Chicago: University of Chicago Press.

1988. *Limited Inc*. Trans. S. Weber. Evanston: Northwestern University Press.

Descartes, R. 1985. *The Philosophical Writings of Descartes*. Ed. and trans. J. Cottingham, R. Stoothoff, D. Murdoch, and A. Kenny. 3 vols. Cambridge: Cambridge University Press.

Devitt, M., and K. Sterelny. 1999. *Language and Reality: An Introduction to the Philosophy of Language*. 2nd ed. Cambridge, MA: MIT Press.

Dowty, D. R., R. E. Wall, and S. Peters. 1981. *Introduction to Montague Semantics*. Dordrecht: D. Reidel.

Dummett, M. 1973. *Frege: Philosophy of Language*. New York: Harper and Row.

1991a. *Frege: Philosophy of Mathematics*. New York: Harper and Row.

1991b. *Frege and Other Philosophers*. Oxford: Clarendon Press.

1995. "The Context Principle: "The Context Principle: Centre of Frege's Philosophy." In *Logik und Mathematik: Frege-Kolloquium, Jena, 1993*, ed. I. Max and W. Stelzner, 2–21. Berlin: de Gruyter.

Evans, G. 1975. "Identity and Predication." *Journal of Philosophy* 72: 343–63.

Feigl, H., and W. Sellars (eds.). 1949. *Readings in Philosophical Analysis*. New York: Appleton-Century-Crofts.

Feuerbach, L. 1975. *Werke in Sechs Bänden*. Ed. E. Thies. 6 vols. Frankfurt: Suhrkamp.

Fodor, J. 1981. "Some Note on What Linguistics Is About." In *Readings in Philosophy of Psychology*, vol. 2, ed. N. Block, 197–207. Cambridge, MA: Harvard University Press.

1983. *The Modularity of the Mind*. Cambridge, MA: MIT Press.

Frege, G. 1879. *Begriffsschrift, Eine der Arithmetischen Nachgebildete Formelsprache des reinen Denkens*. Halle: Louis Nebert.

1882. "Über die Wissenschaftliche Berechtigung einer Begriffsschrift." *Zeitschrift für Philosophie und philosophische Kritik* 81: 48–56. Reprinted in Frege 1980, 91–7, and translated in Frege 1972, 83–90.

1891. *Funktion und Begriff*. Jena: Hermann Pohle. Reprinted in Frege 1980, 17–39, and translated in Frege 1952, 21–41, and 1997, 130–48.

1892. "Über Sinn und Bedeutung." *Zeitschrift für Philosophie und Philosophische Kritik* 100: 25–50. Translated in Frege 1952, 56–78, and 1997, 181–91.

1904. "Was ist eine Funktion?" In *Festschrift: Ludwig Boltzmann gewidmet zum sechzigsten Geburtstag, 20. Februar 1904*, ed. S. Meyer, 656–66. Leipzig: A. Barth. Reprinted in Frege 1980, 81–90, and translated in Frege 1952, 107–16.

1918. "Der Gedanke." *Beiträge zur Philosophie des deutschen Idealismus* 1: 58–77. Translated in Frege 1997, 325–45.

1949. "On Sense and Nominatum." Trans. H. Feigl. In *Readings in Philosophical Analysis*, ed. H. Feigl and W. Sellars, 85–102. New York: Appleton-Century-Crofts.

1952. *Translations from the Philosophical Writings of Gottlob Frege*. Ed. and trans. P. Geach and M. Black. Oxford: Blackwell. 2nd ed., 1970. 3rd ed., 1980.

1972. *Conceptual Notation and Related Articles*. Trans. and ed. T. W. Bynum. Oxford: Clarendon Press.

1976. *Wissenschaftlicher Briefwechsel*. Ed. G. Gabriel, H. Hermes, F. Kambartel, C. Thiel, and A. Veraart. Hamburg: Felix Meiner.

1978. *The Foundations of Arithmentic/Die Grundlagen der Arithmetic*. German Text with English translation by J. L. Austin. 2nd ed. Oxford: Blackwell. 1st ed., Breslau: Wilhelm Koebner, 1884. Portions translated in Frege 1997, 84–129.

1979. *Posthumous Writings*. Trans. P. Long and R. White. Oxford: Blackwell. Translation of Frege 1983.

1980. *Funktion, Begriff, Bedeutung: Fünf logische Studien*. Ed. G. Patzig. Göttingen: Vandenhoek und Ruprecht.

1983. *Nachgelassene Schriften*. Ed. H. Hermes, F. Kambartel, and F. Kaulbach. 2nd ed. Hamburg: Felix Meiner. 1st ed., 1976.

1984. "Compound Thoughts." Trans. R. H. Stoothoff. In *Collected Papers*, ed. B. McGuiness, 390–406. Oxford: Blackwell. Originally published 1923, "Logische Untersuchungern. Dritter Teil: Gedankenfuege." *Beitraege zur Philosophie des deutschen Idealismus* 3: 36–51.

1997. *The Frege Reader*. Ed. M. Beaney. Oxford: Blackwell.

Friedlander, E. 2001. *Signs of Sense: Reading Wittgenstein's Tractatus*. Cambridge, MA: Harvard University Press.

Gabriel, G. 2002. "Frege, Lotze, and the Continental Roots of Early Analytic Philosophy." In Reck 2002, 39–51.

Garver, N. 1994. *This Complicated Form of Life: Essays on Wittgenstein*. La Salle, IL: Open Court Press.

Garver, N., and S.-C. Lee. 1994. *Derrida and Wittgenstein*. Philadelphia: Temple University Press.

Bibliography

Gaukroger, S. 2001. *Francis Bacon and the Transformation of Early-Modern Philosophy.* Cambridge: Cambridge University Press.

Gazzaniga, M. 1985. *The Social Brain: Discovering the Networks of the Mind.* New York: Basic Books.

Geirsson, H., and M. Losonsky. 1996. *Readings in Language and Mind.* Oxford: Blackwell.

Gerl, H.-B. 1974. *Rhetorik als Philosophie: Lorenzo Valla.* Munich: Wilhelm Fink.

Glendinning, S. 2004. "Philosophy as Nomadism." In *What Philosophy Is*, ed. H. Carel and D. Gamez, 155–67. London: Continuum.

Glock, H.-J. 2003. *Quine and Davidson on Language, Thought and Reality.* Cambridge: Cambridge University Press.

Grandy, R. 1973. "Reference, Meaning and Belief." *Journal of Philosophy* 70: 439–52.

Guyer, P. 1994. "Locke's Philosophy of Language." In *The Cambridge Companion to Locke*, ed. V. Chappell, 115–45. Cambridge: Cambridge University Press.

2000. "Absolute Idealism and the Rejection of Kantian Dualism." In *The Cambridge Companion to German Idealism*, ed. K. Ameriks, 37–56. Cambridge: Cambridge University Press.

Habermas, J. 1981. *The Theory of Communicative Action.* Trans. T. McCarthy. 2 vols. Boston: Beacon Press. Translation of *Theorie des komminikativen Handelns* (Frankfurt: Suhrkamp, 1981).

Hacker, P. M. S. 1989. *Insight and Illusion: Themes in the Philosophy of Wittgenstein.* Oxford: Oxford University Press. Reprint, Bristol: Thoemmes Press, 1997.

2000. "Was He Trying to Whistle it?" In Crary and Read 2000, 353–88.

Hale, B., and C. Wright (eds.). 1998. *A Companion to the Philosophy of Language.* Oxford: Blackwell. 1st ed., 1997.

Hamann, J. G. 1993. *Vom Magus im Norden und der Verwegenheit des Geistes: Ausgewählte Schriften.* Ed. S. Majetschak. Bonn: Parerga.

Hare, R. M. 1952. *The Language of Morals.* Oxford: Clarendon Press.

Harnish, R. M. (ed.). 1994. *Basic Topics in the Philosophy of Language.* Englewood Cliffs, NJ: Prentice-Hall.

Harris, J. 1751. *Hermes; or, a Philosophical Inquiry Concerning Language and Universal Grammar.* London: H. Woodfall.

Harris, R., and T. J. Taylor. 1997. *Landmarks in Linguistic Thought: The Western Tradition from Socrates to Saussure.* 2nd ed. London: Routledge.

Harris, Z. S. 1954. "Transfer Grammar." *International Journal of American Linguistics* 20: 259–70.

Heal, J. 1997. "Radical Interpretation." In Hale and Wright 1998, 175–96.

Heidegger, M. 1944. *Erläuterung zu Hölderlins Dichtung.* Frankfurt: Klostermann.

Heinekamp, A. 1972. "Ars Characteristica und natürliche Sprache bei Leibniz." *Tijdschrift voor Filosofie* 34: 446–519.

Henry, D. P. 1974. *Commentary on* De Grammatico: *The Historical-Logical Dimensions of a Dialogue of St. Anselm's.* Dordrecht: D. Reidel.

Herder, J. G. 1960. *Sprachphilosophische Schriften*. Ed. E. Heintel. Hamburg: Felix Meiner Verlag.
   1967. *Sämtliche Werke*. Ed. B. Suphan. 33 vols. Hildesheim: Georg Olms. Facsimile of Berlin, 1891.
Hobbes, T. 1839. *Opera Philosophica Quae Latine Scripsit Omnia*. Ed. W. Molesworth. London: John Bohn.
   1996. *Leviathan*. Ed. R. Tuck. Cambridge: Cambridge University Press.
Humboldt, W. v. 1965. *Wilhelm von Humboldts Briefe an Christian Gottfried Körner*. Ed. A. Leitzmann. Vaduz: Kraus Reprints. Reprint of Berlin: Eberling, 1940.
   1968. *Wilhelm von Humboldts Gesammelte Schriften*. Ed. A. Leitzmann. 15 vols. Berlin: de Gruyter. Facsimile of Berlin: Behr's Verlag, 1916.
   1988. *Wilhelm von Humboldt's Gesammelte Werke*. Ed. A. V. Humboldt and C. Brandes. Berlin: de Gruyter. Reprint of Berlin: G. Reimer, 1846.
   1999. *On Language: On the Diversity of Human Language Construction and Its Influence on the Mental Development of the Human Species*. Ed. M. Losonsky and trans. P. Heath. Cambridge: Cambridge University Press.
Hume, D. 1996. *The Philosophical Works of David Hume*. 4 vols. Bristol: Thoemmes Press. Reprint of the 1854 edition.
Jahn, I., and F. Lange (eds.). 1973. *Die Jugendbriefe Alexander von Humboldts. 1787–1799*. Berlin: Akademie Verlag.
Jardine, L. 1974. *Francis Bacon: Discovery and the Art of Discourse*. Cambridge: Cambridge University Press.
   1982. "Humanism and the Teaching of Logic." In *The Cambridge History of Later Medieval Philosophy*, ed. by N. Kretzmann, A. Kenny, and J. Pinborg, 797–807. Cambridge: Cambridge University Press.
   1988. "Humanistic Logic." In *The Cambridge History of Renaissance Philosophy*, ed. C. Schmitt and Q. Skinner, 173–98. Cambridge: Cambridge University Press.
Jesseph, D. 1996. "Hobbes and the Method of Natural Science." In *The Cambridge Companion to Hobbes*, ed. T. Sorrel, 86–107. Cambridge: Cambridge University Press.
Jolley, N. 1999. *Locke: His Philosophical Thought*. Oxford: Oxford University Press.
Kanger, S. 1957. *Provability in Logic*. Stockholm: Almqvist and Wiksell.
Kant, I. 1904. *Kants gesammelte Schriften*. Ed. Königlich Preußische Akademie der Wissenschaften. 29 vols. Berlin: Walter de Gruyter.
   1965. *Critique of Pure Reason*. Trans. N. K. Smith. New York: St. Martin's Press.
Katz, J. J. 1981. *Languages and Other Abstract Objects*. Totowa, NJ: Rowman and Littlefield.
   1984. "An Outline of Platonist Grammar." In *Talking Minds: The Study of Language in Cognitive Science*, ed. T. Bever, J. M. Carroll, and L. A, Miller, 3–66. Cambridge, MA: MIT Press. Reprinted in Katz 1985, 172–203.
   (ed.). 1985. *The Philosophy of Linguistics*. Oxford: Oxford University Press.
Kneale, W., and M. Kneale. 1962. *The Development of Logic*. Oxford: Clarendon Press.

Bibliography

Knowlson, J. 1975. *Universal Language Schemes in England and France, 1600–1700*. Toronto: University of Toronto Press.

Kretzmann, N. 1967. "History of Semantics." In *The Encyclopedia of Philosophy*, ed. Paul Edwards, 7: 358–406. New York: Collier Macmillan.

——— 1968. "The Main Thesis of Locke's Semantic Theory." *Philosophical Review* 77:175–96.

Kripke, S. 1959. "A Completeness Theorem in Modal Logic." *Journal of Symbolic Logic* 24: 1–14.

——— 1982. *Wittgenstein on Rules and Private Language*. Cambridge, MA: Harvard University Press.

Leibniz, G. W. 1960. *Die Philosophischen Schriften von Gottfried Wilhelm Leibniz*. Ed. C. I. Gerhardt. 7 vols. Hildesheim: Olms.

——— 1962. *Gottfried Wilhelm Leibniz: Sämtliche Schriften und Briefe*. Ed. Deutsche Akademie der Wissenschaften zu Berlin. 50 vols. Berlin: Akademie Verlag.

——— 1966. *Logical Papers*. Trans. and ed. G. H. R. Parkinson. Oxford: Clarendon Press.

——— 1970. *Philosophical Papers and Letters*. Ed. L. Loemker. Dordrecht: D. Reidel.

——— 1982. *New Essays on Human Understanding*. Trans. and ed. P. Remnant and J. Bennett. Cambridge: Cambridge University Press.

——— 1988. *Opuscles et fragments inédits*. Ed. L. Couturat. Hildesheim: Georg Olms. 1st ed., Paris: Felix Alcan, 1903.

Lenzen, W. 1990. *Das System der Leibnizschen Logik*. Berlin: de Gruyter.

——— 1992. "Leibniz on Properties and Individuals." In *Language, Truth and Ontology*, ed. K. Mulligan, 193–204. Dordrecht: Kluwer.

Lewis, D. 1969. *Convention: A Philosophical Study*. Oxford: Blackwell.

——— 1983. *Philosophical Papers*. 2 vols. Oxford: Oxford University Press.

Locke, J. 1975. *An Essay Concerning Human Understanding*. Ed. P. H. Nidditch. Oxford: Oxford University Press.

——— 1976. *The Correspondence of John Locke*. Ed. E. S. Beer. 9 vols. Oxford: Clarendon press.

——— 1990. *Drafts for the* Essay Concerning Human Understanding *and Other Philosophical Writings*. Ed. P. H. Nidditch and G. A. J. Rogers. Vol. 1. Oxford: Clarendon Press.

Losonsky, M. 1989. "Locke on the Making of Complex Ideas." *Locke Newsletter* 20: 35–46.

——— 1992. "Leibniz's Adamic Language of Thought." *Journal of the History of Philosophy* 30: 523–43.

——— 1993. "Passionate Thought: Computation, Thought, and Action in Hobbes." *Pragmatics and Cognition* 1: 245–66.

——— 1994. "Meaning and Signification in Locke's *Essay*," In *Locke's Philosophy: Content and Context*, ed. G. A. J. Rogers, 23–41. Oxford: Oxford University Press.

——— 2001. *Enlightenment and Action from Descartes to Kant: Passionate Thought*. Cambridge: Cambridge University Press.

Loux, M. 1974. "The Ontology of William of Ockham." In Ockham 1974, 1–21.

Łukasiewicz, J. 1935. "Zur Geschichte der Aussagenlogik." *Erkenntnis* 5: 111–35.
Lyons, J. 1984. *Language and Linguistics*. Cambridge: Cambridge University Press.
Mack, P. 1993. *Renaissance Argument: Valla and Agricola in the Traditions of Rhetoric and Dialectic*. Brill: Leiden.
Magee, N. 1996. "William of Ockham and the Death of Universals." http://web.syr.edu/~nmagee/ockham.html.
Marenbon, J. 1997. *The Philosophy of Peter Abelard*. Cambridge: Cambridge University Press.
Martin, R. M. 1952. "On 'Analytic.'" *Philosophical Studies* 3: 42–7.
Martinich, A. P. (ed.). 2001. *The Philosophy of Language*. Oxford: Oxford University Press.
McDowel, J. 1976. "Truth Conditions, Bivalence and Verificationism." In *Truth and Meaning*, ed. G. Evans and J. McDowell, 42–66. Oxford: Oxford University Press, 1976.
McGuinness, B. 2002. *Approaches to Wittgenstein: Collected Papers*. London: Routledge.
McRae, R. 1988. "Locke and Leibniz on Linguistic Particles." *Synthese* 75: 155–81.
Merleau-Ponty, M. 1964. "On the Phenomenology of Language." In *Signs*, trans. and ed. R. McCleary, 84–97. Evanston: Northwestern University Press.
Merquior, J. G. 1986. *From Prague to Paris: A Critique of Structuralist and Post-Structuralist Thought*. London: Verso.
Mill, J. S. 1863. *System der Deductiven und Inductiven Logik*. Trans. J. Schiel. 2nd ed. Braunschweig: Friedriech Vieweg und Sohn.
  1974. *Collected Works of John Stuart Mill*. Ed. J. M. Robson. 33 vols. Toronto: University of Toronto Press.
Monfasani, J. 1989. "Was Lorenzo Valla an Ordinary Language Philosopher?" *Journal of the History of Ideas* 50: 309–36.
Montague, R. 1968. "Pragmatics." In *Contemporary Philosophy: A Survey*, ed. R. Klibansky, 102–22. Florence: La Nuova Italia Editrice. Reprinted in Montague 1974, 95–118.
  1970a. "Pragmatics and Intensional Logic." *Synthese* 22: 69–94. Reprinted in Montague 1974, 119–47.
  1970b. "English as a Formal Language." In *Linguaggi nella società e nella tecnica*, ed. B. Visentini et al., 189–224. Milan: Edizioni di Communità. Reprinted in Montague 1974, 188–221.
  1973. "The Proper Treatment of Quantification in Ordinary English." In *Proceedings of the 1970 Stanford Workshop on Grammar and Semantics*, ed. K. J. J. Hintikka, J. M. E. Moravcsik, and P. Suppes, 221–42. Dordrecht: D. Reidel. Reprinted in Montague 1974, 222–46.
  1974. *Formal Philosophy: Selected Papers of Richard Montague*. Ed. R. Thomason. New Haven: Yale University Press.
Moravcsik, J. M. 1981. "Frege and Chomsky on Thought and Language." *Midwest Studies in Philosophy* 6: 105–23.
Mullaly, J. 1945. *The Summulae Logicales of Peter of Spain*. South Bend: University of Notre Dame Press.

Müller-Sievers, H. 1993. *Epigenesis: Naturphilosophie im Sprachdenken Wilhelm von Humboldts*. Paderborn: Schöningh.
Ockham, W. O. 1957. *Philosophical Writings*. Ed. P. Boehner. Edinburgh: Thomas Nelson.
  1970. *Opera Philosophica et Theologica*. Ed. Stephen Brown. 2 vols. St. Bonaventure: St. Bonaventure College.
  1974. *Ockham's Theory of Terms: Part I of the Summa Logicae*. Trans. M. J. Loux. Notre Dame: University of Notre Dame Press.
  1980. *Ockham's Theory of Propositions: Part II of the Summa Logicae*. Trans. A. J. Freddoso and H. Schuurman. Notre Dame: University of Notre Dame Press.
Parret, H. (ed.). 1976. *History of Linguistic Thought and Contemporary Linguistics*. Berlin: de Gruyter.
Partee, B. H. 1997. "Montague Grammar." In *Handbook of Logic and Language*, ed. J. van Benthem and A. ter Meulen, 5–91. Cambridge, MA: MIT Press.
Passmore, H. 1966. *A Hundred Years of Philosophy*. 2nd ed. London: Duckworth.
Pears, D. 1987. *The False Prison*. Vol. 1. Oxford: Oxford University Press.
Pécharman, M. 1992. "Le discourse mental selon Hobbes." *Archives de philosophie* 55: 553–73.
Pinker, S. 1994. *The Language Instinct: How the Mind Creates Language*. New York: Morrow.
  1995. *The Language Instinct*. New York: HarperCollins.
Plato. 1971. *The Collected Dialogues of Plato*. Ed. E. Hamilton and H. Cairns. Princeton: Princeton University Press.
Pombo, O. 1987. *Leibniz and the Problem of a Universal Language*. Münster: Nodus Publications.
Preyer, G., and G. Peter (eds.). 2002. *Logical Form and Language*. Oxford: Oxford University Press.
Quine, W. V. O. 1936. "Truth by Convention." In *Philosophical Essays for A. N. Whitehead*, ed. O. H. Lee, 90–124. New York: Longmans, Green. Reprinted in Benacerraf and Putnam 1983, 329–54, and Quine 1976, 77–106.
  1949. *Methods of Logic*. Rev. ed. New York. Henry Holt.
  1953. *From a Logical Point of View*. Cambridge, MA: Harvard University Press. 2nd rev. ed., 1980.
  1960. *Word and Object*. Boston: MIT Press.
  1969. *Ontological Relativity and Other Essays*. New York: Columbia University Press.
  1976. *The Ways of Paradox and Other Essays*. Rev. and enlg. ed. Cambridge, MA: Harvard University Press. 1st ed., 1966.
  1987. "Indeterminacy of Translation Again." *Journal of Philosophy* 84: 5–10.
  1989. "Three Indeterminacies." In *Perspectives on Quine*, ed. R. Barrett and R. Gibson, 1–16. Oxford: Blackwell.
  1990. *Pursuit of Truth*. Cambridge, MA: Harvard University Press.
Quine, W. V. O., and R. Carnap. 1990. *Dear Carnap, Dear Van: The Quine-Carnap Correspondence and Related Work*. Ed. R. Creath. Berkeley: University of California Press.

Ramberg, B. T. 1989. *Donald Davidson's Philosophy of Language*. Oxford: Blackwell.
Ramsey, F. P. 1931. *The Foundations of Mathematics and Other Logical Essays*. London: Kegan Paul.
Reck, E. H. (ed.). 2002. *From Frege to Wittgenstein: Perspectives on Early Analytic Philosophy*. Oxford: Oxford University Press.
Ricken, U. 1994. *Linguistics, Anthropology and Philosophy in the French Enlightenment: Language Theory and Ideology*. Trans. R. E. Norton. New York: Routledge. Translation of *Sprache, Anthropologie, Philosophie in der Französischen Aufklärung* (Berlin: Akademie Verlag, 1984).
Ricketts, T. 1996. "Pictures, Logic, and the Limits of Sense in Wittgenstein's *Tractatus*." In Sluga and Stern 1996, 59–99.
Robey, D. (ed.). 1973. *Structuralism: An Introduction*. Wolfson College Lectures, 1972. Oxford: Clarendon Press.
Robins, R. H. 1990. *A Short History of Linguistics*. 3rd ed. London: Longman. 1st ed., 1967.
    1976. "Some Continuities and Discontinuities in the History of Linguistics." In Parret 1976, 13–31.
Rogers, G. A. J. 1988. "Hobbes's Hidden Influence." In *Perspectives on Thomas Hobbes*, ed. G. A. J. Rogers and A. Ryan, 189–205. Oxford: Oxford University Press.
Rogers, K. 1997. *The Neoplatonic Metaphysics and Epistemology of Anselm of Canterbury*. Studies in the History of Philosophy, vol. 45. Lewiston, NY: Edwin Mellen Press.
Romanos, G. D. 1983. *Quine and Analytic Philosophy: The Language of Language*. Cambridge, MA: MIT Press.
Rorty, R. (ed.). 1967. *The Linguistic Turn: Essays in Philosophical Method*. Chicago: University of Chicago Press.
    (ed.) 1992. *The Linguistic Turn: Essays in Philosophical Method with Two Retrospective Essays*. Chicago: University of Chicago Press.
Rosch, E., and C. B. Mervis. 1996. "Family Resemblances in the Internal Structure of Categories." In Geirsson and Losonsky 1996, 442–60.
Rossi, P. 1960. *Clavis Universalis*. Milan: Ricciardi.
Rousseau, J. J. 1964. *Oeuvres complètes*. Ed. B. Gagnebin and M. Raymond. 5 vols. Paris: Gallimard.
Rousset, J. 1962. *Forme et signification*. Paris: José Corti.
Russell, B. 1903. *The Principles of Mathematics*. London: George Allen and Unwin. 2nd ed., 1937.
    1905. "On Denoting." *Mind* 14: 479–93. Reprinted in Martinich 2001, 212–27, and Harnish 1994, 161–73.
    1945. *A History of Western Philosophy*. London: Allen and Unwin.
    1988. *The Collected Papers of Bertrand Russell*. Ed. J. G. Slater. London: Unwin Hyman.
Russell, B., and A. N. Whitehead. 1910. *Principia Mathematica*. 3 vols. Cambridge: Cambridge University Press. Abridged version of volume 1 in *Cambridge Mathematical Library* (Cambridge: Cambridge University Press, 1997).

Rutherford, D. 1995. "Philosophy and Language in Leibniz." In *The Cambridge Companion to Leibniz*, ed. N. Jolley, 224–69. Cambridge: Cambridge University Press.
Ryle, G. 1949. *The Concept of Mind*. London: Hutchinson.
  1963. "The Theory of Meaning." In Caton 1963, 128–53.
Salmon, N. 1991. *Frege's Puzzle*. Atascadero, CA: Ridgeview Press.
Saussure, F. de. 1955. *Cours de linguistique générale*. Ed. C. Bally, A. Sechehaye, and A. Riedlinger. 5th ed. Paris: Payot.
  1959. *Course in General Linguistics*. Trans. W. Baskin. New York: Philosophical Library.
Scheman, N. 1996. "Forms of Life: Mapping the Rough Ground." In Sluga and Stern 1996, 383–410.
Schilpp, Paul Arthur (ed.). 1963. *The Philosophy of Rudolf Carnap*. La Salle, IL: Open Court.
Schlick, M. 1930. "Die Wende der Philosophie." *Erkenntnis* 1: 4–11. Trans. D. Rynin, "The Turning point in Philosophy," in *Logical Positivism*, ed. A. J. Ayer (Glencoe, IL: Free Press), 53–9.
  1932. "The Future of Philosophy." *College of the Pacific Publications in Philosophy* 1: 45–62. Reprinted in Rorty 1967, 43–53.
Searle, J. 1969. *Speech Acts: An Essay in the Philosophy of Language*. Cambridge: Cambridge University Press.
  (ed.). 1971. *The Philosophy of Language*. Oxford: Oxford University Press.
  1977. "A Reply to Derrida." *Glyph* 1: 198–208.
  1987. "Indeterminacy, Empiricism, and the First Person." *Journal of Philosophy* 84: 123–46.
Seidel, S. (ed.). 1962. *Der Briefwechsel Zwischen Friedrich Schiller und Wilhelm von Humboldt*. 2 vols. Berlin: Aufbau Verlag.
Shannon, C. E., and W. Weaver. 1949. *The Mathematical Theory of Communications*. Urbana: University of Illinois Press.
Skinner, Q. 1996. *Reason and Rhetoric in the Philosophy of Hobbes*. Cambridge: Cambridge University Press.
Skorupski, J. 1989. *John Stuart Mill*. London: Routledge.
Slaughter, M. M. 1982. *Universal Languages and Scientific Taxonomy in the Seventeenth Century*. Cambridge: Cambridge University Press.
Sluga, H. 1980. *Gottlob Frege*. London: Routledge and Kegan Paul.
Sluga, H., and D. Stern (eds.). 1996. *The Cambridge Companion to Wittgenstein*. Cambridge: Cambridge University Press.
Stainton, R. J. 1996. *Philosophical Perspectives on Language*. Peterborough, Ontario: Broadview Press.
Steiner, P. 1982. *The Prague School: Selected Writings, 1929–1946*. Austin: University of Texas Press.
Strawson, P. F. 1950. "On Referring." *Mind* 59: 320–44.
  1959. *Individuals*. London: Methuen.
Tarski, A. 1933. *Pojęcie Prawdy w Językach Nauk Dedukcyjnych*. Warsaw. German translation in Tarski 1936 and English translation in Tarski 1956.
  1936. "Der Wahrheitsbegriff in den formalisierten Sprachen." *Studia Philosophica* 1: 261–405.

1944. "The Semantic Conception of Truth." *Philosophy and Phenomenological Research* 4: 341–75.

1956. "The Concept of Truth in Formalized Languages." In *Logic, Semantics and Metamathematics*, trans. J. H. Woodger, 152–97. Oxford: Oxford University Press. 1st ed. in Polish, 1933.

1994. *Introduction to Logic and to the Methodology of the Deductive Sciences*. Ed. J. Tarski. Trans. O. Helmer. 4th ed. Oxford: Oxford University Press. 1st ed. in Polish, 1936.

Tobriner, M. L. 1968. *Vives' Introduction to Wisdom: A Renaissance Textbook*. New York: Teachers College Press, Columbia University.

Tonelli, G. 1974. "Leibniz on Innate Ideas and the Early Reactions to the Publication of the *Nouveaux Essais* (1765)." *Journal of the History of Philosophy* 12: 437–54.

Tooke, J. H. 1806. *The Diversions of Purley*. 2 vols. Philadelphia: W. Duane.

Trabant, J. 1990. *Traditionen Humboldts*. Frankfurt am Main: Suhrkamp.

Trendelenburg, A. 1867. "Über Leibnizes Entwurf einer allgemeinen Charakteristik." *Historische Beiträge zur Philosophie* 3: 1–47.

Trinkaus, C. 1970. *In Our Image and Likeness: Humanity and Divinity in Italian Humanist Thought*. Vol. 1. Chicago: University of Chicago Press.

Valla, L. 1934. *De Libero Arbitrio*. Ed. M. Anfossi. Florence: Olschki.

1962. *Opera Omnia*. 2 vols. Turin: Bottega d'Erasmo.

1982. *Laurentii Valle repastinatio dialecticae et philosophiae*. Ed. G. Zippel. Padua: Editrice Antenore.

Vives, J. L. 1964. *Opera Omnia*. 8 vols. London: Gregg Press. Reprint of *Opera Omnia*, ed. G. Majans, 8 vols. (Valencia: Benedicti Monfort, 1782–90).

Walker, D. P. 1972. "Leibniz and Language." *Journal of the Warburg and Courtauld Institutes* 35: 294–307.

Waswo, R. 1987. *Language and Meaning in the Renaissance*. Princeton: Princeton University Press.

1989. "Motives of Misreading." *Journal of the History of Ideas* 50: 324–32.

Weyant, R. G. 1971. Introduction. In Condillac 1971, v–xx.

Whorf, B. 1956. *Language, Thought, and Reality*. Ed. J. B. Carroll. Cambridge, MA: MIT.

Wiggins, D. 1997. "Meaning and Truth Conditions: From Frege's Grand Design to Davidson's." In Hale and Wright 1998, 3–28.

Wilson, C. 1989. *Leibniz's Metaphysics*. Princeton: Princeton University Press.

Winch, P. 1958. *The Idea of a Social Science and Its Relation to Philosophy*. London: Routledge. 2nd ed., 1994.

Witherspoon, E. 2000. "Carnap and Wittgenstein." In Crary and Read 2000, 315–49.

Wittgenstein, L. 1922. *Tractatus Logico-Philosophicus*. German and English facing pages. Trans. C. K. Ogden. London: Routledge and Kegan Paul. First published as "Logisch-philosophische Abhandlung," *Annalen der Naturphilosophie* 14 (1921): 199–262. 2nd ed., 1933. New translation by D. F. Pears and B. McGuiness (London: Routledge and Kegan Paul, 1961, rev. 1963 and 1971).

1953. *Philosophische Untersuchungen/Philosophical Investigations.* Trans. G. E. M. Anscombe. New York: Macmillan. 3rd ed., 1958.

1961. *Notebooks, 1914–1916.* Ed. G. H. v. Wright and G. E. M. Anscombe. Oxford: Blackwell. 2nd ed., 1979.

1980. *Culture and Value.* Ed. G. H. Von Wright. Trans. P. Winch. Chicago: University of Chicago Press.

Wolterstorff, N. 1996. *John Locke and the Ethics of Belief.* Cambridge: Cambridge University Press.

Woolhouse, R. S. 1983. *Locke.* Minneapolis: University of Minnesota Press.

Wright, C. 1997. "The Indeterminacy of Translation." In Hale and Wright 1998, 397–426.

Yablo, S. 1998. "Does Ontology Rest on a Mistake?" *Proceedings of the Aristotelian Society*, suppl. vol., 72: 229–61.

Yolton, J. S. 1990. *A Locke Miscellany: Locke Biography and Criticism for All.* Bristol: Thoemmes.

Yolton, J. W. 1991. *Locke and French Materialism.* Oxford: Oxford University Press.

Zweig, A. 1967. *Kant: Philosophical Correspondence 1759–99.* Chicago: University of Chicago Press.

Index

a posteriori, 141, 160
a priori, 105, 112, 138, 141, 165, 181, 207, 216, 251
Aarsleff, H., 48, 53, 68, 80, 83, 95, 106, 111
abbreviation, 122–3
Abelard, P., 31–2, 34, 42
abstract idea, 3, 13, 16
abstract term, 130, 142
abstraction, 3, 12, 36, 45, 88, 106, 123, 242
abuse and imperfection of language, 3, 9, 17–20, 46–7, 49, 105
accidental sign, 75–6
Adamic language, 54–7
affirmation, 27–8, 58, 133, 139, 154, 174
agglutination, 98, 100
agreement, 33, 44, 58, 74, 94, 142, 227, 236
algebra, 60, 149–50
ambiguity, 37, 79
analytic philosophy, 1, 2, 141, 148, 151, 155, 166–7, 169, 172, 177, 188, 202, 215
analytic/synthetic distinction, 114, 137, 144, 160, 203, 215–16, 218–19
analyticity, 137–8, 141, 144, 147, 209, 219–21
animal, 9, 26, 69–70, 73, 75–6, 80
annexation of names, 13–15
Anselm, 30–2
anthropology, 82, 84, 222
Aquinas, T., 33, 41
Arabic, 28, 98
arbitrariness of language, 18, 22–3, 30, 54, 56, 60, 62, 64, 66, 72–4, 78, 166, 226, 249
argument and value, 175–7, 199, 201
Aristotelian logic, 35, 119, 151

Aristotle, 26–9, 31–2, 36–8, 40, 43, 53, 136, 148, 149
arithmetic, 50, 58, 61, 63–4, 82, 108, 149, 152, 159–60, 162, 165, 171, 185, 251
Arnauld, A., 58, 72–3, 77
art of discovery and judging, 60
artificial language, 54, 66, 153, 182, 220–1
assent and dissent, 224
assertion, 26, 126, 128, 135, 155, 174, 207, 210–11, 215, 244–5, 247
attribute, 103, 129–34, 139–40, 142, 168, 232
Augustine, 230
Austin, J. L., 240–6
autonomy of language, 89, 101, 148, 183, 184, 247–8
autonomy of meaning, 127, 247–8
axiomatic systems, 90
Ayer, A. J., 35

Bach, K., 182
Bacon, F., 17, 42–5, 47, 119
Bauch, B., 185–7
Beaney, M., 148, 154, 158–60, 186
behavioral sciences, 118
Berkeley, G., 2, 132, 188
Berlin Academy of Science, 106
Bianchi Identities, 187
biology, 7, 84–8, 91, 217, 234–6, 244
Black, M., 166, 172, 194
Boehme, J., 55–7
Boethius, 28–30, 32–3
Boole, G., 149–50, 156
brain, 7, 85, 171, 184, 251
Büchner, G., 171
Burnett, T., 52

269

Index

calculation, 59, 198
calculus, 49, 53, 58, 66, 206, 231–2
Carnap, R., 159, 171, 179–80, 196, 199, 202–16, 218, 220
category, 17, 28, 36, 62, 66, 87, 97–100, 104–5, 108, 120–1, 169, 185, 224
category mistake, 47
Cavell, S., 236
Chinese, 98–100, 237
Chomsky, N., 7, 70, 83, 90–1, 95, 182–4, 251
Chomsky thesis, 182
Cicero, 37, 119, 128, 133, 140
circularity problem, 73, 77, 79
classification, 12–14, 16, 87–8, 93, 97, 99, 143, 247
cognition, xiii, xiv, 5–7, 12, 28, 38, 45, 49–50, 74, 77, 80, 93–4, 104, 108, 114, 214
combinatorial structure, 58–60, 66
common usage, 19, 35–6, 38–9, 42
communication, xiii, 4, 5, 12–13, 16–18, 21, 72, 86, 101–3, 120–2, 234
community, 101, 236
competence, 183, 251
complex idea, 3, 9, 11–12, 16, 58, 68, 123
compositionality, 3, 123, 134, 181
comprehension, 169–70
computation, 50, 149, 171
concept, xv, 29, 32–3, 36, 40, 49, 60, 66, 86, 89, 93–6, 99–100, 102, 104, 112–14, 137–8, 141, 152, 156, 159, 163, 174, 176, 183–4, 186, 189, 199, 201–3, 219–20, 223, 232, 236
conceptual content, 153–8, 163, 185, 224
conceptualism, 32, 34
Condillac, E. B. de, 11, 48, 52, 68, 69, 73–83, 85, 111–14, 120, 224
conditional, 215
Condorcet, 116–18
confusion, 17, 21, 43, 45, 157, 205
conjunction, 87, 95, 97, 149
connotation, 35, 128–30, 132–4, 140, 147, 160–1, 168–9
consciousness, 76, 89, 130–1, 145, 173, 246
constative, 240–2
context, 34, 61, 115, 134, 169, 180, 216, 219, 220, 223, 243, 245, 247
contradiction, 28, 73, 137–8
convention, 18, 23, 26, 55, 72, 136, 140, 142, 206–7, 212, 215–16, 243, 245, 247–8
conventionalism, 23, 63, 77
conventionality, 21, 23–4, 26, 31, 33–4, 39, 41, 54, 56, 63–4, 73–4, 140, 207–8, 212, 244, 245

copula, 61–2, 65, 71, 133, 154
Cordemoy, G. de, 73–4
cosmic exile, 218
Coste, P., 53
creativity, 70, 89, 101, 117, 183, 250
culture, 88, 110, 171, 235–6
customary speech, 35, 37
Czech, 214

Dalgarno, 62
Dascal, M., 11, 45, 61–3, 66–7
Davidson, D., 180–1, 191, 224–9, 247–51
decision theory, 226–7
deduction, 6, 42, 45, 48–50, 60, 62, 66, 135–6, 153–5, 208
deep or underlying structure, xii, 22, 42, 52, 61, 66–7, 81, 115, 122, 230
definite description, 177–8
DeMorgan, A., 150
denial, 26, 154, 174, 204
denotation, 35, 128–30, 132–4, 140, 142, 147, 159, 161–72, 176–8
Derrida, J., 38, 191, 229, 239–40, 243–51
Descartes, 69–73, 75, 82, 125
designation, 120, 167, 205, 208
Destutt de Tracy, 111
determinism, 28, 184
  linguistic, 38–9, 81
diachronic, 239
disjunction, 149–50
diversity, xv, 18, 22, 31, 60, 81, 83, 87–8, 94, 96, 115, 117, 122, 145–7, 238, 243
dual aspects, xii, xv, 115, 211
dualism, 38, 74, 115, 184
Duns Scotus, 33

eggplant, 248
Einstein, A., 187
empiricism, 114, 132, 145, 160, 171, 187–8, 202
Engel, J. J., 109, 113
English, 53–4, 98, 121, 167, 180, 206, 223, 249
Enlightenment, 69, 109, 214
  Counter-Enlightenment, 104, 108–9
enthusiasm, 86, 146
epistemology, 2, 5, 6, 8, 12, 21, 24–5, 40, 43, 45, 137, 141, 152, 168–9, 171, 188, 225, 234
essence of language, 230, 237
Euclid, 157
existentialism, 2, 213
extension, 72, 169, 177, 228
external question, 209, 215, 218

Index

fabric, 43, 217, 219
falsity, 27, 207
family resemblance, 232
Feuerbach, L., 171–2
Feyerabend, 2
Fichte, 188
figures of speech, 41
first philosophy, 25, 48
first person, 8, 250
force, 3, 26, 36, 44, 88–9, 97, 109, 239–41, 243, 246, 248
  assertoric, 174
  illocutionary, 243, 245, 247
form of life, 234–7
formal language, 36, 50, 178, 230
formal mode, 204–6
formal notation, 150–1
formal property, 42, 199–202
formal system, xii, 82, 90, 148, 150, 180–3, 225, 252
formalism, 146, 171
freedom, 39, 70, 89, 91–2, 96, 101, 107, 117, 146–7, 163, 184, 206–7, 211, 216, 220, 240, 247
Frege, G., 1, 2, 35, 67, 121, 124, 148–78, 181, 183–8, 190–1, 194, 197–8, 219, 230, 239, 251
functional expression, 176, 179
function-argument structure, 157, 174, 177–84, 191

gender, 65, 86, 94–5, 99
general idea, 12–15, 17–21, 123
general names and terms, 3, 12–13, 15–16, 18–19, 34, 123, 128, 130, 142, 223
generative linguistics, 83, 89–90, 95, 101, 122
Geneva School, 239
Gerl, H.-B., 38–9
Goethe, 85, 234
grammar, 36–7, 42, 60, 64, 72, 86–7, 90, 107, 110, 121, 157, 182, 249
  grammatical form, 22, 26, 65, 67, 88, 91, 94, 98, 107–8, 148, 157
growth of languages, 142
Gruppe, O. F., 171

Hamann, J. G., 104–6, 108, 113
Harris, J., 85, 119, 165
Harris, Z., 182
Hebrew, 28, 98, 240
Hegel, F., 171, 188, 240
Heidegger, M., 2, 213
Helmholtz, H., 171
Herder, J. G., 78, 104, 106–8, 113
hermeneutics, 224

Hobbes, T., 10, 22, 27, 42, 45–50, 63, 71, 73, 77, 79, 120, 128, 133, 149
holism, 85, 102, 134
humanism, xiii, 22, 35, 37–8, 40–2, 67, 252
Humboldt, A. v., 85
Humboldt, W. v., 2, 80, 83–105, 108–15, 117, 127, 134–5, 144–6, 148, 155, 194, 211, 252
Hume, D., 2, 5, 137, 145, 252
Huntington, E. V., 167
Husserl, 162

idealism, 38, 132, 171, 188, 204
identity, 3, 31, 87, 92, 122, 126–8, 138–40, 147, 150, 158, 164–6, 222–3, 246
illocutionary act, 241
illusion, 44, 104–5, 156
imagination, 9, 27, 30–1, 71, 73, 76, 78, 96, 110, 112
import of proposition, 121, 124–6, 128–30, 133–5, 139, 141, 147
indeterminacy of translation, 222, 227
indirect discourse, 169
individuality, 101–3, 110, 117, 146–7, 247
induction, 36, 43, 117, 135–6, 152–3, 181, 251–2
inference, 124, 135–7, 147, 150, 153–4
infinity of language, 90, 92, 100, 182, 215, 221, 233
inflection, 62, 64, 98, 100, 110
information theory, 90
inner form, 55, 95, 97, 99, 108, 115
inscription, xiv, 94
intellect, 31, 56, 82, 146
intellectualism, 106, 252
intensionality, 170–1, 208, 219, 220
intention, 8, 216, 221, 225–6, 243, 245–8
internal question, 209, 215, 217–18
interpretation, 10, 161, 178–80, 205, 224–6, 232, 248
introspection, 8, 80, 184, 252
isolation, 98, 100, 163–4
iterability, 244, 250
Ith, J. S., 84–5

Jacobi, F. H., 110, 113
Javanese, 87
Jevons, S., 160
John of Salisbury, 32
justification, 6, 152, 234, 237

Kanger, S., 180
Kant, I., 5, 6, 62, 86, 104–5, 108, 110–11, 114, 131, 137–8, 141, 160, 165, 172, 186, 188, 203, 252
Katz, J. J., 181, 251

Index

Kawi, 87
Kneller, J., 109
knowledge, xv, 2–4, 6–8, 10, 17, 19, 21, 24, 26–7, 48–9, 55, 58, 60, 69, 71, 73, 77, 82, 97, 104–5, 114, 118, 124–5, 131, 134–6, 141–2, 144, 152, 166, 187, 210, 212–14, 217, 219–20, 246, 250, 252
Kretzmann, N., 5, 11, 31
Kripke, S., 180, 233
Kuhn, T., 2

labyrinth, 237–8
Lancelot, 72
language acquisition, 7, 93, 211, 216
language and action, xiv, xv, 77–9, 81, 86, 88, 107, 109, 114, 115, 167, 181, 206, 211, 224, 235, 252
  language and volition, xiii, 33–4, 54, 57, 75, 78–9, 82, 88, 207, 213
language and logic, 28, 42, 45, 119, 147–8, 153, 156–7, 172
language and mind, 21, 27, 41, 43, 45, 52, 67, 69, 72–4, 78, 81, 92, 102, 106, 108, 111, 120, 122, 127, 173, 222
language game, 231, 235–6, 238
language of nature, 55–7, 60
language of thought, 60
  mental language, 29, 33–4, 55, 107
Laromiguière, P., 113–14
Latin, 4, 28, 36–8, 47, 54, 65, 71–2, 114
Leibniz, G. W., 10, 22, 48, 52–4, 57–68, 72, 79, 81–3, 91, 104, 109, 114, 117, 125, 127, 135, 137–8, 148–9, 154, 170, 185–6, 188, 219, 240, 251
Lesniewski, 178
Lewis, D., 216
Liebig, J., 171
life, 35, 54, 67, 70, 86, 89, 91, 103, 105, 118, 140, 155, 213, 234–7
limits of language, 21, 39, 213, 234
lingua characteristica, 185
linguistic behavior, 79, 81, 91, 184, 222, 224, 228, 232
linguistic framework, 208–12, 214–18, 222
linguistic philosophy, 1, 148
linguistic relativism, 2, 81, 83
linguistic relativity, 81, 206, 208, 212
linguistic turn, xiv, xv, 1–4, 6–8, 21–2, 25–6, 35, 40–2, 47–50, 52, 72, 74, 81, 109, 114, 136, 215, 229, 251
linguistics, xi–xiii, 27–8, 80–1, 83, 85, 90, 92, 147–8, 180, 182, 189, 229, 244, 251–2
literal meaning, xiv, 247–8

Locke, J., 2–22, 24–8, 40–2, 47–50, 52–3, 60–2, 67–9, 74, 79–81, 104, 122–3, 125, 127, 129, 224, 251
locution, xiv, 29–30
locutionary act, 241–2
logical analysis, 1, 202–3, 205
logical constant, 197–9, 223
logical form, xii, 61, 66–7, 81, 115, 134–6, 148, 154, 157, 185, 191–3, 195–6, 198, 201, 212, 218, 230
logical object, 191, 197–8
logical positivism, 202–3
logical structure, 22, 42, 61, 135, 147, 149, 157, 177, 199, 202
logicism, 153, 190
Lotze, H., 174, 185–8
Loux, M., 33

Malagasy, 87
malapropism, 249
Malayan, 87
Malebranche, 75
Martineau, J., 146
Marx, K., 171
material mode, 204–6
materialism, 75, 80, 171, 187–8
mathematical function, xii, 174–5
mathematical logic, 148–9, 151, 182, 191, 200, 230, 237
mathematics, 67, 82, 105, 148, 152, 164, 171, 181, 186, 190, 203, 211, 216, 219, 251
Maupertuis, P. de, 106
meaning and belief, 226–7
meaning of language, xv, 2, 18, 27–9, 31, 34, 70, 72, 74, 121, 125, 127, 130, 135, 140–1, 143, 146–7, 158, 169, 172, 174, 177, 180, 191, 203, 209, 221–2, 225, 244–5, 248
meaning postulates, 220–2
memory, 2, 3, 7, 21, 59, 76, 86
Mendelssohn, M., 109
mental activity, 90, 93, 95, 112, 114, 154
mental proposition, 9, 11
mentalism, 252
Merleau-Ponty, M., 2
Mersenne, M., 70
metalanguage, 196, 198, 201
metaphor, 47, 95, 126, 172, 221, 239
metaphysics, 5, 8, 12, 25, 28, 35, 40, 68, 80, 104–5, 111–12, 114, 116, 130, 137, 152, 201, 203–4, 208, 210–11, 213, 240
method, 3, 46, 72, 77, 100, 118, 120, 198, 201, 237–8

Index

Mill, J. S., 2, 35, 66, 115–19, 121, 124–48, 152–5, 159–62, 165, 167–9, 171–2, 194, 208
Mill, James, 145
mind and body, 73–5, 80, 238
mirror, xiii, 56, 60–1, 127, 173, 192, 195, 251
modal language and logic, 36, 95, 179, 208, 220
mode of presentation, 166
modularity, 7
Moleschott, 172
Molyneux, 53
Mont Blanc, 177
Montague, R., 180–1, 251
Montague thesis, 182
morality, 5, 14, 20–1, 40, 50, 54, 110, 118, 141, 207
music, 69, 89, 196
mystery, 13, 39, 68, 103–4, 131, 212, 214, 250
mysticism, 104, 201, 214

naming, 15, 16, 23, 140
nation, 29, 86, 103, 172, 214
natural history, 146
natural language, xii–xiv, 21–2, 24, 26, 27, 35, 40–2, 45, 49–50, 52, 60, 65–7, 69, 73–4, 77–82, 89, 91, 108, 114, 119, 135–6, 143, 147, 153, 155–7, 165, 173, 180–1, 184, 224, 225, 231–2, 249
natural languages, 24–5, 50, 52, 54, 57, 61–2, 65, 67, 74, 81–2, 115, 142, 147, 168, 180, 182, 225, 230, 236
natural meaning, 23–4, 33, 56
natural order of ideas, 58–62, 65
natural science, 80, 117, 171, 184, 198, 201, 203, 230
natural sign, 73, 75–6, 78
naturalism, xv, 23, 35, 80–2, 85, 88, 132, 140, 171, 181, 188, 217, 239
naturalization, 181
necessity, xiii, 28, 54, 62, 92, 147, 180, 187
negation, 28, 61, 133, 149, 174, 179, 180
Newton, I., 49, 53, 68–9
Nicole, P., 72–3, 77
nomenclature, 107
nominal essence, 14, 18
nominalism, 34, 36
noun, 29, 34, 65, 94, 97–8, 123
Nugent, T., 68

object of belief, 124–7, 155
object sentence, 204–5, 207

occasionalism, 75
Ockham, 33–4
Ohio, 221
ontology, 25, 187, 192, 208, 223
operation of human understanding, mind, 6, 60, 69, 72, 78–80, 118, 120, 123, 126, 137
ordinary language, xiii, 22, 24, 30, 33, 38, 45, 56, 67, 104, 156, 174, 180
ordinary usage, use, 22, 38, 40, 42, 52, 194
organic theory of language, 86–7
organon, 105
origin of language, 106

paper truth, 63
Parmenides, 22, 25–6
particle, 61–2, 65, 67, 123
parts of speech, 26, 28–9, 95, 102, 120–3
passing theory, 250
peace, 20, 45, 238
Peirce, C. S., 150
perfect language, 24, 100
performance, xiii–xv, 109, 181, 183–4, 206, 229, 234, 236–43, 246–7, 249–51
performative, 240–3
persuasion, 35, 41
Peter of Spain, 37
phenomenology, 2, 8
philosophy of language, xi–xiii, xv, 3, 21, 24–5, 27–8, 38, 40, 47–8, 52, 54, 64, 67, 74, 82, 85–6, 89, 91, 97, 104, 106, 110, 113–17, 134, 136, 144, 146, 151, 153, 158–9, 180, 185, 189, 215, 218, 225, 229, 234, 238–40, 242, 247
philosophy of mind, 8, 25, 69, 109, 171
phonology, xii, 2, 18, 70, 102, 115, 121, 135, 246
phrase structure, 182
pictorial form, 192–3, 195, 197, 218
plasticity, 146
Plato, 22, 24–6, 29, 38, 53, 119, 142
Platonism, xv, 163, 181, 183–4, 191
Poe, E. A., 115
poetry, 99, 172
possibility, 26, 38, 62, 66, 91, 129, 192, 193, 196–7, 200
possible worlds, 180
postmodernism, 38, 191
power, 3, 9, 55, 70, 75–6, 86–9, 92–4, 96–7, 100–1, 108–9, 112, 117, 132, 236
pragmatics, 42, 52, 180, 217
Prague Circle, 1, 239

prayer, 26
predicate, 58, 97, 99, 130, 133–4, 138–9, 154, 175–6, 196, 199–201, 205, 209, 220
predicate calculus, 150
predication, 95, 151
Priestley, J., 146
principle of charity, 227
principle of humanity, 227
private idea, 12
private language, 233
problems of philosophy, xiv, 1, 24–5, 30, 35, 40–1, 45, 49, 72, 191, 206, 208, 238
progress, xi, 88, 89, 116, 118, 152, 211
proper name, 120, 128–30, 147, 167–8, 171, 176
propositional function, 177–8, 199
propositional logic, 149–50
propositional structure, 104, 198
Protagoras, 22
Prussian Royal Academy, 106
pseudoconcept, 200
pseudoproblem, 203–4
psychologism, 171
psychology, 6–8, 21, 22, 27–9, 50, 61–3, 67, 80, 84–5, 112, 137, 148, 168, 171–4, 183, 186, 191, 194, 203, 208, 224, 232, 246, 250–1
public language, 26, 33–4, 38, 93
Pythagoras, 22

quantification, 150–1, 176, 223
quantifier, 150–1, 157, 176, 178
Quine, W. V. O., 25, 151, 171, 191, 202–3, 214–25, 227–8, 251
Quintillian, 35–6

radical interpretation, 226
radical translation, 222–3
Ramus, P., 60
rational characteristic, 57
rationalism, 82, 114, 252
real essences, 18–19
realism and irrealism, xii, 38–9, 184, 215, 227, 251
reasoning, 10–11, 23, 35, 37, 42–3, 45–8, 59, 61, 63, 67, 71–4, 77, 79–81, 84, 114, 124, 127, 135, 137, 172
rectify, 19, 21
reference, 17–18, 24, 167, 227–8
  direct, 130
reflection, 2, 3, 8, 11, 25, 56, 58, 77–80, 106–7, 111, 127, 141, 143
reform, 50, 56, 142
Reid, 2
relation of ideas, 137

religion, 5, 20, 39, 54, 57, 110, 186, 187, 211
representation, xv, 47, 59, 92–4, 101, 107–9, 112, 114, 126, 131, 146, 155, 163–4, 172–3, 176, 185, 191–6, 251
resemblance, 23–4, 27, 30, 131, 140, 142–4
rhetoric, 36–7, 40, 42, 45, 119
romanticism, 109, 116
Roscelin, 32
Rousseau, J. J., 73
Royal Society, 48, 53, 55
rule-governed, xii, xiv, 60, 78–9, 95–6, 115, 248–51
rules, 37, 44, 60, 66, 86, 90, 95, 107–8, 150, 171, 181–3, 206–7, 209–11, 215, 220, 231–2, 234, 243, 248–50, 252
Russell, B., 1, 124, 130, 151, 159, 174, 177–8, 190, 195, 197–8, 230
Russian, 122

Sanskrit, 87, 98, 102
Sapir, E., 2, 83
Saussure, F. de, 1, 2, 107, 239
Schiel, J., 161
Schiller, 86, 111
Schlick, M., 1, 202
Scholasticism, xiii, 22, 34–7, 42, 45, 47, 52, 54, 67, 105, 116–18, 129, 131–2, 169, 252
science of language, xiii, xv, 5, 42, 80, 88–9, 91, 106, 109, 115, 148, 212, 243–4, 251
Searle, J., xiii, 8, 245, 250
semantic ascent, 216–17
semantics, xii, xiii, xv, 5, 31, 91, 95, 115, 127, 135–6, 140–2, 147, 162, 177–81, 183, 196–7, 205, 208–9, 212, 224, 228, 247, 251
sense [Sinn], 162, 168, 196
sense and reference, xiv, 35, 241
sensibility, 85, 110–14, 146
sentence, 66, 97, 100, 121, 158, 163–4, 166, 170, 180, 194, 225, 231–2, 242
  declarative, 26, 28, 124, 155, 163, 173–4, 176–8
sentential function, 178–9
sermo, 32, 42
sign, 15–17, 30, 33, 43, 57, 62–5, 69, 70, 72–9, 81–2, 107–8, 111–13, 120, 122, 163, 165–9, 171, 198, 201, 212, 232, 245
signification, 3, 4, 12–13, 17–20, 26, 29, 30, 32–4, 38–9, 41, 46–7, 54–5, 60–1, 63, 66, 74, 122–3, 127, 130, 133, 140, 245
silence, 211, 213

simple idea, 3, 9, 16, 19, 58, 123
skepticism, 56, 229
Slavic languages, 122
Sluga, H., 151, 171, 174, 183, 186, 188
social sciences, 2, 41, 48, 117–19, 214
Socrates, 23–4, 35, 119, 142, 177
sound, 11, 23, 26–7, 29, 31–2, 54–6, 70, 73–4, 78–9, 89–90, 92–5, 97–102, 105, 107, 212, 230, 246, 248
sound form, 94, 96–8, 101–2, 115, 147
speech, xiv, 27, 29–31, 37, 40–2, 45, 47, 55, 67, 73, 86, 91–4, 102, 120, 122–3, 183, 206, 229
  speech acts, 242–7
spiritual word, 55
spoken language, 27, 29, 30, 33, 54, 94
spoken word, 30, 33, 70, 108
spontaneity, 110, 112–13
standards, 19, 20, 22–4, 40, 43, 49, 73, 80, 149, 159, 165, 175, 222, 244, 248
stimulus meaning, 223
Stoics, 150
Strawson, P. F., 8, 167
structural properties, 1, 198, 200
structuralism, 1, 38–9, 229, 239–40
subjectivity, 94, 161, 172, 206
subject-predicate proposition, 151, 157
subordinate clauses, 169–70
substitution of equivalents, 61, 65–7, 170, 219
supposition, 25, 34, 36, 169
syllogism, 28, 36, 43, 58, 149–50
syllogistic logic, 22, 28, 37, 40, 43, 45, 116, 135, 148–51, 154
symbol, 27, 34, 46, 56, 60, 63, 66, 79, 149–50, 158, 200, 206, 229
symbol system, 21, 50, 57, 59, 64–6, 71
syncategorematic term, 37, 61, 79, 123
synchronic, 239
syntactic structure, xv, 74, 91, 95, 102, 115, 147, 198, 202–3, 208
syntactical sentence, 203–5
syntax, 1, 91, 110, 181–2, 191, 199, 202–3, 205, 207–8, 212, 222
system perspective, xiv, xv, 81–3, 88, 106, 183, 185, 211, 228, 229, 236, 251

Tarski, A., 178–80, 196, 208, 224, 227
tautology, 198
theory of meaning, 1, 91, 180, 225, 246
theory of mind, 6, 57, 107
therapy, 238

tolerance, 208, 211–12
Tooke, J. H., 122–3
transcendental, 105, 188, 212–13
transformation rule, 122, 150, 182, 206–7
Trendelenburg, A., 185
truth, 42, 50, 58, 63–4, 67, 71–2, 77, 118, 135–6, 138–9, 141, 146–7, 178, 180, 198, 202, 208, 225, 227, 243
truth-conditions, 227
truths of fact and reason, 137–8
truth-value, 26–7, 136, 169–70, 176–80, 198, 209, 219–20, 242–3

universal characteristic, 60, 65–6, 185
universal generalization, 28, 133–9, 151
universal grammar, 112, 119–23
universal language, 57, 70
universals, 12, 31–2, 34, 232
use and mention, 169
use of language, 22, 36, 38, 42, 60, 70, 86, 105, 140–3, 156, 209, 212, 222, 229, 237, 241, 248, 249
use perspective, 81–3, 106
utterance, xiv, 184, 226, 242, 244, 249–50

validity, 36, 42, 61, 66, 82, 103, 136, 147, 153–5, 185
Valla, L., 35–6, 38–41
verb, 65, 71, 97–9
verbal proposition, 8, 137–41, 144
verification, 203
Vienna Circle, 1, 202
Vives, J. L., 36–8, 40–2
vocabulary, 42, 70, 86–7, 90–1, 211
Voltaire, 68
Voss, A., 187

Waswo, R., 38–9
Webster, J., 56
Whitehead, A. N., 151, 190
Whorf, B. L., 2, 81, 83
wilderness of words, 119
Wilkins, J., 119
Wittgenstein, L., 38, 83, 188, 190–3, 195–8, 200–1, 203–5, 208, 212–14, 218, 228–39, 251
word and idea, 3, 8, 10–12, 17, 31, 51, 63
word and object, 38–9, 228
workmanship of the understanding, 9, 12, 16–17
  mental labor, 89
writing, 9, 31–2, 61, 229, 237, 240, 247
written language, 29, 108